WILD SPORTS
OF
BURMA AND ASSAM

WILD SPORTS

OF

BURMA AND ASSAM

COLONEL POLLPK

(FITZ WILLIAM THOMAS POLLOK)

AND

W. S. THOM

GYAN

Published by

Gyan Publishing House
5, Ansari Road
Daryaganj, New Delhi-110002
Phone: 011-47034999, 9811692060
E-mail: books@gyanbooks.com

Distribution Network
gyanbooks.com
India, USA, Canada, UK, Australia, France

ISBN: 978-81-212-8388-5 (PB)
First Published, 1900

2nd Impression 2023

Printed at: Gyan Press, Delhi.

WILD SPORTS OF BURMA AND ASSAM
Authors: COLONEL POLLPK, W. S. THOM

WILD SPORTS

OF

BURMA AND ASSAM

WILD SPORTS

OF

BURMA AND ASSAM

BY

COLONEL POLLOK

LATE STAFF CORPS,

AND

W. S. THOM

ASSISTANT DISTRICT SUPERINTENDENT OF POLICE, BURMA

WITH ILLUSTRATIONS AND MAPS

LONDON:

HURST AND BLACKETT, LIMITED,

13, GREAT MARLBOROUGH STREET.

1900

COLONEL F. T. POLLOK.

PREFACE

In 1879 Messrs. Chapman and Hall published a book of mine, *Sport in British Burma*, but I was not in the country at the time, and did not see the proofs or the illustrations—and many, though immaterial, errors crept in. Since then, Upper Burma has been annexed, so that from the base of the Himalaya range to Malaya the whole country, including Assam, is now uninterruptedly British. When the proposed extension of our railway system into Yanan is carried out, there will be a great influx of Europeans into Burma, and during the intervals of business most Britons delight in following the *feræ naturæ;* but without a reliable guide, sport is very difficult to be got there, for the conditions between India and that country are very great, and however *au fait* a man may have been on the west of the Bay of Bengal, he will be quite at sea on the east.

No book giving a description of the wild sports of Upper Burma has been written. In fact, it has often been asserted that there was no sport to be had in the whole of Burma, Upper or Lower, but I trust these pages—copied from diaries—will prove the contrary.

Beyond a casual visit to Amrapoora in 1856 and Mandalay in 1858, I know nothing of Upper Burma or its capabilities for sport, but my colleague, W. S. Thom, has resided over six years in that part of the country, and he has been the pioneer in exploiting its big game, as I may say I was of that in Lower Burma. We have therefore jointly written this Guide to the Wild Sports of those countries. I had thirteen years' experience of Lower Burma, and over seven of Assam. Mr. Thom has spent eleven years in the two Provinces (now one).

I have no doubt, as the country is opened and developed from Assam downwards, it will be formed into a Lieutenant-Governor Chief, with separate Commissioners for each Province, and the best men for administering the country, or for exploiting its vast resources, are those fond of a wild life, and who go into the inmost depths in search of the wild beasts of the field.

There is no country—not even Africa—where there is more and varied game than Assam and Burma. The people of Assam, debased as they are, are preferable to Africans in general, and all Europeans who have come in contact with the Burmese prefer them to most Asiatics.

Neither Mr. Thom nor I pretend to be learned naturalists, but we have been keen sportsmen and kept our eyes open, and have studied the manners and habits of the animals we have hunted, and we flatter ourselves that many points which we have noted have been ignored or overlooked in the best Natural Histories.

In Lower Burma, to be successful as a hunter, elephants are requisite, but are seldom procurable, excepting by a very few. In Upper Burma my colleague did all his shooting on foot, tracking up and stalking game with the assistance of skilled *Moksos* or native hunters, partly because the pleasure and excitement gained in this way were greater than could be obtained from the back of an elephant, and partly because this animal was available only for officers of the Forest and Public Work Departments, and that on rare occasions.

I far prefer shooting on foot to shooting out of howdahs, but for tiger-shooting in Lower Burma, and for big game generally there, nothing could be done without those useful slaves. But I was exceptionally fortunate: I had four attached to my Department, I had always one or two of my own, and the right to indent for four from the Commissariat on payment, and as the Commissariat Officer was an old brother officer of mine he allowed me the pick, and as my *jemadar* had been formerly in the Keddah department, he knew many of the *mahouts* and elephants, and helped me to choose the best for sport.

I was not twenty-one years old when I went to Burma: I possessed the constitution of a buffalo, I had private means of my own, and drew exceptionally good pay from Government, and I was, to all intents and purposes, my own master. I had a district extending from our frontier to close on Moulmein, over the whole valley of the Sittang river. I was employed in road-making and surveying from Meaday down to Bassein and Rangoon, and even to Cape Negrais, thus my opportunities of exploring the country and indulging in its wild sports were unrivalled. In Assam I had similar work to do—I had the districts of Nowgong, Tezpore, Durrung, Goalpara, the Cossyah and Jynteah Hills under me, and I was expected to be out in the district at all seasons; and for nearly eight years there were very few square miles that I had not traversed. Thus, for over twenty-one years I was constantly on the move without once taking extended leave to Europe. I was inured to the climate, which is not nearly as deadly as represented; I was constitutionally strong, and I was also a believer in out-door life, and never drank a drop of spirits or smoked, but I should like to have all that I have spent in beer and other (comparatively speaking) harmless beverages. Not that I see the least harm in partaking of spirits or smoking, if not indulged in to too great an extent; but no one can expect to keep healthy in those Provinces who indulges in brandy-panee, and spends half the day in sleep, and who is afraid to venture out for fear of sunstroke,—those are not "the men for Galway."

F. T. POLLOK.

There are would-be sportsmen who have spent most of their time in mercantile pursuits in Rangoon, Moulmein, and Bassein, and who, having shot a snipe or two, think they know everything that is to be known with regard to sport. Hence they criticize, as Munchausen, the records of adventure and exploits that transcend the limits of their narrow experience, and wax anonymously wrathful with sportsmen who are not ashamed to add their names to what they relate. In reply to the criticisms of such, my colleague and I have merely to say, in anticipation, that our records are taken from our diaries, and are as accurate as they can be made.

W. S. THOM.

I am indebted to the kindness of P. Burges, Esq., of Clifton, Sir Benjamin Simpson, Bart., Mr. Hannyngton of the Burma Trading Company, and to Messrs. Watts & Skeen, Rangoon, for the photographs in the book.

F. T. POLLOK.

CONTENTS

UPPER BURMA

[By W. S. Thom]

ASSAM 425

[By F. T. P.]

COSSYAH AND JYNTEAH HILLS . 490

LIST OF ILLUSTRATIONS

MAPS

INTRODUCTORY

WITH the expeditionary force that helped to conquer Pegu and Martaban were many noted *shikaries*, but they found such a difference existing between the Land of Pagodas and India, that they despaired of finding game, if any game did exist, which was denied by many. Not knowing the language was one cause; the endless savannahs covered with elephant grass from 10 to 30 feet high,—the want of such *shikaries* as they had been accustomed to,—the difficulty of procuring elephants, and, when obtained, not knowing where to seek game, were other causes. Dr. Wilson, once out with me, shot a sambur, but otherwise was unsuccessful; so was Speke, brother of the explorer. So was Grant Allan, as good a sportsman and as capable an officer as India ever produced. He had been over Burma more than any man in Pegu, and in all his wanderings all he had seen were two or three sambur. Both Wilson and Speke wrote to the *Oriental Sporting Magazine* in, I think, 1855, deploring the want of game in Lower Burma. I, though but a youngster, and not within measurable distance of those named as a sportsman, yet from the commencement of my service in Lower Burma in July 1853 I had district work to attend to. I kept my eyes open; I treated the people well, and on the few occasions when I was lucky enough to slay a stray sambur, a thamine, or a hog deer, I kept very little of the meat to myself, and gave the rest to the Burmans who were with me exploring for the best routes for roads. I had seen a little game, but from conversing with men and women in the remoter jungles I became convinced that not only did big game exist, but that it was plentiful, so replied, under the name of "Phoongie," that there was no want of the *feræ naturæ*, but that owing to the disturbed nature of the country, want of elephants, and ignorance of the language, it had yet to be discovered; and I set to work to ingratiate myself with the people. I may without boasting assert that I was the pioneer in Lower Burma, as my colleague has been in Upper, in the shooting of big game. I had exceptional facilities. I spared no expense, and was lucky enough to have a stud of never less than four elephants, and my duties took me too over a vast tract. I ventured into jungles which were avoided by most men, as they were said to be deadly. I had had my bout of jungle-fever in India, so was probably "salted"; was of an active habit, up at daylight, and, after a cup of coffee, either on horseback or an elephant the whole day, getting back in time for a bath and dinner in the evening, which generally formed my only meal.

Nothing the Burmese love more than a pōō-ay, or theatrical performance. When I went to a new locality and put up in a zyat, or rest-house, in the largest village, I sent for performers and treated the people to one of their interminable operas. I gave the womenkind (most influential in Burma) bits of jewellery and finery, a looking-glass or a piece of soap, and asked them to use their influence to get me some intelligence of game. One would say: "Why, Moung Oo or Mg. Kyaw, or Mg. so-and-so, is the village *shikarie* at——" some place she would mention; some other girl would give me information of another man. If not too distant, I would go to the locality, and secure the *shikarie's* services by giving him a few rupees, or a little tobacco, tea and sugar, and occasionally a little rum. Many of them were very chary of going out, fearing, if any accident were to happen, they would be blamed; but the few who did, found I was a fair shot and somewhat generous, keeping little of the meat for myself, and giving the rest to them, which they jerked and sold to the people. It was a slow and laborious process, but patience and perseverance, they say, will conquer most things; so it was with me, and in time I got game; the very thoughts of which make my mouth water and a longing to see the like again, old though I be. Very few sportsmen in Burma have sent their sporting adventures to *The Field* and other sporting papers, until at last an editor of *The Field* said somewhere, that if ever game had existed in Burma it was no longer to be found.

There is no royal road to sporting; to be successful you must be plodding. In a new country learn the language and conciliate the people; and without a certain amount of health and strength you cannot cope with the difficulties inseparable from searching for big game; but adopt a few precautions, such as not sleeping on the ground, for which there is no excuse. Get one of Edgington's trestle-cots; ask for my pattern, as it is an improvement on the old, with a large waterproof cover, and two mosquito-curtains, one of fine muslin, to be used as a precaution against sandflies, and another of net for mosquitoes, together with a cork mattress to put inside, and a pneumatic pillow. Avoid chills—if wet through, change—or, if you can't, put on the thickest coat you have. Wear flannel,—be abstemious in your living,—at the same time, live well. If you have elephants, and are accustomed to drink beer, take a supply with you; a bottle of Lager will hurt no man. If you cannot carry it about, take whisky, and use it as a corrective to water; avoid drinking water unless previously boiled. I here preach what I never practised, for I have drunk water little better than urine, from any pools or river, but it is not wise to do so. But thirst is far more unendurable than hunger, and a man with a parched throat does not consider what is good or bad. Indeed, I believe half the talk indulged in now-a-days of *bacilli* is nonsense. If they are so numerous as the learned say now, I ought to have died years and years ago. Then there are also to be considered the best seasons for sport, and the localities where to find it; these differ somewhat each year; the fires may have been earlier, and the rains also. If so, the new grass will have sprung up and the game will be leaving their strongholds in March; but if the fires are late and also the *Chotabursat* has been slight, the grass will not be fit for grazing until May. I have been out more or less every month, but to attempt to shoot during the height of the monsoon is a misery in Lower Burma, and you get very little owing to the nature of the jungles, which are so heavy that you can see no game until you all but touch it, and few animals are so confiding as to let you get to such close quarters. In the north-west of Tongho I have shot game on foot during the cold months, but for real enjoyment the time is May. Then go to the foot of the Yomahs and beat about the savannahs at their base. When you form a line and advance in Burma you never know what you may start or what you may come across; it may be a tiger, a leopard, a bear, elephant, gaur, or tsine, and various kinds of deer. I have come across all I have mentioned in the course of the same day.

Burma is now one of our principal Provinces, and it has a great future. Our *employés* in it now number by hundreds compared to the dozens when I was there. No one has attempted to depict its wild sports as a whole, and I believe that a book treating of the Lower as well as the Upper portion will be welcome and useful to those who have to spend years there. Sport in any shape is fascinating to the Briton, be he English, Scot, Welsh, or Irish. I know the difficulties and expenses I underwent in acquiring the knowledge I possessed when I left. My colleague has been a most successful sportsman in countries beyond the limits of my own experience, and between us I hope that our book will not only give information to those more intimately connected with the Province, but will please those who are fond of sport in general. A reliable book on sport relating to the country is a godsend to the new-comer.

Were I going to Burma again, if likely to be stationed in Lower Burma, I would take a double hammerless Mannlicher rifle, such as are being made by Westley Richards—a Paradox of either 8 or 10-bore,—a double No. 12 rifle, or an Express ·577 for deer and soft-skinned animals, and a 12 smooth-bore carrying either ball or shot; and much the same for Upper Burma, but on that my colleague will give his views. I have no interest in recommending one maker in favour of another. I have had guns of nearly every maker of note. I recommend Westley Richards because I believe his block-breech action is the best, and that he has persistently used the top lever action for the heaviest and largest bores, when other makers declined to make rifles with it, asserting that they were unsafe. They make guns and rifles at prices to suit every pocket, in every way equal, barring finish and fitting up, neither of which are required for jungle work in the wilds of Burma. Rich people might do far worse than go to the East for a two years' shooting-trip. They could get pig-sticking in Tirhoot; elephant and gaur and tsine, shooting in Upper Burma; any amount of tiger and rhinoceros shooting in Assam; capital all-round sport in Lower Burma. The climate is not pestilential like that of parts of the Dark Continent, and since the rinderpest, our possessions in Eastern Africa have lost two-thirds of its game and nearly the whole of the buffaloes. About Lakoja, where we have troops now, there is good sport, and the place is not very unhealthy, but going up the Niger *is*. I far prefer, having tried them all, our Eastern possessions beyond the Bay of Bengal; the people, too, are so much nicer. You can obtain anything and everything you want in Burma, as there are capital shops in Rangoon, Moulmein, Akyab, and Mandalay. Even the small game has a great attraction for me, especially snipe. With Horace Browne of the Commission, I have made fair bags of Phayre's Francolin at the base of the hills near the White Pagoda, a few miles north of Padoung Myo.

One day Blair was my guest at the Sapper and Engineer Mess; there was a large party, of whom I fear but a few survive. We sat up very late, and probably drank more wine and beer than was good for us. When we got up at daybreak next morning to go after snipe, we were conscious of having heads on our shoulders; but pouring a few chatties of very cold water over us, we felt all right, and sallied forth with six or eight Burmese as beaters to hunt up the longbills. As is usual in the early morning, the birds were very wild, neither of us as steady as we ought to have been, and we fired atrociously. The beaters regularly laughed at us every time we missed, and I have no doubt thought us fools for trying to shoot such small birds on the wing. I fancy we were the first Europeans they had ever been out with, and had never seen birds shot flying. Generally, Blair and I could hit many more birds than we missed; but this day the more we tried to hold our guns straight, the worse we succeeded. This would never do; so we called a halt, took a longish rest, breakfasted, and drank a bottle of beer apiece, a thing we seldom did until the day's sport was over; but to-day it was a case of "a hair of the dog that bit one," and we felt greatly refreshed. When we commenced to shoot again, the sun was well up, the birds lay better, and we commenced to knock them over right and left, much to the amazement of our followers; from jeering they took to praising, and though we had done so badly in the morning, I don't think either of us ever shot better in our lives than that day after breakfast, and we took home thirty-four couple between us.

LOWER BURMA

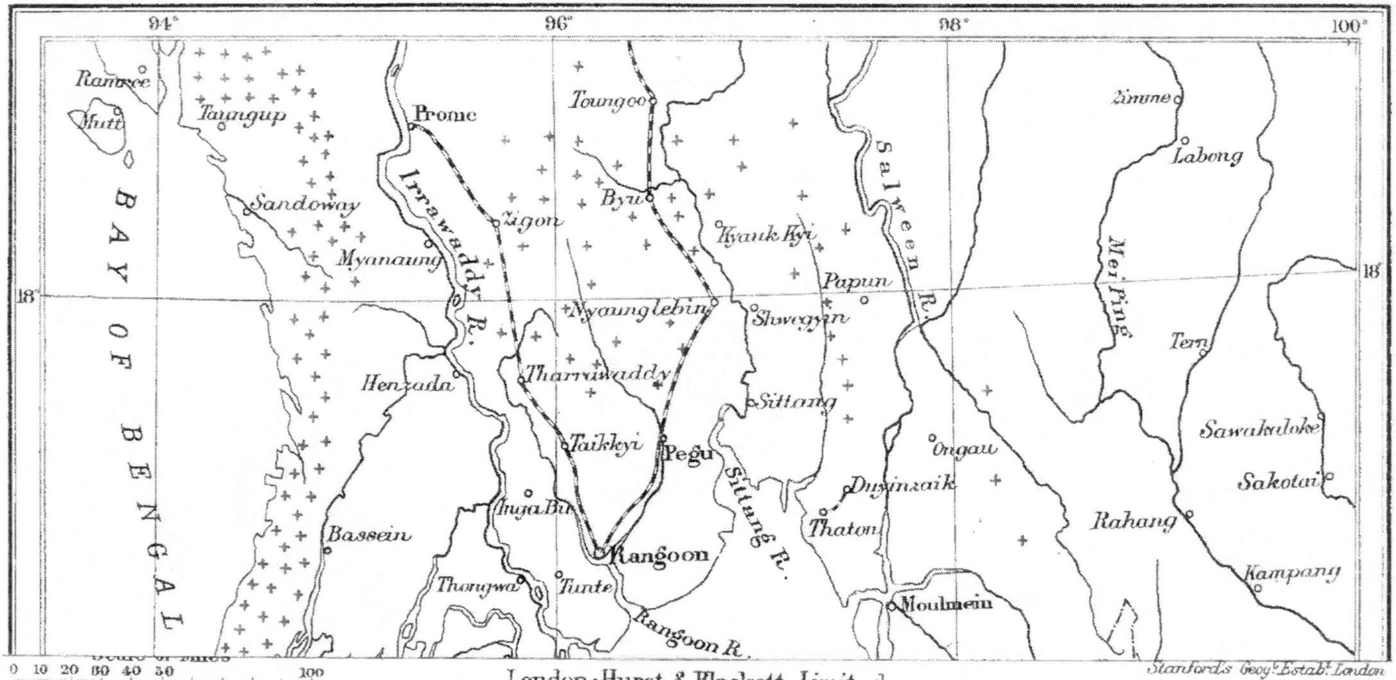

London: Hurst & Blackett, Limited.

Good Sporting areas are marked thus +

WILD SPORTS OF BURMA AND ASSAM

LOWER BURMA

CHAPTER I

In 1826 Arrakan and Tenasserim, provinces of the ancient kingdom, of Burma, were ceded to us. In 1853 Martaban, Pegu, and Bassein were annexed. In 1880 Lord Dufferin made Upper Burma a portion of our vast possessions in the East. Assam was also annexed in 1826.

No great progress was made in Burma until the late Sir Arthur Phayre became Chief Commissioner, but under him it made strides unprecedented in the annals of our rule in India, and now that the whole province from Yunan down to nearly the Straits Settlement is ours, it may be fairly claimed to be considered amongst the most flourishing of our possessions, with a great future before it.

Dr. Mason, a venerable missionary who spent a lifetime in the country, quoting the words of a visitor, says: "It is a beautiful country; in it are views and patches of scenery, green fields and green lanes, that lead back the mind to one's own land. It is a beautiful land when seen on the coast, but it is still more beautiful when seen amidst its mountain streams, streams which cannot be surpassed in romantic beauty even in the annals of poetry." Some of the noblest rivers in the world, such as the Irrawady, Salween, Shwéli, Méza, Myitngé, Mogaung, Mole, and Taeping (these last three are the most important tributaries of the Irrawady), run through its centre or skirt its boundaries, whilst small streams like the Sittang, Shoaygheim, Ghine, Attaran, and many others, aid in its development, and add additional beauty to its scenery.

In Lower Burma, between the sea and the Irrawady are the Arrakan range of mountains, rising to an altitude of 6000 feet, and extending from Chittagong to Cape Negrais. Between the Irrawady and the Sittang, the Yomahs run parallel, and rise to an altitude of from 1500 to 2200 feet, harbouring in their vast solitudes (which have never been explored, except by a few venturesome sportsmen) immense herds of two varieties of elephants, gaur, tsine, two varieties of rhinoceros, buffaloes, to say nothing of the royal tiger, panther, and leopard, and several varieties of deer. Between the Sittang and the Yonzaleen there is the Panloung range, which also extends to the Salween, rising to 7000 feet, and nearer the Shan States to 10,000 feet, and even more. The Salween passes through Karennee and the Shan States, where some of the finest ponies in the world are bred and reared.

The seaports of Burma, namely, Akyab, Sandoway, Bassein, Rangoon, Moulmein, Mergui and Tavoy, invite ships from all parts of the world, and will be of far greater importance hereafter as our trade with China increases.

Lower Burma is rich in minerals, and gold is found in most streams. In recent times it has not been found anywhere in great quantities, but there are the remains of many old workings, which in former days yielded a rich crop of gold to the seekers, and gave a good revenue to the Burmese Government, who used to farm them out. Even now a few nuggets are occasionally found in the Shwégyin river. Quartz of the auriferous deposits is also fairly abundant, and I firmly believe that at some future date Eldorados will be discovered inferior to none of those hitherto found.

Silver is rather scarce in the lower provinces, but, as is well known, it, together with other precious stones and metals, is found in Upper Burma, though the workings have not, I believe, hitherto proved remunerative. Copper, combined with antimony, iron, and sulphur, is found in the islands of the Mergui Archipelago, and also on the banks of the Attaran. Lead is scarce in Lower but plentiful in Upper Burma. Iron pyrites are scattered about everywhere. Tin

RANGOON, AS SEEN FROM DALLA.

From a Photo by Watts & Skeen, Rangoon.

is abundant in the Tenasserim province. Manganese and arsenic are obtainable near Mergui. Coal of an inferior description is found near Mergui, but some eighty miles further inland it is very plentiful and of the finest quality. A vein of excellent coal was discovered near Thayetmyo, but it was soon exhausted. Limestone is plentiful near Moulmein, where are situated the Damathat Limestone Caves, but is scarce elsewhere in the lower provinces. At Yenan-Choung (Stinking Water Stream) are the celebrated earth-oil or petroleum wells, and a few exist elsewhere in the province.

In botany the province, and in fact the whole country, is exceedingly rich. Its teak is inferior to none ; the Amherstia is one of the most beautiful flowering shrubs in the world; whilst many of the orchids, wild-flowers, ground orchids, and flowering shrubs and trees, are amongst the most lovely in the world.

Though it possesses many venomous snakes, such as the hamadryad, cobra, bungarus, and others, they are seldom met with. Its rivers and its coasts abound with the most delicious fish, such as the pomfret, hilsa, mango, and many other varieties, as well as such edibles as crabs, crawfish, eels, etc., and its mountain streams afford capital sport to the lovers of the gentle craft. The Thouk-a-ghat, or drinking-water stream, which falls into the Sittang, a little below Tongho, is full of *mahseir* and of a fish they call *gnamein*, which takes a fly, and is capital eating. Diamond Island has long been famous for its turtle, and I used to turn many when at work at a lighthouse on the Great Coco.

The vast forests and extensive plains covered with perpetual vegetation swarm with mammals and birds, sought alike by the sportsman and naturalist. The wild tea-plant, similar to the indigenous tea-plant discovered in Assam, exists in Karennee, and should one day become a great industry. It has been tried on a small scale in Arrakan, and with most favourable results. In Lower Burma the extremes of heat and cold are not so marked as elsewhere, and there is a total exemption from hot winds. There would be thus nothing prejudicial to the development of leaf, and both the Burmese and Karens are easily led, have no caste, and would readily settle down on an estate, where they were kindly treated and got regular work and fair pay. Tea should therefore be one of the future industries of the country.

HABITS AND CUSTOMS OF THE BURMESE

It is almost impossible to understand a Burman—he is a man of contradictions.

In physical characteristics the Burmese much resemble the Mongolian race, from which they are doubtless descended. They have the same broad faces and high cheek-bones; the eyes are oblique, caused by the structure of the lids; there is seldom any bridge to the nose, the nostrils are rather broad; but since our occupation of the country the people have improved for the better in good looks, for the Burmese women readily accept as husbands all foreigners, so there has been a great mixture of blood, which has shown itself mostly in features. In Arrakan especiálly, years ago the Mongolian type has been modified by a mixture with the Caucasian and the Aryan, and I have seen young girls with remarkably good features and showing but very faint traces of the Mongolian race. But even the unmixed Burmese women, when young, have a pleasing expression, and greatly ingratiate themselves with those with whom they come in contact.

The men, though short, are a fine, robust, athletic race; their frames are well-proportioned, with long bodies and shortish legs, but good length of arms. The head is well set on, shoulders square, chest deep and wide, and legs showing good muscular development.

They wear their hair tied in a knot on the top of the head, and wind round it a piece of muslin or gay silk handkerchief; a jacket hangs loosely from their shoulders over the hips, a *putso* of bright silk is wound round the waist, extending to the ankles, and with one end often thrown jauntily over the shoulder. From the waist down to a little below the knees nearly every Burman is tattooed, in various figures of animals, birds, devils, etc., all enclosed in a groundwork of tracery and flowing lines. This operation commences at an early age

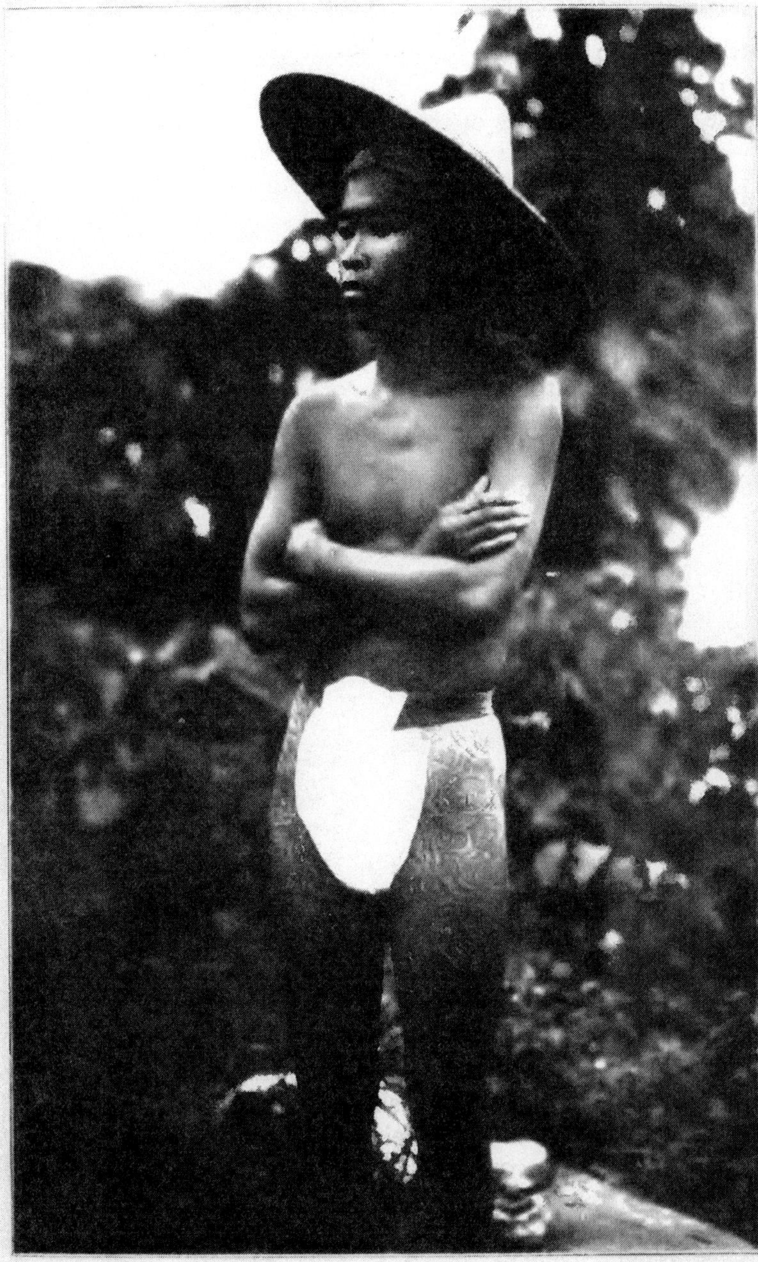

A TATTOOED BURMAN.

From a Photo by Watts & Skeen, Rangoon.

and often extends over several years. It is performed by an instrument resembling a mathematical steel pen. In addition, portions of the arms and upper part of the body are tattooed in cabalistic characters and charms against an enemy, evil spirits, and disease. They also make incisions into which they insert bits of gold and silver and allow the skin to heal over them; this operation they think renders them invulnerable.

The women are fairer than the men, and their features more delicate. I have never in my life seen more perfect figures than those possessed by the young girls. The Hindoos are as good perhaps, and on a larger scale, but the Burmese girls have firm, well-developed busts, small hands and feet, and are well moulded together. Their naturally long black tresses, of which they are very proud, are added to at times with false tails carefully dressed and perfumed, are gathered at the back of the head *à la Chinois*, and gracefully adorned with fresh flowers, sometimes an orchid, jasmine, or a *chumpac*. They are very cleanly in their persons, probably the most cleanly in the world; they bathe once, twice, or even three times a day, and have no disagreeable aroma about them.

They wear, wrapped round the body, a *ta-mein* of silk, woven in vandyke, cable, or serpentine patterns of the brightest dye and varied hues, always blended with great taste. Young girls support their busts by wearing a tight under-jacket. Married women with children dispense with this, and cover their chests by a bodice of a looser material folded in under the left arm. The *ta-mein* is tucked in tightly at the waist, and falls down in front to the ankles, but as the ends only slightly overlap, a portion of the leg, when walking, is exposed, sometimes half-way up the thigh. The bottom of the skirt is of a different pattern, often of a pale pink, with horizontal narrow stripes of dark colours interwoven with gold or silver threads. This skirt trails behind some ten inches or a foot on the ground, and its graceful management, in either walking or dancing, is one of the accomplishments of a Burmese belle. An *enggee*, or jacket, of muslin, silk, or satin, is worn open, and with a *ta-bet* or scarf thrown over the shoulders, partially hides the admirable contour of the bust.

When in full dress, they powder their faces with *sha-nat-kha*, a cosmetic with a fragrance similar to that of sandal-wood, pencil their eyebrows, and rouge their lips. This is all done to make themselves look as fair as possible. They cover themselves over with necklaces, of pure gold inlaid with precious stones, their fingers with rings, and have peculiar ornaments of amber or gold inserted in the lobe of the ear. These ear-tubes are cylindrical, the hollow being large enough for them to insert a cigar. They are inveterate smokers,—even children taking to it before being weaned; they also chew betel-nut and *separee*, with which lime and a little *aitch* is mixed, and yet have small symmetrical white teeth.

Pliability of the arms and body is much prized. By constant practice, a girl is taught to turn the inside of the elbow outwards, and the joint becomes so flexible that it moves with equal facility either way. A girl will stand on a mark, and by bending backwards, pick up a small coin with her teeth which has been placed within a few inches of her heels. They are born actresses, and delight in either seeing or taking a part in theatricals. There is no stigma attached to a girl dancing in public as there is in India to the Nautch girls, who are but courtesans. Their manners are pleasing; there is a mixture of courtesy and freedom, and even the poorest, while frank, are well-bred. In their intercourse with each other they are good-humoured and considerate, and Europeans are struck with the enjoyment, contentment, and happiness of the people. No one is rich, but there are no beggars. The earth is so bountiful that three months' labour suffices to produce enough food for the year. If by any reverse a family is in want, the neighbours assist at once; they are hospitality itself.

They are more truthful than most Orientals. The affection of parents for their children is very great. Filial piety is inculcated as a sacred precept, and much respect is shown by the young to the old. They are fond of amusement and excitement, their motto being, "Sufficient for the day is the evil thereof." Strong, patient, and good-tempered, they are indolent in the extreme, yet they can work like galley-slaves on an emergency. No man seeks to make a fortune; should he by chance do so, he spends it at once in good works, such

A BURMESE BOY BEING TATTOOED.

From a Photo by Watts & Skeen, Rangoon.

as erecting *phoongie* houses or building pagodas, and goes on leading the same life as heretofore, content with a very little. There is no selling of girls when infants for marriage, or worse. The men prefer girls who are fully grown and developed, and the young men and women carry on their courtship openly. About eight o'clock in the evening is courting-time, when the young ladies receive their bachelor acquaintances, and a lamp placed in their casement is a signal that they are at home. The great ambition of a girl is to keep a stall in the market-place. It is her introduction into society, and a sign that she is marriageable; it is the equivalent of our girls being presented at Court or taken to balls and parties. There is a great deal of coquetry on the part of the girl; if she lights a cheroot, takes a puff or two and then presents it to her adorer, it is a sign that "Barkis is willin'"; otherwise, if she refuses to do this act of courtesy, he knows that his attentions are not appreciated, and that he had better seek a bride elsewhere. Parents do not unduly interfere in these matrimonial ventures. Once the couple have agreed to be man and wife there is no delay; a feast is prepared, the happy couple eat out of the same dish before the assembled guests; the bridegroom then presents his bride with *hla-pet* or pickled tea; the compliment is returned, and the ceremony is over. Then follows the interminable *pōōay*, but the couple manage to steal away and go to their home, and as soon as this is discovered, the bridegroom's friends and others assemble round his house, throw stones on the roof and at the doors; this is in accordance with the immemorial custom, but a somewhat inconvenient one to the happy couple, who would prefer their friends' absence to their company; but if it were omitted, doubtless they would afterwards think that a compliment was wanting.

A woman socially is her husband's equal; his superior in the house and in the interior economy, as she buys and sells what she pleases. She has the sole right to any property she possessed before marriage, and also to that acquired afterwards. She can hold real property in her own right, and even obtain legal possession of her husband's if he forsakes her.

For Easterns, I consider the Burmese woman decidedly virtuous. If well and kindly treated, she will seldom commit adultery, and is faithful to her husband unless she has had a *liaison* before marriage, and then, if tempted, she yields, as she thinks the first man has a prior claim on her. If a couple do not agree, nothing is easier than for them to be divorced; they can part by an equal division of goods, or either can go, leaving all the property they possess behind. Occasionally, to be rid of a termagant wife, a Burman will turn priest, or the woman become a nun, or the slave of a pagoda. The man can readily resume his ordinary garb again, and remarry, but not the woman. She can do so, but to have been a pagoda-slave is always a term of reproach, and very few men would marry one, even if she were young and pretty; generally they are old hags. A doctor who visited Burma and travelled in it for some weeks, calls them vestal virgins, which would astonish the old women not a little, as they have probably done their share to multiply and replenish the earth. The people are very sensitive, and put an end to themselves on the slightest provocation, generally by an over-dose of opium. They are omnivorous, will eat or drink anything, from a dead and half-putrid elephant to a snail. They are very fond of fish, and preserve it in various ways; a favourite dish of theirs is *nga-pee*, a horrid decoction of rotten fish pounded with chillies, garlic, and other condiments.

As Buddhists, they are forbidden to take life, and most Burmans would not tread upon a worm, but there are always local *shikaries*, who kill game and bring it in for sale, and no one will refuse to purchase and partake of it, as the sin lies on him who deprived it of life. But between man to man they are most bloodthirsty, and kill and mutilate an enemy with horrid tortures. I have known and seen men who had been strapped down and holes bored through them with red-hot irons. I have seen a string of men, crucified, impaled, ripped open, and left to die with a fire lit under them! They are a mass of contradictions, but for all that, I prefer them to the natives of Southern India.

Burmese burn their dead; only the few who cannot afford to do so, bury them. Directly the breath has left the body,

BURMESE WOMAN.

From a Photo by Watts & Skeen, Rangoon.

the women of the house raise the death-cry; other professional women are called to take up the cry when the relations are exhausted. Coffin-makers are sent for, and do the needful in the street opposite the house. All those who come to offer condolences, contribute to the expenses of the cremation.

After the body has been washed, and, in the case of a girl, her face decorated also, a coin is placed in the mouth. It is then wrapped in a clean white cloth and laid on an open bier in the principal room of the house and left there till the coffin is ready, which is fully two days. When the procession starts for the last obsequies, alms for the *phoongies* and poor are carried in front; then come nuns carrying pickled tea, *pān*, and betel; then the priests, followed by their pupils walking two and two. A band of music precedes the coffin borne by the friends of the deceased, and immediately behind are the relations dressed in white, which is a sign of mourning amongst Buddhists. On the arrival of the coffin at the cemetery it is placed near the funeral pyre with the priests sitting at its head, and the mourners in front of them; the priests then recite the prayers for the dead; the chief mourner pours out water from a cup on to the cloth attached to the coffin, or, in its absence, on the ground, pronouncing at the same time after the chief priest, "Let the deceased and all present partake of the merits of the ceremonies now performing." The assembly reply, "We will." They then retire to a distance, the coffin is placed on the funeral pyre by those whose office it is to set fire to it. Before leaving the cemetery, the alms are distributed to the priests and to the poor, and the pickled tea and *pān* and betel are partaken of by all present. Three days afterwards the ashes are collected, placed in an urn, and buried.

When a high priest dies, he is embalmed and kept for a year, and then burnt with much *tamasha*, as the Indians would say. The whole population of the neighbouring villages turns out; many dummy coffins are made, besides the one containing the defunct, and neatly arranged in a cluster, the one containing the remains of the priest in the centre, with a funeral pyre arranged underneath, in which also there is generally some gunpowder; to this ropes are attached, and on these rockets are laid and fired, all endeavouring to be the first to light the pyre. But before this, as the bier with the dead priest approaches, two sides are formed, ropes are attached to the car, front and rear, and the two pull against one another much as we do when playing at the tug of war; but generally it is a mere pretence, those retarding it give way, and the triumphant party drag the coffin to the pyre and quickly place it in position.

The hubbub and noise are deafening, and the dust fearful. Everybody is dressed to within half-an-inch of their lives, and after some hours' jollification, in which women and children freely mix and take a part, the whole of the structures so carefully and tastefully erected are burned down, the crowd separates, each one going on his or her way rejoicing. The saturnalia begins two days before the cremation, but ends soon after it.

The scene, though repugnant to our ideas of what is becoming at a funeral, is, whilst it lasts, a very gay one, and is meant as a mark of respect to departed goodness. The gorgeous apparel of the men and women, the numerous flags and banners, the structures so gaily painted and resplendent with tinsel, gold-leaf, and silver, help to light up the otherwise sombre scene, or which ought to be one.

Their priests are pure mendicants, they can possess no property, and are supported by the charity of their parishioners. They cannot speak to, or even look at, a woman; they are well housed by the people, and act as village school-masters, and every Burman is taught to read and write his own language.

School commences about an hour before daybreak, and the noise made by the pupils is deafening. When I first heard it I thought it was an attack by Dacoits. Each lad spouts out his lessons at the top of his voice.

A *phoongie* can leave the priestly craft whenever he likes, and become a layman; but this is very seldom done, and one who does it is looked down upon. All the pupils are neophytes, and are dressed in a yellow robe, and go from house to house every morning with a bowl suspended from the neck. He solicits nothing, but accepts silently anything put into the

FUNERAL-CAR OF A HIGH PRIEST.

receptacle, and this forms the daily meal of their masters and themselves.

The women are a merry, pleasant set, and so struck were the stalwart Sikhs, that when, after the war of 1852-53-54, they returned to their own country, many took back with them these, comparatively speaking, plain women, preferring them as wives and companions to the far comelier women of the Punjaub. I have no doubt that our numerous native troops, principally Sikhs, located in Burma, have all taken wives of the country, and have settled down for good in the province.

There cannot be a prettier sight anywhere in the world than a crowd of Burmese gathered together *en route* to a pagoda on a gala day; what with their gay dresses, pretty figures, pleasant faces, banners streaming, flags flying, the beauty of the scenery, and the general jollity, no pleasanter scene could be wished for. The women of course can neither write nor read, because their priests cannot teach them, but I think their ignorance is preferable to what they learn at the schools instituted by Europeans.

I do not myself believe that the missionaries, though earnest, hard-working people, do any good. You cannot convert a Buddhist. If you talk to him of our religion, he will tell you Gaudama and Christ are one, and that the sayings and doings of the latter are but the utterances of the former, who lived some 700 years earlier.

To highly educate people like the Burmese, Chinese, and even Hindoos, is, I think, a great mistake. They were far happier when their minds were unhinged, and they did not ape the vices of the conquering race.

Whilst it is all but impossible to convert a Buddhist, the Karens, having no religion but a legend that the true faith would be preached to them by people ruled over by a queen, have been converted by the dozen. So whilst the missionaries, chiefly American, all but starve on the pittance they get from their Societies when dealing with Burmese, those that preach to Karens live in clover, as they are supported by their converts.

Although the country abounds in large game, it is very

difficult to discover in Lower Burma, because there are no regular *shikaries* in the Indian acceptation of the word. Every village has its local *shikarie*, who lives by trapping and killing game. Taking life is contrary to the precepts of his religion; he is looked upon as one damned by his neighbours, but that does not prevent them buying from him the spoils of the chase.

Their hunting is done principally at night by means of lights and bells, which will be described further on. He also digs pits, lays down snares, uses crossbows, placing them fixed with a string attached across paths frequented by game; or he sits on the lower branch of a tree, and shoots anything passing underneath. For tigers and leopards he uses poisoned arrows, or inserts barbed and poisoned *panjies* along the paths, carefully concealing them with fallen leaves; and so deadly is the poison that if sufficient penetration takes place to obtain but one drop of blood, the beast dies within an hour or two.

At first these local *shikaries* were not willing to accompany Europeans in the chase, because they feared ill-treatment, and believed that if an accident were to happen, they would be severely punished, perhaps even hanged! So few Europeans understood Burmese, and the Burmese dislike having to treat through an interpreter. They don't like, naturally, the jungles in their own vicinity disturbed, because it would interfere with their own sport and profit; but once you can get them to believe in your generosity and kindness, they will attach themselves on to a successful sportsman, who will, in addition to their pay, give them an occasional glass of grog and a cheroot, and all game killed, excepting just enough for camp-followers. This they dispose of at a good profit after converting it into *bilthong*.

They are very useful as guides, but all the niceties of sport must be done by the hunter himself. They are not good trackers;[1] nor do they mark down game, but they know the whereabouts of the beasts, and will take you from one jungle to another and back to camp. The sportsman must trust to

[1] It is different in Upper Burma. *Vide* Chapter III. by my colleague. —F. T. P.

his own knowledge of *shikar* to beat up the game and to kill it. They have very good eyesight, and can generally spy out an animal before any European. They are handy in cutting up game and slinging it on to elephants, and are most useful in rigging up temporary sheds, if required to do so. Tents are seldom taken in Lower Burma.

Good as are these men as pioneers, yet once on a wet, cold misty day, my guides lost their way, and we did not get back to camp for eighteen hours, and should not have got there then had not our men, like most of the Burmese, been able to guide themselves by the stars. We started at 6 a.m. and got back at twelve at night, having been soaking wet from 2 p.m.

CHAPTER II

GAME IN LOWER BURMA

THE following are the Mammalia of the province:—

Elephants. Two varieties
Single-horned Lesser Rhinoceros
Two-horned Rhinoceros
Gaur
Tsine or Wild Cattle
Buffaloes
Sambur
Brow-antlered Deer or Thamine
Hog Deer
Barking Deer
Wild Pig
Serow

Tigers
Panthers
Leopards
Bears
Wild Dogs
Many kinds of Wild Cat
There are no Hyænas, no Antelopes, or Spotted Deer
Jackals are very few, and are only found near Meaday on the old frontier.

In the Tenasserim province are found:—

The Tapir. (Malay)
Mouse Deer

SMALL GAME

Near Prome, Shoaydoung, Padoung, Eeingmah-Pounday, Meaday, Thayetmyo, Mendoon, and along the base of the Arrakan range, along the foot of the Yomahs, the following are found pretty numerously:—

Green Pigeons, five varieties, and Green Doves
Three varieties of Doves
Three varieties of Imperial Pigeons
Ground Doves
Common Blue Rock Pigeons

Woodcock (rare)
Two varieties of Snipe
Jack Snipe (very rare)
Solitary Snipe (very rare)
Godwit
Two varieties of Curlew
Three varieties of Crane

Green-necked Peacock
Yit or Pheasant, allied to the Derricks
Peacock Pheasant
Jungle Fowl
Francolin
Five varieties of Quail
Six varieties of Plover
Duck of various kinds, but never very plentiful in Lower Burma
Geese
Comb Duck or Perching Goose
Three kinds of Teal; three of Bittern
Hares

The following are peculiar to the Tenasserim province:—

Nicobar Pigeons
Double-spurred Peacock Pheasant
Argus Pheasant
Great Fire-back Pheasant

The following are found in the hills only:—

Ruddy-necked Partridges
Three varieties of Francolin

The best places in Lower Burma for game are:—

1. Arrakan range.
2. Mendoon, fifty miles west of Thayetmyo.
3. Ma'ee Pass and along the spurs of the Arrakan range.
4. Eeingmah, Zeagoung, Pounday, along the base of the Yomahs in the Tharawadie district. In the Yomahs north of Pegu, near Cape Negrais, Bassein, north-west of Banlong, inland, along the foot of the Yomahs, in the Yomahs, Mong on the Sitting; inland from Shoayghein and throughout the Yonzaleen. Along the banks of the Attaran river, and in the districts of Mergui and Tavoy. In most of the places I have named there are *shikaries* who will accompany a European, but the difficulty is to obtain elephants, and without them it is useless looking for game in the vast savannahs, covered as they are with impenetrable long grass and reeds ranging from 4 feet to 30 feet in height, and with stems like those of the bamboo, but rather worse, for they are covered with a fluffy sort of down which irritates the skin almost as badly as the Cow-itch.

In the rains elephants and buffaloes wander about, and are met with generally all over the province, especially near cultivated tracts, adjacent to the long grass in which they lie hidden during the day and sally forth to ravage at night. But it is all but useless going after them during the monsoon. The nature of the country is such that no one can traverse the lowlands on foot, owing to inundation and the innumerable tree and swamp leeches which infest these jungles. It is useless trying to kill elephants off elephants, as it is impossible to get the requisite angle. It is very cruel work—I only tried it once, and then I only bagged one at the time, but sent a dozen or so away very badly wounded. Of these, I came across five dead, and nearly shot a Burman who had gone inside one for some tit-bit, and as he crawled out a mass of bloody gore, I thought he was a bear or some other beast, and was just going to fire, when he stood up. The Burmese found three others dead, and these were a godsend to them, for they prefer first the flesh of the gaur and then that of an elephant to all others; but I never tried that mode of sport again.

Green and Imperial pigeons, though most common throughout Lower Burma and the Andaman and Cocos Islands, are very difficult to see when roosting on trees, so wonderfully does their plumage tally with their surroundings. They are at times very good for the table, but the very reverse at others. It depends on the fruit in season. Green doves are very scarce. I don't think I saw above half-a-dozen in twice that number of years. The Imperial pigeons are very large fine birds; some are green, others of a deep metallic or bronze hue, and others blue. The Burmese call them Knit-ga-noa or bullock-birds.

The common Blue Rock pigeons are very plentiful beyond Yenan-Choung, where the earth-oil wells are. The banks of the river are from 150 to 200 feet above the water, and much resemble our chalk cliffs. In these the birds burrow and build their nests, and as there is plenty of grain growing near, they thrive exceedingly, and are very plump and delicious eating.

The Green-necked Peacock is a beautiful variety of the ordinary peacock. It has no bluish purply neck like the Indian bird. It is green all over, but the tail is the same in the two, and grows sometimes six feet long. At Port Blair, Andaman Islands, hybrids between the Indian and Burmese Peafowl were very common, but they were tame in plumage when compared with either of their progenitors.

The Burmese Pheasant, or Yit, is a beautiful bird of silvery grey. When caught young and well fed they are capital birds for the table. They are easily tamed, and often become a nuisance, as their constant cry is very irritating, and as they wander in and out of the house and are off and on to the table even at meal-times. They are common in all hilly parts, but near Zeagoung they were particularly plentiful.

The Jungle Fowl is similar to those in Assam and over the greater part of India, but perhaps a little smaller. It is a game little fellow, and at times affords excellent sport. I used to take up my position on an elephant and have them beaten up towards me, and once or twice I found them as plentiful as pheasants in a preserve in England. Once on the wing, they are very swift and strong fliers, and require a good blow to knock them over.

Phayre's Francolin is also a very handsome bird, something between a painted partridge and a black Francolin as found in Assam. It perches on trees, and its constant cry of "Khā-Kă-Kăh" is to be heard every morning and evening along the right bank from Akoutoung and inland to the Yomahs, but it is not known on the Sittang side.

The Burmese, when they cut their paddy, leave a good deal of stubble, and I have had capital sport about November in the dried-up Dhan Kates, which were situated at the foot of some high land. When flushed, it rises perpendicularly for a considerable distance, and then flies off horizontally. If fired at as it rises, even the best shots are liable to miss it by firing beneath it; but if one waits until it commences its horizontal flight no bird is easier to kill. The Burmese keep these Francolins in cages—why, I don't know, as I never saw them used for fighting, which is so common in India.

Corn Quail are not plentiful in Lower Burma, but I have shot some there, and in the islands in the Irrawady going towards Pagan. The Button and Rain Quail are very plentiful in the season, and afford good sport. It is best to use only very small shot, and not too much of it, or of powder.

Of the Plovers, the golden and the grey are the only ones worth shooting, but the Peewits are very annoying when one is after big game, as they hover about screeching out, "Pity to do it"—and putting every beast within hearing on the *qui vive.* I have then shot them in revenge.

Snipe is, after all, the most pleasant of the small game shooting in Lower Burma, and though plentiful everywhere during the season (which generally lasts from early in August to the end of October, though the birds are found later in certain localities), yet it is not every one who knows the best places to look for them. All paddy fields not too much flooded have them, but these should, in my opinion, be avoided. There is a great deal of knack in knocking the birds over, but more in finding the most suitable places to look for them. I used to go about during the cold season after the paddy had been cut and stored, and noticed places which I thought would be left fallow next season, or I looked up ground slightly inundated and covered lightly with reeds or rushes; and I used to go there and come back in the season with a stick laden with the long-bills when better shots than myself had not a quarter of the birds to show. The Burmese don't cultivate the same fields every year; they leave some fallow for cattle to graze upon, which get manured by their droppings. The ground is always wet, and as they roam about, the cattle turn up the sods with their hoofs, and the snipe—which are never far off—pounce upon the worms, and will not leave such ground if not too much harassed. Some wonderful bags have been made in India, and also in Burma. An officer of the 80th or 18th regiments, I forget which, killed, near Shoaydoung, in 1852, 80 couple in one day; but I think the record bag has been 130 couple to a single gun somewhere near Madras.

I never shot more than 51½ couple in the day, and the most I ever found on my stick on getting home was 49½ couple, the others having been purloined or dropped off. I once thought I was going to make an immense bag. I was shooting at Tsében, and before twelve o'clock I had 36 couple on my stick. I then went to the Zyat, where I was putting up, for breakfast, thinking I should double my bag by the evening; but heavy rain set in; the birds got wild, and I only killed 12 couple more, and *one* hare, which was a rarity on the Sittang side.

I was Executive Engineer for five years at Tongho, our then frontier station. We had as many as 80 Government elephants in the Pheel Khana, and as these had to go considerable distances for their daily *charah*, the surrounding country, soon after the rainy season set in, became a mass of pitfalls, rendering the ground almost impossible for horse or foot to go over.

As I had elephants of my own I could always go about, and more often than not took one or two men with me. One day I was out alone, and had visited the best snipe grounds within a radius of five miles without scarcely seeing a bird. I sat down on a bund, and whilst deploring the bad prospect before me I noticed a small herd of buffalo going along in single file. They passed me, crossed a shallow sheet of water, and entered a forest. Where buffaloes go to graze there is sure to be some marshy spot; I brightened up a bit, and followed. I thought I knew every inch of the country, and never dreamt of there being a marsh in the midst of a forest, but within a couple of miles I came upon a quin or clearance in the forest; it was about two miles long, and perhaps three-quarters of a mile broad. In this the buffaloes commenced to feed. I put my elephant into it, and up rose a wisp of some dozen snipe and lit again close by. I was off my steed in no time, and better sport I never had. I had just got out my first breech-loader, a pin-fire by Westley Richards, and not expecting much sport had not brought very many cartridges with me. The birds lay well, and pitched again within fifty yards. The walking was easy—it was evident it had never been shot over before, and in a very short time, and before I had gone over half the marsh, I had expended all my cartridges and had 39½ couple of birds to show. Within a few days afterwards I took Lloyd, the Deputy Commissioner, with me. We began to shoot about eleven, and left off at four, with a short interval in the afternoon for lunch and rest. Lloyd had then 36½ couple of birds, and I had 36 couple. Going homewards on the elephants, two snipe got up, and I bagged them both with a right and left. The truth is, I lived so much on elephant-back in those days, and for years afterwards, that I could shoot almost as well off one as I could on foot.

A good retriever is worth his weight in gold for snipe-shooting. I bought in 1860 a nice-looking, well-bred, spaniel pup. The parents had been imported by Col. Pinson—a well-known dog fancier.

This pup soon attached himself to me, and as he showed a propensity for retrieving, I took to shooting birds and throwing things for him to fetch, but I had not had him out shooting game until he was about a year old. I was going across the Kabong river to a pet piece of snipe ground which was then only known to me, and to get there I went on an elephant, and took the dog on the pad behind me. Before long the dog was as sick as if he were crossing the Channel in rough weather for the first time, and by the time we got to the ground seemed to be all abroad. Where I dismounted there was a small Zyat. I left my tiffin-basket there, and walked into the snipe ground with the dog at my heels. I had soon several birds on the ground, and bid the dog fetch, but he showed no aptitude at retrieving at all, and would not leave heel. I was very fond of him, but utterly disgusted at his behaviour, as I had expected great things from him, so I went on shooting, and presently missed him altogether. I screamed myself hoarse calling him, but could find him nowhere, nor had the coolies with me seen him go away: so I thought I had lost him, and went on shooting till about twelve, when I went back to the Zyat to breakfast, and there I found my dog curled up close to the basket. I don't know whether I was more pleased at finding him, or angry at his behaviour, but I made much of him, fed him, and took him out again, but it was useless—he would not retrieve. So I thought I had been mistaken in him, and never meant to take him out again. He sat behind me on the pad going home, with 26 couple of snipe close under his nose; he was not sick.

Whether he got used to the elephant's motion and began to comprehend what was required of him from his close contact with the birds I cannot tell, but the very next time I mounted an elephant to go out snipe-shooting, he of his own accord jumped up behind me, and when I commenced to shoot, although rather wild at first, he soon settled down and retrieved as if he had been used to it all his life. In time he became a perfect retriever: he would remain at heel if told—or hunt if desired well within shot. My elephant got quite accustomed to him, and would allow him to jump on and off, but would not allow another dog to come near him.

One day I hit a snipe; it flew some way, then towered and fell into the midst of a very large dense sugar-cane field. I never expected to see that bird again, but involuntarily said: "Go in and seek." He took the fence at a fly—was not in the field five minutes when he returned with the bird in his mouth. Dogs don't last any time in India. I had him for three years, and he then—whilst romping round me—fell dead of heart disease, and I lost a dog that I was as fond of as of a child.

Every now and then we hear a great outcry against snipe-shooting in India. Those who are too lazy and devoid of energy pronounce it unhealthy; but all I can say is, that some of the best-worn and healthiest men in India, even after forty years' service, are those who have been devoted not only to big game shooting, but have also been ardent and constant followers of the long-bills.

Of course if people whilst snipe-shooting drink brandy-panee, smoke incessantly, wear linen, sit in their wet clothes when they get home, probably in a draught or under a punkah, or do other foolish things, they must expect to get ill, as they deserve to do; but for a healthy man who is also ordinarily prudent, not only no harm, but positive benefit, will be derived from following such sport. If a man is incapable of standing a day's snipe-shooting, he is certainly unfit for campaigning, and the sooner he retires and vegetates in his club in London the better. Wading in mud and water is a healthful recreation compared to sleeping through the greater part of the day and constantly imbibing pegs and smoking strong tobacco to excess. It is not men of an active disposition who suffer from an Indian climate, it is those of a sedentary habit. With a proper covering to the head, which can be bought for a rupee or two, a man can defy the fiercest sun, and whilst moving about he need not fear getting or being wet, especially if he wear flannel and change his clothes directly he leaves off shooting, which is the best; or, immediately he gets home, has a tepid bath and puts on clean clothes.

He will not only feel no ill effects, but he will positively be better for the exercise he has taken. But avoid stimulants during the heat of the day, and whilst toiling through mud and water under a broiling sun, for snipe can best be shot with advantage during the hours of ten to four. Before and after that, the birds get wild. The less spirits a man drinks in India the better. There is no harm in his taking a fair modicum of the liquor which best pleases him with his evening meal after the day's fatigue is over, nor indeed a moderate allowance of claret-cup or shandy-gaff (beer and ginger-beer mixed) or even a bottle of Lager beer with his late breakfast or tiffin, but it is best as a rule to avoid drinking anything, water not excepted, whilst actually shooting. The more you drink, the more you want. Tea is a fair substitute, but drink as little as possible. Men who wish to lead a healthy life in India must not be molly-coddles, but be given to out-door sport, be it shooting, riding, cricket, rackets, lawn-tennis, and the like, but they must at the same time lead a sober life. Drink used to be the curse of India, but since the habit has died out Indian lives are accepted by insurance offices as good as those of others who live in more favoured climes. Now that European troops are being gradually concentrated on Hills, single stations for native troops are getting more numerous, and I think in choosing a place where six or eight officers are to be bottled up for several years, thought ought to be had for their amusement and recreation. If a lot of officers get together in a locality devoid of sport, and with nothing to distract them except their daily routine of drill, it is placing them at a great disadvantage, and the chances are, however efficient and good they were when first they arrived at such a station, they will soon deteriorate. If there be neither shooting nor riding to be had, then I think the Government should provide a racket-court, a swimming-bath, and lawn-tennis grounds. For be sure that all work and no play never answers anywhere, least of all in India.

How can a man who takes no exercise ordinarily be fit to take part in such a campaign as that of the North-West, where we have met more than our match in the wild savages who are at home in their crags, and to whom climbing mountains, or a twenty-mile trudge, is but child's play? Pick out men who show bodily activity and endurance. Pluck, all Britons and Irish possess: but more is wanted. Put all men useless for such work on half-pay; they are no use as leaders of men, and the only use of officers is to lead the way, and how can they do that if they are not physically fit by constant exercise? and where can that be obtained so well as in following wild field sports? Moreover, a man accustomed to meet the denizens of the forest has his wits about him, or he is snuffed out. He will exercise all the cunning he has learned in wood-craft to outwit not only the beasts of the field, but the enemies of his country.[1] All the cramming he has learned under the present system is not worth a year's experience of sport, followed up by a six months' campaign. Our officers and men have shown pluck, but the enemy opposed to us are just as plucky and have out-fought and outwitted us, solely because they were physically more fit than ourselves.

Godwits are seldom seen. Only one of the Curlews is fit for the table, in my opinion; but some people like the Raj Curlew, a large black bird. Of the Cranes, the Coolin or Kurruk, though plentiful in India, is very rare in Lower Burma; there are two or three kinds of Bittern, one very small, but they are seldom shot. As for the Waders, Storks, etc., their name is legion.

Of all the small game shooting in the lower province, Duck-shooting is the poorest. Notwithstanding that the country is greatly inundated during the monsoon and from the flooding of the rivers, it dries up about the time the annual migration of the duck tribe takes place. There are no large bheels or tanks during the cold season, so the ducks pass over to India where there are suitable places for them, and where they swarm; but a very few only remain in Pegu. During September I have seen a good many of the Comb Duck, which often, like the Whistling Teal and also the small Blue-winged Teal (commonly called Cotton Teal), perch on trees, but they are not thought much of for the table. There are also a few

[1] *Vide* the Boers, who are born sportsmen, and they have outwitted us as they have been in the habit of doing the *feræ naturæ* of their country.

D

Brahminee Ducks in pairs along river-banks, but neither are they appreciated. There was a large bheel a little below Shoaydoung where a few ducks could be picked up by going after them in dug-outs. In the delta of the Irrawady a few also are found.

The water-fowl, as distinguished from the ducks and teal, are very numerous, but none of them are worth mentioning excepting the water-pheasant.

The hares on the Irrawady side are fine large beasts, many of them nearly as large as English ones, and are fairly plentiful; whilst those on the Sittang are very rare, much whiter, and not much bigger than a rabbit. If properly cooked, an Indian hare is not half bad eating, but though in most things culinary the native servants and cooks are unrivalled, they are not adepts at cooking game.

When I was sent to Namyan—five miles south of Prome—to clear it out for building a Station, there was very fair sport there. I have shot snipe, hares, francolins, jungle fowl, and occasionally a barking deer, on the same day.

BIG GAME OF LOWER BURMA

Naturalists acknowledge but two species of elephants, the African and the Asiatic—in which they are undoubtedly correct; but why they assert that the Muckna or Hine is identical with the Goondas I do not know. Mr. Sanderson—for whom I have the greatest respect as a sportsman and observer—remarked in his *Thirteen Years among Wild Beasts*, that the having tusks or not was merely accidental, like whiskers in a man; but I maintain that the two beasts are varieties, though of the same species. Any good mahout, whether Indian or Burmese, laughs at such a theory. There are marked differences, not only amongst the males, but those differences extend to the females. In Ceylon they are almost all Mucknas, also in Sumatra; in Burma there are more Hines than Goondas. In Assam, Goondas predominate, but there are plenty of Mucknas too. In India the latter are decidedly in the minority, and, I think, if further search be made, it will be acknowledged that Mr. Sanderson made a mistake in saying they were identical. The Goondas, male and female, have a broader expanse across the forehead ; the bump between the eyes and the root of the trunk is more prominent, but the hollow between the eye and ear, commonly called the temple, is less marked. Its countenance is more pleasing, its eyes brighter and kinder-looking; it seldom grows to the height of the Muckna. The males have large tusks, the females rudimentary ones.

The Muckna, called " Hine " in Burma, has the head much longer and narrower, the temple very much depressed; the trunk is longer, more ponderous, possessing immense strength, as if to compensate the beast for the want of the formidable tusks possessed by its rival. Both males and females have rudimentary tushes only, longer and thicker in the male than in the female; the eyes are small and sleepy-looking, and its general appearance morose; and even when quite young it has an old look. In size, they grow taller and are more leggy than the Goondas. The two varieties herd apart, but interbreed at times, the males often fighting for possession of the females, and the result of the cross-breed is that you get large males with very poor tusks, but still tusks, as distinct from tushes, which adorn the Mucknas.

In Ceylon there is not above one tusker to three hundred Mucknas. I doubt if there would be that number even, had not tuskers been imported from the mainland for work in the timber yards, as only tuskers can carry and stack the heavy squared logs. Some of these in days gone by have probably got loose or have had intercourse with the female elephants of the country, and a throw back is now and then the result. But from long association with both varieties I am convinced, in my own mind, that they are varieties, and not identical.

If Nature has not given intellect to these animals, it has given them an instinct next thing to it. One has only to hunt them in their wilds to learn how wonderfully Providence has taught them to choose the most favourable ground, whether for feeding or encamping, and to resort to jungles, where their ponderous bodies so resemble rocks or the dark foliage by which they are surrounded that it is most difficult for the hunter to distinguish them from surrounding objects; while their feet are so made, that not only can they trample over any kind of ground, whether hard or soft, thorny or smooth, but without emitting a sound. Some of their encamping grounds are models of ingenuity, surrounded on three sides by a tortuous river, impassable for ordinary mortals by reason either of the depth of water, its precipitate banks, quicksands, or entangling weeds in its beds, whilst the fourth side would be protected by a tangled thicket or quagmire. In such a place (as I have found them in) the elephants are in perfect safety, as it is impossible to get at them without making sufficient noise to put them on the alert. Their mode of getting within such an enclosure is also most ingenious. They will scramble down the bank where the water is deepest, and then, either wading or swimming up or down stream, ascend the opposite bank a good half-mile or more from the place they descended, thereby increasing the difficulty of following them. I was over an hour once endeavouring to get into such a fastness as I have attempted to describe, in which some twenty or more elephants were assembled, within a space nowhere more than four hundred yards square, but so well were all the approaches protected, that when at last I did succeed in getting over the preliminary difficulties, the noise we made was sufficient to have awakened the seven sleepers, to say nothing of disturbing a herd of elephants always more or less on the *qui vive*, that I had the pleasure of seeing them make their exit one way as I entered that on the opposite, and I never even got a shot, for such was the intricate nature of the country, it was useless—indeed all but impossible—to follow them with any chance of getting within range. They prefer forests by day and open ground by night, and feed on bamboos, wild cardamam, plantains, null, branches of certain trees, the ficus preferred, or long grass, which is abundant in all the plains; but if there be any cultivation within reach of their stronghold they will go for it and do more harm by trampling it down than by devouring it, which is not inconsiderable either. It is marvellous too how they remember the seasons when certain fruits are ripe. I have noticed this more in Africa than in India, but it is true of both. Before this fruit or vegetable appears there will not be an elephant within fifty miles of the locality; directly it ripens, down come the lordly beasts and hover about till the season is past or the succulent morsels devoured.

To hunt these animals successfully on foot is very hard work, and requires a man to be not only in good training, sound of wind and limb, but also to be possessed of determination, undaunted pluck, a quick eye, and very sharp ears; he must also have learnt the art of walking over ground covered with fallen timber and *débris*, and through dense jungles and forests without emitting the slightest sound.

Huge as are these beasts, none are easier to kill if the hunter comes across one whilst on foot at sufficiently close quarters, and if he knows the right spot to aim at and hit, and the angle to fire. A knowledge of the two must be combined; one without the other is useless. Although I have lately read in Mr. Chandler's *Through Jungle and Desert* that with the Mannlicher ·256 rifle, his comrade Von Hohnel killed elephants at 300 to 400 yards, I need not say such would be impossible in India, because you would never see them at such distances. The golden rule is to get as close as possible —the distance should not exceed 20 yards, better if it be some ten paces closer. General Michael, the great elephant-shot of Southern India, lays down certain rules for shooting them in the *Encyclopædia of Sport.* They differ very slightly from mine already published in *Sport in Burma*, and *Fifty Years' Reminiscences of India.*

General Michael's.	Mine.
1. "If the animal be directly facing you, with both eyes visible, and standing on the same level as yourself, or a little above you, plant your ball low in the rounded bump which is so conspicuous on an elephant's forehead just above the trunk. At that spot there is a convenient opening in the	1. The bump between the eyes, which should be fired at from the front, low down and upward.

General Michael's.	Mine.
skull through which the bullet will pass slightly upwards, direct to the brain.	
2. "If he be facing you, with both eyes visible, but standing on a lower level than yourself, plant your ball in the concavity of the forehead just above the rounded bump.	2. Not noticed.
3. "If the animal be standing at three-quarters face towards you, with only one eye visible, shoot into the hollow of the temple in a line between the eye and the orifice of the ear, at such an angle that the bullet may cut the middle of the imaginary rod passing through the ears.	3. The temple, between the corner of the eye and top of ear. This shot should be fired either from the right or left face, from the front, slightly upwards and backward, or in the centre of the hollow or temple equidistant from the corner of the eye to the top of the ear. Of all shots this is the easiest to kill with, and the safest to the hunter, because being on one side, if the shot does not prove fatal, and the elephant either charges or involuntarily rushes forward, as most animals are apt to do on suddenly receiving a wound, the sportsman will not be in the line of charge or flight, and will be less liable to be trampled upon than in firing the front shot.
4. "If he be standing exactly broadside on to you, shoot straight into the orifice of the ear.	4. This corresponds with my No. 5, which is—fire straight across into the orifice of the ear. For this shot the gun should be on a level with the ear.

General Michael's.	Mine.
5. "If he be standing with his head three-quarters turned away from you, and if you can still see one eye, shoot behind the ear when he flaps it forward, at the level of the orifice. If his head be so much turned away from you that you cannot see his eye, do not fire.	5. This corresponds with my No. 3, which is—a spot just behind the ear at the junction of the head ; but this is a shot one seldom gets.
6. "Get as close as you can," etc. (In all of which I agree, but have already stated them.)	6. I have mentioned two other vulnerable spots—a shot fired from a moderate height downwards in a forward direction, striking the back of the head at the junction of the spine—when death will be instantaneous. A ball placed behind the shoulder at the point of the elbow. I have seen this done by native *shikaries*, successfully. A shot fired into an upraised foot will cripple the beast and make him an easy victim to succeeding shots.

It will be seen that we differ very little, if at all; but I would advise the young sportsman to be guided by General Michael in preference to myself, because he has seen so much more of elephant-shooting than I have. The spots I have mentioned and the angles were all successfully tried by myself, but I don't pretend to pit my experience against his. My colleague's remarks also deserve attention.

Although the trumpeting of elephants at night leads one to suppose that they are close at hand, yet this noise is very deceptive. They wander about so silently, and, as a rule, they go such immense distances, that a stern chase is, with them, the proverbially long one. Although I shot several elephants in Lower Burma, yet, as my colleague will relate his adventures which will be new, whereas mine would be stale, I leave them out.

Elephants are at all times a wandering race; they consume so much, and waste so much more, that no single forest could long support them, hence their roving propensities. During the rains they are very destructive to the paddy crops; when the harvest has been gathered, they retire to their hill fastnesses; it is best to follow them there, but somehow—with a few exceptions—sportsmen now-a-days fear discomforts and fever more than a generation or two back. There is no royal road to sport—risks must be run, if you wish to be successful and are at heart a *shikarie*. You must first learn to shoot quickly and accurately; then study the habits of the beasts you wish to follow, and the right way to circumvent them, and then to rough it.

Elephants have a very keen sense of smell and of hearing,[1] and so they must be approached up wind; and in the dry season, owing to the number of fallen twigs and leaves, it is almost impossible to come close enough to a herd to be able to kill one. If they hear the slightest noise, off they go, but after the jungles have been burnt and a shower or two has fallen, particularly when they are feeding on bamboos, they are easier to get at. A friend of mine once got so close to a tusker's quarters, that he gave him a pat to make him turn out, which he did, only to fall dead instantly.

The tree leeches,[2] so plentiful in forests inhabited by these beasts in Lower Burma, are a sad drawback to the pleasures of sport—as I never found anything which could keep them out for long. I tried the crude petroleum as obtainable in Burma; that did for a while, but directly it got washed off by the dew, in they got. The best—though by no means an

[1] Their sense of hearing or sight is dull, in my opinion, compared with their sense of smell.—W. S. THOM.

[2] None in Upper Burma.—W. S. THOM.[1]

---

[1] He has found plenty lately in the Arrakan Yomahs.—F. T. P.

absolute—preventative, is wearing first thick worsted stockings, and over them drawing on a pair of closely knitted cotton or silk stockings, and saturating them with either petrol or a thick decoction of salt and very little water. But then if they can't get at your legs or feet, they will crawl down your back, or get in anywhere, where a loophole is left. They not only deplete one, but the bites very often fester. In fact they, ticks, and mosquitoes, are the plagues of a sportsman's life, and caüse him frequently, I fear, to use many and often big, big D's.

Some remarks on elephant-shooting by that excellent sportsman Col. McMaster are so apropos that I take the liberty of inserting them here.

"Those who only think of elephants as they have seen these domestic giants working at any of the innumerable tasks on which these almost reasoning slaves may be employed, can hardly imagine how puzzling a matter it is to distinguish them amongst the dark shadows and irregular outlines that fill up any portion of a landscape in their forest haunts.

"I was for some moments, it seemed to me hours, waiting in long grass and reeds within a *few feet*, not yards, of the head of a fine tusker, without being able to get a satisfactory shot at him, or even see more than an indistinct dusky outline of form, or a dark shadow as his trunk was raised aloft, when the mighty beast suspected that he scented mischief. Having at length made sure that there was something uncanny near him, he uttered a shrill cry and wheeled right round on the very spot on which he stood, without exposing any more vulnerable target than his enormous hind-quarters, at which it would have been wicked and wanton cruelty to fire—rushed down the hill, followed by his family (eight or ten unwieldy wives and sturdy children), whose progress, as they crashed through the dense undergrowth of long grass, caused a noise sufficient to startle any one whose nerves were not tightly braced, and which my pen is certainly too weak to describe."

The following is an extract from the *South of India Observer*, by "Hawkeye"—General R. Hamilton, I believe;

a brother of that famous draughtsman and *shikarie*, General Douglas Hamilton, better known as "Velvet Foot" of the old sporting magazines.

"On another occasion I was *blown* at by a wild elephant, who threw her trunk out from behind the jungle lining the narrow path along which we were running to intercept the herd, and blew her nose so suddenly in the chest and face of the leading man, that he fell back right upon me. We had cut this elephant off from her companions, and having a young calf to take care of, she had loitered behind the herd. In this case we noticed what I have before alluded to—the wonderful and extraordinarily quiet manner in which these gigantic animals noiselessly move through the forest when trying to avoid observation or danger."

The height of an elephant is all but twice the circumference of the front foot as it rests on the ground. This is not quite exact, but near enough for all purposes. Elephants vary much in size. We hear of 12, 13, and even 14 feet, as mentioned by some writers; the same credence can be placed on that statement as of the 12, 13, and more feet tigers. I do not think that elephants grow to the same size as they used, for one of 10 feet is now very rare, and a taller all but unknown; but there is the skeleton of one in the Calcutta Museum of Natural History which measures 11 feet, 2 or 3 inches in height, and must have been, when living, close on 12 feet. The tallest elephants I have ever seen, wild or tame, were Mucknas. There was one in the Commissariat, a very old decrepit one, 10½ feet, but 9 feet for a male is a fair size—rather over than under, and 8 feet for a female. For Lower Burma elephants are a *sine quâ non* for hunting. There are places where game can be followed on foot, when you get there, but to reach the localities you must have these giants to take you there.

I have never known an elephant that could be invariably depended upon for dangerous shooting; they are like women —"Uncertain, coy, and difficult to please." I have had them as staunch as possible one trip; perhaps the very next—without the slightest cause—they would run from a deer and even from a hare!—whilst if a peafowl or partridge got up with a whirr under their trunks, they would quake with fear and hesitate to advance. One of my elephants, a very massive, powerful female Koonkie, did not care two pins for a tiger, but if she saw a pony coming towards her at a canter she would run for her life, and nothing could stop her.

Be careful with your gear for all your elephants; have the guddies made to fit each individual animal. No two have the backbone alike; in some it is far more prominent than in others; the portion over the spine must be left open, and the pad, lined with pith, should be well stuffed and sufficiently thick to prevent anything placed on it pressing on the back ridge. If you don't see to this, and your beast gets a sore back, you can't use him. The lump formed has to be lanced and the pus let out, and if an elephant is once cut he is never so staunch afterwards as before the operation—at least, that is my own experience after having kept them for twenty-one years. A good mahout will instil pluck into a cowardly elephant, whilst a coward will cause the pluckiest animal to run away. We all know what influence a man has on a horse—it is doubly so on an elephant, which is a far more impressionable beast, and with not half the spirit of a thorough-bred horse. The behaviour of the animal is but a reflex of that of his rider. I here give an instance, though it did not occur in Burma, but in Assam.

Col. J. Macdonald, Deputy Superintendent of Surveys in Bengal, a capital sportsman, was on a tour of inspection, and as he was anxious to kill a rhinoceros or two, I took him with me into the dooars where I had to go on duty. The Luckeepore Zemindar lent him for the trip one of the largest and staunchest elephants in the province, off whose back tigers, rhinoceros, buffaloes, etc., had been killed by the dozen. His history too was a curious one. He was born in captivity, his mother having been caught but a few months before his birth, which took place on the same day as the Zemindar's eldest child. The natives are very superstitious, and the Brahmins foretold that the prosperity of the family depended on their keeping possession of the elephant, who rapidly developed into a very fine and high caste animal, but with only one tusk.[1] When young he had been considerably maltreated by a huge Muckna; but when he was about twenty he walked off into the jungles and was not heard of for two years. There was great grief in the Zemindaree, and all efforts to find him proved vain; but after he had been given up and mourned over as one lost for ever, he returned to his shed as quietly as if he had never left it. The first thing he did was to go in for his old enemy the Muckna, and after a severe fight he vanquished his opponent and reigned supreme, and has shown no inclination to revert to a wild life since. Macdonald was decidedly in luck getting him, as his owner did not often lend him to people. With him came the mahout who had been with him since his birth.

On May 6 we arrived at Soonapilly, where in general rhinoceros were plentiful; we started very early on the 7th, and came across fresh marks at once; but as it was a boisterous day, the beasts themselves had retired into the long grass, where it was not worth while to follow them, as shooting them in that was out of the question. Whilst looking for these pachyderms we came across some marsh deer, and afterwards fell in with a herd of buffaloes, and duly accounted for some of each. We found there was a party of elephant-noosers camped not far off, who had disturbed the game, so we moved camp to Basbarie, going across country ourselves, and sending our traps by village pathways. I told Macdonald to lead the way as soon as we came across the fresh track of a rhinoceros, and it was fortunately travelling the same way as ourselves. I had a Cacharie mahout, Sookur by name, a very plucky fellow, and about the best tracker I ever saw. Although the marks were those of the morning and we followed up as fast as we could, we did not come across our quarry under six or seven miles, and then found her with her little one lying down in a mud-hole. We both fired a couple of shots each, and the hubbub that followed was deafening. The rhinoceros grunted its peculiar cry, and even the redoubtable Maina, who had heard this cry times without end, turned tail; mine did the same, of course. By

[1] The natives prize these more than those with two tusks, and call them Gosein.

HOWDAH ELEPHANTS.

From a Photo by P. Burges, Esq.

the time we got back we found the big beast dead, and as the young one had also been hit, we had to kill it.

On the 9th we started at daybreak, going along the banks of a stream, and soon hit off a trail, Macdonald leading, and I keeping a little on one side, ready to pour in a volley if required. In about an hour we came upon a fine male. Macdonald fired and hit, but he ran into grass about 20 feet high, and into this we followed, but there were so many tracks in every direction that we soon lost the one we had been following. We still continued our course, and presently came to a patch of unusually high and dense grass into which Maina refused to enter, and mine hung back too. So we knew there was something ahead of us. We told Maina's mahout to push his beast in, but he declared it would not go in, so Sookur called out: "Get out of the way: it is you who are afraid, not the elephant!" Giving Lutchmie a few vigorous prods he drove her headlong into the entangled thicket. I looked about everywhere, and had perhaps gone through half the patch without seeing anything, when something induced me to look back, and there within ten yards of me stood a full-grown rhinoceros, craning its neck and staring up at me in a peculiarly idiotic manner; a lucky shot dropped her dead, and then we discovered that there was a young one with her: so leaving the carcase and the butcha undisturbed, we sent an elephant back to the village for nets and men to catch the calf, and went on ourselves. It was, as I have said, a boisterous day, and a nasty drizzling rain set in; the grass was so blown about that to track any animal was useless, so we were thinking of returning to camp when we came upon two very fresh spoors. We could not resist following them for awhile, Macdonald still leading. We had to go further than we thought, and again came upon very heavy grass. Maina suddenly turned off to the left and went off full score. I called out, "Where are you going? that is not the way the rhinoceros have gone." But I got no reply, and the elephant and his rider vanished. Sookur, after abusing Maina's mahout, went straight on, and within a hundred yards I came upon two full-grown rhinoceros. I could see their ears and indistinct forms, looking towards me, so guessing for the chest of the larger, I let fly. A shriek and a headlong charge was the result—Lutchmie spun round like a teetotum and went off at her best pace. I had just time to turn round and fire as the rhinoceros' nose was within a foot of my elephant's posterior. I was using a muzzle-loader—a double, two-groove No. 10 rifle by Joseph Lang, the bullets hardened with a mixture of quicksilver. The bullet entered the back and passed out at the belly and floored my antagonist, but the row she kicked up frightened Lutchmie to such an extent that although I got her to go back, the least movement on the part of the mortally wounded beast made her scamper, and correct shooting was impossible. I knew the beast could not survive, and not wishing to get my elephant cut, I left her and made the best of my way home.

I bathed, lunched, and still there was no news of Macdonald, but as he had our breakfast-basket behind his howdah, containing all that was requisite for refreshing the inner man, I knew he would not starve, but wondered what had become of him and Maina. He returned about 6 p.m. Maina, on smelling the rhinoceros, had turned off abruptly, and going at his best pace straight across country, had returned to our yesterday's camp some twelve miles distant!—crossing in his course several nasty nullahs without slackening his speed, and shaking his rider into a jelly. The mahout had lost all control over him.

After resting awhile, and having something to eat, Macdonald wanted to return by the direct route we had followed, but nothing would induce the animal to leave Soonapilly unless he had a man walking ahead of him, and by the long and circuitous pathway made by the villagers.

Now what had upset this usually staunch animal? I can only account for it in this way: Macdonald had a theory, knowing how fond of opium the Assamese are, that if he took some of this drug with him and kept doling it out, the mahout's zeal and pluck would be increased. I fancy he gave no thought to what the mahout had previously taken—the two combined proved too much for the man's nerves, and he got demoralized and communicated his funk to the animal he bestrode.

AN ORDINARY JUNGLE.

From a Photo by P. Burges, Esq.

I have seen Maina many times since in all sorts of scrimmages, and I never saw him show the white feather again, though with the same mahout on his back; but I fancy the Zemindar, when he heard what disgrace had been brought on his pet *shikarie* elephant, gave the mahout a bad quarter of an hour. During the night the villagers brought in the young rhinoceros, and when I saw him the next morning he was the impersonification of all that is savage. He was securely tethered, but he tried to get at everybody—a tiger could not have been more savage. Yet in the course of a couple of days he quieted down, ate plantains out of the hand, and in a week followed Sookur about everywhere. I sold him to Jamrach's agent for £60, but I believe I ought to have got double.

CHAPTER III

THE CARNIVORÆ

THE TIGER

THE Burmese assert that there are two varieties of tiger: those of the plains that live on the village cattle being much the larger, and with a longer tail; those that roam over the hills and live principally on such game as they can outwit, being much smaller and with shorter tails; but, if anything, more fierce than the former. Tigers are plentiful all over the country, but very difficult to find; and where cattle and game abound they do little or no harm to human life. But in the remoter districts, especially in the Yonzaleen, man-eaters are very plentiful. Captain Watson of the Artillery, Assistant Commissioner of Yonzaleen, assured me he seldom crossed over the Hills to get to Kyoukee in the plains without losing one or more men. In Assam they are more plentiful than in Burma and more get-at-able. Generally each tiger has his beat, and will tolerate no other male on his preserves. If an intruder puts in an appearance a battle-royal takes place, and if one is killed, he is often eaten by the survivor. The length of tigers has been greatly exaggerated. I have never seen one more than 10 feet 2 inches as he lay dead, and the largest I ever heard of from a reliable authority was 10 feet 4 inches.

I here give an instance. A tiger we shot measured as he lay dead 10 feet 1 inch; when the skin was taken off it was 12 feet 6 inches; when pegged out and dried it became 13 feet 4 inches—these measurements having been noted at the time in my note-book. He was an unusually big brute, with a very loose skin on him.

The size of a tiger of course depends a great deal on the

quantity of food available. Where cattle abound they are very destructive. I have known one tiger to kill five bullocks off the reel, to drag them into the dense bush where vultures would not get a sight of them, and there to leave them and partake of them when he was so disposed. If anything, I think they prefer their game high. I read when a boy that a

TIGER SKIN.

tiger never condescended to partake of anything not killed by himself, but there cannot be a greater fallacy; they drag away and eat the cattle that have died of murrain, and which are thrown to a distance from the village. There is not a surer bait than a buffalo or a gaur or even an elephant or rhinoceros that has been shot and left; but generally he won't go for them until putrefaction has well set in. I heard of one officer who had shot three tigers one night by sitting up over the body of an elephant he had shot five days before. And as for the legend that man-eaters are old mangy brutes who take to homicidal practices when they are unable to pull down game or cattle, and that they are sans teeth, sans vigour, sans everything but hunger, it is a myth. I have known them shot as sleek as a well-cared-for cat, young, active, and vicious, and as portions of the cloth of the victim slain were taken out of him, there could be no mistake as to his identity.

Occasionally white tigers are met with—I saw a magnificent skin of one at Edwin Ward's in Wimpole Street; and Mr. Shadwell, Assistant Commissioner in the Cossyah and Jynteah hills, also had two skins quite white. I have also heard of *one* black tiger having been killed. Some have coats far more fulvous than others; a few, greatly prized for their rarity, have double stripes, or very nearly double.

Tigers have a wonderful knack of hiding themselves. I have known one to be in a bush which we passed quite close and unseen, although it was so bare that one would have thought a hare could not have been in it unobserved. Man-eaters, as a rule, are probably more cowardly than the cattle-lifters, but occasionally they are the very reverse. Witness the following, as related by Colonel McMaster, who was at that time Adjutant of his regiment, and a bold, successful sportsman, and good naturalist, whether with the rifle or the spear or pen:—

"The 36th Regiment was *en route* from Samulcottah to Berhampore in the Northern Sircars, and was approaching Tonee. An officer's servant, who with the men's kit had, as is often the case, preceded the corps to the next encamping ground, was—just at dusk and close to the mess-guard—carried off the high-road by a tiger; an infant, then about eighteen months old, which he had in his arms when he was seized, was quite unhurt in the awful rush that took place. It would be interesting to know what effect the recollection of the scene may have had on the child in after life. On hearing of the tragedy next day, when we reached our encamping ground, three of us went back to the spot, about three miles off, to try and recover the body. Except that we made our way in Indian file through thick thorny bushes, under which we had to creep sometimes on hands and knees, the trail—marked with fragments of clothes, the cap, keys, purse, blood

A PRIZE INDEED.

From a Photo by P. Burges, Esq.

and hair of the victim—was an easy one. The body was very little mangled, so it was determined to wait for the return of the tiger, and in the meanwhile to put up a small platform in the only tree near.

I had office work to attend to in camp, so left my two comrades, who took breakfast and shelter from the sun (it was then near mid-day) under a bush close to, but not within sight of the body, which was not a pleasant spectacle during their meal; their gun-carriers were about the spot, collecting the rough materials at hand for the Mâchan. While all were thus employed, the tiger carried off the body from their midst in open day and through not very thick brushwood, without being observed by any one. I returned to them soon after, as they were trying to follow the trail, this time without success, for the body had now neither blood nor rags to mark the path, and the ground was hard. It is difficult to conceive how the beast could have outwitted them, but so it was. I still think, from the trail as we had it first, that this was a small tiger—probably a tigress."

The peculiar cry of the jackal (which is generally called the "phēal"), so unlike its usual unearthly howl, has caused much discussion. It is only the frightened cry of a jackal. As the yelp of a dog undergoing chastisement, or under sudden fright is totally different from its bark, so when the jackal is attempting to poach on the preserve of his master, the tiger, and the latter puts in a sudden appearance, the "provider," as he is called—the purloiner would be a truer title—goes off with his tail between his legs, uttering the cry of a "phēal." Of this I am sure, as it once occurred before me, when a leopard made a spring at a jackal; and once when General Blake and Mr. Barry were watching over a dead bullock, near Rungeah.

Tigers are chary of attacking wild buffaloes, but they often kill isolated tame ones; but if the herd be near, they will charge *en masse*, and I once saw a tiger so killed.

Nor does a tiger care to tackle a wild boar in the open—the bodies of the two have been found near each other dead. Scott of my regiment, when with Peyton, 9th Regiment, the crack shot, on the Bison Hill up the Godavery, saw a boar trotting up the hill-side champing his tushes and looking round every moment—so he stepped behind a tree to see what was up; as soon as the boar had reached the crest of the hill, which was quite flat and open, then he turned round and halted. In a few seconds up came a large tiger, but the pig would not move; as the tiger walked round him, so the pig turned, presenting a bold front. Scott was so absorbed in the spectacle, wishing to see its *denoûment*, that he never thought of firing; but whether the tiger funked or whether he got a taint of the biped, he suddenly sprang down the hill-side, and the boar galloped off on that opposite. Before Scott could raise his gun to fire, both animals had disappeared. I here relate a story of a tussle we had with a tigress.

On May 11 we moved to Myetquin from Banlong on the Sittang, Burma.

Madden and Osmer of the 69th went out to try and secure one or two of the numerous deer we could see scattered over the plain, whilst Boyle and I stayed at home.

Between 3 and 4 p.m., just as we were thinking of having our daily bath, a mahout on a small elephant hurried up, saying his *confrères* on the other elephants had surrounded a tiger close by. We could see them grouped in a circle not more than a quarter of a mile away. We had no time to spare, as the sun sets about 6 p.m. There is no twilight in the east, and it would be dark at 6.30. Boyle, brother of the defender of Arrah, had not undressed, but I had on only my pyjama suit and no socks, and a pair of slipshod slippers.

Seizing a couple of guns each, we mounted the elephant without changing, and in a few minutes were at the scene of action. Boyle got on to a large commissariat tusker—on a pad. I got on to my own elephant, and sat on the charah, or green fodder, which was piled on his back ready to be taken to camp. No sooner did we advance than I saw the tigress creeping along in front of us, but she saw us as soon as we spotted her, and before we could fire, with a short half-roar, half-growl, came at us open-mouthed. I think her object was to frighten our steeds, and in this she fully succeeded, as every beast we had turned tail and bolted; but both Boyle and I fired, and one of our shots went through her foot. She then took refuge in a patch of long grass. As soon as we got control over the elephants, we formed line and again

ELEPHANT WITH HIS CHARAH OF WILD PLANTAINS. *From a Photo by P. Burges, Esq.*

advanced, but although my elevated position gave me a great advantage as far as seeing was concerned, yet my seat was very insecure—the charah wobbled about, and I had two weapons to look after. We had my howdah in camp, but there was no time left to send for it. We had great difficulty in inducing our elephants to advance; they kept trumpeting, shuffling their feet along the ground, knocking the tips of their trunks on the hard earth or against their feet—showing, in fact, all the symptoms of being in a blue funk. The tigress had shown good generalship in her tactics, for she had succeeded in thoroughly demoralizing our steeds, and had rendered the task of slaying her a most difficult one.

However, we forced them into the long grass and started her again. No sooner was her rush heard than all the hathēēs except mine formed a close phalanx and ran for their lives, taking Boyle with them. Mine did not retreat, but he was very unsteady, swaying about and kicking up the earth with his fore-foot. To shoot accurately off his back was impossible; he was a fine young tusker of the very highest caste, but had not been broken in for shooting. I told my mahout, a Mussalman, to force his steed into a patch of grass into which the tigress retired. Before I reached it, Boyle, with the other elephants, joined me. I could see the grass moving as the tigress swayed her tail to and fro, and I knew she meant mischief. Shoayjah, a Burman *shikarie*, had come up, and mounted one of the leading elephants; he urged me to fire at the moving grass. I did so, and as the movement ceased I thought I had made a lucky shot and slain the tigress. I told the mahout to push his elephant in; we had not gone above 10 yards, when the tusker began to protest by sundry shakings of his body and pitiful cries, but still his head was towards the foe.

She rushed out like a shot from a catapult, and although I fired and hit her, she closed, and seized the elephant by the right foot; but he, with a mighty effort, jerked her off, and threw her to a distance of some 10 or 12 feet. As she lit on her back, close to Boyle, whose steed was in full flight, he fired and shot her through the stomach. I too, fired, and hit her somewhere. But she picked herself up and went into a thicket close by. By this time I was getting riled, and repented of having got on to the charah, but there was no time for delay, if we wanted to bag the tigress.

I stood where we were until I saw the other elephants coming back, though at a snail's pace, protesting the whole time. My mahout had been punishing my beast, and I think he got his pecker up, as he did not hesitate to push his way into the thicket. No sooner had his head entered than the tigress sprang clean off the ground, lighted between his tusks and, clinging to the trunk and forehead with her claws, she set to work to maul him about the jaws. I had hit her as she sprang, but she seemed to bear a charmed life, and to be still full of fight. Those who are familiar with elephants will realize the row mine kicked up at this mark of affection on the part of the feline.

He suddenly threw himself on his knees, and began to drive his long tusks into the ground, imagining, no doubt, that he was pounding the tigress to death; but she was perfectly safe where she was, and was mauling him dreadfully. As the tusker dropped on his knees, the charah toppled over and I was sent flying. I lit on the broad of my back, holding on like grim death to my gun—the rifle had fallen off with the charah. I had half-cocked the weapon as I felt falling off, but re-cocked it directly I embraced mother earth. When I picked myself up I was about four feet in front of the infuriated elephant and the equally enraged tigress. To shoot was impossible, so rapid were the movements and so intricately mixed were the two—and I might perhaps shoot the mahout or the elephant—so I thought discretion the better part of valour, and retreated backwards.

Boyle had seen me disappear, and thought I was in the clutches of the tigress; he was thrashing his mahout to come to the rescue, but not a beast would budge an inch in the required direction. I expected every moment the tigress would leave the elephant and attack me, so I kept my eyes steadily on the combatants and my gun at the ready. I had no shoes or socks on—my slipshods had disappeared—the ground was hard and lumpy and covered with the stalks of the grass which had just then been burnt a short time back. The stumps were sticking out of the ground like panjies, and cruelly lacerated my feet; there were thousands of trailing creepers with hook-like thorns, and these kept tripping me up, and every few paces I went a cropper backwards. Every time I fell, Boyle thought the tigress had me, but could do nothing to help me; after about as nasty a hundred yards' trudge as I ever wish to undergo, I got to where the elephants were congregated; the soles of my feet and my legs (pretty well denuded of my pyjamas) were torn and bleeding.

Fortunately just then a large commissariat tusker, who had been with Madden and Osmer, came upon the scene. I jumped on to the pad on his back, and he—not having been in the scrimmage—advanced pretty rapidly towards where the elephant and tigress were still fighting. Before I had gone 50 yards I saw my elephant, who had shaken off the tigress, coming towards me at his best pace, dragging the charah along the ground and the mahout hanging on to his hind-quarters, instead of being seated on the neck as usual. As he passed me he called out—

"She has bitten me!"

I of course hurried to the front; no sooner had I got within about 20 yards, than without waiting to be shot at, she charged. I hit her and stopped her for a second; had the elephant stood, I might have killed her, but he spun round like a teetotum. She rushed on and seized him high up on the inside of the thigh, and hung on like a bulldog.

Using the gun like a pistol, with one hand, whilst I held on with the other to the ropes of the pad, I tried to shoot her; but her body swayed about so that I missed; and she fell off and went into another patch of grass. As soon as I could get this elephant—who was nearly 10 feet in height—round, I again returned to the charge, but it was already getting dusk; she did not allow us to get very close, but rushed at me with short, coughing roars that sent the steed flying.

To make a long story short, this vixen mauled my second mount several times, receiving herself a bullet each time; but no great damage was done either way. I was as savage as the tigress, and would have advanced on foot had it been practicable; but the grass, though burnt here and there, was too long in her vicinity, for she did not throw a chance away for a man to have had any chance. My elephant at last refused to budge—it was all but dark—so we judged it better to leave her and look her up in the morning.

My poor mahout's foot was fearfully bitten—almost crunched to bits. He bore his wounds like a Spartan, and all he said was that it was his "nuseeb"—pre-ordained luck. He hoped I'd get the tigress on the morrow. Madden was afraid at first that he would have to amputate the leg, but the man begged him to spare it, even if so doing cost him his life. So Madden, who was as good a doctor as he was a companion, took out as many of the broken bones as he could, and bandaged up the foot, but he had no medicines, instruments, or appliances with him. I sent off a man at once to Tongho; he went all night and reached the station next day—getting all he was told to bring. He got into a dug-out, and after an absence of only thirty-six hours he was back again, having covered one hundred and some twenty miles in that time, and was fully satisfied with the reward, 20 rupees, which I gave him.

Thanks to our medico's skill and kindness, the man recovered, but his foot was never very sound, for every now and then a sore would break out and pieces of bone come away; but he remained with me whilst I was employed in the Provinces.

The elephant's wounds caused by the tigress were bad enough, but the worst were where he had been cut by the ropes of the charah. I have been in many scrimmages afterwards, and he behaved fairly, but was never a very good shooting elephant, as he would not remain perfectly still.

At daylight next morning we were back at the scene of combat. There lay the plucky tigress on her back—dead. She must have died soon after she drove us off, for the body was quite offensive; but I have known this to happen a few hours after death.

She had thirteen wounds; we took out eleven bullets—two had gone right through. I recovered my double rifle, but never saw my slipshod slippers again.

The tigress was only 9 feet long as she lay dead, but her tail was very short, and the Burmese said she was a hill tigress, who had probably wandered into the plains after game; and that those of her caste were all more savage than the tigers of the plain, who fatten upon the kine of the people.

Thus ended as pretty a scrimmage as one cares to be in.

Charlie Hill's escape from a man-eater has been told by me too often to bear repetition here *in extenso*, but I give a brief summary of it.

He was with a party of Burmese Police in chase of our Shan levies who had mutinied and absconded with their arms. One morning, just after daybreak, he was marching along ahead of his men with only a stout stick in his hand, and his boy and an orderly carrying his gun and rifle, with orders to keep close: of course they loitered.

He was following a narrow path along a hill-side fringed with grass which much resembles bamboo when young, and thought he heard a slight noise, and thinking it might be a yit or a jungle fowl, he turned round and told his lūgălāy to hand him his gun. Before the lad could do so, out came the head of a tigress almost within striking distance; and unfortunately not only he, but his detachment and his boys saw it too, and halted, crying out—"A tiger! a tiger!—he will be killed!"—without coming to his assistance. Seeing that he could get neither his weapons nor help from those behind him, he pretended to hit the brute a back-handed blow, yelling at her the same time. So far from intimidating her, she rushed in, and Hill—who was then in the zenith of his manhood and stood 6 feet 2—gave her a crack on the side of her head which either felled or turned her, and then he turned round and said—

"Give me the gun."

Hardly were the words out of his mouth when his stick was knocked out of his hand, his right arm pinioned to his side, and the brute was standing over him with her paws on his shoulders, growling like the very devil. He bent his back, and hit at her with his left arm over his right shoulder; but with a whoop, she came down on his back and he fell as if shot, the tigress going a complete somersault over him. He lost no time in picking himself up—on all-fours; the blood was pouring down his face and beard from two holes in his neck. As the tigress and he got up, they were facing one another;

she did not care two pins for a man, but she suddenly found him transformed into a four-footed beast, more uncanny-looking than herself—put her tail between her legs and ran for her life and escaped, but was eventually killed by some Karens, after killing a great many people, and being for the time the terror of the hills. Here was a case of a man-eater showing no fear of even a detachment of troops, who, as they were all armed and loaded, might have killed her when she first appeared, had they possessed an atom of pluck. Hill was carried in to Shoayghein and eventually recovered, but he had a more than fortunate escape, for only the upper fangs penetrated his neck, actually grazing the jugular. Had not Hill fallen so suddenly and she had made good her grip, the artery would have been severed, and he must have died in a few minutes.

When a tiger kills a beast he never goes far off, so if it is intended to sit up for him, great circumspection should be used in erecting the machan to avoid noise; it is best to take a native charpoy or couch, which is light and fairly strong, and either sling it on to a tree or to fasten it to the branches. When moving the carcase of the kill, care must be taken not to allow human hands to pull it about—not that a really hungry tiger would care, but if he has had a good meal lately he will be dainty, and smell the carcase all over, and if he detect the least taint of a human being he will go away and perhaps not return for several days. Sitting over a fresh kill is bad enough, but to do the same over a putrid corpse is sickening, and more than most men can stand. So if there be no suitable place for sitting up where the garah lies, and you have to move to a more favourable locality, throw a noose over the horns and drag it to where your mart has been erected. In my young days I did a good deal of machan and mart work, but with little success, and I strongly advise no man to sit up unless the moon be very bright; and to use luminous paint for his foresight. It seems ridiculous—you can see the smallest objects moving at a distance by moonlight, yet you can't see the foresight of your rifle. I tried many dodges—all failed—but the best was luminous paint. With everything most carefully worked out the chances are greatly in favour of the tiger getting off, and you have had all your worry and annoyance from mosquitoes—not to say of the risks you run from malaria fever—for nothing.

However careful a man may be, however cool and collected and a crack shot, the chances are not equal when he meets a tiger on foot. Many tigers, notably in the Madras and Bombay Presidencies and in Central India, are killed yearly in this way, but scarcely a year passes without some fatal accident. Enough has been said of the stealthy nature of the animal to prove that he can hide in an inconceivably small space; and once within springing distance, in at all thick jungle, one pat of a tiger's paw or one grip of his tremendous jaws are sufficient to kill an ox. Then what chance has a puny man? Such is the vitality of one of these cats, that though shot through the heart, he is still capable of killing half-a-dozen men before giving up the ghost himself. At times tigers will, like every other animal, seem ridiculously easy to kill; but at other times the more balls he gets into him, the more lively he seems to be. I look upon shells as very effective for tigers and soft-skinned beasts, but useless for pachyderms.

Tigers were at one time very numerous at Pegu. An officer of the Commission, Dangerfield, had a large powerful bulldog—which at night was chained to the foot of his bed—killed under the bed and carried off by a tiger; and Dr. Le Presle, Assistant-Surgeon of H.M.'s 84th Regt., baited a trap with a duck and caught a large tiger!

The two Hamiltons, brothers, Richard and Douglas, were second to none as *shikaries.* One of them, writing to the *South of India Observer*, says:—

"Some years back, at Pykara, not far from the bungalow, a tiger took a fancy to a Todah in preference to the buffaloes he was tending. Two of the Todah's comrades were witnesses of the affair, and they described how the tiger behaved like a cat with a mouse. Having caught the man, he amused himself for some time by letting him go, and then dodging him as the poor victim tried to escape, before killing him outright, notwithstanding the shouts and yells of the lookers-on. It is a moot question concerning man-eating tigers as to what induces them to take to preying on human beings: some affirm that it is only when age overtakes the animal, and he finds himself unable to cope with his ordinary victims, deer or cattle, that he falls upon man; and it is stated in support of these views, that these man-eaters are mangy and decrepit beasts without possessing a single point that makes the tiger the formidable creature he is in his prime. This is partially true, but man-eaters have also constantly been found to be sleek, lusty, and at their full strength and vigour, quite as often as the reverse; it is not therefore entirely dependent on age and concomitant weakness that the tiger takes to this habit. I think the argument advanced by many observers and naturalists, that the animal—either accidentally or by press of hunger—having once seized a man and found out what an easy capture he had made, and, in addition, that the flesh is palatable, takes advantage of this acquired knowledge, and thenceforth becomes that dreaded monster, a man-eater—is equally reasonable, and may be accepted, perhaps, as the more probable of the two.

"There are divers opinions as to the exact mode by which a tiger takes its prey. Popularly he is supposed to lie in ambush and spring on his victim as it passes his lair; or watching by a pool, awaits the arrival of animals in quest of water. These would offer but precarious chances even to so cunning and stealthy a foe as the tiger, as all wild animals are so wonderfully cautious in their approach to such resorts. The tiger, too, betrays his presence to them by that peculiar smell attaching to him, so that the odds are greatly against our striped friend's success: though of course he occasionally is rewarded by catching some unwary, over-thirsty animal that rushes to the water heedless of the consequences. But this will not apply to the tiger on the hills, where no paucity of water ever occurs to such an extent as to drive the game to any one spot to drink. That the tiger's principal food in certain localities is game there can be little question, but how he takes it is not well known, and perhaps may never have been witnessed by any one.

"I have a theory of my own upon this point—let us ventilate it. In the first place, the tiger must have room to spring on his victims: in the sholas many are sufficiently clear to allow this; and no doubt he takes advantage of such spots when a chance offers in them, but in general the woods are dense with undergrowth interspersed with trees so close together that the spring of the tiger and the force of his blow must, I should say, be greatly interfered with. Then again, his presence—as before said—is so liable to detection by the deer that his chances of capture are remote; but at night the deer are out in the open, and then, perhaps, the wind being by chance in his favour, he may succeed; and I am disposed to believe that this is the most likely time for him to do so, though he is in no way restricted as to time or place, for he slays buffaloes oftener during the day than the night, and at times close to their habitations. All deer possess an acute sense of smell, and against it a tiger has to contend before he can provide his larder with game; but how does he manage it? We cannot give him the credit of the intellect of man, who in pursuit of game is well aware nothing can be done down wind; and also, not a sambur or deer would be left alive—the tiger would bag them all, just as he pleased: in fact, he would then be able to kill any deer when he wanted it.

"We have so far considered the acuteness on the part of the game to ensure them against total destruction, and I have only one further observation to record, and that is, how often the presence of a tiger is indicated by the actions of the sambur and other deer; if disturbed by him in a shola during the intense heat of the day, the deer immediately resort to the open, watching with eagerness the wood they have quitted, and generally warning the neighbourhood with loud consecutive bells.

"That the tiger is stealthy and quiet in his movements we all know; that velvet paw of his, so soft, yet so formidable, enables him to tread the woods and forests so noiselessly that even the sharp-eared deer may often be taken by surprise and fall a victim to its blows.

"There is also another mode of craftiness adopted by a tiger in approaching game, and that is, the tiger often replies to the bell of a sambur or the call of a deer, and he does so with a short, impatient grunt, at the same time quietly stealing on towards the sound of the deer's call. This answer of his seems to elicit a reply from the deer, and so the tiger, ascertaining with tolerable precision the position of his prey, is guided accordingly, stops his growling, and perchance secures a victim.

"There is a peculiar and singular distinction in regard to the mode of breaking up their prey between the tiger and the panther, the former invariably commencing on the hind-quarter of the animal slain, and the latter at the fore-quarters or chest. There is no known reason for this strange difference, but it is a well-established fact, and perfectly recognized by all sportsmen, Europeans as well as natives."

An officer thus describes the striking down of a cow which he and others saw:—

"We were walking along the northern bank on our way to our posts when we were stopped by the cry of 'Bagh hai!' and looking down to the bed of the river we saw what apparently was a very large tiger, stalking a herd of cattle that had come down to water. We crouched down and had the luck to see the whole affair. The tigress, as she proved to be, when first seen was stealthily stalking a white cow, which was some little way off from the main body of the herd, and, taking advantage of the slightly undulating bed of the river, had probably approached across an open space of perhaps 500 yards before this cow had seen her; the rest of the herd were behind one of the islands and could not yet see the feline. The white cow allowed the tigress to approach to within about 80 yards before she appeared to notice her danger, and at first seemed to be fascinated by the appearance of the brute creeping towards her, and it was only when the tigress commenced to increase her pace to a trot that the cow made off; the trot increased immediately to a lumbering gallop, as the tigress had now got on to the firmer ground that surrounded the islands, and in a very short time she skirted over a small ridge into close proximity of the herd, which was then commencing to scatter, on the news received from the white cow. The gallop turned into a charge, and in a few seconds the tigress had picked out a fine young cow, on whose back she sprang, and they both rolled over together in a heap. When the two animals were still again, we could distinctly see the cow standing up with her neck embraced by the tigress, who was evidently sucking her jugular; the poor cow made a few feeble efforts to release herself, which the tigress resented by breaking her neck. The remainder of the herd, after rushing wildly away, now returned to within 50 yards of the tigress, who was silently slaking her thirst off the cow. Finding, after a few minutes' survey, that the animal embracing the cow was probably a dangerous one, they scuttled up the south bank and commenced grazing again."

LEOPARDS AND PANTHERS

Naturalists have come to the conclusion that there is but one species of leopard, but two well-marked varieties. The larger with more symmetrical rings arranged in rosettes, the fur deep, and tawny in hue, length from $6\frac{1}{2}$ to $7\frac{1}{2}$ feet, of which the tail is $2\frac{3}{4}$ feet, or 3 feet. It hovers about villages in the plains, and is most hurtful to cattle, and dogs especially. The panther is a smaller and more active animal, living principally on such game as it can capture. It is lighter in colour, and the rosettes are not so regular. In size it ranges from 3 to $3\frac{1}{2}$ feet to root of tail, which is $2\frac{1}{2}$ feet; height, $1\frac{1}{2}$ to 2 feet. The head is rounder, and it is most common in the hills, and particularly partial to goats and dogs.

In parts of India the panther is more destructive to human life than tigers—it will remove thatch, enter a house, kill and eat the people. At Shillong, Major Montagu, the commissariat officer, caught in the same trap, in his own compound, twelve leopards and a small tiger in twelve months. Mason gives instances of people sleeping in trees being killed and eaten by panthers.

The black panther is but a melanoid of the true panther, and a female has been known to produce occasionally a black and at other times ordinary panthers. Although these are *lusus naturæ*, they are far commoner in damp heavy forests such as those of Mergui and Java and Malaya than in more open country. It is well known animals and insects get assimilated in colouring to their surroundings. In the Malaya Peninsula an ordinary leopard would soon starve, for he has to prey upon Gibbons and other monkeys, that live aloft, and if of an ordinary hue, he would be conspicuous, and his prey would quickly scamper away; but now and then, in places far apart, and under totally dissimilar conditions of climate and foliage, a black panther is occasionally come across. I have known of several instances, and tried to shoot a black panther that used to roam the heavy jungle at the outskirts of Namyan towards Shoaydoung; she had with her two cubs, a black and an ordinary one, but she outwitted us. One melanoid, in the People's Park, Madras, had several litters, but she never produced one like herself whilst I knew and took an interest in her.

When wounded, a panther is more dangerous than a tiger—it is equally ferocious and far more active.

Whilst a griff, I lived with two other officers in a large house, with a terraced roof, at Secunderabad. We had a small menagerie, consisting of a sambur, a bear, and a panther. The latter had been caught when quite a baby, and used to sleep on our beds and go about like a tame cat; but as it got bigger it showed signs of treachery. We used to take it upon the roof of an afternoon—one of us would sit down with his back towards the animal, which was then let go. As soon as the panther thought he could do so unperceived, he stalked the sitter immediately, crouching down and crawling along on his belly. We took care never to let him get within springing distance, and at a signal the one sitting down would jump up and confront the beast, and it was amusing to see the utterly innocent look he would put on, and gaze upon the surrounding objects, but never towards the person he had been stalking. At last he became so big and dangerous we had to chain him up at the foot of a tree in the compound, and he spent the greater part of the day and night in its branches. I had just purchased two thoroughbred English greyhounds, and paid a stiff price for them: they got loose one night, and attacked the panther, who in a few minutes rendered them *hors de combat.* He did not succeed in killing them, because we rushed out and belaboured him well until he let go and ran up the tree, but the dogs were useless ever after. He also one day sprang down on the sambur and would have killed it, had it not been rescued. He took a decided dislike to one of my chums and would always go for him, but with us others he was usually friendly. At last we let him loose on Mole Alley racecourse and speared him, which was also the fate of the bear. In Burma I only saw a very few, and only killed one, and wounded but lost another. In Assam, large towns like

PADDING A LEOPARD.

From a Photo, by P. Burges, Esq.

Burpetta and Hazoo had swamps and cane-brakes in their centres, where two or more panthers always lurked. Mackenzie and Campbell shot a good many at Burpetta, which was their head-quarters. I also shot one there, and two at Hazoo. My colleague has slain several in the Ruby Mines district. Cooksley killed a lot in Assam, and I shot a few, but not many. I killed many more in India, but this relates to wild sport of the countries east of the Bay of Bengal only; so beyond a casual mention of what game exists there, which is also found in Assam and Burma, we do not treat of them.

The Chita, or hunting leopard, is not found in these damp moist countries subject to a heavy rainfall, nor the hyæna; the jackal only in Assam and parts of Upper Burma—it does not penetrate into Pegu. One or two were killed near Meaday, and I was one of the first to assert its existence, as I had heard its cry, but had not seen it; but D'Oyly did come across one or two; and Boswell of the Artillery shot one, and sent its skin to Colonel Phayre.

BUFFALOES

I look upon this animal in its wild state as, if not the most dangerous, certainly one of the most formidable of the *feræ naturæ.* Not only are they savage, but they are treacherous and most difficult to kill. Solitaries are invariably morose. He will lie in wait in a dense patch of grass and attack anything that comes in his way. He is, if anything, worse than a rogue elephant. There are seldom any buffalo bulls kept in Burma or Assam, but the people trust to the wild ones to keep up the breed. There is therefore but little difference, if any, in size and ferocity between the so-called tame cattle and the feral.

Even the tame cow buffalo, that will allow itself to be driven about and thrashed by a little native urchin, will go for a European. I have frequently been chased when out snipe-shooting, and poor D'Oyly once meeting a cow that seemed inclined to prove aggressive, in a narrow lane, rode at her on his pony; she met them half-way and tossed them, and killed the pony, but D'Oyly escaped with a shaking.

Baldwin, author of *Large and Small Game of Bengal*, when shooting small game on foot near Loqua Ghat in Assam, was pounced upon by one, and all but killed. I have known natives, going up incautiously to what they supposed to be a defunct buffalo, get killed.

During the rutting season a bull takes possession of a tame herd, feeding and associating with them during the day, and even following them to the place where they are picketed at night; he soon loses all fear of man, and at times will not allow the gwala to approach the cows even to milk them. This applies to Assam and not to Burma, for the Burmese don't use milk in any way, though buffaloes are milked by the Karens.

Dr. Mason says that he thinks the feral ones are but descendants of tame ones run wild, but the people think otherwise, and I agree with them. The Burmese bulls have heavy horns, much curved as a rule, but the long-horned variety is also frequently met with. The wild buffaloes resort to the valleys in the Yomahs, and only venture into the plains after the monsoon has commenced, in fact just as sportsmen are going back home, so they are not often met with. We shot a few during the last three or four of our trips towards the end of May, but having to visit the same localities once in July and August, I came across any number of them.

Tigers fight shy of the wild buffaloes, and will not attack one if the herd is near, as they rush to the rescue, and often Master Stripes comes off second best. In that trip during the monsoon I shot a very large cow whose withers had been nearly wrenched off, and her back was scored all over with claw-marks, which must have been done by a tiger.

Although buffaloes inhabit remote and swampy localities, they at times do a great deal of damage to cultivation, and as they are very fearless, refuse to be driven off. I have seen elephants, buffaloes, and rhinoceros feeding about in the same plain.

The buffalo's forehead is narrow and convex, horns black, very rough except towards the points, colour blackish-slate, hair scant; there are albinos occasionally among both tame and wild, but in the latter, very seldom. In size they are almost the same as a rhinoceros. A very large bull—probably the largest I ever shot—measured, as he lay dead, 12 feet to the root of the tail from the tip of the nose; tail, 2½ feet; height, 6 feet 2 inches!

The thickest horns I ever got, either in Burma or Assam, were from the very first buffalo I killed in Burma; they were not long, but each horn measured, round the greatest circumference, 27 and 26½ inches respectively.

These brutes have given me more trouble to kill than any other animal, and the fights I have had with them have been innumerable.

We were shooting once near Myetquin near Banlong; Madden and Boyle of the 69th were with me. We had killed a couple of gaur—had padded the head of one, and were about to commence operations on the second, when a herd of buffaloes appeared. These were the first wild ones we had seen; we chased them, but to no purpose, as they outran us, so we returned to the dead gaur. We were a long way from camp when I espied a huge solitary bull buffalo. He looked at me, but went on feeding placidly. I beckoned to the others, who had loitered behind, to hurry up, and when we got within 50 yards, we let fly. He was rather hard hit, but did not charge, and whilst my comrades went in full chase I jumped off the elephant under a tree to load. I had only muzzle-loaders in those days, and it was drizzling. Before I had loaded and remounted, I heard several shots, the trumpeting of elephants, and a voice calling to me to come sharp, so I made my beast go as fast as he could, and when I got near I found that the buffalo had charged and knocked the legs from under Madden's elephant, very nearly upsetting him, and had then charged Boyle's, who however got away. Neither steed would budge an inch towards him, and were restrained from running away with difficulty. I followed, but I was on a very slow Hine female, which, though steady enough, could not, or would not, go faster than about three miles an hour. The bull did not hurry himself, and when I got within 50 yards I opened fire and let him have the contents of my battery, but he neither took notice nor hurried his pace. I had to stop to load, for I was on a pad, and when I was ready to proceed, the bull had disappeared. I followed on his track, and soon saw his shadowy form in a heavy patch of long grass, intently listening. I got as near as I thought safe—about 30 paces off—stood up on the pad, and fired into the broad of his back, hoping to break his spine. On receiving the bullet he was round and into my elephant, just as I had time to throw myself into a sitting posture astride the pad. He then shifted his position, and came to the side and looked up into my face. I put down the heavy rifle, and, touching his forehead, pulled the trigger, and for the only time, it missed fire. The next instant my elephant was driven forward a good two yards—I told the mahout to take her out into an open space close by, but the foolish beast would not budge, but kept yelling "blue murder" whilst the bull was cruelly punishing her. At last, seeing the other elephants—which had at last approached—she condescended to go towards them, and the bull did not venture to follow her into the plain. There I got on to a fresh elephant and went back; the bull was decidedly seedy, but charged once or twice, but we managed to stop him, and at last to lay him low; but even when on the ground he struggled so, that we had to pour in volley after volley before he gave up the ghost. We had fired some 39 bullets into him. He was fully 18 hands high, and it was as much as four men could do to lift his head on to a pad elephant. My elephant was laid up for several months. I never used her again for sport. Though staunch, she was not fast enough, and nothing breaks a sportsman's heart so much as being on an elephant that has not a go in him or her.

On another occasion, when out with General Blake, we came across several, and killed three; one of these charged my elephant, but he promptly knocked him over. In Assam, in the first six months, I shot twenty-two, and then the sport had not the same attraction, and I seldom molested them unless they disputed the right of way, or were inclined to be pugnacious, which was not infrequent. I shot altogether over two hundred.

After the wild bulls have served the cows, instead of retiring, they often insist on remaining with their harem. They then become a nuisance, and the Assamese have recourse to various devices to get rid of them; they dig pitfalls, hang a dart weighted on the branch of a tree under which they notice

A DEAD BUFFALO.

From a Photo by Sir B. Simpson, Bart.

he wends his way, in the hopes that it will fall on him and impale him, which it sometimes does. But if any one (European) is near, they go to him and ask him to shoot the intruder, which I have done for them many a time; but as that has generally to be done on foot, it is somewhat dangerous, and some hairbreadth escapes have been recorded in *Incidents of Foreign Sport.* The very big bulls are not so numerous now as formerly, yet still bulls with horns close up to 12 feet measurement from one tip to the other round the outer curve and across the narrow forehead are still to be found; the cows have longer horns, but not so thick. The largest on record is, I believe, one I gave to Lord Mayo when Viceroy of India; the measurements of which were 13 feet 8 inches and 6 feet straight across between the tips. Although not so numerous as formerly, yet there are vast herds of Bubali roaming about the dooars and churs (islands in Assam). Archie Campbell, for years in the Assam Commission, had the elephant he was riding knocked down by a bull, and who followed him up by scent, as a hound might have done. Just in time he came to a small tree, and climbed it as the enemy bore down upon him.

Once near Tseben, a favourite site of mine for snipe, I found an albino cow, belonging to a villager, that had immensely long horns; when she threw back her head each horn lay alongside the dorsal ridge nearly to her croup. I offered the maximum price in those days for a cow, namely, 50 rupees, but her owner, seeing how anxious I was to possess her, raised her price to 200 rupees, which I declined to give. I tried to get her horns measured, but although quiet enough with the natives generally, yet when she felt them handling her horns she became restive, and so the measurements were never taken.

So alike are the tame and wild buffaloes, that once we came across a herd far, far away from any village. I did not like their looks and declined to fire, but my comrade killed two, and had to pay 50 rupees each. They had been let loose for breeding purposes. Huge and strong as are these beasts, the cowardly Assamese catch them in nets, the string of the meshes being of hemp twisted of the size of one's little finger. The adult bulls they kill, and also full-grown cows, selling the flesh to the Cacharies, but the young ones they tame. The young bulls are castrated, and employed, when of a size fit for the purpose, in ploughing.

RHINOCEROS

Although I have heard it stated in Lower Burma that there are three varieties of the rhinoceros, I think it doubtful. There is certainly the lesser rhinoceros (*R. sondaicus*), and the (*R. sumatrensis*), and an allied one, which was secured by the late Captain Hood in Chittagong, and sold by him to the Zoo. The two are very similar in appearance, and both have strong incisors, like tusks. I only shot one *R. sumatrensis* in Burma, and that near Cape Negrais, but I have been after them several times; but the nature of the ground was such, that our animals (elephants) could not go through the quagmires, whereas the rhinoceros would half wade, half swim through them with ease: but my colleague will write about them more, as his experience with these animals is greater than mine in Burma.

I may here mention about them in Assam—as I intend to give a short sketch of wild sport in that Province—that I shot there forty-four to my own gun, and probably saw some sixty others slain, and lost wounded fully as many as I killed.

The first is the great Indian rhinoceros (*R. indicus*), which is very plentiful in the Bhootan Dooars, but it is also found in the Churs of the Brahmapootra, and along the foot of the Garrow Hills, and also in the swamps along the base of the Cossyah and Garrow Hills. It has only one horn, seldom 18 inches long, generally a good deal less; this horn, which is said to be a conglomeration of hairs, is liable to get detached through injury or disease, when another one grows in its place. The skin is exceedingly thick, with a deep fold at the setting on of the head, another behind the shoulders, and another in front of the thighs; two large incisors in each jaw, with two smaller intermediate ones below, and two smaller outside the upper incisors, not always present. General colour, dusky black. The largest I bagged measured as follows: extreme length, 12½ feet; tail, 2 feet; height, 6 feet 2 inches; horn, 14 inches.

All rhinoceros delight in swamps, and lie in mud-holes for the greater part of the day. In a good-sized mud-hole one day I saw a rhinoceros lying at one end, and a buffalo at the other. I have never shot the lesser rhinoceros on the right bank of the Brahmapootra, but I have no doubt it exists, as it is also found in the Soonderbunds not far from Calcutta; but it is fairly plentiful on the left bank south of Goalparah, where I have killed it.

As a rule, rhinoceros are inoffensive; they do a good deal of damage to grain if any is grown within a reasonable distance of their haunts, but generally they inhabit such remote localities that they can do no harm. It is naturally a timid animal, more anxious to escape than fight, and it is by no means difficult to kill. Of course, when a rhinoceros has been severely wounded and is closely followed up, it will turn; but so will a rat, or, as they say, even a worm; but its principal anxiety is to get away and lie in some mud-hole, where it wallows, and where it probably dies. The horn is only used for grubbing up roots; when they wish to attack they use their incisors, which with them answer much the same purpose as tushes in a boar. They can inflict a clean deep cut, and they appear at certain seasons to fight amongst themselves, for I have killed both males and females scored all over.

It used to be said that the skin of the rhinoceros will resist an ordinary ball, but that is all sheer nonsense; a spherical ball out of a smooth-bore, if rightly placed, will kill one of these animals far easier than it will a buffalo. It is not the hide, but the enormous muscles, mass of flesh and bones, that cover the vital organs, that render the use of heavy rifles and immense charges so necessary to penetration. But as Von Hohnel killed two rhinoceros in East Africa with one ball, using a Mannlicher rifle, a similar weapon should account for them in the East. Colonel Campbell, an old Assamese *shikarie*, had the credit of also having killed two rhinoceros with one ball; but it was not quite certain, for he did fire two shots, but at animals some way apart; whereas the two killed were standing alongside of one another. I have sent a hardened bullet right through one.

If the bullet, with a sufficiency of powder behind it, is placed in the centre of the shield over the shoulder, rather low down, the ball penetrates the heart. If behind the shoulder the lungs are perforated, and the beast succumbs after about five minutes, and can easily be recovered by its stertorous breathing, which it utters before it gives up the ghost. This noise, once heard, can never be forgotten.

Although the horns are almost useless as trophies, for many of them are but knobs, the natives prize them very much, and will buy them, giving as much as Rs. 45 a seer (2 lbs.). The young ones are easily caught after the mother has been killed, and though very savage at first, soon get tame, and are worth a lot of money. They cost next to nothing to keep and rear. The footmarks much resemble those of an elephant; but they are a little smaller, and a little longer, and have but three toes against the elephant's five. Although many castes in India—Brahmins and Marwaries in particular—partake of only grain, they have asked me to dry the tongue for them; this they pulverize and bottle, and take a pinch of it when ill.

The Assamese, bigoted Hindoos as they are, used to follow us about in gangs like flocks of vultures, and directly they heard shots, rush up, all fighting for certain tit-bits; not a morsel would be left; even the hide they cut into lengths and roast over embers, and eat as some people eat the crackling of a pig.

Considering the value put on the flesh and horns of this animal by the natives, I am surprised there is one left alive, as it deposits its ordure [1] at one spot only until a mound is formed, sometimes several feet in height, and as it visits that spot night and morning, by digging a pit near, nothing could be easier than to shoot it.

Whenever I went into the dooars I was followed by native *shikaries* who kept out of my ken, but hovered about near; as I had seldom time to hunt up wounded beasts, they would trace them up, and either shoot them, or, if they found them dead—as was oftener the case—they would appropriate the horns and flesh. They thus stole a magnificent horn (for Assam), 18 inches long, off a beast I had severely wounded

[1] My colleague states he has not noticed these dung-heaps. I have seen them, I may say, always, where either variety of rhinoceros have taken up their residence. He has since come across them in the Arrakan Yomahs.—F. T. P.

A DEAD RHINOCEROS.

From a Photo by P. Burges, Esq.

and lost, and I should have known nothing of it, had the men not quarrelled over the spoils, and one run back and told the Deputy Commissioner, but the man was over our frontier before he could be overtaken and seized.

The lesser rhinoceros is distinguished by being somewhat shorter in height and their shields being less prominent, and the skins at times are covered with square angular tubercles. This animal extends throughout Assam, down Sylhet, the Garrow Hills, Tipperah, Chittagong, Arrakan, and Burma to Malaya, and probably into Yunan and the western provinces of China. The Burmese assert that it devours fire.

The two-horned rhinoceros extends from Chittagong downwards. It is not known further north. Its skin is as smooth as a buffalo's; the anterior horn is fairly long, the posterior generally a mere stump. I do not see why they should not be utilized, as they are easily domesticated. A dhooby in Gowhatty used to take his clothes from the wash about on one (*R. indicus*, *R. unicornus*), but I think he sold it to an Afghan, who was one of Jamrach's agents.

The variety obtained by Mr. Hood had tasselated ears. It got bogged in trying to cross a river, and was secured by means of Keddah elephants.

Doctor Mason asserts that the larger single-horned rhinoceros (*R. indicus*) has been caught in Arrakan, and that he has also seen it along the banks of the Tenasserim river. The Burmese have told me the same, but Blyth declared that they had mistaken the smaller *Sondaicus* for the *Indicus*.

The bigoted Hindoos store their horns in their Namghurs, the point downwards, the base forming a kind of bowl in which they pour water and use as a charm. The Chinese also put a fictitious value on them. Knowing how valuable they were, Major Cock[1] bought up a lot of the white African rhinoceros horns, which are at times 3 feet long, which he saw for sale in the Bazaar in Calcutta, and sent them to Becher in Assam for sale, but the natives would not look at them, not believing that they were what they professed to be!

[1] A rare good sportsman; afterwards killed in one of the fights in the Naga country.

THE GAUR (*miscalled Bison*)

This animal, one of the noblest game-beasts in the world, has probably a more extended range than any other beast which is an object of chase; yet until very lately very little was known about it, and the accounts hitherto published of it have referred to the animal found in Mysore, the hilly ranges of Southern and Western India. It is plentiful in Travancore; a few were to be found in the hills not far from Vellore; in Central India, near Warungul and the Nirmal jungles in the Nizam's country; very many exist in the hilly regions of the Northern Circars of the Madras Presidency, at the foot of the Bhootan Hills in Assam, in the hills along our North-Eastern Frontier, and downwards through Burma to Malaya. In this extended range there is but one species, but two well-marked varieties. Mr. Blyth, probably one of the best naturalists that ever lived, thought for a long time that the Gayal (*Bos sondaicus*) took the place of the gaur in Burma, but he quite altered his views. I sent him some heads, and when he visited the Province he procured others, and came to the conclusion that not only did the gaur exist, but that it was a far larger and finer beast than those in India.

I have shot a great many of them in various parts of Southern India, and in Lower Burma and Assam, but nowhere did I see such splendid specimens as in Burma. I háve seen very fine heads brought down from the Mishmee Hills, and their owners must have been noble bulls indeed. I have no doubt that the abundance of food procurable in the vast forests and hilly ranges of Burma has contributed to increase their height and general bulk. Whereas in Southern India the largest bull is recorded as 19 hands and 2 inches, cows have been shot in Burma 19 hands. My colleague has shot them in Upper Burma up to 20 hands, and I shot one near Banlong only ½ inch short of 21 hands, or 7 feet. It is difficult, of course, to measure such a beast accurately, but I always took the greatest care to make the measurements as correct as possible. I used to stick a straight bamboo in the ground at the top of the ridge over the shoulder, stretch the beast out, and another at the heel of the fore-foot, and measure directly across with a measuring-tape. I did the same to those I shot in India; but on an average the Burmese bulls and cows far exceeded them in every way; besides, there are other differences. The dorsal ridge is more pronounced, and extends further back to within a span of the croup or hip-joint; the head is longer, the nose arched like a

GAUR HEAD.

ram's (some of those in the Western Ghauts have this too, but in a less degree). The cows in India differ from the bulls in having slighter and more graceful heads, while those in Burma have longer heads, and noses more arched than the bulls.

It was recognized by most naturalists that the gaur had no dew-lap, and such also was my opinion; but lately it has been proved that some have a well-marked dew-lap, and others none. I don't think the loose skin of the neck in the Burmese animals amounted to a dew-lap, but that depends a good deal on what a man understands by that word. "Smoothbore," an excellent authority, describes dew-lap as follows:—"It originally meant the loose fold descending from the chest, which, when the animal was grazing, swept the dew; thus in *Midsummer Night's Dream* hounds are described as 'dew-lapped like Thessalian bulls'; but in the humped Indian cattle the fold extends from the throat downwards, and in the Mysore draught bullocks and in the Brahmini bulls is enormous; whilst in the ordinary village cattle the development is small."

He also adds, "A planter of many years' experience in

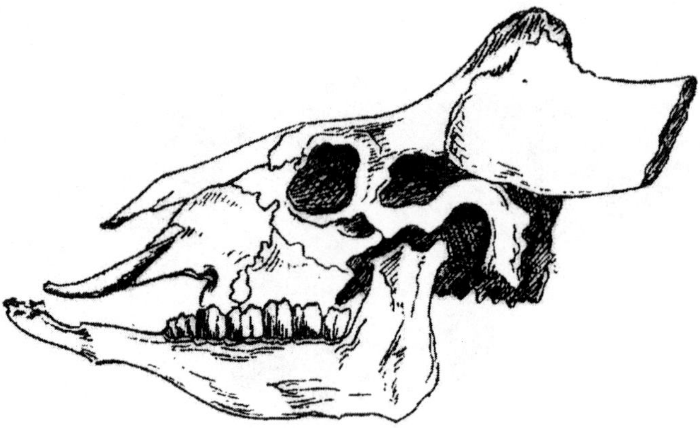

GAUR HEAD.

Travancore, and a keen, observant sportsman, states that in some examples the gaur have scarcely any dew-lap, and that in others it is strongly developed. So marked is this difference, that the natives divide them into two castes, calling one 'Katia Madoo' or jungle cow, and the other 'Kat-ereiny' or jungle buffalo."

The late Mr. Bartlett of the Zoo wrote that the one which was in the Zoo for about a year and a half had a well-developed one. But Elliot, Jerdon, Campbell (the old Forest Ranger), Sterndale, and most authorities have said that the loose skin did not amount to a dew-lap, so I think we may conclude that some have, and others have it not. I have given the measurements of an old bull shot in the Nirmal jungles, and those of a bull and cow in Lower Burma.

MEASUREMENTS OF GAUR.[1]

	INDIAN.	BURMESE.	
	BULL.	BULL.	COW.
Height at shoulder	19 hands ½ in.	20 hands 3½ ins.	19 hands.
Height at croup	18 hands	19 hands 1 in.	18 hands ½ in.
Girth behind shoulder	7 ft. 10 in.	8 ft. 5 ins.	7 ft. 6 ins.
Tail and tuft	3 ft. 3½ ins.	3 ft. 4½ ins.	3 ft. 3 ins.
Snout to crown of forehead	2 ft. ½ in.	2 ft. 3¼ ins.	2 ft. 4 ins.
Length of ears	9 ins.	1 ft. 1 in.	1 ft. ½ in.
Length of fore-hoof	8¼ ins.	8½ ins.	7¾ ins.
Horns (outside curve)	2 ft. ½ in.	3 ft. 1 in.	2 ft. 1 in.
Terminal between the tips	2 ft. 7 ins.	3 ft. 4 ins.	1 ft. 9 ins.
Girth of horn at base	1 ft. 6 ins.	1 ft. 11 ins.	1 ft. 5 ins.
Nape to root of tail (straight)	7 ft. 5½ ins.	7 ft. 10 ins.	6 ft. 10½ ins.
Girth of fore-leg near chest	2 ft. 8½ ins.	3 ft. ¼ in.	2 ft. 4 ins.
Total length from upper lip over forehead to tip of tail, following curve of hump, dorsal ridge, etc., etc.	14 ft.	14 ft. 4 ins.	13 ft. 8 ins.

The following is Jerdon's description:—"In length it is about 9½ or 10 feet long from the nose to the tip of the tail; the tail 34 inches long, ranging down a little below the hocks; the skull is massive, the frontals large, deeply concave, surmounted by a large semi-cylindric crest rising above the base of the horns. There are thirteen pairs of ribs. The head is square, proportionately shorter than in the ox, and the bony frontal ridge is 5 inches above the frontal plane. The muzzle is large and full, and the eyes small, with a full pupil of a pale blue colour. The whole of the head in front of the eyes is covered with a coat of close short hair of a lightish greyish-brown, which below the eyes is darker, approaching almost to black. The muzzle is greyish, and the hair thick and short. The ears are broad and fan-shaped, and the neck—which is sunk between the head and back—is short, thick, and heavy. Behind the neck, and immediately above the shoulder, rises a fleshy gibbosity

[1] The ears of the Indian bull were much torn and slit, and the tips had disappeared altogether—the horns of this bull also were much worn. The ears and horns of the Burmese gaur were quite perfect.—F. T. P.

or hump, of the same height as the dorsal ridge. This ridge rises gradually as it goes backward, and terminates about the middle of the back. The chest is broad, the shoulder deep and muscular, the fore-legs short, and the joints very short and strong, and the arm exceedingly large and muscular. The hair on the neck and breast is longer than on the body; and the skin of the throat is somewhat loose, giving the appearance of a slight dew-lap. The fore-legs have a rufous tint behind, and laterally above the white, the hind-quarters are lighter and lower than the fore, falling suddenly from the termination of the dorsal ridge. The skin on the neck, shoulders, and thighs is very thick, about 2 inches, the horns pale-greenish, with black tips curling outwards, upwards, and slightly backwards, and finally inwards. General colour, dark chestnut-brown, or coffee-brown; legs, from knee downwards, a dirty white. I have already noted in what respects the Burmese differ from the Indian."

I think the following notes on the gaur will be interesting. They are from the pen of Mr. A. F. Martin of Travancore, who wrote to "Smoothbore":—

"When the Kaunan Desan Hills in North Travancore were opened out for tea and cinchona some years ago, the felling of the forest restricted the wild beasts, particularly the elephants and gaur, when passing across the estate, to one or two pathways. One particular track was, however, left to them for about ten years, when further cultivation led at last to the blocking up of even this right of way. The animals were at first much puzzled, and both elephants and gaur took to wandering about the cultivation. The elephants accommodated themselves to the altered conditions, and used the estate paths. The gaur, more suspicious, took a straight line for their grazing grounds over the rotten felled timber and through the older cinchona plantations, but were often brought up by the sight of whitewashed walls surmounted by a corrugated iron roof.

"At last they settled down to a pathway between the old cinchona and a natural belt left between it and the new clearing. A pit 10 feet long, 8 feet wide, and 8 feet deep was dug on the boundary, covered with a mat made of reeds and bamboos, over which earth and dry leaves were scattered. The smell of the fresh earth, however, turned them off. Once a gaur got his fore-feet down the side of the pit, but made a bold jump and cleared it.

"After some months the tracks of a large herd were found making for the pit, and it turned out that a gaur had fallen in, but had managed to jump clean out again. It was evident 8 feet was not deep enough, and rock in the bottom prevented its being sunk deeper. Another pit was therefore dug some distance away on the same boundary. The ground was on the side of a steep hill, so that whilst the lower wall was 10 feet, the upper was 14 feet deep.

"After a while a cow gaur fell in, but whilst Mr. Martin was watching her, and waiting for coolies to help in putting logs across the pit, she managed to scramble out; and although she followed the path to the old pit, she avoided it and escaped. Two days afterwards a bull fell in and was secured. Getting logs across the top of the pit, with the gaur charging madly about, was exciting work, but the feat was successfully accomplished only after the utmost difficulty and danger. The appearance of any one near the pit always caused a furious demonstration on the part of the gaur, who dug big caves in the side of the pit with his horns, and thus an approach to the edge was rendered dangerous. In ten days' time he had become somewhat tame. He tossed about the grass thrown in to him and trampled it into the mud, eating but a small quantity. His only drink was water poured into the pit, and which collected in the holes he had made in the mud with his feet. Matters were very little improved by having bundles of grass lowered by a long piece of cane fastened round, for he charged them furiously, and got a lot of the grass on the ground only to trample it into the mud.

"By degrees he began to eat more and to throw less about. Water was a great difficulty: any attempt, too, at lowering a bucket to him was futile, and only ended in the bucket being flattened out. It became imperative, therefore, to get him out of the pit. To attain this end, a stockade about 30 feet square was made round the pit, consisting of stout poles, 15 feet high at the lower, and 10 feet high on the higher part of the ground. They were each sunk about 3 feet in the ground, 18 inches apart, and lashed together with cross sticks and fibre, and formed an almost solid wall. A sheet-iron trough was fixed in one corner; when complete, large quantities of brushwood, ferns, and grass were thrown into the pit, until by degrees it became half full, and the bull was enabled to jump out. His first act was to charge the corner whence he was being watched, but the only harm was done to himself, his frontal ridge being slightly cut. His attention was then attracted by the water-trough, which he knocked about considerably, but finding the water, he took one good long drink before finally knocking it to pieces. During the examination of his new quarters he once more fell into the pit, and this enabled us to repair damages; but before they were quite completed he jumped out again and caused a general stampede. Having twice hurt his head against the stockade, he never again made any attempt to test its strength. The sheet-iron trough seemed to annoy him more than anything else, and was soon rendered useless. A three-cornered wooden trough was then inserted in a corner and protected by stout poles across the corner of the stockade, and this having been satisfactorily arranged, the gaur soon became comparatively tame. He allowed the measurements of his horns to be accurately taken through a window left in the stockade, and very fine horns they were too, measuring 34½ inches across, from outside to outside of sweep. Although the pit was filled up level with the ground, his previous experience led him to conclude that it was dangerous, and he never crossed it. The result was, that the narrow space between the pit and the stockade became ploughed up, and he was up to his hocks in mud. It therefore became necessary to enlarge the enclosure for about 100 yards in length, taking a bit of jungle for shelter, and a small ravine which would hold water. A small shed was erected with sliding bars on the outside and inside, with a view of introducing a domestic cow as a companion, and so—if he approved of her—she might be let into the stockade.

"He took to his new quarters very kindly, and soon got to know that grass was left for him at the inner gate of the shed.

In a short time it was found that he liked having his nose and head rubbed, and licked the clothes of the person who rubbed him. He took salt from the hand, but did not at first seem to care for it, probably because it was not mixed with earth as in salt-licks, which he was accustomed to, spitting it out if he got too much in his mouth at one time. After two months he became quite tame, and permitted his captor to come into the enclosure, not even moving if he happened to be lying down. After the third month he began to shed his hair, and liked it rubbed off with a wisp of grass, allowing the operator to sit on him whilst cleaning him, but he did not like his hind-legs or tail to be touched, kicking out as if he were tickled when this was done. A shed had been built in one corner of the stockade, with a view of introducing a domestic cow to bear the gaur company. In this shed was kept guinea grass, to be given to him in the mornings. One night, however, he thought he would prefer having the grass of which he was inordinately fond, instead of waiting till daybreak. He managed to push aside one of the sliding bars of the gate, break a lower one down, and raise the top bar sufficiently for himself to get through; he ate the bundle of guinea grass, and when this was finished he repeated the performance with the outer bars of the shed, and walked out to freedom. So we lost this magnificent specimen. He stood 16 hands 1½ inches fair vertical height."

Whilst in the Indian cows the bony frontal ridge is scarcely perceptible, it is most pronounced in the Burman ones. All gaur have very small feet for their size, not much bigger than those of a large sambur. The old bulls have the bases of the horns much truncated with rough ridges, and each ridge, the *shikaries* affirm, represents a year of its life after the sixth year, before which none are apparent. If this theory is correct I must have killed gaur over thirty years of age. The old ones have little hair on their backs, they look as if shaven; the skin also exudes an oily substance, slightly offensive. Never sit on a dead gaur, for this substance will cause a stain which is ineradicable. These cattle browse on the young shoots of the bamboo, and graze on such grasses as they can find. They inhabit in Burma mountain ranges like the Yomahs, but after the annual fires, when the new grass has sprung up, they descend to the forests lining their base. They feed during the night and early morning, and also in the cool of the evenings, but during the heat of the day they retire to the deep forests; or if gadflies are very troublesome they force their way into the heaviest elephant grass they can find, and lie there to avoid their tormentors.

The wind being favourable, they are not difficult to approach on an elephant, because they see them roaming about so often in the vast plains which are their joint homes. I never saw one in Burma charge an elephant, but I did see something of the sort in the Nirmal jungles when I was a youngster, but I have heard of their doing so. Sportsmen following up a wounded solitaire, have occasionally been killed.

Now and then if frightened they run amûk. A herd in the Goalparah district, moving from one locality to another, found themselves in the vicinity of a village, and the plain dotted about with natives. Whether they thought they were being surrounded or what, I do not know, but they charged the people right and left, and killed several and wounded many others. One man I saw in the dispensary had scarce a whole bone in his body. I forget whether he lived or died, but natives do make wonderful recoveries. It is best to start after them before daybreak, and try to get them before they retire to their strongholds. The solitary bulls are the best worth seeking; they are larger and older beasts, and have the best heads.

When alarmed, their enormous strength enables a herd to crash through bamboo and forest, knocking down everything of a moderate size. Often, when disturbed suddenly, they will gallop forward for about 50 yards, then pull up, turn round, snorting and staring at the intruder, and then go off for good. Once I came across a herd of about sixty at the foot of the Yomahs on the Sittang side, and a prettier sight cannot be conceived. There were stupendous bulls, graceful cows, pretty calves, all peacefully grazing on the short, crisp, succulent young grass. When they saw me they snorted, stamped after the manner of deer with their fore-feet, and then went off. I jumped off the elephant, but I had been wet through for five

DEAD BULL GAUR (ASSAMESE).

From a Photo by Sir B. Simpson, Bart.

hours, and was so benumbed that all I did was to take a step or two and then measure my length on the grass; every one got away.

The marrow-bones and tongue of a gaur are a *bonne bouche.* I am told that the flesh on either side of the so-called hump along the dorsal ridge, where it is in three layers, is very good, especially the middle piece; but I cannot say that I ever partook of it. The tail makes excellent soup; the hide, when cured, is very good for soling shooting boots. In hilly districts there are depressions somewhat like small nullahs, where a species of white clay impregnated with natron is found; and wherever this exists, other conditions also being favourable, you will find not only gaur, but deer and also members of the *felidæ;* whether the latter go after the fauna, or for the sake of the earth I do not know, but the natives assert that they, too, partake of the earth, and have pointed out to me their droppings in which some of this has been evacuated with portions of hide and hair of animals.

On one trip in Burma we noticed numerous marks of Tsine in a quin about two miles from our camp. Close examination showed that the cattle were in the habit of resting during the heat of the day in a tope of trees lying in the centre of the quin. So I determined to try and circumvent one of these wary brutes. Getting up at 3 a.m., we walked through the long grass, getting to our destination soaking wet, and there we had to sit shivering with cold till past ten o'clock before the beasts put in an appearance. At last two or three cows leisurely feeding along came in sight, but the bull did not appear till close on mid-day, and it was fully an hour later before he got within shot. I then fired behind the shoulder, and as he fell to the shot I blazed into a cow, and she too dropped, but the bull picked himself up and went off full score. I followed, and the cunning brute very nearly had me, as he hid in a patch of long grass and charged me as I passed. I had just time to throw myself behind a prostrate tree, as he cleared it and fell into a deep nullah on the other side. There I had no difficulty in despatching him. In the evening I came across a herd of gaur; they got up out of a heavy patch just in front of my elephant. I fired at one going away, tail on end; the bullet struck close to the root of the tail and traversed the whole length of the body—we cut it out of the neck. The animal fell like a stone to the shot.

THE GAYAL

(*Bos frontalis*)

These wild kine are plentiful in parts of the Chittagong Hills and in parts of Tipperah extending towards Munipore and along our North-Eastern Frontier, where they are kept in a state of semi-domestication by the Dafflas, Looshaies, Mishmes, and other wild tribes. Very many of them are caught in nets when mere calves, and are herded with their tame kindred. Huge lumps of rock-salt are thrown about near the villages, and these have an extraordinary fascination for them. After domestication they are picketed on the outskirts of the forest near the village, and are let out to graze during the day and recalled towards night, by the tinkling of bells or the striking of gongs.

The forehead of the gayal is not concave like a gaur's, but quite straight, and is destitute of the semi-cylindrical crest. The horns grow straight out and then curve very slightly upwards: the forehead is broad, and its colouration is almost identical with that of a gaur. I suppose it is a cousin many times removed. It browses more than the *Bos gaurus*, and has a slight but distinct dew-lap. The dorsal ridge is prominent, but not nearly so much as in the larger animal. At a distance one might easily be mistaken for the other, and unfortunately both are called Mithun by the Assamese and hill tribes, the only distinction being that if pressed, they say the gaur is the Asseel Mithun, and the other Mithun only. This has led even such a careful observer and good *shikarie* as Mr. Sanderson to say that the gayal is not found in a feral state, and that the gaur has also been tamed—an error propagated by Mr. Blanford and also by the Royal Natural History. Mr. Blanford has also asserted that it is found in a wild state in the Tenasserim Provinces, but there I am nearly certain he is mistaken, for it is not mentioned by either Mason or General Fytche, and the Burmese have no name for it. I never heard of it during my thirteen years' wanderings. Whether the bull gayal in the Zoo is a pure one or only a hybrid, he is about as fine a specimen, barring the height, which is somewhat less, as is to be found in the East.

At the foot of the Bhootan range wild hybrids are plentiful and very savage. The Bhooteahs and other hill people bring down tame ones to the fair at Oodulgheery in Darrung, and Europeans often buy them. If you transport them to Shillong at once they will live and thrive moderately, but if kept in the plains in the hot weather they die very soon. They don't give much milk, but what little they do give is very rich. I had a pure-bred gayal cow and her bull calf; they were very handsome; the cow strangled herself accidentally, and the calf died. I have seen numbers dead of the murrain, of which Assam is never free, but I never shot but two, and those fell to a right and left.

THE TSINE, OR *BOS SONDAICUS*

The wild cattle extend from the hill tracts of Chittagong downwards, and are found in Java, Sumatra, Borneo, and the

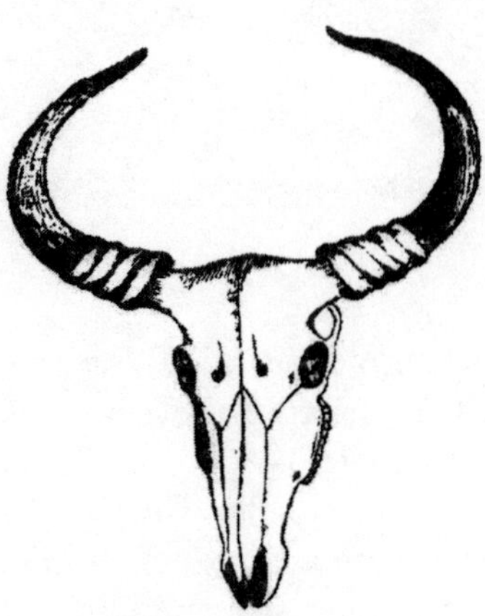

BURMESE WILD BULL.

Celebes. Father Barbe, a learned missionary, wrote to Mr. Blyth that the gaur, gayal, and tsine were to be found within a measurable distance of each other on the borders of Chittagong and Tipperah, and that whereas the gayal was not found further south, the tsine was not found further north, and I believe he is perfectly correct. These are true cattle, very handsome, of a deep red (the very old bulls get almost black in their second childhood), with white rings round the eyes, white under the belly and under the tail, along the buttocks, and with dirty whitish stocking below the knees and hocks; a slight hump, which is lost in the ridge, which is not very prominent, and a slight dew-lap which is not always apparent.

TSAING OR TSINE.

The head is very like that of a wild stag, the facial angle quite straight, and at a little distance they look like a herd of tame cattle. They are very hard to get at in Lower Burma, as they feed in the open quins, but the Burman *shikaries* note the paths they follow, sit upon a branch, and pot them as they pass. As during my long residence in Lower Burma and the many years I hunted them, I killed but five tsine, whilst my colleague killed twenty-five in less than five years, I will leave him to tell his adventures with them.

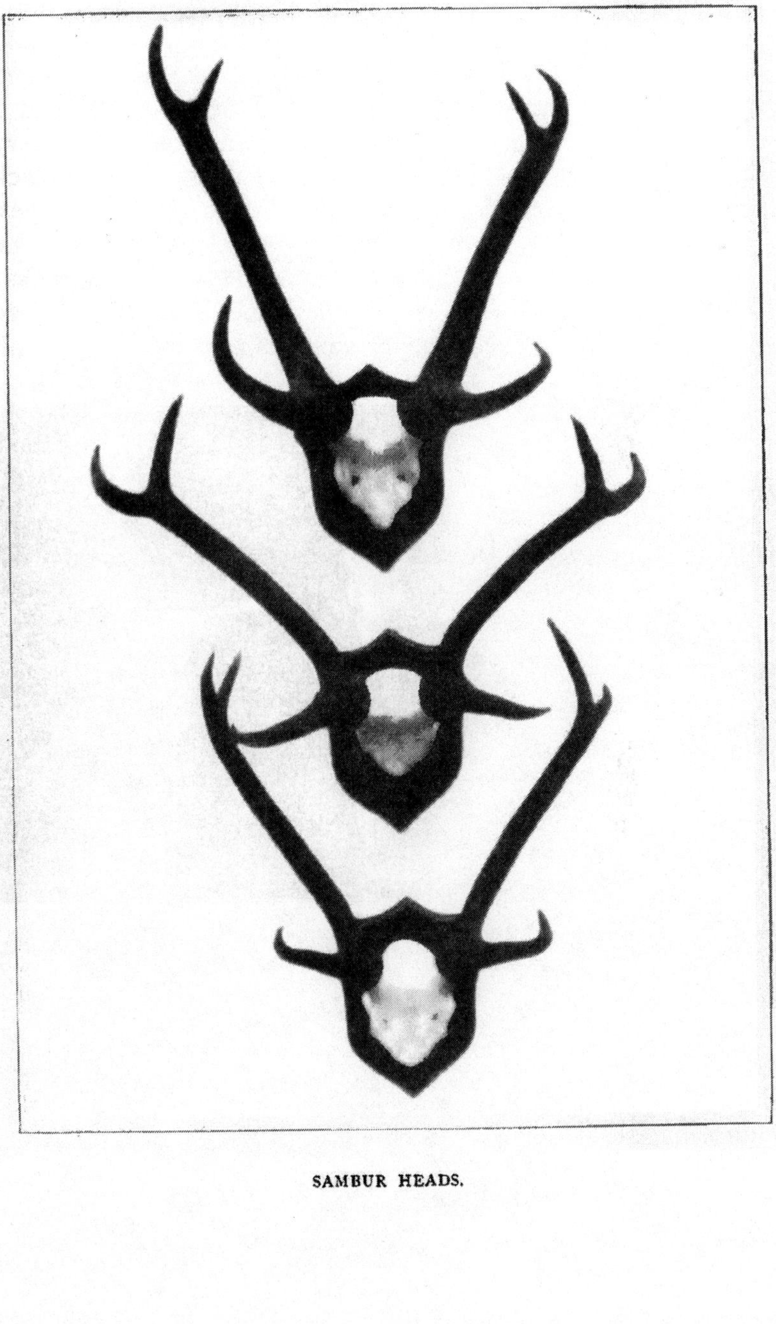

SAMBUR HEADS.

THE DEER TRIBE

SAMBUR

In Burma I am convinced there are two varieties of this noble stag. Those which inhabit the higher ranges of the hills of the country are identical in appearance, and carry heads as large as those of the Neilgherry hills, but those called "Sapt"—found in the plains of Burma (Lower)—although as bulky as the others, have but poor heads, and are wanting in the mane, so conspicuous in their brethren of the mountains.

We used to hunt them generally during May, but I have shot them at other seasons; they shed their horns during June, and are in hiding till September; the velvet is not worn off till October, which is their rutting season. Another peculiarity I noticed in these animals was that every one we shot had an abrasion of the skin of the neck underneath, of the size of an eight-anna piece, about the same size as a shilling, caused, the Burmese said, by the sambur rubbing the part to get rid of parasites. They are gregarious, living in communities of six or eight, only one being a stag. When passing through a forest, the stag brings up the rear. They are possessed of immense vitality, and will go away with wounds that would stop most animals. Col. Campbell, "the old Forest Ranger," mentions an instance of a stag going off with thirteen well-placed bullets, and I have myself put eight belted balls out of a 10-bore double rifle by old Joseph Lang into a moderate-sized sambur before he fell. I also once shot one through the heart, and he ran for 200 yards without showing a sign of having been hit, and then rolled over dead.

The very best stags are the solitaires that lead a hermit's life, and are usually in almost inaccessible posts. A really fine stag is a trophy indeed, but out of upwards of a hundred that I shot in the plains of Burma I did not get a single head worth mentioning, nor did I see a good pair of horns on any of the stags shot by others, nor any on the many skulls we came across killed either by tigers or which had died of the rinder-pest. The "bell" of a Rusa can be heard a long way off, and when disturbed suddenly, or when they see or smell a tiger or a leopard, they make the surrounding country resound with their notes of alarm.

Steaks of the sambur, cooked like those of a cow or bullock, are scarcely to be distinguished from a real rump-steak so dear to the heart of Englishmen. They are very inquisitive, and often advance towards an object they cannot quite make out. I have seen them stamp their fore-feet as if to intimidate before running away. But the Rusa shot in the Arrakan mountains are in no way inferior to those of India.

HOG DEER

(*Cervus porcinus*)

These are equally abundant both in Assam and Lower Burma. When I saw them first in the latter country they were in their monsoon coat, and as I only got a glimpse now and then as they flitted past, I thought they were a variety of spotted deer—for the young are spotted, and so are the mature deer during the rains. They possess great vitality, and I have seen one run 100 yards with its entrails trailing behind. When in long grass they lie very close and creep along in front of one's elephant, and now and then I have mistaken the movement for that of a tiger. When in moderate-sized grass, and you are in want of meat, a charge of No. 2 or even No. 4 shot will do for them, but that is butchery and not sport, and only justifiable on an emergency. I remember when I was in Baghdooar I had a large camp following, and by going on the Churs of the Manas river—which was fast filling—I shot eight of them in an hour. They are not at all bad eating—a native cook will give you cutlets and chops from them which you would not know from prime mutton. They never carry much fat; very good broth can be made from their heads.

BARKING DEER

(*Cervus muntjae*)

These deer are usually found only in hilly localities, but I have occasionally come across a few in the plains some distance from the Bhootan Hills, and also in Burma in the vicinity of the Yomahs.

If alarmed or wounded, they will call, with an imitation of a dog's bark, and can be heard a long distance off. They have peculiar horns and long canine teeth, Roman noses, a decidedly ugly head, two dark lines down each cheek, and a tuft of black hair—as a sort of brow—over the eyes. If anything, the female is uglier than the male. These are also good eating—the females for choice. A serang at Port Dalhousie shot one, and converted nearly the whole of it into a dry curry, which he assured me would keep good for a year. It was certainly very good to eat when I tasted it, shortly after it had been made.

MOUSE DEER

(*Memimna indica*)

This pretty little deer is found towards Tavoy and Mergui, and further south in Malaya they are so plentiful that often a dozen can be bought for a rupee. I did not care for its flesh, as it had a peculiar taste.

THE SWAMP OR MARSH DEER

(*Rucervus davoucilii*)

This fine deer has an extended habitat. I have shot them in the Northern Circars, Madras Presidency; they are found in the forest land at the foot of the Himalaya, in the Central Provinces and Goomsoor, but nowhere are they so abundant as in Assam and the Bhootan Terai. Some years ago they were found within twelve or fifteen miles of Vizianagram, but have been exterminated there.

The horns are large and moderately stout, curving well outwards—pale, with basal antler, and a more or less branched summit; the lower branches sometimes simulating a medium tine: colour, dull yellowish-brown in winter, bright rufous-brown or chestnut in summer—paler below and inside the limbs, white under the tail. The female is lighter, of a pale dun or whity-brown colour; the young are spotted. Length, nearly 6 feet; tail, 8 to 9 inches; height, 11 to 11½ hands; average length of horns, 3 feet or a little more. Fourteen or fifteen points are not uncommon; I have shot many with eighteen, and once saw a head with twenty-seven, but many of the tines were merely excrescences. It is the one deer in India that carries a lot of fat; on hitting one I have seen balls of fat come out of the bullet-holes. I have seen them in herds of thousands in the Bhootan Terai both north and south of the Manas. The Churs of the Brahmapootra river have on them generally many of these deer. They lose their horns in September and October, and the new are not perfect till about the middle of June, though I have got good heads towards the end of May now and then. They hide in the heaviest patches of long grass during that period, and lie very close. Tigers kill very many of them. A saddle off a fat doe is not to be despised.

THE THAMINE

(*Cervus frontalis*)

This is a very handsome deer, somewhat less in height than the swamp deer, and for their size they have very large and graceful horns. The basal antler is directed forwards and is very long, and the horns are very divergent, with terminal branches. A variety is found in Munipur; the basal antlers of the latter are longer, and form a curve with the main horn, and very often there are no terminal branches at all, even in old stags; whereas in the Burman (except with the very young) there are always terminal branches.

BROW-ANTLERED DEER (BURMESE).

I have shot them with six tines on each horn. In the Munipur deer the basal and the main horn form a continuous curve, whilst in the Burmese they form more of an angle, generally. They are gregarious, and feed in quins, or open spaces, surrounded by the jungle. If there are any patches of long grass they lie down in them during the heat of the day—otherwise they go into the forest and rest under the grateful shade of the trees. A herd of from twenty to thirty is not unusual. When the rains commence and the gadflies abound, they are so tormented that their whole attention is taken up in knocking them off; and then, provided the wind be favourable, a wary hunter can get within easy shot, and I know of no greater pleasure than bagging one of these handsome stags after a careful stalk. I have shot them off elephants, but very rarely, and then only when they had retired for their mid-day siesta.

They drop their horns later than the sambur, and are then in hiding. I do not remember ever coming across one at that season. I have seen them feeding in company with hogs, hog-deer, and wild cattle or tsine. They are plentiful at the foot of the Yomahs both on the Irrawady and Sittang sides. Hodgson says he procured them from Nepaul, but I think he is mistaken, as they are never found amongst hills or mountainous country like Nepaul. They, like the swamp deer, are fond of marshy spots, feeding on aquatic plants, and generally they are very wide-awake and most difficult of approach.

THE SEROW

(*Nemorhædus rubida*)

The serow is found in all the higher ranges in Arrakan, Pegu, and Tenasserim, and my colleague has shot them in the Ruby Mines district. They are also found in Assam, not only in the higher ranges, but we killed three in some hills only about 1700 feet high, near Ranee about 17 miles from Gowhatty.

A large male was caught swimming the Sittang near Shoayghein. It was a savage, intractable beast, and died soon after capture. The horns were about 10 inches in length, much curved backwards.

THE WILD HOG

(*Sus indicus*)

Pigs are numerous in Burma, but I have never known them in ridable ground there. In our jungle trips we used to shoot a few as a change of diet for ourselves and also for our Burmese and Madrassie followers, who rather admire their flesh. In the remote jungles they are, as a rule, clean feeders, simply because they can get no offal; but shoot a beast and leave it, and a sounder of hog will soon find it and devour it. I am speaking of the heavier jungles, where vultures had not caught sight of the slain. The Burmese boars are very large and possess splendid tushes. They are wonderfully plucky. One day at Burpettah news of a kill by a tiger was brought us, and Campbell and I on a huge Muckna, and Farquharson on one of mine, went out to try and get a shot. To get to the kill we had to go three miles along the Government road which I had but lately constructed; the country was open on both sides. We had done about two-thirds of the distance, when we saw an old grizzly boar walking along, and he crossed the road about 60 yards ahead of us, and after going some 50 yards or so, he pulled up, staring at us. When we got opposite, in fun I called out "Whoof whoof!" Up went his bristles, down went his head, and he, with a "Whoof whoof!" also, charged down upon us. We could not help laughing at his audacity. He pulled up after going some 20 or 30 yards, eying us viciously, so I yelled out "Whoof whoof!" again. This was more than his hogship could stand, and he made for us as straight as a dart. It was time to stop his little game, so we up with our rifles and gave him a broadside. Being severely wounded, he turned off and made for the forest, but we did not allow him to escape, but followed him up and killed him. Now considering he was not 3½ feet in height, and our elephant over 10 feet, the pluck of the beast may be imagined.

Between Pagan Myo in Upper Burma and a range of hills to the east, I have seen wild pigs out feeding, and as the ground was perfectly ridable I see no reason why pig-sticking, the noblest of sport, should not be carried on there.

WILD DOGS (*Canis*)

(*Cuon rutilans*)

These are fairly plentiful in the country not subject to wholesale inundation, but although closely allied to the wild dogs of the neighbouring hills and other parts of India and Assam, I do not think they are identical. A bitch McMaster had and presented to the People's Park, Madras, was a nasty, savage brute—very offensive; and neither in size nor looks to be compared to her kin in the Wynaad.

Dr. Mason also mentions another variety of wild dog in Karennee. D'Oyly heard of them too, and after a great deal of trouble two were brought to him by some Karens. They were hairy—something like skye-terriers; in size about a medium-sized spaniel, black and white in colour. They used to dig out holes on the side of an embankment, crawl in backwards, and lie there perdu, with only their ferrety eyes and sharp-pointed noses visible. They were quite young when D'Oyly got them, but they would never allow themselves to be petted or handled. They eventually escaped, and we were never able to replace them. I got another dog from Karennee, but it was only one of the ordinary pariahs of the East; it had a very good nose, and would hunt fairly. In Assam I have frequently seen them in the Dooars.

JACKALS

(*Canis aureas*)

These are not found in Lower Burma, although a few exist near Meaday and Prome on the frontier. In Assam they are in thousands. My colleague will be able to say whether they are in Upper Burma. Everybody has heard in the East the unearthly cry of "A dead Hindoo! where, where?—here, here!" uttered by these obscene animals; but there is another cry they give utterance to, called the "Pheeal"—it is the frightened yelp of the ordinary jackal, and not that of a variety, as many have asserted. Although it is asserted to be the Tiger's-provider, I think the reverse is truer; they follow the royal beast and hope to pick up the pieces, but he generally lies up close and will not allow any one to intrude on his larder; but occasionally when he has gone for a drink, or is absent for some other cause, a jackal nibbles at the quarry; and if the tiger puts in an appearance suddenly, off he goes with his tail between his legs, uttering the cry of the "Phēēal."

The hyæna is not known in Assam, or in Lower Assam.

The porcupine is found in both countries.

The snakes are innumerable, and of very many kinds. Many very venomous, but are seldom met with or seen. I have seen a Hamadryad in the streets of Shoayghein being exhibited by a snake-charmer, over 16 feet in length, and equal to a man's thigh in thickness.

CHAPTER IV

ELEPHANTS, HOWDAH, AND MAHOUTS

MAHOUTS are the best abused servants in India, not altogether undeservedly, but I do not think due allowance is made for all they have to go through. They are very apt, unless well looked after, to allow an elephant to forage for himself, rather than be at the trouble of bringing in his charah or green food, of which he requires fully six hundred pounds a day, and afterwards bathing his elephant, and securely tethering him. If this is not insisted upon, the elephant will either get no food, or, in wandering about in search of it, he will destroy property for which you will have to pay fourfold, and he will also stray away and not be caught till late next morning.

But mahouts have their good points. They are, as a rule, plucky, being principally Moslems; and as such, fatalists. It must be remembered the sportsman, safely ensconced in the howdah, runs or incurs little risk, while the mahout, sitting on the elephant's neck, with his legs dangling down, is in very great danger from a charging tiger. He is unarmed, save with his driving-hook—guzbuz; and the frequency of accidents proves that his berth is not a sinecure. The friction caused by sitting on the animal's neck, perhaps for twelve hours on stretch, is excessive. He also gets bitten by numerous gadflies and mosquitoes, and is exposed to the sun all day, and he has perhaps to readjust your howdah several times during the day, if it gets out of the perpendicular, as is but too often the case. Being in a crooked howdah is not only misery to the rider, but it is impossible to feel at home, and to be able to shoot correctly when you are lopsided.

After reaching camp he may have to go miles to get the charah, which should have been cut and collected by his assistant; he has to stack this carefully on the elephant's back and bring it home, to bathe and well scrub the animal, to anoint his head with oil, and then to give him his grain—which, if properly done, takes a considerable time, as the rice should be tied up in small bundles of grass or plantain pulp and then put into the beast's mouth. If allowed to feed himself, an elephant blows the rice through his trunk down his throat, without masticating it, and he derives no benefit from it. He must then be securely tethered for the night, and his charah placed within his reach. It is only after this that the mahout is at liberty to cook and prepare his own food. All these duties combined constitute a hard day's work, and this continues perhaps incessantly for a month or more whilst in camp. Is it a wonder, then, that a mahout sometimes shirks some portion of his daily task? In the management of his elephant a mahout should not be interfered with too much. If you have a stud, engage a head man or jemadar, one who held some responsible position in the Government Keddah for choice. If you are known and liked he will readily come to you if you give him a rupee or two more a month than he has been receiving. Leave the physicking and interior management to him. Do not keep a mahout you cannot trust, or who shows the slightest signs of funk; he will only ruin your animal.

I think more can be done by judicious kindness and general supervision than by bullying or nagging; but, when necessary, don't hesitate to make a severe example of a man who wilfully disobeys your orders, or takes advantage of your kindness to neglect his duties. Treat natives as you would children, with a mixture of kindness and firmness, and be liberal in sharing all Government rewards amongst them, and they will do anything for you; but avoid extremes—one is as bad as the other.

Many of the mahouts enter into the spirit of the chase, and like a successful sportsman for a master, because the more wild beasts he slays the more they expect to get. I know my men's pay was frequently doubled whilst out, and this adds

PUTTING ON HOWDAH.

From a Photo by P. Burges, Esq

to their zeal, and without hearty co-operation of your mahouts you will get little or no game.

Elephants differ greatly in make and size; and a really good mahout will tell pretty accurately whence the animal came by merely looking him over. Elephants utter peculiar sounds to denote certain meanings. A whistling noise produced by the trunk indicates satisfaction; when they trumpet or utter a hoarse, sharp scream it is a sign of rage; a noise made by the mouth like "pr-rut-pr-rut" is a sign of alarm, so is the striking of the trunk on the ground accompanied by a pitiful cry, whilst a noise like "urmp-urmp" denotes impatience or dissatisfaction. Elephants are never still, their bodies are always swaying to and fro, the ears and tail are constantly flapping or brushing off flies, the trunk is in incessant use, the legs are constantly rubbed one against the other; but if the same animal, so full of restlessness, becomes suspicious, he becomes for the moment as rigid as a rock, with his trunk raised and ears cocked forward, using his olfactory and acute hearing to the utmost. I do not think their eyesight is very good, they trust more to the two senses I have just mentioned, but if an elephant runs away and all other means fail to stop his flight, try blindfolding him. I have known it succeed several times.

Elephants when asleep often snore: they are very human-like in many of their ways; for instance, I have seen them use a foot as a pillow on which to rest their head. They get a piece of wood and use it as a toothpick, they will plug a wound with clay, they scratch themselves with the tip of their trunk, or if they cannot reach the irritable part with that, they take up a branch and use it. An elephant often thrusts his trunk into his mouth and extracts a quantity of water which he squirts over his body, and often over his riders.

Before starting on a day's shooting, see that your howdah is correctly, tightly, and straightly put on: if it is at all crooked, have it taken off and re-adjusted: it is better to have it correctly done in camp where you have men to assist than to have to do it in the jungles where the hands are few. One great source of the howdah getting out of gear is the constantly making an elephant sit down to enable the rider to dismount;

to avoid this, take a howdah ladder with you. It is about 8 feet long and ingeniously constructed; there is a groove into which the rungs fit when the ladder is folded up, and then it looks like a stout stick slung on to one side of the pad. They are obtainable in most of the principal towns in India from which parties start out hunting.

An elephant is naturally very gentle, and would not hurt a worm, but they can be taught anything. Never allow your beast to make a football of a dead beast between his legs; he will do it at first with reluctance, and only when forced, but it teaches him bad habits, and if frightened he might do it to his own master. No elephant will tread upon anything if he can avoid it; they are wonderfully sure-footed, and will go up and down the steepest places which to any other beast would be impossible. The way they slide down the steep side of a nullah with fore-legs stretched out in advance and the hind doubled backwards dragging them along, or ascend an equally steep place by bending the fore-legs and walking as it were on their knees, has to be seen to be believed.

I would rather be on an elephant that runs away than on one given to charging. I have been run away with dozens of times, and have had some narrow squeaks. Unfortunately, if an elephant gets into a panic, and he sees a forest anywhere near, he will make for it straight across country as hard as he can amble along, for they cannot canter or gallop; but it is astonishing how fast they can go at their shamble. A good runner might have a chance on a smooth sward, but he would have none over rough ground. An elephant cannot jump—a deep ditch of over 7 feet is to him impassable unless he can go down and up it.

As a rule, they are frightened at seeing fire, but an elephant of the battery in Debrooghur in Assam would help to put out a fire, and she would do what I never saw any other elephant do, and that was—after a fallen buffalo's throat had been cut through to the vertebræ, she would, when told, put her foot on the neck, twist her trunk round the horns, and wrench the head off and hand it up to the mahout. Some few elephants will pick up birds after being shot and hand them up, but not as a rule.

ELEPHANTS GOING UP RIVER BANK

From a Photo by P. Burges, Esq.

A howdah should be made as light as possible consistent with strength. It should not rest on the spine, the part across that should be hollowed out. The weight must be distributed equally on each side of the back longitudinally on bars resting on the pad, which should be well stuffed, and under it there should be a thick guddelah, and another above, to prevent the howdah slipping. It is better to have these guddelahs stuffed with wool than with cotton.

The bars which form the foundation of the howdah have eyelets through which a rope with a piece of soft leather attached to it is passed under the throat, and a similar one under the tail; these form a crupper and breast-piece as in a horse, and keep the howdah from shifting either to the back or front. The body of the howdah should be raised at least four inches above these bars, and be quite clear of the pad. I prefer the floor of a howdah to be planked; the motion of the elephant is not so much felt; but some prefer standing on the guddie, which is, I think, a great mistake. Round the sides of your howdah tack a strong Charsootie cloth or light canvas, and give it two coats of green paint, which renders it not only less conspicuous but also waterproof. On the two longitudinal iron bars connecting the front with the back of the howdah sew two strips of good waterproof cloth to serve as flaps to throw over the guns if rain falls. They are not in the least in the way, as they hang down outside till wanted. Sew on a few bullets to the lower edge to prevent the wind blowing them off or about. By taking this simple precaution I have kept my weapons perfectly dry in the wettest weather. The front should not be too high, and should be in accordance with the height of the person who is going to use it; it should be just clear of his elbows when he stands up. The back part should be about a foot lower. Now that breechloaders are universal a double howdah is not requisite; it was intended for two—in the front the sportsman, and in the back an attendant for loading, but at the best it was a bad arrangement. When a beast charges, oftener than not the elephant turns tail, and to avoid a collision, it is necessary to turn round sharply and fire down over the elephant's tail, and this cannot be done satisfactorily if there is a man behind.

For good shooting and for comfort, everything depends on the height of the seat from the floor—the edge should just fit into the bend of the knee: if less and the elephant jolts suddenly forward, the rider is apt to go backwards; if higher the constant friction against the back of the thighs is very annoying and apt to throw a man forward; but if of the height I have mentioned you feel firm, the body sways to and fro, and you feel at home and able to shoot here, there, and everywhere. Until you feel at home in a howdah on an elephant's back and can do without holding on to the sides, you will never make good shooting. Four guns in a howdah are ample, two on each side of your seat, where racks are fitted just large enough for the butt-end of your stocks; these racks had better be lined with felt to prevent rattling. In the fore-part there is a bar with notches for the barrels; these should be lined, or the polish will soon be taken off the gun. In a box, also lined, your cartridges should be arranged; in a scrimmage there is no time to pick out cartridges—it is best therefore to have your weapons of the same bore, with perhaps the exception of an Express, whose cartridges cannot be mistaken for any others. There should be a lid to let down to keep off dew or rain. The less noise, other than the unavoidable one the elephants make in going through the long grass, the better; most of the game in Burma and Assam are accustomed to hearing and seeing the elephants moving about, but if they hear the rattling of gun-barrels or of plates, etc., they soon know there is something uncanny approaching, and make tracks.

Take a light zephyr waterproof coat to put on if heavy rain sets in. The best protection overhead is a large native umbrella with a long handle; on either side, between your gun-stocks, drill two holes, one on the seat and the other in the floor; by opening the umbrella and inserting it on one side or the other according to the sun's inclination, you will have shade, which is only required when going over large tracts where there is no game expected. When not wanted, take the umbrella out of the holes, fold it up, and put it head-downwards on the floor, the handle sticking out behind the back of the howdah, and it will not be the least in the way.

Never picket your elephants long in the same spot; standing on their own dung and soil impregnated with their urine will very soon soften or rot the soles of their feet; which, though spongy, ought to be at the same time as hard as ivory.

If you see an elephant eating earth, stop his grain, he will pass in a few days a quantity of bots, and will then be all right again.

The period of gestation in an elephant and the age it lives to, have been accepted on very meagre grounds, which are not, in my opinion, conclusive, or even likely. Mr. Sanderson says the average age of an elephant may be reckoned at 150 years. Mr. Nuttall, Mr. Sanderson's predecessor for thirty years in the Government Keddahs, held a different opinion. Writing to the late Frank Buckland he said:—

"When the British captured Ceylon, a memorandum was found left by Colonel Robertson, who was in command of the island in 1799, which stated that the elephant attached to the establishment at Matura had served under the Dutch for upwards of 140 years, during the entire period of the occupation from the expulsion of the Portuguese in 1656, and found by them in the stables when they took possession of the island."

Even if this were the case, as one swallow does not make a summer, it does not follow that because there was one Methuselah amongst elephants, all should live to the same period. But as Mr. Nuttall continues:—

"The stories of elephants living to an immense age in India I put no trust in, because with any favourite elephant in former days (when the jemadar had the naming of them) they had special names for these animals, and as their vocabulary of names was but limited, they used to give three or four elephants the same name, as, for instance, Pobun Peary, No. I, Pobun Peary, No. II, and so on. 'Pobun' means 'the wind,' and an elephant in the depôt possessing swift and easy paces would go by the name of Pobun, and when Pobun I. died, Pobun II. became I., and so on. These names appeared in the office books, while the casualty rolls were kept merely on fly-sheets, and were after a while disposed of as waste-paper, and therefore no check was possible to the true identification of an elephant, and as no trace could be found except in the office books, which simply showed the same names of elephants running on continually year after year, it appeared as if the elephants reached an extraordinary age. But all this has now been altered, and the books better kept. I consider an elephant to be at its prime about thirty-five or forty, and capable of working up to seventy or eighty years of age. An elephant's life may extend rather longer than a human being's, but not by much; but I do not believe in animals (except a very occasional one) living up to 150 years. There are mahouts whose fathers, grandfathers, and great-great-great-grandfathers were all mahouts, and my opinion is founded on theirs, supplemented by my own observations of the past thirty years."

One of the reasons given for believing that an elephant's age extends to 150 years is that the gestation takes from twenty to twenty-four months. When I pointed out that although the mare took eleven months, and the human race only nine months in gestation, and that there could be no comparison in the ages attained by man and horse respectively, Mr. Cameron says this comparison is inadmissible, because cattle and mankind respectively belong to different natural orders. Cattle are born in a condition to take care of themselves, while mankind are born helpless, like naked birds in a nest, and pass, so to speak, through a period of extra-uterine gestation; which, if we are to compare them with cattle, must be added to the intra-uterine period.

If so, add a year or a year and a half, by which time a child is about as capable of taking care of itself as a calf or a colt at birth, and we should get a far longer period of gestation for man than even the elephant, and if so, why should not men's days be 150 years instead of three-score years and ten?—but I am not learned enough to argue on such subjects. About 1890, when I was at Bangalore, an officer there showed me some photos of a male elephant *in coitu* with a female. He had served several, and several photos had been taken. This is a most unusual occurrence, and as the elephants belonged to the Government stud, the commissariat officer doubtless made a note of the date, and should be now in a position to state how long gestation took place; and if the young ones brought forth from this connection live, the generation living about 2136 or thereabouts should be able to settle as to the longevity or otherwise of these most useful beasts.

There is, or was, a saying that no one had ever seen in England a dead donkey or a postboy. Many sportsmen who have spent a lifetime in jungles infested with these pachyderms wonder what becomes of the remains of elephants who die a natural death. Sanderson, Sir S. Baker, and others, all assert that they have never come across a dead elephant. Mr. Cameron says:—"The remains of defunct elephants may escape the casual notice of a comparatively few sportsmen absorbed in the eager, and not seldom dangerous, pursuit of living game; with the dead elephant, as with a dead stag, carnivorous animals consume the decomposing flesh; deer and oxen chew and scatter the dismembered bones; the grass grows, and withers upon what is left; a bone here and there may arrest the passing eye, yet tell no story to the preoccupied mind."

He mentions also that Captain Swayne, visiting the exact spot where a large bull elephant had been killed two years previously, found after careful search nothing but the jawbones with the grinders embedded in them, and was assured by his Somalis that the skeleton had been completely disposed of by the domestic cattle and the koodoos.

This may apply to sportsmen solely, but in my own case it is different. I was not only a sportsman but an engineer employed in opening out countries little known; for this purpose I had hundreds of men employed in cutting traces through the enormous savannahs of Assam and Burma—countries where wild elephants are probably more numerous than in Ceylon or Southern India. I had to traverse these at all seasons, even in the rains; if I could not go by elephants I had to go by boat. I had to burn these jungles yearly—in all for over twenty-one years. Yet I have never come across the body of an elephant that died a natural death, though I have seen hundreds of carcases of deer, gaur, gayal, buffalo, and tsine lying dead—and also the remains of elephants killed by either myself or others.

In Somaliland there are numerous hyænas, in Assam and Burma not one. I cannot credit deer and cattle demolishing the enormous head and pelvis of an elephant. I instance the case of a large Muckna shot by Herbert Bainbridge in Assam, which was in evidence for about eight years, although shot in a vast plain, far away from all civilization and subject yearly to inundation in the rains and to fire in the dry weather. Why should not deer, of which there were plenty about, and buffaloes which roam about in herds, have demolished those remains like the tame cattle and koodoos are supposed to have done in Somaliland? If the bones are eaten, what becomes of the tusks? these would be a tough morsel, and could not be demolished at a sitting. Why has not a gnawed one ever been found? The truth is, we are all in the dark on these subjects, and theories are founded on conjectures.

Elephants are subject to many diseases, the worst being Zurbād, a dropsical swelling which appears generally first under the belly; if taken in time the animal may be temporarily cured, but the disease is sure to return and kill. It also seems infectious; the best thing to be done is to sell the beast off for anything you can get for him. In *Sport in British Burma* I gave the contents of a treatise by Dr. Gilchrist of the Madras Army of the diseases elephants are subject to and their treatment, but I myself don't pretend to know much about them. I know a murrain broke out in the Pheel Khana in Tongho, and though the elephants were scattered as fast and as far apart as possible, some forty out of eighty died. To make up these losses, the commissariat officer, Major Mackellar, an old brother officer of mine, was directed to purchase others. There is as much rascality in selling an elephant as there is in selling a horse; a vicious elephant is drugged, and in that state sold as docile, whilst ginger and arrack even are given to make a sleepy worn-out beast look bright; every trick is resorted to—a useless brute that never carries flesh when worked is fed up with massala and sugarcane, on which he speedily gets fat, and is then sold, only to fall off again as rapidly when these stimulants are discontinued and the beast is worked.

Some elephants are vicious by nature—those born in a state of captivity more than those caught wild ; the former, whilst losing their dread of man, get treacherous and almost useless for sport or for ordinary traffic, owing to their fears of all wild beasts, which those caught have been used to. When D'Oyly and I lived together at Tongho, he used to hire elephants in preference to indenting on the commissariat for them, for his jungle trips. One beast he hired was particularly vicious; he had killed several mahouts, and at last ran away into the jungles, became quite wild, and did a great deal of damage to the crops, so a reward was offered for his death.

As he haunted the jungles in the vicinity of Tongho many officers went for him, but though he was frequently wounded, no one succeeded in producing his tail; but he suddenly disappeared, and every one who had fired at him claimed having killed him. Nothing was heard of him for a good six months, and the ryots had peace, and supposed that he had either died in the remoter jungles or had wandered away elsewhere. After the epidemic, placards were posted at the Cutcherie that all elephants brought in and passed—if moderately cheap—would be purchased: so good, bad, and indifferent were brought in for sale. I was always looking at them, taking an interest in all animals, and elephants in particular. Amongst those for sale was a sleepy-looking brute with lumps about his head which looked suspiciously like embedded bullets, and he moreover reminded me of the one D'Oyly used to hire. (He, poor fellow, was no more.) I spoke to Mackellar, advising him to have nothing to do with the brute in question, but he did not know one beast from another, and moreover was completely under the thumb of his head Gomashta, a Madrassie, a very able man, who had all the Burmese in that part of Burma in the palm of his hand, and said he would cause inquiries to be made. Armagum, the Gomashta in question, said I was altogether mistaken, the elephant was well known, very quiet (too quiet, I thought), and ridiculously cheap. So he was bought and taken off to the Pheel Khanah. In a few days he began to show signs of vice, and one day when being taken for his charah, he threw his mahout and prodded at him with his long sharp tusks; by wriggling on one side, the man just escaped, and the brute impaled his own trunk right through. The alarm was quickly given, and he was soon recaptured by the other elephants, and after being securely tethered, his trunk was released, but mortification set in and he died, and on examination numerous bullets were found embedded in him. The truth then came out. I was right in my conjecture—it was D'Oyly's old beast. A knowing Burman had watched the brute, and noticed that he followed certain paths going to and from the cultivation, so he threw down goor well impregnated with opium in the paths. The elephant ate thereof, and became partially stupefied; he was caught and taken here and there, far away, for sale, being always under the influence of opium, but everybody fought shy of him, and as nobody would purchase him, the man was about to turn him loose when he heard that the Government wanted elephants, so first drugging him well, and doubtless by means of palm-oil, he succeeded in selling him and got clear away with the money—some Rs. 1500.

Elephants take strange antipathies; here is a case in point, from the *Oriental Sporting Magazine*:—

"A female elephant which I had lately bought had, partly from not having been long caught, and partly by bad management by the mahout, so great a dislike to Europeans that she was with much difficulty approached by them, even to mount her; and when feeding, she would start off if any European came near her. It was supposed it was their dress which alarmed her, and the plan proposed was to dress her attendants like Europeans. To test this, a native, calling himself a Portuguese, was sent towards her. To the surprise of everybody she allowed him to approach and caress her without any signs of dislike, though he was dressed in European clothes. It was evident it was not the dress, but the colour of the face which alarmed her. A friend and myself now approached her slowly, with black crape tied over our faces, and no signs of dislike were shown. While patting and talking to her I slowly drew back the crape so as to uncover my face. The first effect of this was the quick

ELEPHANTS SPARRING.

From a Photo by Sir B. Simpson, Bart.

wrinkling of the muscles of the face, the foot half raised, and the body swung back as if for a start; but she came back slowly to the 'stand at ease,' with the peculiar grumbling which they make when satisfied with anything. This singular experiment was made several times, and always with the same result, and in one instance a red handkerchief was used.

"Nothing was given to her that evening by us, but the next day she came without any trouble to the verandah, and when called forward, came up and took fruit from our hands with her mouth, as all well-trained elephants do. There is something very much resembling reason in this change in the animal's behaviour; she got over her fright as soon as she discovered that white and black faces could be made to appear at pleasure."

When a male makes up to a female and she does not chime in at once with his wishes, he often seizes her by the tail and wrenches it off. I have seen several instances of this.

Considering that elephants and rhinoceros and buffaloes herd and feed almost together, why the first should have—when domesticated—such a dread of the second, I cannot think, but it is a fact. They dislike the smell, but the grunting noise made by these thick-skinned beasts they dread far more. I have known an elephant's leg cut to the bone by the tush of a rhinoceros, and also one knocked over by a buffalo. But the *shikar* elephants in Burma and Assam do not dread the bubali so much, as the tame ones are nearly as large as the feral, and equally savage, but whilst going for Europeans, they take no notice of elephants or of the native children who herd them.

I have known of a female suckling her own calf and that of another cow that had died. Some say the females are vicious to the calves; it may be the case with old maids, but I have never seen it in the case of a female who had had young of her own. An old bull elephant will at times knock over a presuming hobbledehoy who annoys him, but generally they are very sociable and peaceable amongst themselves. Full-grown males cannot, however, be trusted to live in amity; thus, for greater security, the tips of Government elephants' tusks are sawn off.

JUNGLE TRIPS ON ELEPHANTS, LOWER BURMA

Early in May 1860 I asked our Brigadier, Glencairn Campbell, C.B., brother of the old Forest Ranger and cousin to that great Nimrod, Gordon Cumming, if he would like a few days' sport in Burma. He had seen much fighting, especially at the Cape against the Kaffirs, and had also been a noted sportsman and athlete. He was still well preserved, and a capital shot. He gladly consented, and as Lloyd—also a keen sportsman, who had lately come up as Deputy Commissioner—wanted to go too, we agreed to go together, and asked Liardet of the 2nd N. I. to accompany us.

The Brigadier, Lloyd, and Liardet started on the 2nd, but I could not get away until the 4th, but I got into my loung or racing boat, and reached Banlong by 8 p.m. The others had finished their dinner, and whilst I was partaking of mine, Lloyd told the result of their sport. On the 3rd they had tried stalking thamine, but got none. On the 4th, at Shoayjah's instigation, they got on to the elephants on pads—there were no howdahs in Burma in those days—and went through several savannahs, where the grass was only about four feet high, and saw much game; but none of them had been accustomed to shoot off elephant-back; on a pad you can only fire comfortably and with any chance of success to the left front, and as a rule the deer are seldom obliging, but will insist on going off to the right. They had fired a great many shots; but the Brigadier had shot a stag sapt (sambur), Liardet a buck and a doe sambur, and Lloyd a hog deer, d'ala'el of the Burmese, but he lost three sambur badly wounded.

On the 5th the Brigadier did not feel well, so Lloyd, Liardet, and I went alone.

Banlong is on the river; on three sides are extensive paddy fields; beyond them, forests, and beyond again are quins, or open spaces, formerly cultivated but left fallow for many years past; these are covered with short grass, a few trees, and occasionally a little pool of water. In the quins are herds of brow-antlered deer, hog deer, and hogs; in the outlying savannahs there are numerous sambur, hog deer, hogs, and tigers now and then; occasionally gaur, and even tsinc. We saw some thamine and tried to stalk them, but they were too cunning, and we failed to bag any. On entering the savannah opposite, I shot a hog deer with rather nice horns.

We then breakfasted, and on resuming hostilities all the luck fell to my comrades, and they fired away as fast as they could load, and they missed at least half-a-dozen, whilst I did not get a shot. Liardet then bagged a sambur; up to three o'clock Lloyd and Liardet monopolized all the luck. Lloyd got nothing, whilst Liardet was credited with a buck and a doe. At last I killed one and wounded another, which we followed on foot. Lloyd came upon her and killed her. Towards evening I took a snap-shot, and killed one more. As we were then seven miles from Banlong we went towards home, and got there at dark.

We had a long confab with the local *shikaries*, who were Shoayjah, Moung Wine, and Moung Oo; they said if we would go twelve miles further inland we'd get better sport; so we moved camp next morning, Liardet and I on one elephant going ahead. We agreed to fire at no deer, as near Myetquin we might expect to come across big game such as buffaloes and gaur. We saw herds of deer, but true to our compact we did not fire at one; but Lloyd could not resist the temptation, and blazed away, but had nothing to show for his expenditure of ammunition. The next day (7th) we were out early. Lloyd would fire at deer, so we all took to blazing away at anything we saw. The Brigadier bagged three sambur, Liardet also three, Lloyd one, and I two.

On the 8th we followed up tracks of gaur and tsine, and so got out of the kine grass into the heavy forests, and so lost much time. By the evening Lloyd had two, Brigadier two, Liardet lost two; I only got a hog deer.

We moved back to Banlong on the 9th, and I at once saw the capabilities of Myetquin as a head-quarters for sporting purposes, and as soon as I got back I sent out materials and carpenters and had a bungalow built there. There is a large bheel at Myetquin, and between it and the Yomahs there is to be had the best sport in Lower Burma. We only shot a few deer *en route*.

On the 10th we came across our first gaur (pyoung); we had shot several deer, when some lumbering beast went through the heavy grass. Lloyd called out, "A bison!" and fired. As the bull passed an open spot, the Brigadier fired and killed it. There was a dispute as to whether it was the Brigadier's or Lloyd's, Lloyd claiming it as having fired at it first. I believe myself that Lloyd missed, and that the beast was the Brigadier's; but the elder man had shot too much game to be jealous, and gave it up.

On the 11th Liardet and I went stalking on foot, and I was as near getting a sunstroke as possible. We had a long walk over dried paddy fields, then through rather an open forest for a mile, then through a quin devoid of game; but in the tree-jungle beyond I shot a thamine and hung it up. I then wounded another and tried to run it down, but the ground was a mass of hummocks covered with trailing and thorny vines, and I soon measured my distance on the ground, having come a cropper. We saw many deer, but they were on the *qui vive*, so we had miles of walking over the most difficult ground under a blazing sun for nothing. I was thoroughly done, and we were miles from camp. I told my comrade to get home as fast as he could and send an elephant for me; but he did not like to leave me in my present condition, so we stumbled along. At last we came to a buffalo-hole in which those cattle had been wallowing; it was half mud, half water, well impregnated with urine, but such as it was I was glad to pour it over me, and even to drink it. It was to me a weary trudge, but I was too obstinate to give in, and finally reached the Zyat more dead than alive. I rushed into the bath-room, poured all the ghurrahs of cold water over me, and soon got all right.

May 12.—We were late in starting, several of the mahouts sick. We did not do much—got out of the kine grass, and into dense forests, but about 8 p.m. we saw five gaur chewing the cud and flapping the flies off themselves with their tails. The Brigadier jumped off and stalked them; he had to go through long grass fully ten feet high.

SPECIMEN OF HUNTING GROUND.

From a Photo by P. Burges, Esq.

We remained to cover him, if he were charged. The plucky old man got to within ten yards, but could not see them. The bull, hearing a noise, advanced, and we expected every moment that he would be on the Brigadier. We did not like to open fire, as we wanted the General to get first shot, but suddenly the bull spun round, and with tail on end went off full score followed by his wives. We fired a volley but did no harm. That was the last chance we got at gaur that trip.

May 13.—Moved towards home, going *viâ* Tagoondine.

May 14.—Brigadier and Liardet went shooting. Lloyd and I up the Puechoung to see the waterfalls. We came back by rafts.

May 15.—Nouksedouk, a good place for big game. I left my comrades there, and rode back to Tongho, having work to attend to.

In October I received orders to visit an old fort, Zayawadie, and I persuaded Dyke of the 69th to come with me. I sent on the elephants several days before, and told them to meet us at Banlong. We started on my birthday, the 19th October, by boat, and after sundry adventures got to our destination only to find that the elephants had not arrived, but we had my servants and some food and beer, and made ourselves as comfortable as possible. We slept on the floor of the Zyat, and used logs of wood in lieu of pillows. Our elephants did not turn up till the afternoon of the 20th. The mahouts told us the roads were nearly impassable, and that they had taken eight days to do what they generally got over in three, or three and a half. We called the *shikaries* together, but they told us it was madness trying to shoot at this time of the year; but as I had to go, I thought I'd try and get some sport. I was luckier than I deserved, for I bagged a couple of sambur with one ball each; but it was pure luck, for all we could see were the ears. The stags had dropped their horns and were in hiding.

The next day it took us fourteen hours to do eight miles, and we did not get to Zayawadie till 5 p.m., and our attendants did not arrive till dark. We had our beds rigged up and took refuge under the curtains, for the mosquitoes were numerous and ravenous. Our dinner was not ready till 8 p.m., and it was handed to us under the curtain, in bed.

I examined the fort well, and then moved on to Tagoondine on the Pue. The next day we got into the midst of at least three hundred elephants, all hines. We tried to shoot them off elephants, but signally failed to bag more than one at the time, though in all, I believe, eight died, and were picked up by the natives, who delight in their flesh. It was cruel work, and I have never since fired at an elephant off an elephant. Had I thought of the ear-shot, I might have been more successful, but shooting at the temple is useless at that angle.

October 25.—We moved to Kyenkein and came across two of the elephants dead, but the short tushes had been stolen, and I very nearly slew a Burman; he had crawled inside one of the carcases for some tit-bits, but hearing us talking he came out backwards on all-fours, and as he was a mass of gore I mistook him for some beast, and was just going to fire when he got up on his feet!

The next day we shot only one stag, but saw many sambur. Jungle is too thick at this time of the year. We found out a new quin where the men said in May and June big game was plentiful. The *shikarie's* name, Moung Mon—he lives at Kadeingzee. The quin is called "Pojahgalay Quin." We then wended our way home, shooting lots of snipe *en route.*

I have occasionally shot deer by going three or four miles out of Shoayghein, and once bagged a leopard. The fishing in the pure crystal waters of the Shoayghein river was very good; fishing a little way up stream with spoon-bait, mahseer are to be caught. By using a fly, I have caught, in the course of an hour or two, several gna-mien, weighing from 3 to 6 lbs. They are silvery and have no scales, but are capital eating, with but one bone to speak of, and that like a sole's; they have barbules on the mouth, and the flesh is coloured—slightly pinkish. The larger fish of the same kind take a spoon, but are not nearly so good for the table as those of about 5 to 7 pounds; with a little melted butter and anchovy sauce, I know no better fish. The most delicious fish in

SENDING OFF BEATING ELEPHANTS.

From a Photo by P. Burges, Esq.

the East is the hilsa; they ascend the rivers at spawning-times, and in the Delta they are caught in thousands. I have seen a Burman boat almost gunwale under water from the number caught in nets. Although most delicious to eat, they are probably the most bony fish in existence, but there are four bits, each about the size of a table-spoon, which can be extracted by the *cognoscenti*, which are totally devoid of bone. The best plan is to lay the fish flat, and with a fork to run it down its length with the bones, extracting the flesh and leaving the bones behind.

The fresh-water crabs are not bad. There are no lobsters, but immense prawns and crayfish are caught off the coasts, and are delicious eating. The best thing I ever got for jungle work was dried prawns; the smell was against them, but after soaking them for twelve hours, and then making them into a curry, they were very good indeed.

Night-fishing by blazing out of a boat is not bad fun. I used to go out to the lime-kilns some fifteen miles distant from Tongho; as the boats we went in were mere dug-outs, upsets were frequent, so we were arrayed in bathing costume. If you strike at and miss a fish you are sure to go overboard, but that is not of much consequence in India. The Thouka-ghat, or drinking-water stream, is one of the most beautiful I have ever seen. Its waters are always icy cold, and the scenery, as it debouches from the mountains, is lovely. I built a bath in it, staking it all round and making it quite private, and connecting it with the shore by a bridge. It was a favourite place even for ladies to bathe. Stakes were necessary, as the current was rather swift. I removed the materials every year before the rains. I had a house there, 17 feet off the ground, and whilst it was unbearably hot in Tongho, we were glad of blankets there.

Determined to try the shooting localities at various seasons, Lloyd, Clarke, and I went to Banlong in January. The first day I shot a doe thamine. The next day we went to Myet-quin, where our future hut had just been commenced. I got one deer *en route*. As the grass was very high and the annual fires had not commenced, we tried what beating would do. We sent the elephants round and took up our positions in trees, but nothing came our way. In the evening Lloyd and Clarke got a deer apiece.

January 23.—We went towards Gna-Eein, a pool not far from the base of a spur of the Yomahs. At first we had not any luck: we saw lots of deer, but they kept out of shot, but Lloyd shot a sow for the pot. I had all the luck to-day, and bagged several deer. One stag I thought I had missed—he doubled back and ran on as if untouched; but hearing a noise as of something kicking against a tree, I went back, and found it lying dead between two trees. We came upon a sambur just killed by a tiger; we beat for him everywhere, but failed to find him. We came to the conclusion that this was not the season for sport in those jungles.

24th.—We again tried for the tiger, but had no luck. We only shot a hog deer and a pig between us.

The Burmans attributed our indifferent luck to the influence of evil spirits, so we gave them a few rupees to do pojah with. I had found somewhere—I forget when or where—two small images (twin-jointed) of Gaudama, the only ones of the sort I ever saw. I had them with me, and placed them in the fork of a tree overhanging the Gna-Eein. The Burmese were delighted, and said as long as they remained there, the pool would never dry up. Nor did it for three years, but when we went there the fourth, they were gone and the pool hard and dry! Whether the *shikaries* in their wanderings had seen the pool dry and removed the images, I do not know; but I strongly suspect they did, to verify their own prophecy.. It is a fact that for the three years they (the images) were there, the pool always had water in it, though it was more liquid mud than *aqua puris.* It was full of a coarse fish, and our mahouts used to jump into it and catch numbers of them. There were also salt-licks about, so it is no wonder that game abounded near that spot. We came across three elephants, one a fine tusker, but could not get near them for a certain shot. I fired very badly to-day, and Lloyd and Clarke got three deer between them. Tired of this work, we mounted our ponies and rode back into Tongho.

We next thought we would try spring shooting, so Lloyd

HOMEWARD BOUND. CHANGING FROM HOWDAHS TO PADS.

From a Photo by P. Burges, Esq.

and Mrs. Lloyd started in a boat over-night, and Clarke, Dr. Madden, and I early next morning in my loung. We got to Banlong at 7.30 p.m. The Lloyds had only just arrived. We had time to bathe before dinner, and soon after, all turned in. The next morning we started early, but the jungles had not been sufficiently burnt, and though we put up a lot of sambur and thamine we saw little more than the tips of their horns. I got the only deer killed. The next day I got nothing, and Lloyd killed one deer.

March 20.—Clarke, Madden, and I went ahead to Myetquin, our house then being ready. I wounded a stag thamine, and jumping off the elephant, ran after it with a Burman dalweil, or fighting sword, and with one blow I nearly cut its neck right through. As I wished to fire off my muzzle-loaders, we fired at a group of deer fully 400 yards off. We saw none fall, but from the thud I said I thought one had been hit in the head, and we found a young buck shot right through the head with my two-groove rifle which had been fired by Clarke.

March 21 and 22.—During these two days we only shot two deer, but the jungle fires were still raging, and the game on the move. I took Mrs. Lloyd in my howdah, which I had just had made. Lloyd fired at a peacock with ball and missed, but Mrs. Lloyd knocked it over very prettily. She is good all round. We only shot two or three deer, not worth the expense of coming all this distance at this time of the year. On the 25th I again took Mrs. Lloyd in my howdah; she shot a hog deer, and then, as it was getting very hot, she got on to a pad elephant and went back to camp. I killed three deer to-day. On the 26th and 27th we again shot with indifferent luck, bagging in the two days only seven deer between us. The next day I rode back to Tongho.

In April I had to go to Shoayghein, and got to Ka-een-kine at 5 p.m. The next day we went across country, making for Myetquin. I started a tiger, but failed to get a shot; the heat was awful, and not a drop of water to be had anywhere. We were getting to the edge of a tree-jungle, and well out in the quin was a herd of tsine (wild cattle), the first I had seen. They are beautiful creatures, and I have described them elsewhere. I got off and attempted to stalk them, but a pad elephant trumpeted, and off the herd went. I followed them up for some time, but had to desist. We got to Myetquin at 2 p.m. The large bheel there was all but dry. In the evening I shot a stag, but as it had not been hăl-lāl-ed, the Mussalmen mahouts turned up their noses at the flesh, so my servants and *shikaries* fared all the better. I had wounded a doe also, but lost her in the dark. We found her remains next morning; she had evidently been eaten by a tiger. I hunted for it, got a glimpse and wounded it, but it got into the tree-jungle and got away. I had an appointment to keep at Shoayghein, so could not delay any longer *en route.* We made for Chowteah, and I shot a stag *en route.* On the banks of the Koonchoung we disturbed a herd of gaur, but they got away. To try the accuracy of my two-groove rifle I fired at a couple of peafowl right and left, and brought them down. I saw some Coolen to-day, but could not get near them.

April 14.—Moved to Thabew, where I had a bungalow. *En route* I bagged two deer and a pig, as well as two jungle fowl. I saw the fresh marks of bears about, but not the beasts themselves. A tiger killed a cow in the open and I went out at once. Close by there was a clump of long grass, and near it I had a pit dug, and sat in it with my *shikarie.* About 6 p.m. the tiger appeared, and after spying about everywhere, he slowly approached the kill. He was an old male with fine whiskers; he had evidently been wallowing in a pool, as his body was encrusted in mud. When within a few yards of the kine he stood still and took a look round again; as his head was slightly turned away, he presented a splendid shot. I pointed to the shoulder for Shoayjah to fire at; I aimed at the junction of the head and neck. I fired just ahead of the *shikarie*, and the tiger rolled over dead. We walked back to camp. I had ordered the jemadar to send a couple of elephants directly a shot was fired, but they were too busy cooking their own food to hurry themselves. I told them to be more careful to obey orders in future, but to finish their meal, and to go out to bring in the tiger immediately afterwards. I had just finished my dinner when the mahouts returned, saying the tiger was not dead, but eating the cow! It was too dark to do anything then, but I told them to be ready at daylight. There was my tiger, dead enough, but the cow had been demolished, and her bones scattered about. I asked where the mud-pool was that the tiger had bathed in, and a villager said close by. I went up to it and started the tigress at once, got two snap-shots, but failed to bag her; and as I was pressed for time and she had got into a tangled forest, I told the local *shikarie* to look her up. I left the greater part of my impedimenta here, and after seeing the tiger's skin pegged out, I started on pony-back for my destination, with just my bedding and a few necessaries which had been sent on in the early morning on a fast pad elephant. I got to Shoayghein by the evening, and put up with Watson of the Artillery. I was very busy there looking after a bazaar that I was constructing, for three days, and then rode back to Thabew, getting there by the evening. I had three good ponies, two as relays. The tigress had not been recovered, but the local man had a couple of panther cubs; he offered them to me for a rupee, but as there was no milk to be got, I refused them. I believe he got his own wife to suckle them till he got a goat from the Karens, but whether he ever reared them I never heard.

April 20.—I started early for Chowteah. I went straight across country, and it was very hard work for the elephants to push their way through the long and entangled grass, which evidently had not been burned for years. The stems were more like bamboos. Elephants are the only beasts which can make their way through these heavy prairies, and in the tracks they make, gaur and buffaloes follow. I soon lost sight of the other elephants, and coming on a recent track I told my mahout to follow it. There seemed no prospect of sport, so I was sitting down reading, when there was a snort; I dropt the book, and just saw the tail of a gaur disappearing. I had no time to fire. It is a very reprehensible habit, reading in a howdah, as many shots are lost by it. When too late, I put the book away, and took up the rifle, but for an hour I saw nothing, and was all but smothered by the dusty fluff from the reeds, which is also very irritating. We got out of the heavy grass and through a quin, then through a belt of trees that fringed the Koonchoung which we crossed. We then saw several tracks; as one seemed fresher than the other, I told my man to stick to it, and in half-an-hour came upon five gaur lying down chewing the cud under the few trees that were there. We had approached so silently that they only saw us when we were almost on them. I fired at the nearest—a cow; the herd sprang up and were off, but not before I caught the bull a crack, and one more ball finished the cow. The mahout cut her throat and declared she was hăl-lāl-ed, that is, lawful to be eaten, but she was dead as a herring before he approached her. I had her flayed, and took her tongue, a strip of the hump, and the marrow-bones for myself. The mahout took enough meat for the whole camp, and tied it on behind my howdah. Before we had gone a yard, down came the vultures—first in ones and twos—then in tens and twenties—and soon in hundreds. At times we found them a perfect nuisance: they used to follow us about—flying ahead, lighting on the topmost branches of the trees, and the flapping of their wings disturbed the whole country and frightened game away; thus proving, from their greediness, their own enemies. Had they remained in the sky, they would have got far more pickings. I once threw out a very large tiger, and in eight minutes there was not a particle of meat left on the bones. We reached our camp at 4 p.m. and found our baggage animals had arrived before us; they too had seen gaur and wild elephants. The villagers complained that three men, woodcutters, had been killed by bears lately, but they did not know where those beasts lived.

April 21.—We made for Myetquin. We lost much time looking for a rhinoceros, which the people said was always about Ananbo, but we failed to make his acquaintance. We saw plenty of hinds, but it was useless shooting them here, as we had plenty of meat and could get as many as we wanted at Myetquin. Out of one patch, not 20 yards square, I put out three sambur and a tiger; he had been rolling in the ashes of the grass fires, and I did not recognize him for a feline till he was all but out of shot. I hunted him for

VULTURES ON A DEAD CARCASE. A DEAD TIGER DEMOLISHED IN EIGHT MINUTES.

From a Photo by P. Burges, Esq.

a couple of hours, but failed to see him again. About five miles beyond I saw a gaur standing alone; I got off and stalked him. I was within 50 yards, and should have got nearer, had I not tripped over a vine, and the noise startled not only him but seven others. They ran about 20 yards —the country was just there quite open—and then faced about. I lay full length on the ground. I had my trusty Lang, and fired at the chest of the big bull, and, as they spun round, at the shoulder of another. Both balls told, but nothing fell to the shots. I picked myself up, and running along, without a loaded barrel, I all but stumbled over the prone bull, but he was fortunately *in articulo mortis.* I jumped back—reloaded—and then found his spirit had fled. I waited for the elephant, and got into the howdah. I had not gone 100 yards, when I came upon the cow—gave her two more bullets, but she led me a long chase, but I eventually bagged her. I took the usual tit-bits for myself, and the tail in addition, whilst the mahout—who had again performed the hăl-lāl—took a couple of hind-legs, which I had the pleasure of helping him to tie on either side of my howdah. When I got to camp I found my other elephants had come upon the bull and brought in the trophies, thus saving me the trouble of sending for them. Shoayjah here met me with the skin of the tigress I had fired at on the 13th, but the skin was not worth the keeping, and I told him to take it to the Cutcherie for the reward.

I had left Boyle and Dr. Madden at Myetquin, and gone back to Tongho for a few days, as my eldest boy was ill and his mother very anxious. I stopped there from the 16th to the 21st, and then, as my people were all but well, I got into my boat and returned to Banlong. I found no elephant or pony for me, though I had requested Madden to send them to meet me; but I had a cold fowl, some beer, and rusks with me, and lay down on the floor of the Zyat and slept till daylight, when I got up, and after my ablutions I walked into Myetquin, only to find my two comrades out shooting. They did not return till 2 p.m. They had seen a lot of buffaloes, had dismounted and wounded several; fortunately they were not charged. They failed to bag.

On the 23rd heavy rain all night, and for the greater part of the day, but we went out all the same. About 8 a.m. I came upon five gaur lying down, and wishing the others to get shots too, I stood perfectly still, beckoning to them to hurry up; but one of the elephants trumpeted whilst my back was turned, and off the gaur went without my getting a shot: so much for forbearance out shooting. We followed them, and at last a monster gave me a broadside shot. I put two belted balls in him; he ran about 300 yards and then pulled up, breathing heavily. Madden was on a fast elephant, I was on a very slow one; he ran ahead—came alongside the bull, and in his excitement missed with both barrels! A young one joined the old bull and cleared the way for him, and eventually we accounted for them both.

We then moved to a village called Thep-pat. We saw sambur and a lot of gaur, but the grass was too high, and we could only see the tips of their horns as they bounded along. The country not having been burnt, it was useless remaining there, so we made tracks back to Myetquin. We agreed to fire at gaur, buffaloes, or tigers only, but there were so many stags about that the temptation proved too much for my comrades, and they opened fire. The reports of their fusillade disturbed a gaur to my left. He presently joined four others in an open glade, so we jumped off our steeds and stalked them on foot. We got within 80 yards—there were three standing near one another—one stood at least a foot higher than the others, and they were all full grown! The head and shoulders of the monster were behind the trunk of a tree. I could not see them from where I was, but Madden and Boyle could. At a given signal we fired. I aimed at the hip-joint—down he went. He looked very old, very emaciated; all his ribs stuck out, but he was colossal. The others went away with their tails in the air. I ran forward, and by the time I got within 20 yards he had partly struggled up, his hind-quarters were down and his fore up, resting on his heels. I let fly into his shoulder; up he jumped, and went off on three legs, one of the hind ones flying about anyhow, broken at the joint. As there was long grass about we mounted the elephant, and went in chase. I got two more shots, and he left pools of blood behind, but he managed to crawl into a cane-break, where elephants could not penetrate. We went after him on foot—came upon where he had been lying in a mass of gore; but he had enough life left to play at hide-and-seek with us, and as it was getting dark we had to desist and go home. Next morning a large herd was reported as close by, but in the opposite direction to where we had left the wounded one. Convinced that he was dead, I sent Shoayjah on an elephant to ascertain, and we went after the herd. We were rather late in starting, as we were to move homewards to-morrow. We agreed to fire at nothing less than gaur, buffaloes, or a tiger, but we searched far and wide and did not see the kine, so my comrades got tired of not firing, and coming upon a fine sambur, let fly. I was disgusted and turned towards home, but had not gone more than a couple of miles when I saw a couple of gaur. I tried to stalk them, and in so doing put up a herd of about eight. They ran on, tail on end, for 50 yards, and then wheeled round. I fired a right and left at two of the largest, and when the smoke cleared away the herd—all but one—was gone. I went up to it and killed it; my ball had struck the dorsal ridge, and had paralyzed it. I knew another was wounded, and followed the herd, but seeing no marks of blood, went home. Had I gone about 100 yards to the right I should have come upon him lying down. There in that position I found him next morning, but he had strength to get clear away, but left pools of blood behind him.

May 27.—We determined to go home *viâ* Pojahgalay Quin; I had heard much of it, so putting everything we had, including servants, on elephants, we went straight across country and put up the wounded gaur as just stated. But my gun was in its waterproof cover, and I could not get it out in time for a shot. Beyond the tree-jungle, about five miles on our way, we came to a sort of half pond, half bheel, in which were lying down some dozen wild buffaloes; we dismounted and opened fire, but failed to persuade one to remain behind; further on, we came to two of those Boyle and Madden had fired at—dead, just dry skeletons.

We got to Pojahgalay Quin late in the afternoon. I had

ordered a hut to be built here for us, but we could not find it for fully two hours—none of us knew where it had been erected. The village was six miles off. The verandah had evidently been used as a stable by a herd of tsine, as they had left their cards behind them. The shed itself was so full of fleas that a white cloth placed on the ground became almost black in a few minutes. We had the verandah well rubbed over with the wild cattle manure, and by slinging our hammocks well off the ground, managed to pass the night in tolerable comfort. We took our meals out in the open. We sent on a couple of elephants to find the village, and to bring us supplies and the best *shikarie.* We went out shooting and came upon three buffaloes—those we had fired at yesterday—dead. We each got a buck sambur. In some places the gadflies were so numerous they drove our attendants, our elephants, and ourselves nearly mad. Marks of gaur, elephants, and tsine plentiful. Our people returned with supplies, but told us the head *shikarie* had died, and that the others did not profess to know these jungles. The next day we went to Ka-een-kine, and thence back to Tongho.

Hill persuaded me to go after rhinoceros to a place called Thayet-pen-Kin-dat. Starting from Shoayghein I went to Thanzeik, and on to Upper Bogatah. I got a gaur and a fine sambur, and lost another gaur there. From Kyoukee we started for the Yonzaleen—the country exceedingly pretty, but all the way up and down hills intersected by numerous watercourses. Groves of betel-nut and delicious oranges everywhere. The mode of irrigation perfect. A bad road for laden elephants. There was a false alarm of a tiger in the night—they are much dreaded, being all man-eaters. Watson, the Deputy Commissioner, told me he had never crossed over this part of the country without losing one or more men from tigers.

The next day the first hill was a buster; it took us three hours to reach the top, and then we had to descend nearly as much again. At last we got to the Pemah-ben-choung at ten. The Têh or rest-house here was stockaded, and with a *chevaux-de-frise* round it of pointed bamboos to keep off the felines. We halted there till 3 p.m., in the hope that our elephants would come up with our breakfast, but as there were no signs of them we went on, and got to the police-station of Thayet-pen-Kin-dat at 5 p.m. The elephants did not arrive till after dark; one of the mahouts had helped himself to our liquor, got drunk, made his elephant—a bad-tempered brute—charge the females, and broke no end of wine and beer, crockery-ware, etc. To teach him to behave better in future, I tied him up and gave him a dozen well laid on. The whole place we found full of bugs, fleas, and gadflies, and to make matters worse, the ravines where the rhinoceros live were quagmires through which elephants could not go, so we did not bless Hill, but went sadly back to Kyoukee the next day.

April 16.—Started for Ananbo—got there at 9.30—breakfasted, and went on to Thabew. We put up a lot of deer, but the jungles wanted more burning, so gave the head-man ten rupees, with instructions to see it done. We shot various deer, and one day coming to a Karen village far away in the interior, we stopped there for an hour or two. Knowing that the Karens are famous for making a spirit from rice, we asked them to sell us some, but they, thinking it was a trap laid for them, swore they had none. After getting round the buxom daughter of the old chief, who was a hoary old sinner of about seventy-five, we got a bottle. It was, my comrades declared, equal to mountain-dew or the real potheen. I am no judge, as I never take spirits. The old rascal told us, on our asking him where we could find a stream to bathe in, that he had never used water for ablutions in his life, and that he only changed his garments once in five or six years. He was accustomed to get drunk three times every week for the benefit of his health. Yet the old fellow, for his age, looked lusty, and had several fine women for wives, and many daughters and sons. I shot a couple of deer, and next day, leaving my comrades to continue their sport, I went on to Shoaygheіn, where I had work to attend to.

On another trip—May 3—I rode out to Za-oo-goon, on the Pue river, thirty-three miles from Tongho. Felt a sharp shock of earthquake as I sat in the open, eating my dinner.

May 4.—Made for Myetquin across country. We had not gone a mile when a tiger was put up, but not near me, and it got away into bamboo jungle. I then made two good shots, and rolled over a couple of sambur. I saw lots of marks of gaur and some tsine in the distance. Got to camp at twelve—the heat awful. I went out in the evening, but only got rather a fine hog deer with the best horns I ever saw. Water is very scarce. Numbers of sambur lying about dead of some disease.

May 5.—I made straight for the Gna-Eein, and saw during the day seven gaur, three buffaloes, a tiger, a boar, and numbers of various deer. Near Zelokee a gaur got up, but too far off to fire at. When near the tangled jungle I saw three gaur go along and lie down under some trees, so got off and told Shoayjah to stop there till he heard me fire. I took Moung Wine with me; when I reached the point where I expected to find the kine, they were gone! Looking round for the cause, I found Shoayjah quietly seated in my howdah close behind; he had of course frightened the beasts off. I was in a rage, and gave Shoayjah something not to do the like again, and made him trudge on foot after us the greater part of the day. In half-an-hour I again saw a gaur, but could not get within gunshot. The heat was awful—the sun like a fiery furnace—not a breath of air and no water—I did not feel amiable. The mahouts were clamorous for water for themselves and their beasts, but there was none near. I had just descended one bank of a nullah and ascended the opposite, when I saw a very large bull staring me in the face not more than ten or at the most fifteen paces off. I took a careful aim with the two-groove Lang, but as I pulled the trigger the gaur threw up his head, swerved, and ran about 30 yards. I again fired, and then he lay down. I went up with a new breech-loading rifle, which Westley Richards had just made for me; as he jumped up and attempted to run across, I gave him the contents of both barrels, and he fell dead. He was within a half-inch of 7 feet at the shoulder. I could not see a shot-mark on his forehead, and the *shikarie* declared I had missed with my first shot, but that I could scarcely credit. On opening his mouth to extract the tongue, we found the bullet had gone up the right nostril, leaving no external mark, and had lodged in the neck at the back of the head. The palate was furrowed all along. I went a long way, and seeing no signs of big game, I blazed at a pig and fired over it—on which up jumped a gaur and went off at his best pace. I then came upon three buffaloes, and broke the hind-leg of one, and put it up several times afterwards, but did not get a shot at it again. I was at the edge of a small but deep nullah with a heavy and dense forest beyond, when there was a sudden roar, and the elephant bolted down the nullah, and it was as much as the mahout could do to prevent her running into the forest. I saw the tiger, and might have had a good shot at him had my elephant only been steady, but I could not risk the chances of a smash-up amongst the trees, so refrained from firing. I told the men to make for home, and in an hour I saw another gaur chewing the cud under some trees. My first idea was to dismount and to stalk the bull, but he very conveniently moved behind an immense bush, and keeping this between us I advanced rapidly on him and got within fifty yards, and moving a little on one side I got two shots and did for him. He was a big brute, but not as high as the former. I got back to camp at 7 p.m., after a hard and unpleasant day's work.

May 12.—Persuaded Hill to go back with me for a few days' sport. We determined to go *viâ* Thabew and Chowteah. I tried short cuts, but did nothing but go astray, but at last got to Thabew at 1.30 p.m. I had just time to get a lot of people to repair the thatch, when a perfect deluge set in, so we made ourselves comfortable, and read and lounged all the afternoon.

May 13.—We agreed not to fire at deer to-day. If we came across wild elephants, we were to dismount and shoot them on foot. I saw a porcupine, and thinking it looked different from those in India, I very foolishly broke through our rule and shot it. Hill then fired at a stag and disturbed a gaur, and whilst he took up the spoor I travelled alongside about 50 yards off on his left. I had got ahead slightly, and on looking back I saw a splendid tusker walking straight up to Hill's elephant. As the ground was most favourable, I jumped off, thinking my comrade would do the same; but he got so excited that he blazed into the cranium of the tusker without dismounting, and of course did no harm, but effectually frightened the elephant, who went of as fast as his legs could take him. We tried to overtake him and followed on his trail for fully two hours, but never saw him again. We saw lots of footmarks of gaur and elephants. We were not far from Chowteah when, in an open quin, we saw a herd of tsine; we drew back into the forest, dismounted, and made the best stalk we could. There were a few clumps of long grass scattered about, and one large white-ant nest, and nearest to it the bull of the herd. We crawled up to it; and fired together. Hill shot it through the body—I near the hip-joint, a favourite shot of mine, and broke its hind-leg. Off went the bull, and we after him; we came upon him within 200 yards standing under a tree, and directly he saw us he snorted and began to paw up the ground and to toss his head, and trotted towards us. It was a pretty sight, but the poor brute had not a ghost of a chance. Hill had my double breech-loader, I had my two trusty two-groove rifles, and in a few seconds he was on the broad of his back—stone dead. He was just 16½ hands high—bright red, with white under the tail and along the inside of the thighs and belly; legs, from the knee downwards, whitish-yellow or a dirty white; white rings round the eyes, with a game-like head and a deer's eyes; the facial angle quite straight, the horns somewhat like a cow bison's, but not nearly as massive; hump lost in the dorsal ridge, which was distinct, but nothing like as prominent as in the gayal even; no dew-lap, or scarcely any. Opinions differ as to whether the loose skin of the neck amounts to a dew-lap or not. We skinned him and cut off his head. The marrow-bones and tongue were very good for the table; the beef I did not try. This was the only one I shot, till—years after—I got four. The bull's horns were truncated, as shown in the engraving, p. 102.

On the 14th, 15th, and 16th we saw gaur and tsine, but got no shots, but shot several deer each day.

May 17.—We put up three tigers to-day. We shot five deer between us, and got home to our hut just in time, as a regular downpour set in. George turned up, looking like a drowned rat; he had had a tiger walking in front of him well

PADDING A TIGER.

From a Photo by P. Burges, Esq.

within shot for some time, but his guns were wet through, and not one of them would go off. At Tuen he and Lloyd had killed two gaur and two stags; Lloyd had been recalled, but said he would follow in a day or two.

May 18.—Hill rode back to Kyoukee. George and I went out; we killed some deer, saw a herd of tsine and followed it on foot for hours, but failed to get within shot: the old bull in the distance looked black. We then mounted our elephants, and saw gaur, but had no luck. On getting back to camp found Watson and Hill there, and Lloyd also arrived in the evening.

May 19.—We all started very early in the pouring rain. George broke the leg of a sambur, and I killed it for him; a little further on, a gaur got up almost under the trunk of Lloyd's elephant, and everybody, with the exception of myself, fired shot after shot at it, but it got away. We soon saw another herd of gaur, but the jungles had been over-burnt—we could not get nearer than 150 yards. I wanted Hill to bag a gaur; I told him to fire at a monster which was nearest to us. Hill let fly and hit his. Lloyd fired at another and wounded his; they took opposite directions, and off went the ardent sportsmen full chase. As Hill was alone, George and I followed him; Lloyd, having Shoayjah, could find his way about, but Hill could not. I had mounted Hill on my fastest elephant, and he soon distanced us and got out of sight, but as he kept up a constant file fire, we followed in his wake. In the other direction we heard Lloyd popping away, whilst we two did not get a shot. Hill pulled up after leading us a wild-goose chase for two hours, and did not bag his beast after all. He had the tiffin basket behind his howdah. We sat down to breakfast not in the sweetest of tempers, for Hill had led us away from all the best ground; and Lloyd, equally unsuccessful, turned up in an hour. He, too, was savage that neither of us had gone with him, as he said, with help he could have got his beast, whom he had reduced to a walk; but it had got into a brake and escaped. On the way back I shot two hamadryads nearly 10 feet each, with ball right and left; these are the most venomous of all poisonous snakes. Lloyd shot a sucking-pig, which proved capital eating. We also got several deer.

May 20.—Heavy rain; but we went out in the afternoon and shot a pig, a sambur, and a dala'el or hog deer.

May 21.—Heavy rains; only Lloyd and I ventured out. We had each shot a stag, and were going through a patch of long grass, in which we saw the movement of some animal. We thought it was a hog deer, but coming to a small but deep nullah, over bounded a tigress, and Lloyd, taking a snap-shot, broke her back, and I put her out of her pain. She had a deep cut inside her thigh, inflicted on her evidently by the boar. We padded her and sent her to camp, which was in sight. She was offensive two hours after death. I got a fine stag thamine and put up a gaur, but did not get a shot at it.

May 22, 23, 24.—Too rainy to do much, but we killed a few deer. Lloyd and George went to Banlong. Hill and Watson to Kyoukee, and I to Tuen, and thence to Tongho.

In October, Lloyd, Duval, and I went south. The grass was too high and the country under water; we shot three buffaloes and some deer, but this is not the season for shooting in Lower Burma.

These are a few of the records of our trips—just sufficient to give the reader an idea of what the sport is like.

CHAPTER V

SPORT IN UPPER BURMA

RHINOCEROS SUMATRENSIS—THE ASIATIC TWO-HORNED RHINOCEROS. [W. S. THOM]

To those desirous of becoming better acquainted with this rhino's haunts, habits, and appearance, Blandford's description of the animal in his *Fauna of British India* may not be amiss here. He describes this animal as the smallest of living rhinoceros and the most hairy, the greater part of the body being thinly clad with hair, and the ears and tail more thickly covered. The two horns are some distance apart at the base; both are slender above, except in the case of females, which have mere stumps a few inches, and the anterior horn of the male in fine specimens elongate and curve backwards. The skin is usually rough and granular; the folds, though much less marked than in the one-horned species, are still existent, but only that behind the shoulders is continued across the back. Colour, varying from earthy-brown or black. Dimensions, somewhat variable. The type of Sclater's *R. lasiotis* was 4 feet 4 inches high at the shoulder, and 8 feet long from snout to root of tail; its weight about 2000 lbs. An old female from Malacca was only 3 feet 8 inches high; the average height of adults is probably 4 feet to 4 feet 6 inches. The largest known specimen of the anterior horn measures 32 inches over the curve. Skull, 20 inches; basal length, 11·25 inches zygomatic breadth.

Varieties.—Specimens from Chittagong and Malacca were living at the same time in the Zoological Society's Gardens, London, in 1872, and the former was distinguished by Sclater as *R. lasiotis*, by its larger size, paler and browner colour, smoother skin, longer, finer, and more rufescent hair, shorter and more tufted tail, the ears having a fringe of long hair and being naked inside; but above all by the much greater breadth of the head.

Unquestionably the difference was considerable; but by far the most remarkable, the shape of the head is shown by Blyth to be variable in both *R. unicornis* and *R. sondaicus*, for he figured and described a broad and narrow type of each, as well as *R. sumatrensis.*

The other distinctions scarcely appear to me of specific value, and I am inclined to regard the two forms as varieties only.

Distribution.—Rare in Assam, though one specimen has been recorded on the Sankosh river, in the Bhutan Duars (*P. Z. S.* 1875, p. 566). Another was shot 20 miles south of Comillah in Tipperah, in February 1876. From Assam the species ranges to Siam, the Malay Peninsula, Sumatra, and Borneo.

Habits.—Very similar to those of the other species. This rhinoceros inhabits forests, and is found at a considerable elevation, having been observed 4000 feet above the sea in Tenasserim, by Tickell. It is a shy and timid animal, but easily tamed when adult.

Details obtained by Mr. Bartlett concerning a young animal born in London, induced him to regard the period of gestation as probably a little over seven months. This differs greatly from Hodgson's account of the period in *R. unicornis,* but no details are furnished in the case of the last-named species, whilst the evidence is stated in that of *R. sumatrensis.* Still, for so large and apparently so long-lived an animal, seven months of uterine life appears short.

Anderson, in his *Fauna of Mergui and its Archipelago,* mentions having heard of a two-horned rhino seen swimming in the sea near High Island in the Archipelago. Probably all rhinoceros are good swimmers. (They certainly are.—F. T. P.)

The story of the Chittagong rhinoceros that was unable to swim must be, I think, a mistake. The account given by Mason, and repeated by Blyth, of this or any other rhinoceros attacking fire should be received with great caution. To my personal knowledge Mr. Blyth's principal informant had a weakness for relating *shikar* stories which were frequently good, but not always authentic.[1]

I was fortunate enough, during my five years' sojourn in the Ruby Mines district, to come across four of these animals, three of which I succeeded in getting. I had also many opportunities, when spending my short leave out in camp, of studying the habits of these ungainly mammalia. They are not easy to find, and are always very timid and shy, but when found they are easily stalked and killed, provided you are armed with a heavy rifle. They are capable, when alarmed, of dashing away through the densest jungle at a great pace, and often travel for many miles over the roughest country before they come to a halt. Mud-wallows, swampy ground, and dark, damp, cool jungles amongst the hills, up to an elevation of 4000 feet, are the spots they usually frequent. (I found them at the base of the Arrakan range, near Cape Negrais, at a very slight elevation only.—F. T. P.)

Three or four animals may sometimes be found in one locality within a mile or so of each other. But as a rule they are solitary; I have on one occasion come across two females wallowing in the same mud-hole.

These mud-holes are usually found at the source of some small stream, where the soil is swampy, or of a clayey nature. A spring or a marshy piece of ground by some stream is often utilized in the same manner, and one rhinoceros may have two or three wallows, or mud-holes, which he visits in turn: principally during the months of May, June, July, and August.

The sportsman will be notified of the near vicinity of a wallow by the caked mud which has been rubbed off the rhino's body by the bushes and tree-trunks as the animal passes.

Should the rhino be in his mud-bath, the sportsman will sometimes be made aware of the fact by hearing peculiar, low,

[1] I do not agree in this statement. Mr. Blyth to my certain knowledge was a most painstaking and able naturalist, and did not accept all he heard, but most Karens and Burmese assert that this rhinoceros rushes at a fire and scatters it.—F. T. P.

rumbling, humming sounds, the noise being very similar to that made by a species of large hornbill when soaring through the air, or like the sound made by a vulture's wing when stooping to the earth.

These rhinos sometimes wander great distances to feed, but are most frequently found within a mile or so of their wallows. They feed principally on bamboo-leaves, shoots, young cane, thorny shrubs, and a bush called "Kyau-sa." It was in the Sagadaung jurisdiction of the Shan State of Momeik, Ruby Mines district, that I first made my acquaintance with these animals. I had previously, in other parts of the district, when out looking for gaur and elephant, come across old tracks, but had never had the luck to find any fresh ones, or to light on a fresh mud-hole.

One evening, in the beginning of the rainy season, Moung Hpe turned up in the "zayat," or rest-house, whilst I was lolling in my long arm-chair, under the soothing influence of a good dinner, cigarette, and a cup of coffee, and said—"Thakin, hnepen taung-daw thwa gya-zo, mane-ga wakok the-ma hnit-yauk kyan-kyi-ya ah thit twe ge de" (Sir, let us go into the hills to-morrow; two bamboo-cutters saw fresh rhinoceros tracks yesterday). This was excellent news, and Moung Hpe was immediately made the recipient of a bottle of Younger's Monk Brand beer, an old shooting-jacket, and five rupees.

Poor Moung Hpe, as fine a tracker as ever stepped! I wonder what he is doing now? Ah, those glorious days, gone like a fleeting dream!

As the locality in which the rhino's tracks had been seen was distant in the hills above Sagadaung only some eight or ten miles, I made up my mind to pay a flying visit to the spot, leaving early next morning, and camp out only one night in the jungle, as I had a good deal of work on hand.

At 6 a.m. next day I was well on my way into the hill, having first arranged with my camp-followers and servants as to the spot to be chosen for our camp. Moung Hpe and an old retired Shan *shikarie,* whose knowledge of the hills was extensive, accompanied me. He was a curious old fellow,

A SHAN TRADER.

From a Photo by Watts & Skeen, Rangoon.

this Shan, and never better pleased than when smoking away at a long Shan pipe and drinking raw spirits.

I was armed on this occasion with only an old single ·450 sporting Martini-Henry carbine, which belonged at one time to poor Tucker of the police, as daring a sportsman and as good a shot as Burma has ever seen, and a double 12-bore shot-gun by Joseph Lang, which burned a maximum charge of 4½ drams of powder, and carried a spherical ball with great precision and penetration up to 30 or 40 yards.

After reaching the outlying spurs of the Shwe-u-taung range we struck the Tunkachoung stream, along whose banks we walked. As luck would have it, we had not gone a quarter of a mile before Moung Hpe, jumping down into the sandy bed of the stream, exclaimed—"Thakin, thakin, kyi-ba-thee ma, kyau-kyi-ya, ah-thit gane ma net saw zaw thaw-ge-de" (Sir, sir, look here, fresh rhino tracks; the animal passed early this morning). On examining the tracks I noticed that the water in them was still a little clouded at the bottom, and that they must be very fresh tracks. I knew that Moung Hpe very rarely made a mistake as to the freshness of a track, and I was convinced, from the decided way he had spoken about the tracks, that he was quite certain in his own mind that they had been recently made.

We decided to wait the arrival of our camp-followers before taking on the tracks, as there was a suitable piece of ground for pitching camp on the banks of the stream, and I wanted to warn them about making any noise which might disturb the rhino.

After waiting about an hour and a half our followers turned up, when we informed them of the fresh tracks, and after cautioning every one not to cut down bamboos or make any preparations for chopping firewood, etc., till they had heard me fire, we started off on the trail.

The ground in the neighbourhood was very hilly, and at times we had to push our way through cane-jungle and over swampy ground.

After covering some two miles of country the track showed that the animal had been feeding round in circles,

[1] All rhinoceros feed in circles.—F. T. P.

and at times tracking was made to my eyes almost impracticable, as the animal had crossed and recrossed its own tracks dozens of times. So mixed in fact had they become, that sportsmen unaccustomed to tracking would be under the impression that two or three animals instead of one had been in the vicinity. We succeeded eventually in hitting the right trail out of this maze, and after travelling for over three hours, came on unmistakable signs of a mud-wallow. Moung Hpe now fell back and requested me to lead, warning me at the same time to be careful, as a wallow was not far off, and, indeed, numerous traces of it were apparent. The surrounding jungle was composed of cane, bamboo, and tree forest.

Following a small game track I pushed my way cautiously along the side of the hill through the foliage, which fortunately was not very dense here, Moung Hpe and the old Shan hunter following in my traces.

I felt as if my heart was going to burst from suppressed excitement, at the thought of seeing for the first time a real wild rhinoceros. Of course I had seen the larger species of rhino in the Zoo, but had never seen one in its wild state. Moreover, the animal I was tracking had two horns, and, if I remember rightly, no specimen of the *Rhinoceros sumatrensis* was in the Zoological Gardens when I paid my visit.

Rounding a clump of overhanging canes on a sloping ridge, I caught sight of the edge of the basin or wallow on the brow of the hill, a few feet above the level of my head, and at a distance of about 25 yards. There were numerous fresh signs of the rhino's presence in the splashes of yellow clayey mud all round the edge of the basin and on the surrounding trees, but no sound emanated from the wallow, which appeared to be deserted.

Turning round and holding up my hand as a signal to Moung Hpe and the Shan to stay where they were, I cocked both barrels of the smooth-bore, bent low, and moved cautiously forward about ten paces. My coat unfortunately caught on a hooked thorny cane-creeper, and knocked down a small decayed branch, which fell to the ground with a faint rustle.

The scene was changed in a moment. An ugly, small-eyed, piggish, horny-looking-beast reared itself up out of the wallow in a sitting posture, only exposing its head and shoulders, and blinked at me stupidly for a few seconds in an undecided manner, as if debating in its own mind what manner of animal I was. I did not give it time to consider long, but jumped from my stooping attitude and aimed hurriedly at the huge head, firing both barrels in quick succession. A tremendous commotion in the wallow immediately ensued, followed by sounds like the drawing of corks from very large bottles, the sound being caused by the rhinoceros pulling its feet out of the clayey soil as it rushed out of the wallow and bolted, in full flight, down the hill-side, through cane-brake and bamboo, carrying everything before it. At first I was greatly disappointed, being under the impression that I had made a clean miss.

Moung Hpe, who was also greatly disgusted at my shooting, came up with a very long face, taking it for granted that I had missed, and said, "Thakin, thakin, thee-tokan-now ka-bedaw ma ya bu kyan hue dine ma twe hnine bu ma, hman bu tin de" (Sir, sir, you will never have such luck again; it is not every day that you see a rhinoceros, I think you have missed it). But I had not missed, for after following up the tracks for about 100 yards, we found, much to my delight, blood on either side of the track, which proved beyond a doubt that one of my bullets had gone clean through the animal's head.

It was simply marvellous to think that any animal could have received such a shock without staggering or showing any signs of having been hit, and then make off, down a steep hill-side through dense undergrowth, like an express train.

We had not been an hour on the trail before Moung Hpe pointed out the rhino to me, lying down on its stomach amongst some bushes, breathing heavily. I could just see a dirty yellow patch, which I immediately fired at.

On receiving the shot it jumped up and made off again. We came up with him after going about 300 yards further; it was standing broadside on, and I put in a right and left behind the shoulder. I was obliged to use my smooth-bore, as the striker of the Martini carbine was out of order, and would not explode a single cartridge. The last two shots seemed to waken it up pretty considerably, as it travelled some distance before we again overhauled it. We had some difficulty on this occasion in finding the tracks, as it had entered a stream and waded down for a considerable distance. We now found that the rhino was heading back in the direction from which it had come, and we could distinctly hear our camp-followers talking and laughing in the hollow below, and some of them now joined us in trying to find the lost tracks.

While we were thus scattered about up and down stream examining the ground, my attention was suddenly drawn by Moung Hpe to the rhino, which was standing with heaving flanks on the bank of the stream, within ten paces of a rock upon which I had climbed. I could see from its stertorous breathing that the poor beast was done for and quite helpless, so wading quietly up to within a yard or two I fired behind the shoulder, aiming for the heart. The rhino stood motionless for about four seconds, and then sank dead on to its knees, with a long-drawn sigh.

On examination I found that it was a female, and that only one of my two first shots had taken effect, but this one had gone clean through the head, and only missed the brain by a very narrow margin.

The rhino was 4 feet 6 inches from heel to shoulder, measured between uprights, and had two distinct horns, the front one about 4 inches in length, and the hinder one a mere horny protuberance.

In the male the front horn varies from 6 to 12 inches. The folds were much less marked than in the one-horned species, and commenced behind the shoulders, continuing across the back; there was also a slight overlapping of the skin on the posterior. The colour of the skin approached a light earthy brown; the ears had a long hairy fringe, but were naked inside.

The male rhinoceros, according to Burman hunters, consort with the females about the middle and end of the rain.

On another occasion I saw three animals within the space

of an hour and a half on an outlying spur of the Shwe-u-taung hill, two of which I succeeded in bagging. We had been camping in a cave on the top of the hill, and were moving down a spur intending to pitch on new ground as soon as we came across traces of rhino or gaur.

I had been out on a shooting expedition for over a month, having been granted leave from April 3 to May 17, and during that time I had succeeded in getting two elephants, six gaur, one tsine, one sambur, two barking deer, one leopard, and one serow—not a bad bag. Moung Hpe and I left camp early and started walking leisurely down the ridge, leaving the remainder to pack up and follow at a respectable distance.

We had gone about two and a half miles, when Moung Hpe, suddenly stooping down and examining the ground carefully, exclaimed, "Kyan hnit kaung, mane ga ma net saw zaw thwa ge de" (Two rhinos passed this way early yesterday morning). We immediately called a halt and held a consultation, chose a suitable spot for our camp, and arranged for tracking up the animals. Eventually we agreed that our carriers and camp-followers, numbering in all some twenty men, had better follow our trail in single file, in silence, and at a respectable distance, until we came on fresher tracks, when we could fix on some more convenient spot near a stream for our camp. On this occasion I was armed with a 12-bore rifle, and a double 8-bore burning twelve drams. Moung Hpe carried the 12-bore, whilst I took the heavier weapon. After warning our followers to remain perfectly quiet whilst on the march in our rear, Moung Hpe and I started off and took on the tracks of the rhinos, with every hope of being able to come up with them in some mud-wallow before dark. Moung Hpe as usual took the lead, and whenever he was at fault, which very rarely happened, I assisted him by making wide casts till the trail was recovered. We had greater difficulties to contend with than I had expected to find. The ground was not only covered with a thick layer of leaves, which in places had either been scratched up by jungle fowl and pheasant, or scattered by the wind, thereby obliterating all foot-prints, but at times it was very hard and rocky. After covering some three miles of precipitous but fairly open and rocky country, I felt tempted to give it up in disgust, as we had not as yet come upon tracks which were only an hour or two old. Patience is however usually rewarded in the end, and after many twistings and turnings, backwards and forwards, up-hill and down dale, often going over the same ground twice, we came on fresh tracks, and were suddenly startled by hearing in our immediate neighbourhood the peculiar low, muffled humming sound repeated at intervals; and Moung Hpe at once recognized them as proceeding from the rhinos. To walk noiselessly down the ridge in the direction of the sound was the work of a few moments, but I was afraid our camp-followers would catch us up before we could get sight of the animals. Fortunately, however, they had all seated themselves on the ground for a rest. The peculiar low, buzzing or humming noises now became more distinct, and as we rounded a rocky ridge which overlooked a shallow ravine, wooded with bamboo and an undergrowth of bush and prickly cane, a large mud-wallow, in a small clearing bordering the cane-jungle, came into view, and in this two rhinos were disporting themselves. One animal, the larger of the two, was standing half in and half out of the slushy mud; the other was lying in it half submerged, rolling about from side to side, and uttering the peculiar noises which had attracted our attention. Telling Moung Hpe to fire at the animal standing on the brink of the wallow, I aimed at the other, and fired both barrels. Moung Hpe's shot rang out simultaneously with my own. There was a terrific commotion for a second or two in the wallow, accompanied by unearthly grunts and screeches, something like the bray of a donkey, and then both animals bolted away in different directions through the cane.

We rushed down and examined the ground and bushes in the neighbourhood of the wallow for blood, several big splashes of which we discovered on the line of flight taken by the rhino which I had fired at. We took on this animal's tracks immediately, and had not gone very far before I caught sight of the beast, limping along with a broken fore-leg ; a right and a left behind the shoulder brought it to a standstill, and a third shot completed the business. After marking the spot carefully we returned to the wallow, intending to take on the tracks of the animal fired at by Moung Hpe. We found that his bullet (Moung Hpe having fired only one shot, being unaccustomed to a double rifle, and naturally finding the firing of a second shot with any degree of precision well-nigh impossible) had passed through a creeper about the thickness of a man's calf, which would naturally lessen the penetration of the bullet, although he used a steel-tipped one.

After arranging a suitable spot for camp with our followers, who had in the meantime joined us at the wallow, and who were in great glee at the thought of dining off rhinoceros flesh, Moung Hpe and I started off after the other rhino, which, from a spot of blood found on a cane-bush near the wallow, had evidently been hit.

We were rather ludicrous-looking objects after we had been following the trail for some time, our clothes, hands, and faces being plentifully besmeared with the clayey mud whilst following in the wake of the rhino, which deposited a portion of its coating on the bushes and branches at every step. After puzzling over the tracks for three and a half miles of very rugged country, up and down hill, through cane brakes and ravines, we gave it up in disgust, as not only was it getting late, but the animal had not shown any signs of having been badly wounded. An animal, as a rule, when severely wounded lies down once or twice to rest after the first mile or so ; an experienced Burman hunter can often tell by the footprint of an animal such as the gaur or tsine whether it has been wounded or not, the slot of a wounded beast being often deep and irregular, though this very rarely occurs in the case of a wounded elephant or rhino, which, as a rule, only lie down when about to die or unable to stand ; though I did once follow a huge "Muckna" which lay down to rest no fewer than three times within the distance of two miles.

I did not succeed in coming up with this animal, although it had received three 8-bore spherical hardened bullets well placed behind the shoulder.

It was now about 4 p.m., and as we had not eaten any food since 10.30 a.m. we proceeded to dispose of our respective breakfasts, mine consisting of cold salted gaur tongue, biscuits, dried figs, and some cold boiled rice, washed down with beautifully cool, clear hill water. Moung Hpe opened out on boiled rice, cold smoked gaur, and last, but not least, that highly odoriferous national dish, a "bonne bouche," amongst Burmans known as "ngápee." Whilst in the middle of our well-earned meal we were startled by hearing the peculiar, muffled humming sound already referred to, and which seemed to proceed from no great distance.

We both jumped to our feet with alacrity, sending the remains of our meal flying. I seized my 8-bore and, after pocketing a couple of spare cartridges, moved cautiously in the direction of the sound, Moung Hpe bringing up the rear. After wading through a swampy piece of ground for about 40 yards I caught sight of another wallow, from which the sounds seemed to issue. Arriving within half-a-dozen paces of it I saw a spectacle which made my heart throb at a tremendous pace—a rhinoceros lay submerged in the mud, with its ears and the top of its head occasionally showing as it rolled about from side to side, uttering each time its nostrils and mouth rose above the surface low, peculiar, long-drawn grunts. I cautiously withdrew and beckoned to Maung Hpe to approach a little closer so that he might be of some assistance in case of a charge, and, after seeing him ensconced behind a tree within a few yards of the wallow to my right, I took a steady aim for what I took to be the shoulder of the animal, but which afterwards turned out to be its stomach, and fired.

A tremendous grunting, screaming, snorting, and splashing ensued after my shot, and I was so near to the wallow that several splashes of mud struck my hat and coat.

The rhino, after making several rapid gyrations in the wallow as if trying to bite its own tail, shot out of the pit through mud two or three feet deep, and rushed down the side of the hill as fast as any pig could travel, followed by a second bullet from me and a right and left from Moung Hpe, all of which, as I afterwards found, took effect in various parts of his body.

Notwithstanding all this we had a long, stern chase, the rhinoceros keeping up a tremendous pace for nearly three miles, and leading us through some of the most awful jungle which it has ever been my fortune to travel over. All things must, however, come to an end some time, and we eventually came up with him standing stock still on the side of a deep ravine looking very sick. I was very thankful that we had come up with him, and I am certain that I should not have been able to keep up the pace another mile over such country as that we had traversed, encumbered as I was with the heavy 8-bore. I was literally dripping from head to foot, and almost blinded with perspiration from the violent exercise we had just undergone, enhanced by copious draughts of icy water *en route*.

As the rhino was standing facing away from me, I worked cautiously round till I could obtain a good shoulder shot. I succeeded in getting partially round, but was discovered by the brute, which wheeled round with a loud grunt and walked quickly with lowered head towards me. This was a most unusual proceeding, and entirely unexpected, for I was always under the impression that a rhino was a harmless beast. As may be imagined, I did not wait to see any more, but delivered a quick right and left. On the smoke clearing I saw that the rhino had not only come to a standstill, but was about to fall. In fact, after a preliminary roll or two from side to side, a loud gasping sigh as it collapsed slowly on to its knees proclaimed its decease. A kill of two rhinos in one day was not bad work, but to crown all we found that we, or rather the rhino, had been travelling round in a circle, and that instead of being five or six miles from camp we were only some two or three hundred yards from it. I returned highly elated, but feeling a little knocked up, a dip in the stream which flowed past our encampment (an erection of leaf huts, "taungzin pet" leaves), and a good dinner brought me up to par once more. Many a long yarn did my *shikaries* and I spin over the flickering camp fire far into the night, before I dropped off into a well-earned slumber.

With regard to a doubt expressed by some naturalists as to rhinos being able to swim, I can say, from what I have seen and heard myself, that they are undoubtedly good swimmers.

I remember very well on one occasion, whilst out with a party of police tracking a gang of dacoits, coming upon some fresh rhino tracks leading into the Kin river and emerging on the opposite bank at a crossing where the water, it being then well on in the rainy season, was quite four to five feet deep. One of my hunters informed me that he had once watched two rhinos, a young one and its mother, cross a stream. Before entering the water, however, the mother had to prod up the little one from behind with her snout several times to induce it to venture in. Being unarmed at the time he was unable to shoot them. He noticed particularly that both swam very strongly and swiftly across, the young one in front, and that only a portion of the snout and head of each animal was visible. The young one on arriving at the opposite bank lay down and rolled over and over again on the grass, in the same manner as a horse would do, but the mother walked steadily on after reaching the bank, leaving her young one to follow. It is said that rhinos deposit huge mounds of ordure,[1] visiting the same spot daily. I have not noticed this with regard to the *R. sumatrensis* (I found the mounds at the foot of the hills near Negrais, and in Assam they were very plentiful wherever there were rhinoceros.—F. T. P.), although I have come across their droppings in the ordinary course of my wanderings, and they all seemed as if left on a single occasion. The morning after the death of the rhinos I had rather a novel experience on the top of the Shwe-u-taung hill with a tiger.

My hunters and I were engaged tracking a solitary bull gaur which, after browsing on young bamboo shoots and leaves in the valley, had left the cover for the more open grassy slopes on the ridge. The grass here, which was never at any time higher than one's knees, had been burnt, and the young green shoots which had sprung up after recent showers attracted sambur and an occasional solitary gaur.

The tracks after winding about for some time through this

[1] Mr. Thom, since this was written, has found these mounds in the Arrakan Yomahs.—F. T. P.

open country led us to the top of the ridge, from whence a glorious view was obtained, the surrounding country lying like a map at our feet. Here and there might be seen the river Shweli with its tributaries glistening in the sun like silver threads, the Kin and the Momeik, whose combined waters eventually empty themselves into the Irrawady, and an occasional glimpse of the broad waters of the latter some thirty-five miles off. It was while standing admiring the grand panorama stretched out before us, that my attention was drawn to five or six doe sambur, which, emerging in single file from the dense woods at our feet some 400 yards off, began feeding slowly along up the side of the hill quite unconscious of our presence. After the last animal had disappeared over the ridge I was just about to try a stalk, as our stock of fresh meat required replenishing, when another animal emerged from the wood, trotted up to the top of the ridge near where the sambur had passed, and lay down. Thinking that this was another sambur and that it would be easily approached, I took my 8-bore, having no other weapon with me at the time, and began the stalk. For the first 200 yards or so it was easy enough, but after that there was little or no cover behind which I could screen my advance. Whilst pondering how I was to get any nearer without being discovered, I noticed the animal's tail flick upwards once or twice with a quick spasmodic jerk, and then only it dawned upon me that the animal lying basking in the sun a couple of hundred yards from me was a tiger. This was rather a shock, and something I had not bargained for. I was determined, however, not to back out or show any signs of funk, as my men were watching my every action, and it would not have done to let them have the impression that I was afraid to face any animal. I succeeded, after a great deal of tortuous manœuvring, in lessening the distance between us to about 150 yards, and flattened myself out behind a small clump of ferns. I lay like a log in this position for over three minutes, in the hope of seeing the tiger get up and move in my direction, near enough to enable me to get home an accurate shot. What would I not have given at that moment for a good ·577, ·450, or even ·256 rifle! I was not a good enough shot, nor yet sufficiently accustomed to the heavy 8-bore, to be absolutely certain of hitting at any distance beyond 80 to 100 yards, much less of reaching a vital spot. Besides, the tiger, as he lay on all-fours, did not present a very large target. At last I made up my mind to chance a shot, as I was getting rather cramped and uncomfortable from the position in which I was lying. So putting up the 150 yards sight and cocking both hammers quietly, I raised my rifle to the shoulder, both elbows on the ground. The tiger at the same moment faced round and stared hard in my direction. I remained as if turned to stone. What a magnificent appearance he presented, his whiskers and a grand ruff round his face showing quite distinctly.

After gazing hard in my direction for a few seconds he rose slowly to his feet, peered down into the valley below him, where I could still see some of the sambur grazing, and on one of which I had no doubt he had intentions of making a meal. After a preliminary yawn or two and a jerky flick, flick of his tail he stretched himself, and, to my delight, faced round and started to walk along the ridge in my direction. I had never had the chance of bagging a tiger before, although I had seen several and knew a good deal about their haunts and habits, consequently I was rather excited at the opportunity now afforded me.

I waited till he had covered half the distance between us, and then slowly raised my rifle, intending to fire at about 50 yards, but I reckoned without my host, as the brute's quick eye detected the movement, and, halting dead, he turned half round as if uncertain what to do. I immediately fired, taking a full sight, as I am rather inclined with a heavy rifle to shoot low. The distance would be about 100 yards. A short hoarse growl was the reply to my shot, and the tiger, whose fore-leg I had broken, charged away down the hillside into the dense jungle, where all hope of pursuit on foot was quite out of the question. I sent a second shot after him as he disappeared into the jungle, but missed, as I saw the spot where the bullet knocked up some earth a foot or two behind him. It would have been utter folly to have attempted to walk him up, accompanied by any of my men, in jungle where you could not see two yards ahead, and where some of us would in all probability have been badly mauled. If I had had an elephant it would have been an easy matter to rout him out. My hunters were very much astonished to see the supposed sambur change into a tiger.

While returning to camp the same evening, strolling listlessly along ahead of my men, I suddenly came face to face with a herd of gaur. I was never so utterly disgusted with myself, for I had not a rifle with me; a huge bull, which was standing some twenty paces off, sounded the alarm with a terrific snort, and the whole herd thundered away with a crash through the jungle at a tremendous pace, the deep thud, thud of their hoofs being audible for some time.

The stampede of a startled herd of gaur through bamboo jungle, once heard will never be forgotten, so terrific is the noise. The loud whistling snort of alarm emitted by an old solitary bull, standing 19 or 20 hands at the shoulder, when heard at close quarters for the first time by a sportsman, is grand, and fills him at the time with an indescribable mixed feeling of fear and awe. I made a vow from that hour I would never walk anywhere where there was the least likelihood of coming across game, without having a rifle of some sort in my hand. I had, moreover, good reason to congratulate myself on having my 8-bore in my hands half-an-hour later. As we were nearing camp, I had not expected to see any game, and was talking in a low tone to Moung Hpe, when a slight noise in the jungle ahead attracted our attention, and almost immediately after a dark-coated animal, which I at first took for a young gaur or sambur, passed in front of us at a quick walk, apparently quite regardless of our presence. I immediately fired for the shoulder, the bullet taking effect rather low down, breaking the leg. The goat, for it turned out to be a serow or Burmese goat antelope, the *Nemorhædus sumatrensis*, on receiving the shot, uttered two or three shrill screams and made a most determined charge straight down the hill towards me, evidently intent on getting at me. I had, in fact, to jump to one side and deliver a second shot before it fell. Even then it seemed to be very tenacious of life, for it struggled hard, and butted right and left with its horns whenever we tried to get near it.

A blow on the back of the neck from a heavy male bamboo finished it. The horns were about 8 inches long, and curved slightly backwards. Measurement from tip of tail to snout 5 feet 5 inches, and length at shoulder 3 feet 4 inches.

It was a very old female animal. The skin and hair of the body was almost black, with a silvery fringe of long, coarse, scanty hair running along the whole length of the back: it was longer and there was more of it at the top of the neck. The legs were of a rufous colour from the thigh and fore-arm downwards. The muzzle was jet black. This animal was shot at an elevation of about 4000 feet.

After skinning and cutting up the animal we left for camp, which was reached as a heavy thunderstorm broke over our heads. During the night we heard gaur bellowing not far from camp.

BLAZING DEER (*MEETOUNG*) AT NIGHT

A BURMESE MODE OF HUNTING DEER, AND HUNTING THE BURMESE RHINOCEROS IN LOWER BURMA. [F. T. P.]

The Burmese professional *shikaries* pot a great deal of game, but prefer hunting deer by torchlight. I may here describe the *modus operandi*. It is most fatiguing, and one that few Europeans would care to follow as a pastime. Whilst at Haingye I crossed over to Dalhousie. This was one of the great Proconsul's follies; not satisfied with Burma, having already ports like Moulmein, Rangoon, and Bassein, Lord Dalhousie determined to construct another to bear his own name at the entrance of the Bassein river. After several lacs of rupees had been spent, a tidal wave swept all away in a night, and all that was visible in 1863 were a few culverts far apart, and the place had reverted into jungle. A boat's crew was kept there to aid shipwrecked mariners.

By appointment some *shikaries* met me one day towards dark at Dalhousie, and we set out to "blaze" deer. Their hunting-grounds were a long way off, and we had to walk over deep and loose sand for fully six miles, and then to cross numerous tidal nullahs, spanned by bridges consisting of a single bamboo with a small handrail attached; not an easy task at any time, and very unpleasant on a pitchy dark night. We then turned inland, and stumbling about over most uneven ground for another mile, I was told that we had arrived at our hunting-ground. One of the men put a broken chatty (earthenware pot) in a framework on his head, fastened it under his chin, and set some rags well impregnated with earth-oil alight. As soon as the fire blazed up, he—with a man on either side ringing bells—started off at a fast jog-trot in zigzags, and a man armed with a dah and I followed in the rear. The country was a mass of holes and ant-hills covered with short grass and jungle. They were quite invisible, for the light from the pot was thrown ahead, whilst all in the rear was impenetrable darkness. I should be sorry to say the number of falls I had, but unaccustomed to the work, and unused to such exertions on foot, I could scarcely keep up with the men, who never slackened their pace. Presently they redoubled the noise with the bells, their zigzag pace became faster, and the man whispered to me to get up closer. Out of the darkness I saw two eyeballs glaring at me, and as we got nearer I distinguished a dark object which I took to be the body of a sambur. I fired into it at a distance of 10 or 12 feet, and on receiving the ball the poor brute bounded forward, upset one of the bell-ringers, and disappeared. As the beat was for me, I was allowed to shoot, but, as a rule, the man with the dah crawls behind and hamstrings the beast. If in these night-beats the men come across a tiger, they squat down together and extinguish the light, and the tiger slinks away; they then continue their sport and generally make a fair bag. We continued our eternal jog-trot, and in about half-an-hour came upon another sambur. I fired at it, but it, too, got away. By that time I had had enough, so leaving the three to go on, I, with the fourth, walked back to the Zyat where I was stopping, getting there at 2 a.m. thoroughly tired out. The Burmese hamstrung another sambur after I left, and the next day the two I had fired at were found dead—a stag with a fair head of horns and a doe.

One day a Karen brought in the head of a two-horned

rhinoceros, which he had shot, he said, not far off and where there were many others. This was our slack season. I was then employed in constructing the Coco lighthouse in the Bay of Bengal, and during that monsoon I was at Haingye, a large island at the entrance of the Bassein river. Having nothing particular to do I agreed to go with him, but as everything had to be carried by men—not easy to procure—I went in very light marching order. I don't know what his idea of a short distance was, but he took me at least fifty miles, by short cuts, over mountains and down dales, until we were not far from Cape Negrais. The guide and I marched ahead, leaving the six porters to follow about a couple of miles in the rear. The first day I killed a kakur, or barking deer, and several yit—the silver pheasant of the country, a beautiful bird not only to look at, but also good for the table.

We were much troubled with tree-leeches, gadflies, and mosquitoes. As there was no village, we camped in a bamboo forest, and fortunately it did not rain. The next day's march was a very fatiguing one, but I saw a good deal of game. I killed a bull gaur and two pheasants, lost a cow gaur, and saw others and a few sambur. It is a country not often traversed, and the game, seldom disturbed, was comparatively tame. On reaching a Karen village we halted, and sent the villagers back for the deer. The following day we reached our destination, a valley between two high ranges with an extensive swamp in the middle; skirting this, the man pointed out a mound composed of rhinoceros droppings, some three feet high and several feet in diameter, and he assured me that these beasts always deposit their ordure in the same spot whilst living in the vicinity, which I afterwards ascertained to be a fact. He also pointed out other similar mounds, but as none were as fresh as the first, we determined to watch there at night. Whilst two men were set to dig two pits, we went across the valley and ascended the opposite range of hills. We found their surface pretty flat and covered with grass from three to five feet high, and there were many forms of sambur about, and a few clumps of trees and bamboos. From a patch of grass near some magnificent canes, a bull gaur jumped up, ran about 20 yards, and then faced about. A ball, No. 10, two-grooved, from my double Lang brought him down; we cut off his head and hung it up and went on. We left the table-land and entered a sholah, where I got three shots at sambur, but only succeeded in bagging one. On getting back to the village we sent for the gaur's head, and the villagers returned staggering under the weight of the beef they carried. After a bath and an early dinner we went to sit up—the Karen in one hole and I in the other. Such a night as I spent! I would not do it again even to shoot a dozen rhinoceros, if each of them had four instead of two horns. It was a bright moonlight night; the pachyderm came about eleven, and as he passed, the Karen gave him the contents of one of my rifles; in his fright the rhinoceros ran into a very boggy part of the swamp close to me, and, stepping out, I killed him easily with a shot behind the ear. It was no use stopping longer, and I had had quite enough of the mosquitoes, who were not only very large, very noisy, but very bloodthirsty. We secured the head next day, and made tracks homeward by a circuitous route. We saw nothing the first day, but came across several elephants. I mortally wounded a tusker, but lost him for the time; the jungle was so dense and the tracks so numerous, that we took up the wrong one, and never succeeded in regaining the correct one. I heard afterwards that the Karens found him and appropriated his tusks, which were rather good ones—not long, but thick. We put up in a Karen village, and the men said if I'd remain for a day or two they would beat a ravine in which there was generally a tiger, and they could also show gaur and sambur. As I was in no hurry, I assented. I was duly posted next day, but, instead of a tiger, a panther showed himself, and I dropped him dead. He measured 7¼ feet to the tip of the tail. Returning to the hut, I breakfasted, and then went out stalking. I wounded a gaur but lost it, and got a sambur and a barking deer. The next day I got back to Haingye.

CHAPTER VI

MISCELLANEOUS SPORT ON FOOT

THERE are very few spots in Lower Burma where sport can be indulged in on foot. In the forests in the Tharawadie district at the foot of the Yomahs occasionally elephants can be hunted, and also from Pegu. In the Banlong district thamine can be stalked and shot, but for really good sport, elephants are a *sine quâ non.* But to the north-west of Tongho, as in the case of General Blake, I have known big game to be met with in localities where locomotion is possible. Raikes of the Artillery and Hill of the 69th Regiment had shot a tusker and various other game at Lepangon near the Pabay Creek. I once got into the middle of a herd of elephants there, but failed to bag one out of the herd ; but the next day, starting very early, we got on to the trail of a solitary male, and as he appeared to be in no hurry, but fed along, I was in hopes we should soon overtake him; but we walked fully fifteen or sixteen miles before we came upon him standing in the bed of a small rivulet, browsing on the wild plantains. It is a curious coincidence that plants which in India only grow at an elevation of 1500 feet and more are found in the plains of Burma. The wind blowing down the streamlet, I crawled close up to him, and sat down under a bamboo clump growing out of the river bank. His broad quarters were facing me, and I could see no vulnerable spot, but I sat patiently with my rifle at full cock and a spare one handy, perfectly confident that he would expose his forehead presently, and that I should bag him to a certainty. I watched his every movement for fully five minutes, then without the least warning he spun right round

—evidently he had scented me. I threw up my rifle for the front shot, but a pendant bamboo caught the barrels and my rifle exploded in mid-air, and before I could bring the left barrel to bear, he was off and away.

How I cursed my own awkwardness! I tried following him up, but there was a large plain of interminable long grass near into which he rushed, and, as I heard various trumpetings, I fancy he joined the rest of the herd, and he was lost to me for ever. Of course, as is usually the case, he had splendid tusks.

The next adventure relates to the same locality; but it is not my own, it occurred some years after I left the Province, but I had coached my friend where to go, and he had a wonderful four days' sport. This is the last but one record of sport on foot in Burma that I shall relate, with the exception of those of my colleague, who will have something quite new to say of sport in a portion of country which to me is unknown.

Tongho, an eastern frontier station, was always a quiet place in the old days, for the communications with the outer world there were very tedious. No rail had been constructed, and a boat trip up the Sittang, extending as it did from twenty to thirty days, was not enviable. After the annexation of Upper Burma the garrison was greatly reduced, and as there were constant requisitions on the part of the civil officers for troops to quell a rebellion or to chase dacoits, we could not depend on any prolonged stay in the station, and could not even obtain the usual privilege leave.

I had several times applied for temporary leave of but a week or ten days, and it had invariably been refused. But one day I met Shoay Boh, a local *shikarie*, who said since the recent disarmament of the people game had become very plentiful, the jungles near Lepangoung were just in a nice state for stalking or beating, and if I could come with him he thought he could show me good sport. I went instantly to my commanding officer, who was also the commandant of the station, and solicited three days' leave from Monday. That day was Friday. I was not on duty on Saturday or Sunday, so I calculated that if I were successful in my application I could sniggle in those two days as well. For a wonder, the leave asked for was granted. I hurried off to a Madras contractor who had some carts, and who now and then let them out on hire, but he charged Rs.2 a day for the cart in addition to the keep of the cattle and the pay of the cart-men, and in case of an accident to either cart or bullock, I was to make good the loss.

It did not take me long to collect my impedimenta. Sending word to Shoay Boh that I had obtained leave and intended to start early on Saturday, I told him if he had anything to put into my cart, to take it to my house at once. I sent him a few rupees as a *douceur*. When everything was ready for starting, I was appalled by the amount of goods the *shikarie* had sent down—they required a cart for themselves; but, wishing to conciliate him, I bade my boy hurry off and get another cart, and what with my own traps, and those of my servants and the Burmans, I found the two carts well laden. So I sent them on ahead, as Shoay Boh was taking out a lot of ngàpee not only for his own consumption but also for sale to the villagers, and if there is one thing more offensive than another it is this Burmese delicacy!

I sent on a syce and an extra pony to Tseben. My servants would sleep there that day, Friday, and I meant to ride through and have some sport on Saturday, where they ought to be before me.

I told my boy when he arrived at Lepangoung not to put up in the village, but in a Zyat on a nullah, about a mile beyond. I was up and away by 5 a.m. on Saturday. The country all round is a dead flat, there are no made roads; the first cart of the season marks out a track which forms the highway for the fine season; during the rains it is much obliterated and cut up by the commissariat elephants going for their daily charah.

My ponies were good amblers, and I got to Tseben in two hours, and by nine I reached the Zyat, just after my men, but my boy had a cold collation ready for me. Shoay Boh was also in readiness, and told me he had sent on fifteen beaters, all he could collect, to some low-lying hills, through which meandered numerous water-courses which were all dry at that season, and where, he said, there were always sambur, ghee (barking deer), and occasionally a panther or even a tiger. Meat was scarce in the village, and as the *shikarie* had been absent for some days, he had failed to bring in any venison for sale; so he had promised on my behalf that if they beat properly almost all the meat of animals killed by me would be given to them, and, in addition, that each one would be paid eight annas for the day's work, with which they could purchase ngàpee, which he had so considerately brought out. My orderly had gone on ahead, taking a pet double rifle and gun, and would wait for me at the appointed place.

By 10 a.m. I was off again, and got to my rendezvous by 11 a.m. The *shikarie* went off with the beaters to beat some low hills towards me, and he stationed me under a bush near the bank of one of the streams, telling me to look out, as the game would be sure to come along its bed. The hills were covered with khine grass about three to four feet high, which the deer love to lie in during the day. My position was a favourable one; the bank on my side was almost perpendicular, the bed of the rivulet about seven feet below. I could see 50 yards up it and 30 yards below. In the river's bed there were only a few bushes and boulders scattered about. I am not partial to a *hank* or beat, as I seldom have any luck and the country gets needlessly disturbed, but the day was too advanced for stalking, so as I took up my position I hoped for the best, but did not anticipate much sport. The Burmese, when you can induce them to beat for game, if left to themselves, go very quietly to work, use no tom-toms or other discordant and noisy instruments, but strike the trunks of trees with split bamboos, and make just sufficient noise to induce the game to move quietly ahead. Along the ridge of the hill there were a few trees; three men had been placed as stops, and the remaining twelve, keeping about two yards apart, forced their way through the long grass, tapping now and then the few trees they encountered.

The beat commenced fully half-a-mile from me, and very soon pea-fowl, jungle fowl, and an occasional pheasant (yit) came running along the bed of the nullah. Had I not been hoping for something better, I might have made a pretty bag of these beautiful birds. When the beaters had advanced about half-way, one of the stops indicated that something was coming his way ; his *tat-tat* was succeeded by that of the next, and finally by the last man, and out walked a brocket. As meat was badly wanted, and I had no faith in my luck, I was thinking of murdering this innocent, when there was another tap. So I allowed him to go by, but as the other markers did not respond, I thought the quarry, whatever it might be, had broken back. I had my eyes fixed on the grass beyond the nullah, not on the water-course itself, but as I saw no movement there, I looked up the nullah, and, with his proud head in the air, looking about him, was a veritable jungle-wallah, a sambur, which might have been worthy almost of those in the Neilgherry hills. He was listening intently, with his ears turned backward. I think I could have shot him where he stood, but to make sure, I waited until he should get closer. For fully five minutes he stood like a rock, then, as the beaters came closer, he gave a stamp or two with his feet, and then trotted towards where I was in hiding. He was followed by five hinds. As he came abreast, I bowled him over ; at the report the does rushed here and there in a decidedly uncertain state as to which way to escape. So I had ample time to put in a fresh cartridge and roll over two plump ones. Thinking all was over I was just about to descend, when I heard a vigorous *tap-tap*. I reloaded and crouched down, with my heart beating with excitement, but for some little time nothing showed. But again another tap indicated that there was something afoot ; the beaters were not far off, hurrying on, no doubt, to ascertain what I had slain. Just then there was a dead silence. The last watcher gave no indication, and I was a bit off my guard, when a large tiger sprang over some bushes into the bed of the river almost opposite me and bounded up the bank, his head and face being about five paces from me. He was hanging on by his fore-feet and endeavouring to scramble up with his hind. Instinctively I fired into his face, and the tiger fell backwards. I jumped up, and caught just a sight of a brindled mass disappearing, and took a snap-shot with the left barrel, which the brute acknowledged by a deep growl. So even supposing I had failed to hit with the first shot, I knew I had hit with the second, yet to miss such an object a few yards off seemed to me impossible. But again, had I hit him fairly where I aimed, the tiger ought to have been as dead as a door-nail.

I approached very cautiously the place where "Stripes" had disappeared; it was a little lower down—at a bend—so I could not see any of the deer I had slain. The bushes on either side were sprinkled plentifully with blood, so telling the orderly to stick close to me with the smooth-bore, which also carried ball very fairly, I advanced at a snail's pace, keeping my eyes about me. I would take a step, then pause to listen for a sound, and to look well ahead and all round for the slightest movement. The jungle was not high, but dense, and to get along I had to push my way through the track made by the tiger. Ticklish work, for these treacherous brutes can hide where scarcely a hare could, and lie *perdu* until you are close up to them—then a rush or a spring, and God be with the hunter! But in the excitement of a hot chase, men don't pause to calculate the pros and cons, but do all they can to slay and recover the quarry.

After going along the right bank for about a mile, the feline had descended back into the bed of the nullah by a sloping path leading to a pool of water, made by animals going there to drink. Now I was safer, as I could see pretty well ahead and around me. The tiger had drunk, and then gone on. I was afraid I should lose him, when I noticed some frothy blood, and I knew he had been shot through the lungs, and that the end could not be far off. I followed the tracks up to close on 5 p.m., then I lost the trail. So telling the orderly, a Sepoy of the Mahratta race, to look in one direction, I circled about in another. In about ten minutes the Sepoy shouted; I hurried up and found him standing by the carcase of a tigress stone dead, lying jammed between two rocks. In her death struggle, panting for breath, she must have sprung and fallen where discovered. There was no time to be lost, the sun would soon set, and I only knew the way back to the Zyat by the way we had come.

We soon collected a quantity of grass and other débris and

covered the body over. If the vultures cannot see the carcase it is quite safe from them; there are no hyænas and scarcely any jackals in Lower Burma, so hoping to find my prize intact next morning we hurried back as fast as we could. We got to the path leading to Lepangoung just at dark, and we reached the Zyat a little before 8 p.m., and I was delighted to find not only the bodies of three sambur but also that of a very fine tiger. Shoay Boh informed me that he found the feline dead—evidently the one I had fired at first; the second must have been his mate. I had the tiger carefully flayed and pegged out, every particle of fat cut away, and warm ashes from bamboos well rubbed in. It was then close on 11 p.m.—time to go to bed.

I was up at daylight, and with eight men armed with a long pole I went off to fetch the body of the tigress. Although it was Sunday I took my smooth-bore with me, and I shot several jungle fowl and one yit before we reached the tigress; found her intact, and returned in triumph. I spent the rest of that day in pegging out the skin and in preparing the heads. I have found that by boiling them for six or eight hours, all the flesh peels off, and the skull is left nice and clean and perfectly white. The teeth sometimes get loose, but can be put back and kept in their places by means of beeswax as a temporary measure, and permanently fixed by plaster of Paris. That is also the best way to prepare even deer skulls, taking care not to submerge any portion of the horn.

I had a long talk with Shoay Boh, and it was decided that we were to start for some salt-licks some two hours before daylight, so as to get there by dawn. He said there were pyoung (gaur) there; so about 3 a.m. we got under weigh, and walked steadily for three hours through principally forests of teak, sâl, and other trees and bamboos, without encountering much undergrowth.

We quickly got on to a fresh track leading towards one of the licks, but as we had to go down wind by following the trail it would be labour lost, so we made a long detour, and it was fully 7 a.m. before we ventured to make for the depression where the whitish earth impregnated with sodium

SKINNING A TIGER.

From a Photo by Sir B. Simpson, Bart.

is found. The ground became uneven, the jungle more dense, and we moved along with the utmost caution. In front there was a heavy fringe of bamboo, extending to a considerable distance north and south. We approached it from the east, with the wind—such as it was—in our faces.

The belt was nearly half-a-mile broad; in one part the bamboos had flowered and were dead, but the remainder were most luxuriant and on the point of blossoming, but they also would all be dead before six months were over; for, directly after flowering, all bamboos die—the seed falls to the ground and the young shoots spring up; are protected in a great measure by the dead canes which have fallen down, otherwise they would soon be devoured by the wild beasts. Thus the forest which succeeds is far denser than the one they replace. A forest of bamboos in flower is a lovely sight, but one seldom seen. The seed is very nutritious, and, if within reach of a village, the people collect it and use it in lieu of rice.

Owing to the impenetrable nature of the dead canes, we could not get to the nearest salt-lick, and it was close upon nine before we got to the others. It was then getting uncommonly hot, and the game had all retired to its fastnesses. Shoay Boh said there was usually a solitary gaur about, but up to twelve o'clock we saw no signs of him. It is no use searching for game in the heat of the day,[1] so I sat down, took my breakfast, got into a comfortable position under shade, and went fast asleep. When I awoke the *shikarie* was absent. I could do nothing wandering alone in these solitudes, beyond losing myself, so I made myself comfortable, and with the last *Field* whiled away the time.

Shoay Boh did not return till past four. He then beckoned me to follow, and taking up a pet ·577, carrying 6½ drams of powder and a solid conical in each barrel, giving him the smooth-bore, off we set. He whispered he had seen the marks of the "solitaire"; after going a mile we crossed over a nullah and made for some hilly ground, covered with dense jungle, and with pendant vines, creepers, and rattan cane. We could only progress by following paths made by wild beasts, a most devious course. Although he had not seen the monster he

[1] Unless you are tracking up an animal.

declared he had got close enough to hear it breathing, but the thicket he was in was so dense that he had prepared a light bamboo ladder to enable me to climb a tree close by and to shoot the gaur from that coign of vantage. When we got to the place, the *shikarie* was up the tree in a moment, but, after staring about and listening, he shook his head and descended, and said the bull was no longer there.

After searching about we got on his trail; this led fortunately towards Lepangoung. There was very little wind, and that in our favour. We walked along quickly, for we had not much daylight left; on turning an abrupt corner, close to a banyan tree with numerous drooping roots, before we knew anything about his being near us, the bull charged down upon us from such a short distance off that I had no time to put the rifle up to the shoulder, but fired into his face with both barrels from the hip, and then sprang aside amidst the pendant roots; the bull went but a few yards; Shoay Boh gave him the contents of my smooth-bore. I did not take many seconds to reload, and I gave him again the contents of both barrels; on receiving them, he retired very groggily into the jungle. We followed very cautiously, the Burman most unwillingly, until we ascertained that he was going away from our camp and no longer towards it. So we left him for that evening, and trudged home, where we did not get till after nine. At four next morning we were up, and in for another hard day's trudge. We went by short cuts, and got to where we had parted company soon after daybreak. We had followed the trail about a mile when we heard growling and snarling, so guessed the gaur was dead, and the bone of contention between two felines. We crept upon all-fours, inch by inch; it was still gloomy and dark, and although I could hear I could not distinguish the disputants, but the dead body of the gaur loomed immense in the distance, and after a while I made out two leopards snarling at one another. Raising my body till I was on my knees, I took a shot at the nearest, but just as I fired he sprang at his antagonist, and I made a clean miss, but I fired again, and strongly suspect that the solid conical passed through them both. They separated, and there was blood, but very little, on each trail. I left them for the time being, intending to look them up later on. The giant bull was fully 21 hands high, and the greatest breadth of his horns from bend to bend was 57½ inches. Shoay Boh went off to get men, and returned at 2 p.m., and, to my disgust, with him came an orderly bearing an official letter, saying I must return at once to take command of a force starting next morning for Karennee. There was no help for it, so telling the *shikarie* to preserve the gaur's head for me, and to try and recover one if not both leopards, I mounted my pony, found a change at Tseben, and got back to cantonments that evening. After eight weeks' fruitless wanderings I returned; the alarm had been a false one.

AN ELEPHANT HUNT

In 1856 I had to go to Mendoon on the Matoon, a lovely stream, some forty miles west or south-west of Thayet Myo, which was, until lately, our frontier station on the Irrawady on the right bank. I had been here before, and had had various sport under the guidance of an old Burman *shikarie* who had accompanied Ashe of the Artillery (afterwards killed at Cawnpore) into the Arrakan range, where he shot three elephants.

On my arrival I sent for the man and inquired if there was any game about near, for my time was limited, and I could not remain away long from my head-quarters, which were at Namyan. He professed to be able to show me a solitary bull elephant with large tusks. I asked him how long it would take to overhaul him.

"If we leave to-day," he replied, "there is a têh we can sleep in to-night, and get to the jungle he frequents about twelve to-morrow."

I had been sold before, so only credited about half what he said; but I could spare four days, during which my work-people would be collecting certain timber I wanted, so telling my head-man to dismantle some deserted phoongie houses and to make rafts of the timber for transportation down the Matoon to Prome, and that I'd be back in that time, I put together a few things, which a couple of men carried, and with my two servants started about 10 a.m. Mendoon had been a place of importance, an appanage of the eldest son of the king of Burma, but it had been burnt down and all but deserted during the late war with us. When clear of it we followed by-paths for an hour, then crossed a stream, an affluent of the Matoon, and entered first an Eeinghein and then a teak forest. There was not much undergrowth, and we followed a track for a couple of hours or more made by elephants during the last rains. We then began to climb the spurs of the lower range of hills. Calling a halt I made an *al fresco* meal, giving some food to the Burman, who, having no caste, will eat anything; in fact, they are the most omnivorous people I ever met—nothing comes amiss to them in the way of food.

The meal over, I reclined under a convenient shade and allowed the Burmese to have a smoke, and doled them out a tot of grog. We then started afresh. The ascent became very stiff, and although I was in very good and hard condition, it was very soon a case of "bellows to mend," but I soon recovered my second wind and was then able to trudge along fairly well. Animals construct these paths as if they had been instructed in engineering, for they wind round and round the hills, gradually ascending, and if we had stuck to them all would have been easy, but the guide would take short cuts, which proved very laborious and fatiguing, as the hillsides were covered with fallen branches of trees and débris of all sorts. About 5 p.m. we were probably at an elevation of 1000 feet. Looking back, the lovely Matoon looked almost at our feet, though miles away; to the east, in the distance, the mighty Irrawady appeared a mere thread; to the north and west rose the Arrakan mountains, which reach an elevation of some 6000 feet, and are densely wooded for about 3000 to 4000 feet. We could see mist rising here and there from the valleys which lay between us and the main range.

About 5.30 we resumed our journey, and after a climb of another 200 to 300 feet began to descend, and soon came to some townyahs, or clearances, made by Karens for growing their hill paddy. These people are very destructive to forests, as they change their location every two years, trusting to the ashes of what they have felled and burnt to manure their crops for that period, then they seek fresh pastures.

Just before dark we came to a têh, a raised platform fully 20 feet off the ground, but as there was space on it only large enough to accommodate a couple of men sitting, I did not think it worth while to ascend it, and although I was told there were man-eating tigers about, I decided to take my chance at the bottom, taking precautions to light fires all round. My dinner was soon ready, and whilst I partook of it, all hands but one servant set to work to collect wood.

My meal finished and washed down with a bottle of that divine nectar as it then existed, Bass's pale ale; alas! that firm seems to have forgotten the knack of making the ale which made them so famous in days gone by,—or I cannot get it,—for the beer of the present day cannot hold a candle to that which used to be exported in hogsheads to India in the middle of this century, and which, when mature and cooled, was a drink for the gods! Never sleep on the ground if it can be avoided, it is so simple to erect a platform of bamboos or other wood a foot or two off the ground; this done, I wrapped a *cumbly* round me, and with an air-pillow under the head I was soon asleep, and slept like a top till within an hour of dawn, when we were all astir. Drinking a cup of *café noir*, for no milk was procurable, we resumed our march by daylight, and it was a case of ascending and descending all day. The lower spurs of all considerable mountains consist of a mass of teelahs; no sooner have you come to the crest of one than down you go into a valley, cross a rivulet, and ascend a hillock higher than the last, and so on, till the intermediary stage is passed and the base of the mountains itself is reached, which may be at any altitude from 600 to 1000 feet or more. About 6 p.m. we halted at the top of a slope, a stream running down close by. We must have been fully thirty miles from Mendoon. The water of this rivulet was deliciously cool and clear, and I utilized it for cooling a bottle of beer. I delight in water for lavatory purposes, but at my meals I prefer something stronger.

Here we soon rigged up sleeping berths and shelter overhead, and were glad to avail ourselves of razais as covering, for the air was decidedly chilly. At the elevation we were there were few or no mosquitoes and no sand-flies.

The *shikarie* warned us to be very quiet, as elephants and gaur and occasionally tsine wandered about here, and we could see from their droppings that this was rather a favourite beat of theirs. So only such fires as were requisite for cooking our food were lit in a secluded glen, and then by 8 p.m. extinguished. The night passed without disturbance.

By 5 a.m. we were up and away. We neither ascended nor descended, but went along the edge of the plateau towards where the *shikarie* said were some salt-licks, always favourite resorts of almost all animals. Leaving the cleared spot where we had rested, we entered into a gloomy forest consisting of sal and buttress trees; from the latter an oil or varnish is extracted. These monarchs are of immense girth and height, often 100 to 150 feet above the ground without a single branch; the roots grow out of the main stem fully 5 or 6 feet, and form buttresses which extend to some distance before disappearing into the ground. On the lower lateral branches there are often huge bee-hives pendant, many of them 7 or 8 feet long by 3 or 4 in depth. These attract the bears, that climb up the trees by sticking their claws into the soft bark, and thus rob the bees of their store of food.

The Burmese and Karens copy these beasts; fill a haversack with bamboo pegs, drive one in, rest on that, drive another higher up, and so on, till they reach the site of the coveted prize; they then smoke the bees until they are stupid and partially unconscious, and then walk off with the honey. The process of thus climbing seems hazardous in the extreme, but an accident seldom happens.

Besides these trees there were stupendous clumps of both the male and female bamboos; the former are much prized for shafts for hog-spears, and the latter are converted into a thousand and one articles, in fact an entire house, including the roofing, is often made from bamboos alone—many of them are 3 feet in circumference and make capital buckets.

From an inspection of the country I came to the conclusion,

before I could bag my elephant my work lay before me. I had at that time a two-grove, No. 10-bore double rifle, made by old Joseph Lang. I was so pleased with it that I had another made like it afterwards, but at that time I only had one of his and one of Sam Smith's, both noted makers in India. The *shikarie* carried one weapon, I the other. They were muzzle-loaders, of course, as breech-loaders had not come into use then. He led the way, I next, and the coolie about 100 yards in the rear, keeping us just in sight.

About 7 a.m. we came upon the fresh spoors of two elephants; they had been feeding quietly and moving along leisurely, so we had no difficulty in tracking them. Those who wish to slay these leviathans in their forest homes need be sound of wind and limb, for it is no child's play following them up, for quietly as they feed along they are ever on the move, and get over the ground far faster than one would believe. Occasionally, when the weather is very oppressive, a beast may take a siesta and be caught napping, but where we were the heat was not outrageous, and these two had not made any considerable halt, so it was close on four before we came in sight of them, standing a few yards apart, pulling down and browsing on the tender shoots of the bamboo. The noise they made in rending the bamboos and then converting them into pulp by beating them on a foot, deadened the sound of our footsteps, and I had no difficulty, the wind being in our favour, in reaching a buttress which afforded good shelter and was within easy shot. The two animals differed greatly, they might have been father and son. The one nearest me was an old emaciated male with long tusks, the other was in his prime, very handsome to look at. What a beauty he would have made for a howdah elephant! We had no means of entrapping him, but it seemed a shame almost to devote him to death for the sake of his tusks alone; but what will not a hunter do with the furor of the chase upon him!

Motioning to the *shikarie* to stand close, ready with the spare rifle, I waited until a movement of the old one exposed the temple shot; then, stepping aside, I took a quick but steady aim and let fly.

Down he fell! His companion turned at the sound and gave me a front shot; dropping on one knee, I fired, and he fell stone dead. I thought the first also was as dead as Julius Cæsar, and, as I was going towards them, he picked himself up and charged full at me. I fortunately had the spare rifle, and gave him a right and left, and threw myself under the lee of a buttress; as the monster passed, he all but trod on me. He only ran a few yards, and then right-about faced and bore down towards me again, but I had shifted my position further back behind another buttress or he would have had me. I now noticed that he was hunting for me by scent, for one of my last shots had knocked out one eye, and the other had, to a certain extent, paralysed the trunk, and the blood was pouring from the wound into the sound optic. So I retreated behind another tree some 20 yards further, where I found the *shikarie*, who had loaded his rifle. I soon loaded mine—the bullets fitted beautifully—and in pushing them down they made no noise. Being ready for battle again, I stepped clear and gave him the contents of both barrels into the temple, but as I fired he threw up his head, and neither missile reached the brain. On receiving these wounds he blindly rushed forward, a buttress caught his fore-feet, and down he went, such a cropper! I seized the other rifle and gave him two shots as he was attempting to rise, but he bore a charmed life, and I again failed to kill. He then retreated. As soon as I had both weapons ready I took up his trail. Considering the terrible nature of his wounds, inflicted at a distance of only a few yards, and the cropper he had come, it was marvellous at what a rate he went away. We had to follow at a trot, and when he heard us coming he either hid and then rushed at us, or spun round and charged blindly. I fired no less than eleven more shots, but failed egregiously to put him out of his misery. It was getting too dark in the gloomy forest for accurate shooting, and the monster kept his head tossing about as if possessed of a perpetual motion. To hit the brain, except by a fluke, was hopeless, so we left him, determined to follow him to the death on the morrow.

We could not find the coolie with our food; he had disappeared during the scrimmage. To return to camp was not to be thought of; sleeping out for a night is no great hardship to a real hunter, so we went back to the elephant I had slain. We collected sufficient débris to keep our fires going all night, and then, declining to partake of any portion of the flesh of the elephant, which the *shikarie* had cut off and partially cooked, I lay down alongside the elephant, and using one of his ankles as a pillow, and bidding the man light a couple of fires and keep them going, I was soon fast asleep.

When I awoke just before dawn I felt a little hungry, and missed my cup of coffee, but tightening my belt and washing my face in the first little stream we came to, we resumed our chase. He must have got ahead fully ten miles, which we had to make up, so we walked along at a pretty brisk pace. When I was all but exhausted I espied a peacock and bowled him over. We carried him till we came to water, and then kabobed some of its flesh over some embers and made a hearty meal.

We did not overtake the tusker that day, so slept in the jungle again, but felt the cold considerably, for we had been steadily ascending. To make matters worse our fires died out, and we were pretty well benumbed by the morning, and glad to resume our pursuit. Every now and then we came upon where the poor stricken brute had struck the boles of trees, the result of his more than half blindness, and also where he had lain down in a mass of gore. We noticed also that his stride became shorter and shorter, and that he had leant against a tree or two for support—all signs of increasing weakness—so we pressed on with renewed hopes.

The country we were in was pretty open forest, with here and there patches of long grass. We had just passed one, with our eyes riveted on the ground, when there was a fiendish screech, and a bloody form all but tottered on to the top of us! I jumped aside, and fired both barrels into his carcase, close to the shoulder. This reduced him to a slow walk, and he struggled along with his trunk pendant and limp, and altogether his aspect was a woebegone one. I seized the other rifle, ran forward, and as he flopped an ear forward I fired into the space behind it, and staggering along two or three yards, he fell forward—dead!

Poor old beast! Thank God he was at last dead, for he must have suffered fearful agonies. One eye was shot out, the other all but closed by coagulated blood, and he had received numerous wounds, yet the gallant brute never uttered a groan, and died fighting to the last. His tusks were 4 feet 8 inches and 4 feet 6 inches respectively, but thick and straight. By the foot measurement he was just 10 feet 2 inches high.

But now where were we? The *shikarie* climbed a tall tree, took a good look all round, and when he descended, said if we walked quickly we should get to the camp by night. Before we had gone far a sambur crossed our path, which I killed, and as I felt very tired and hungry, I preferred camping out another night in the jungle and to have a square meal at once, to tramping on on an empty stomach, with the chance of reaching camp that night.

The Burman soon broiled the liver, cut in slices, which we ate, but Adam's ale was our only drink! We rigged up a shelter overhead, lit a fire, and slept the sleep of the weary till close on daylight. We partook of another meal before starting, and finally reached camp after mid-day.

The coolie had returned and reported that he had seen me trampled to death by the elephant, so my boy had gone to where the encounter had taken place to pick up master's bones, but finding one elephant dead and evidences that we were in chase of another, he wisely returned to camp and stuck to it until we should return.

After a day's rest I took all hands, and as decomposition had commenced we had no difficulty in extracting the tusks, and soon made our way back to Mendoon, and thence by boat to Namyan, where I got only a day after I was due, but as I was my own master that did not signify.

GENERAL BLAKE'S ADVENTURE

"When coming up here (Tongho) I telegraphed for elephants to meet me at Shoayghein, thinking I might as well have a go in at Myetquin on my way up, but they were

TRAVELLING IN OUT STATION (JUNGLE ROAD).

From a Photo by Watts & Skeen, Rangoon.

not forthcoming, so there was nothing for it but to get carts and come here as fast as I could.

"Starting from Shoayghein on the evening of the 26th, going to Thanzeik that night and reaching this on the 30th, is not bad going, but it was a case of continual move, and threatening the bandy-men, one of whom I did walk into in uncommon nice style; I having given him three hours' start, and he having taken out his bullocks to graze after having gone about two miles out of Kyoung-bya.

"From Moulmein to this I did not see a single head of game of any sort, large or small. I just arrived in time to see Lloyd with a party of six start for Myetquin. For me to remain quietly here whilst *shikar* was going on was quite out of the question, so as I could not go with them I took my old line, and went to my former haunts on the banks of the Pabay river, going to Tseben the first day. When I got to my destination there was nothing there, the *shikarie* said; however, that night our ears and eyes told us of elephants being there, a large tusker showing himself just below the huts at one corner of the small tounyah (clearance) and another at the other corner. In the morning I was after them, and followed them backwards and forwards through the kine grass till I was ready to drop. It was fearfully hot. I then took on myself the task of getting up to them. I went through the grass at one end and got round them; at least, this was my intention, but I found they had crossed my path and got into some rattan jungle. I followed sharp, saw them, ran up towards them, and as I was then in the midst of the herd and could see no tusker, let fly and knocked over one. It was a bad shot through rattans and their hanging leaves and creepers. Immediately on this there was, of course, a tremendous rush, and a huge Muckna came and stood about 20 yards to my left; he was quite in the open, and there was not a bush between us; but though quite clear he did not give me a good shot, as he was a little too far past me for a good temple shot; however, I fired, and he and all the rest bolted. I walked up to where I had floored the first one, and he, too, was gone, so you may suppose how disgusted I was. I followed them right through the elephant grass out on to the other side, and imagined they had bolted slick away. Amongst the wild ones was Armoogum's little elephant that he had lent me, for the little brute had been grazing in the grass the night before, and had gone off with the herd. The mahout said he knew his elephant, as it was hobbled, and as it could not have gone away with the rest, he went into the long grass after it. Great was his horror—for he was an awful coward—when he found himself amongst the whole herd, which were resting quite silently. Up a tree he went, and the herd ran back again. I went round, and whilst moving on quietly I heard an elephant, and, strange to say, though I called their attention to it several times, the *shikaries* did not hear it. So, taking only one Sepoy to carry a reserve gun, and accompanied by the mahout, I walked towards the sound; and, sure enough, I came upon an elephant in the Pabay, which is merely a nullah here. At length it showed its head. I asked the mahout if that was his elephant; he said he could not tell; at length I saw her move her fore-legs, and saw that they were hobbled. I said to the mahout, 'Run forward and get hold of your own elephant;' but he said, 'There is a large elephant close to her.' I saw what the fool mistook for a janwar was a bough of a tree, but he was in a great funk, though I went into the kine with him; no sooner had he mounted than he bolted home sharp.

"I heard the herd at a little distance ahead of me, followed, and saw them coming towards me, when a female saw, I think, a Sepoy who was with me—gave a trumpet, and all rushed back. I again followed and came upon them standing quite quiet, and then, for the first time, I saw a splendid tusker. I had left every one except one man behind, and thus was waiting for the huge brute to turn his head for me to take the shot. He would not do so, but moved forward about 10 yards, putting his head behind a tree and his body under cover of that of a female. There was no moving quietly, a burning hot day, and the ground covered with fallen leaves; I think, therefore, that they must have heard me, for they suddenly wheeled round and were off at score. I followed for some distance, but felt myself so done that I could scarcely raise my big rifle, so gave orders for home, and when I did get back to my halting-ground was so done that I could scarcely speak, and was obliged to take a tot of brandy to bring me to. I do not remember ever to have been more thoroughly used up. The day was one of those cloudless, furiously hot ones, and if there was any wind it was not to be felt in the high grass, and I was running and walking all day with a heavy rifle in my hand, so it was not very wonderful that I did not go out the next day. But on the following I took up the trail of the hathees, and though I knew they had one day's and two nights' start of me, yet followed on, and soon got upon fresh tracks of bison, and, on turning a corner of the kine, came upon a huge bull about 10 yards off.

"He was more astonished than I was, gave a sort of roar, and bolted before I could finger trigger. I ran forward, but he had dashed down into a nullah and was away. Wonder where I should have been if, instead of bolting, he had come at me! Soon saw that he had gone off with no intention of allowing me to see him again that day, so took up the elephant track again, and in about half-an-hour afterwards, in a perfectly open piece of ground, and in the middle of the road that the elephants had made, came upon a tiger lying down. As we were upon no fresh track, I was not carrying my gun, and before I could get it he was away into the jungle. I followed for some little distance, but found he had gone into a dense thicket, in which there was no seeing anything. I went somewhat further, and seeing that the elephants had never stopped to eat or drink, and ascertaining that the nearest water was something like six or eight miles off, I gave it up and got back into the Pabay stream, and walked back without seeing anything.

"Next morning I was out after bison again. Before long got on a fresh trail, but it was long before we came upon the brutes themselves. They were in a burnt-up-looking bit of jungle on the top of a hill. I saw the white stockings of one, and ran forward as rapidly as I could till I sighted his chocolate-coloured body, which, by contrast with the jungle around, looked black. He was looking at me and so gave me a bad shot. He was about 80 yards off. I fired, and rolled him over. Running forward, I saw another standing broadside on, which had escaped my notice before. I gave this the shoulder-shot with the remaining barrel of my rifle. This one bolted off, and the first one, wounded, picked himself up, joined the other, and they both galloped down the hillside. One fell at the bottom of the hill, but picked himself up again. There was lots of blood, and I hoped to come upon one of the brutes, at least, lying down or dead. The fellow I had as a tracker was the best I have ever met with out of the Wynaad jungle; he held back when we got to some very thick brushwood and bamboos, and kept climbing trees to see if anything could be seen ahead. However, he seemed satisfied when I put my rifle over his head, and he saw that he had nothing to do but to spring back or aside, if the animal charged, for me to receive it.

"Twice we came upon one of the wounded ones, but not close enough for me to get a shot, the jungle was so dense; and after having followed for I can't say how many miles, were obliged to give it up and make tracks homeward, and a precious long distance I found it too, and got drenched to the skin before I got back. I was pretty certain that the muzzle-sight of my rifle had got shifted, and so, before reaching home, I tried the weapon, and found that both barrels threw considerably to the left. So I think very probably, that instead of hitting behind the shoulder, I struck the brute on the shoulder; and the other one, instead of on the chest, on the point of the shoulder, which caused it to fall, though not much hurt.

"Two days afterwards I saw vultures sailing away in that direction, so the probability is that one, if not both, of the brutes died, though I was no gainer thereby. My last day now arrived, for though leeches, gadflies, and ticks were endured, —with what anathemas I will not say,—the rain was now coming down in torrents, and to shoot much longer was impossible, especially as all the carriage I had was a bandy (cart), which in a few days would have been unable to return, as the nullahs would be full and the country flooded.

"I went out before daylight to catch the gaur grazing. I came upon two, not 20 yards from me, and, as they did not see me, I got a cool pot at one, and my favourite shot behind the ribs. Away they went into some dense rattan and thorny jungle. Scarcely any blood on the trail at all; we came upon the two together twice, but did not see them, only heard their rush. At length took up the track of one, and, after going some distance, found it was the wrong one; so back we went again, came upon the right track, put the brute up three times, and at last found it dead. My ball had struck it a little too high and a little too far back, just over the hip-bone, but it had gone in a slanting direction all but through the body, being only retained by the skin at the shoulder. You would scarcely suppose that any animal could have moved after receiving such a wound as that, yet this creature led me a dance for upwards of three hours. Certainly the gaur grow very much larger in Burma than in India; this was a cow, and she was 19 hands, or 6 feet 4 inches, in fair measurement, from heel to the top of the dorsal ridge. Now a very large bull killed by me in India was only of the same size, and an immense old fellow that I saw killed in the Wynaad was only two inches higher.

"Got back about noon, the sun furious till about two, when it came down a deluge. When they went back for the meat of the cow the following day, they found a tiger had drawn it away, and as he growled alarmingly at their intrusion, the *shikaries* wisely let him keep the beef, but I, fortunately, had taken the tongue and head away with me, and uncommonly good the former was, too, to eat."

The above graphic description of sport on foot in Burma is by one of the most accomplished sportsmen I ever knew. But we learn the following:—That all sights on a rifle should be screwed down to the rib to prevent shifting. This I have always insisted on in my own weapons and advocated in my writings. And the second is—never move in the jungle without carrying your own weapon: I have known so many chances lost by transferring for a time your weapon to a gun-carrier. I could not myself trudge through the jungles unless I carried my own rifle. Use is second nature. Had the sights been true, the General would doubtless have killed an elephant or two and a couple more gaur, or bison, as he calls them. Had he had his rifle in hand, he would doubtless have added the tiger to his bag.

A VISIT TO UPPER BURMA

In 1856 I determined to visit Umrapoora, the then capital of Upper Burma. A little distance beyond Meaday, our then frontier station, there was no regular monsoon known, rain might or might not fall at any time, and during the months of July and August a steady breeze blew up the Irrawady, one of the straightest rivers in the world. Sir Arthur Phayre, accompanied by Col. Yule and other officers, had gone there on a mission previously, but although a couple of officers had taken a trip there too, and nothing had been said to them, yet there was a general order that Europeans in Government employ were not to go across our frontier without previously obtaining permission from the Chief Commissioner, which it was understood would not be readily accorded. So four of us determined to run the risk, and, hiring a large cargo-boat and fitting it up to suit our requirements, Furlong, the Superintendent of the road to Tongoop, and Scott and Stephenson, his assistants, and I set out. The Burmese boats can be made very comfortable; they sail before the wind at a great rate, and often have yards 120 feet across, with a sail in proportion, and at times a topsail. The lie of the river is north and south till within one day's sail of Ava, where it takes a bend to the east. The boats hug the shore, and I have seen them often pass a steamer. Leaving Prome, we reached Thayet Myo in a day and a half, and halted there barely twenty-four hours. Starting afresh, we reached Menloon, the first Burmese station, on the second day. There the Burmese had a Custom-House, and all boats going up and down were examined. The officials were very civil and gave us no trouble at all. We called on the Governor, who received us in grand state and was exceedingly polite, and offered to show us some sport if we would remain a few days; we thanked him, but declined, as we said our time was limited; in fact, we were afraid we might be recalled if we dawdled near our frontier.

Portions of the Irrawady between Meaday and Menloon

are very beautiful. The stream is somewhat confined by high banks and studded with well-wooded islands; the water is clear, and we could hear francolins and peacocks calling, and, on landing, occasionally put up a few corn-quail. Beyond Menloon whenever we approached a town we landed to visit the monasteries and pagodas, many of which were very picturesque. On entering a phoongie house we were generally asked to take off our shoes, because Sir Arthur had done so, but on our assuring them that our custom was to take off our hats, and that the doing so was a far greater mark of respect than going in unshod, they made no objection. Although we did not hurry, we did not halt for any length of time anywhere until we reached Yay-nan-choung, or "stinking-water stream," and wishing to visit the petroleum wells we halted for a day. The atmosphere round Yay-nan-choung is fœtid. There are always hundreds of boats that take the oil in bulk. In stowing a great deal is spilt, and the surface of the river is covered with a film of petroleum very unpleasant to one's olfactory nerves. The wells are about three miles inland, so, starting early, we got there about seven, and spent an hour or two in watching the extraction of the mineral oil. The appliances are of the crudest. The wells are fully 300 feet in depth; there are not many of them, and all are owned by some dozen families, who used to intermarry so as to keep their interests intact; but the older inhabitants now complained that the young people were getting independent, that the young men brought home strange girls for wives, and that the girls often marry outsiders, and as each retains his or her interests, the property is rapidly decreasing in value. The produce is a monopoly of the king's, and pays him well. If a well requires deepening there are but two or three men capable of undertaking it, no one can remain down for more than a minute or two at the most, and occasionally a man dies in the attempt. Where these wells are there is not a blade of grass, no vegetation grows within several hundred feet of their vicinity. Although there are other wells known in Burma, none pay but these. Far finer wells were discovered in Assam, but owing to peculation and bad management those who started their working utterly failed; but lately a fresh start has been made, and they ought to pay well, especially when the railroads, now in course of construction, are completed. The crude petroleum is like thick mud and is very offensive. In Rangoon they have refineries now, and manufacture candles, soap, and kerosene and Rangoon oil.

Leaving Yay-nan, the banks of the river form chalk cliffs, rising from 100 to 150 feet above the river bed, and, sailing alongside, we found they were infested with wild blue-rock pigeons, who had formed their nests by burrowing into the chalk formation, and as the country is well cultivated with wheat, cholum, and other grains, we found the birds delicious eating, and shot a good many of them. As most of them fell into the river when killed, our boatmen, who were amphibious, retrieved for us and fared all the better for their exertions, as we gave them a good many of the birds. As there is no regular monsoon, the great staple, paddy or rice, is grown only here and there where irrigation can be resorted to, so the people of Upper Burma are in great measure dependent on the Lower for their great necessary of life. A trip up this great water-way, especially in a large commodious boat, is very pleasant. We never found the heat oppressive; the steady wind acted as a fan, and the scene varied so at every turn and twist as to resemble a kaleidoscope, and we never tired of its beauties. We halted for two days at Pagan Myo, which alone is worth a month's trip to see; along the river bank for fully nine miles there is visible pagoda upon pagoda, and these extend inland for some three miles. Unfortunately, most of these beautiful structures are in ruins; the hill people, who are not Buddhists, have broken into them for the sake of their relics, and but few remain intact; these luckily are probably the most beautiful of all. Yule declares that the Ananda Pya is in its way more lovely than the Taj at Agra. He thinks it was built by Italians acting under the orders of the Court of Ava many centuries ago. Pagan used at one time to be the capital of Burma, but it was captured by the Chinese, and in 1824-26 Sir Archibald Campbell made it his head-quarters for some time. It is only a place of very secondary importance now, but will ever be famous for its monasteries and pagodas. There they make, too, the best of the boxes the Burmese use for carrying betel-nut and ingredients for chewing and other purposes. They are woven from very fine strips of bamboo and then lacquered, an art in which they, the Chinese, and Japanese excel all other people. Some ten miles to the east of Pagan there are hills rising to an altitude of some 2000 to 3000 feet, where it is said game is abundant. I saw boars feeding in the open where, had we had steeds and spears, we could have ridden them easily. Hares, jungle fowl, and francolins were fairly plentiful, and I killed enough to last us for a couple of days. To see Pagan and its vast ruins properly one should spend a month there.

Although paddy is a scarce commodity, wheat, grain of all kinds, and cereals thrive well. We also landed at Saigon and Ava; the former capital is a mass of ruins and overgrown with jungle, with the ramparts tumbling down. The pagodas remain, and a portion of the old town is still inhabited, but it is a sad ruin to contemplate. Umrapoora, the then capital, was a thriving, well-built, handsome city. We called upon Mr. Spears, an English merchant who had long been resident there, and who showed us much hospitality and kindness. He hired for us a house and acted as our *cicerone.* The king was notified of our arrival, and placed four ponies at our disposal, and promised to see us when the stars should be propitious. We went about freely; there was not the slightest hindrance, and we met with the greatest civility everywhere. We visited the White Elephant, who ranked after the king and had a palace all to himself. When dressed for state occasions his trappings are worth several lacs of rupees. His head-piece alone contained rubies and emeralds worth, Mr. Spears told us, over £20,000. I wonder what became of them when we finally occupied Mandalay in 1880, or thereabouts—looted by the soldiers and officers when Mandalay was taken, most probably. One Tommy, who was placed under arrest for looting, said: "Devil-a-bit do I care—I have enough loot for three generations." Very foolishly, the maids-of-honour were allowed to leave the palace unsearched: they took a vast quantity of jewellery and precious stones with them, but the soldiers were on the look-out, and deprived them of everything. The elephant was certainly a very fine one, most symmetrically formed, and with a splendid pair of tusks. I heard that after we annexed the country Messrs. Rogers of Sheffield bought these tusks at auction. I wonder whether they cut them up into handles for knives! He had been *must* some time, so had not been washed or bathed for about a month, and as he was covered with dirt thrown over his body by himself it was impossible to judge how white he was. He had certainly pink eyes—so I fancy he was an albino. He died a few months after we saw him, and was replaced by a miserable little beast who had not much pretence to being white.

In the centre of the town was the king's palace and its outbuildings—all surrounded by a broad ditch and walls flanked with towers. I was disappointed with the palace; it was not half so grand as many of the phoongie houses I had seen. The stables were extensive, but only occupied by some four or five spotted ponies of no value, and such as we see in most circuses. The great idol is a representation of Buddha seated in the usual cross-legged manner, and consists of metal. It was cast in Arrakan, and when we overran that country it was moved across the mountains to its present site, and took, it is said, 10,000 men to carry. I have no doubt it is very valuable. It is, or was when I saw it, very much distorted from the many thousands of pilgrims daily smearing it over with gold leaf. The Chinese had a quarter to themselves, and their Joss-house was well worth a visit, the images inside were very life-like and beautifully dressed. The whole of it, even the stones used in the structure, we were told, had been brought piece by piece from China *viâ* Bhamo, and must have been a work of time and vast expense.

Round the king's palace were built the houses of his *mingyees* or ministers, and each had a neat little garden in front with a trellis-work on which were growing vines. The streets were broad, well laid out, and perfectly straight; the cross roads being at right angles, forming boulevards like those common on the Continent. There were a good many brick houses. The *Mannipuries*, who form the king's cavalry, lived apart by themselves, and their women are reckoned the beauties of the capital. Each trade has a street allotted to it, so you see the same things for sale all in a row, and there is a good deal of competition and importuning to purchase. The site of Sir Arthur Phayre's Embassy was about a mile and a half from the town across a large lake. We had to cross a bridge (wooden) fully a mile long to get to it. In Lower Burma in those days we had not succeeded in rearing European vegetables, so we were delighted at seeing some cabbages growing, and, after a good deal of haggling, I bought one for a rupee and took it home in triumph. My boy, the next day, bought twelve for the same price! The phoongie houses were splendid—the inner posts of that occupied by the high priest were studded with precious stones. Very fine oranges are grown in the hilly districts, and of course all tropical fruits thrive if looked after; but we were then not at the right season for fruit. Our interview with his Majesty was postponed from day to day; either the stars were unpropitious, or a child was born, or some excuse made. So we left without seeing the king of kings after all. Just as we were leaving, the Kulawoon (Minister for Foreign Affairs) presented each of us with a *putso* of silk of the king's own pattern as a farewell gift, and asked us to delay our departure. We thanked him, but would not remain any longer.

The king has one principal wife—his half-sister—and some seven hundred concubines, many of whom he probably would not recognize. If we could believe a quarter of what we were told, great profligacy was carried on by the ladies of his harem, who admitted their lovers freely; and as for the children, not one in a hundred could claim paternity from the Lord of Many White Elephants, etc. So the half-sister was probably no way related, and that I think must be pretty well understood, for I always found that the Burmese had a horror of committing incest, and the greatest opprobrium you can cast on a man is to accuse him of having been intimate with his own sister. No rain had fallen for two months when we were in Umrapoora, though it was the height of the monsoon in the Lower Provinces. I only saw one cultivated fig-tree in the suburbs; at a little distance, I was told, they, as well as peaches, apricots, pomegranates, and other fruits, were to be found.

Although mangoes,[1] or rather the trees, are very common, good mango fruit was in those days very difficult to procure—nearly every one has a beetle inside, and the only grafted ones I ever saw were some imported by me and planted at Tongho. Custard apples thrive opposite Prome. But Burma—except in the hilly districts—was not then a good place for fruit. Very fine mangoes and oranges may now be had in Rangoon, Mandalay, and Moulmein.

In 1858 the Government discontinued the works on the road I was employed on, so I reverted to the sappers and miners. Each company of a European regiment and the sappers had been supplied with a large boat, and Butt and I, with the help of Dr. Ranking, who had formerly been in the navy, rigged ours up as a yacht, and, having obtained a month's privilege leave, we determined to sail up the river and have a look at Mandalay, the new capital. We took two sappers as a crew, and our two servants, and, laying in an ample supply of stores, we set sail. It was blowing great guns when we started, and the wind continued fair and strong the whole way. I was steersman; Butt undertook the management of the sails, etc. Everybody laughed at us, and told us we were a couple of fools for thinking we could get up without the aid of a Burmese crew, but I, who had already been up, knew there were no difficulties in the way, so we felt confident of our ability to do without extra aid. Our yacht was a capital sailer, and being provided with a keel she could sail on a wind, whereas the Burmese boats can only sail with a breeze fair astern. We did not stick to the bank like the Burmese, but went boldly into mid-stream. Seeing us do this, several large native boats followed our example, and in a straight run fairly ran away from us, passing us with a good-natured joke, but directly there was the least bend they all went ashore, whilst we, close-hauled, passed them in our turn, laughing at them and asking them if we should report having seen them at Mandalay. It is no joke if one of these huge craft gets on a lee-shore if there is a strong breeze blowing, for it then takes them sometimes days to get off. We landed at many of the

[1] *Excellent* mangoes are now obtainable in Mandalay, and, in fact, nearly every district in Upper or Lower Burma.—W. S. T.

islands and shot a number of corn-quail, which in the Lower Provinces are very scarce. We also killed hares, jungle fowl, and pigeons sufficient for our wants, and in one place we came across a lot of goggle-eyed plovers, which had been fattening on grain, and found them uncommonly good eating. We spent two days at Pagan Myo, before mentioned, where the pagodas are so numerous that if a Burman wishes to express an impossibility, he says, "Such and such is as possible as for a man to count the pagodas at Pagan."

Including all our stoppages we reached Mandalay without any assistance on the eleventh day. We sailed up a creek and anchored close to the town. The people at its mouth tried to induce us to stop there, but we pretended ignorance of their language and sailed on. We looked up Mr. Spears, and though he was kind enough to offer to put us up, as we intended remaining only a few days, we declined with thanks and remained in our own boat. In 1857 the king had decreed that Umrapoora was to be abandoned, and a new capital formed four miles higher up the river. It was thought that the position of Mandalay would be safer from the guns of our war-vessels than Umrapoora, but the science in gunnery has made such strides of late years, that the new capital could have been as easily battered down as the old one, which was on the river's bank. The new town was in embryo. It had been admirably laid out, and the streets were 100 feet broad, and all laid out regularly in parallel lines with the cross-roads at right angles. The king's palace as usual in the centre. We walked to the site of Umrapoora, where two years ago all had been beautiful to the sight, but which was now a mass of ruins and desolation. The inhabitants had been forcibly removed, the ramparts thrown down, the brick houses demolished, wooden ones burnt. Nothing was left but charred remains and rubbish, and numbers of half-starved dogs, who were lying about; why they had not followed their masters to the new capital I can't conceive. There are large marble quarries near Mandalay, and alabaster is also found, and hundreds of artisans were busy modelling images of Gaudama of every conceivable size, from an inch or two to 10 and 15 feet in altitude. Nothing was finished, but several thousand people were at work excavating the fort-ditch, throwing up ramparts, and making bricks.

The officials could understand Butt coming up to admire the country, but what could have brought me up a second time they could not make out, and evidently looked on me as a spy!

Phayre's abode during his embassy had been burnt down. We saw the hairy woman and her family, and some very clever jugglers, who did the Davenport trick long before that family was heard of. We wandered all over the place, no one objecting, and, after seeing all that could be seen and purchasing knick-knacks, and obtaining a certificate from Spears that we had arrived on a certain date, to satisfy those who had bet that we should not reach the capital, we crossed over the river to Mendoon, where there is the largest mass of brickwork in the world and the second largest bell. The former was intended to be an immense pagoda, and a model alongside shows that it was to have been 600 feet high when finished, but after it had been raised 200 feet, the great earthquake of 1839 shattered it, and the Burmese, thinking it a bad omen, abandoned the work; but there it was, just as it was left, even portions of the scaffolding were still up! Close by it is the great bell, with an inner diameter of 16 feet.[1]

[1] "Since our occupation this bell has been raised, by public subscription, on a proper scaffolding. Steps were taken by the District Magistrate to obtain funds for raising the bell. The appeal having been generously responded to by all classes of the community, and sufficient funds having been raised, the committee appointed to superintend the work entered into a contract with the Irrawady Flotilla Company to raise the bell and re-hang it on iron pillars. The work of raising it by means of powerful jack-screws and levers was successfully accomplished in March 1896, and the massive iron columns and beams from which the bell will depend are now being cast at the Flotilla Company's works at Dalla, opposite to Nangoon. The beams and pillars have been made of a strength sufficient to support a hanging weight of 100 tons, a weight exceeding by 20 tons the estimated weight of the bell. As it has no clapper, it will perhaps be necessary to provide some mechanical contrivance to elicit sound from its huge lips." (Extract from *Wanderings in Burma*, by S. W. BIRD.)

The bell is called Mingun Bell. I never saw a large bell in Burma with a clapper. I have seen them struck with the horn of a deer—generally a sambur.—F. T. POLLOK.

One portion of the deserted pagoda is said to contain images in gold, life-size, of the past and present members of the ruling dynasty; and if so, there must be wealth enough to satisfy even the greed of a miser. The country is hilly, covered with jungle, and we could hear the cocks crowing and francolins calling all around; the people also said that hares were plentiful, but they were of no use to us, as no one was allowed to fire a gun within a radius of twenty miles of the capital. The big gun which I had seen at Umrapoora had also been taken to Mandalay, but no care had been taken of it, and it was badly honeycombed, and I would rather not be the man to fire it. We saw about fifty tusker elephants at work removing teak logs. Adjoining the walls of Umrapoora there were two enclosures, where they used to catch wild elephants, who were decoyed there by tame females. The officials told us that as many as twenty to twenty-five males had been caught there in one year. The Burmese, when going down-stream during the freshets, to save themselves the trouble of rowing, throw overboard branches of trees and attach them with ropes to the prow of the boats; these catch the full force of the stream and drag the boat along at a good rate. I adopted this idea, but constructed a large kite with mats and bamboos, and, weighting it on one side, launched it overboard. It remained upright, and dragged us along about five miles an hour. The river was pretty well at its height; the greater part of the sand-banks had disappeared, so we went down merrily without any exertion on our part, until one afternoon, when a heavy sea drove us back. We could not understand it. We took in our kite and tried the oars, but it was of no use, the waves broke over the boat, so we made for the bank, and, finding a sheltered spot, anchored. The moon rose brightly, it was full; but after a while a total eclipse took place, which we noted in our journals. About 3 a.m. the waves went down; we pulled into the stream, let down the kite, and again went on rapidly. As we passed the different pagodas, notably those of Pagan Myo, we noticed that the Thēs, or umbrellas that surmount their crest, were either down or all askew, and wondered what had caused it. Near Yay-nan-choung the wind veered round to the north and blew half a gale. So we took in the kite, hoisted the sails, and went down at a good fifteen miles an hour till dark, when we furled the sails and brought the kite again into play. No one steered; we lashed the helm amidships, and expected to be at Menloon early next morning. When we woke at daylight we could not conceive where we were, but we thought Menloon was still ahead, but hour after hour passed, and at last to our surprise not Menloon, but Meaday loomed ahead. We had gone eighty miles in twelve hours by the kite alone. As we approached Thayet Myo we saw all the pagodas a mass of ruins, and thought they had been demolished by the Executive Engineer, but we found on landing that on the day of the full moon, about two in the afternoon, an earthquake had shattered the pagodas, and caused the stream of the Irrawady to run up towards its source, which fully accounted for our progress being barred that day.

Thayet Myo is not a nice place to be stationed at. The rainfall is very trifling and the heat excessive. Cholera, too, is very prevalent. There is very poor shooting anywhere near—even snipe are scarce. In the floods there is good boating; but a huge sand-bank formed, and when I was last there the steamers had to lie fully a mile off.

Going from Thayet Myo, fifty miles west to Mendoon, very good large-game shooting can be had. Near Meaday there was very fair snipe and francolin shooting and occasionally some hares. I believe Meaday and Tongho were some years ago connected by a road.

Robberies were very frequent at Thayet Myo. Ponies were frequently abstracted and taken across the frontier. At one time a cordon of sentries with loaded muskets were placed round the station, but the Burmese, who are daring and expert robbers, used to creep through, and a night seldom passed without some one being visited and despoiled.

There is excellent sport between Prome and Rangoon in the vicinity of the railway. When I surveyed that line in 1855 I found yit (pheasants), the Burmese francolin, and jungle fowl abundant in many places. In the Irrawady district at the foot of the Yomahs, in the forests, big game abounds, and in the more open country thamine or the brow-antlered deer were plentiful. Bassein is also famous for its sport. General Fytche has entered fully into the subject in his book, and no man knew the district better than he, and he was not only an expert shot, but an indefatigable and successful sportsman. Crossing from Haingye and the lower ranges of hills to Cape Negrais I have had some capital sport.

UPPER BURMA

CHAPTER I

RANGOON TO MANDALAY: THE COUNTRY AND PEOPLE.

[W. S. THOM]

THE first portion of this work treats of Lower Burma, its people, the sport, and the ways and means by which it may be best obtained. It shall in turn be my endeavour to give to the best of my ability, although I am neither an adept with the pen nor a learned naturalist, a similar account of that portion of the country known as Upper Burma. Six out of the eleven years of my service were spent in Upper Burma, five in Lower; the "Land of Pagodas." I had therefore many opportunities of enjoying to my mind that most enjoyable of all sports, viz. "big game shooting." Most of my short leave and every available hour of my spare time were utilized in this manner. I was thus able to study and note the habits, haunts, and peculiarities of the many wild animals to be met with in the vast tracts of hill, jungle, and dales of Upper Burma. Always in the best of health and condition, and backed by a good constitution, I was enabled to endure fatigue and hardships when in pursuit of game without any very serious after effects, and could at the same time when in the clutches of malaria throw it off after an attack of a few days.

It is not my intention to dwell on statistics relating to the history, trade, products, the people, their language, religion, and customs, etc., as these subjects have partly been discussed and dealt with in the earlier part of this work by my colleague.

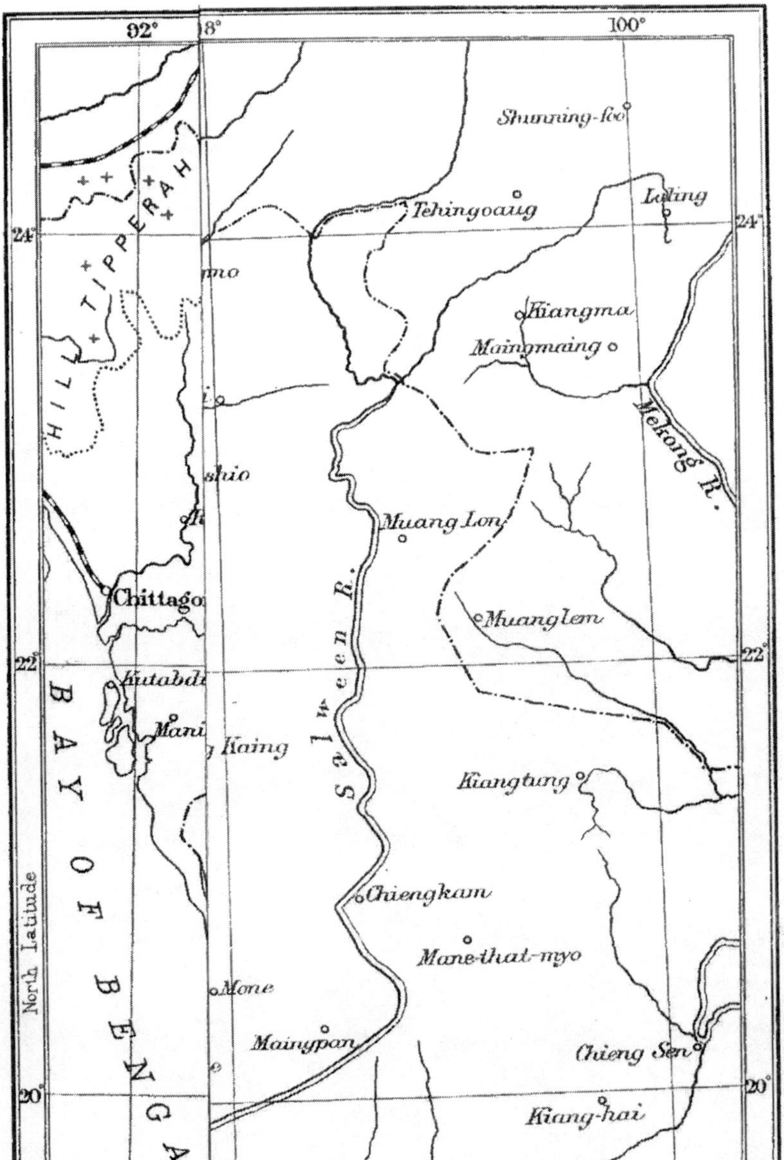

Good Sporting area

Stanford's Geogl. Estabt. London

W. S. THOM.

Mr. Geo. W. Bird, of the Burma Educational Department, has also recently in his admirable work *Wanderings in Burma* dealt with the subject at some considerable length. I shall only touch lightly on these matters as I proceed; the principal object in view being to produce a text-book on sport for those who intend visiting the country.

Rangoon may be reached from England by two direct lines of steamers, the Bibby and Patrick Henderson's. The former line do the passage in about thirty days, calling at Colombo, and are most comfortable. The latter line take sometimes from thirty to thirty-three days, and charge as passage money £30; the food and service on board are everything that can be desired. The journey by the Bibby line, only first-class saloon accommodation, is £50. Passengers have no difficulty in getting their luggage passed through by the Customs officials, who come on board all vessels entering port. Import duty is however charged, if my memory does not deceive me, on all fire-arms, at the rate of ten per cent. on the value of each weapon. Hotels under European management are to be found both in Rangoon and Mandalay. The principal in the former town are Evershed's, Sarkies, Great Eastern, and the British India.

The sportsman on his arrival in Rangoon should first of all make up his mind by what route he intends proceeding to Upper Burma, which may be reached in two ways, viz. (1) by train to Mandalay, a distance of some 386 miles, or (2) by a splendid service of fast steamers, belonging to the Irrawady Flotilla Company, plying twice a week between Rangoon and Mandalay. The journey by rail may be completed in twenty hours or less; by steamer again up the Irrawady several days are required, as the distance is greater and the steamer stops at various stations *en route*. This is, however, a most enjoyable trip, and if the sportsman is not pressed for time the latter journey is certainly to be recommended. The Irrawady Flotilla Company are in possession of as fine a fleet of river steam-boats as any now afloat. The saloon accommodations, furniture, and fittings for Europeans are superb, and last, but not least, most of their vessels are lighted by electricity, and their victualling department, in the way of food, liquor, ice, wines, aerated waters, etc., is everything that the most fastidious could desire.

Let us now suppose that the sportsman has arrived by train at Mandalay with the intention of proceeding up the country. He would first, after his arrival at the station, proceed to the dak bungalow, or rest-house, provided by Government for the use of travellers, where all his belongings would be deposited, and where for a very moderate sum per diem his wants would in every way be most comfortably attended to. The only hotel which merits special notice is the Hotel Europe. The visitor, it is presumed, before leaving the interesting city for fresh fields and pastures new higher up the river, would naturally pay a visit to the various objects of interest to be seen in this town, such as Theebaw's palace, the "Centre of the Universe" as it is called by Burmans, now converted with the various other buildings within the walled enclosure into useful abodes and pleasure resorts for the officials, civil and military, now residing in Mandalay. One portion of the palace proper serves now as the dining, reading, whist, and billiard-rooms of the Upper Burma Club. The roof and ceiling are supported by huge posts of teak, and the whole interior is covered with gold-leaf. Beautiful ornamental tanks, grottoes, rockeries, rustic bridges, and winding paths shaded by grooves of tamarind, mango, bamboo, and other flowering trees meet and entrance the eye on every side. The king's throne is simply a pedestal of wood, of shape similar to those seen in temples, "ponghyi kyaungs" or monasteries, and is about eight feet high. Some of the carved teak-wood spread over the whole area of the palace is very fine. British and native troops occupy various buildings within the enclosure, and other blocks of buildings again are utilized as offices by the Government officials of the various departments, such as Military, Medical, Forest, P.W.D., etc. The building adjoining the theatre, built by King Theebaw for the Parsi Theatrical Company, a room used by the court when witnessing these performances, is now used as the mess-room of the garrison. There are numerous other places worthy of a visit in Mandalay and its environs, such as the Kutho Daw or 729 tablets, the Queen's Kyaung or

RANGOON.

From a Photo by Watts & Skeen, Rangoon.

monastery, the residence of a Buddhist bishop, and the famous Mingûn bell; this huge mass of metal, said to be the second largest bell in the world, is situated about nine miles above Mandalay, on the right bank of the Irrawady. This great bell, weighing over 80 tons, is 12 feet high, from 6 to 12 inches in thickness of metal, and the external diameter at the lip is 16 feet 3 inches. Another very large casting, in the shape of a colossal brass image of Gaudama, may be seen at Amarapoora. This figure, one of 12 feet high in a sitting posture, with limbs in proportion, was once regarded as the palladium of Arrakan, and was brought from thence on its conquest, A.D. 1784, by the Burman monarch. Numerous pagodas, monasteries, and religious buildings may also be seen scattered about over the outer town. The so-called "incomparable pagoda" among pagodas is the most interesting.

As these are however noticed at length in every book on Burma, I may perhaps be permitted to go on to the object I more especially have in view. A short account of what may be seen and purchased in Mandalay, together with a brief outline of the character, habits, and customs of the people there, may not be amiss. Should the traveller be a connoisseur in curios and works of art, such as objects carved in teak, silver, ivory, or brass, some really very useful and pretty articles may be purchased. Silver-mounted, carved, ivory-handled Burmese "dahs" (a short fighting-sabre or sword) and daggers may be obtained to order. Some excellent lacquer-work may also be seen in almost every native or Burmese shop throughout the town, or in the bazaar. Should he desire a better acquaintance with the people and their manners and customs, he has only to stroll out through the town and pay the market, or what in Burma is called the "ze," a visit. *En route* to the "ze" or bazaar some curious studies of the extraordinary motley and variety of nationalities may also be seen in the streets. Here, slouching along, comes a band of sturdy Shans with a decided Chinese cast of features about them, wearing wide-brimmed, beautifully-woven, soft straw hats or "kamouks," a long, crooked, silver-mounted, fighting "dah she" or sword in its wooden sheath, and sling bedecked with bright tassels slung over the shoulder, and wearing the usual dark blue or white, baggy trousers, tattooed from the waist to the ankles. Again, if we look down that side street, the Chinese quarter, the prosperous, smiling, pig-tailed celestial will be seen, child-like and bland, jabbering away to his neighbour in the most voluble manner. There again, on their daily begging rounds, accompanied by their novices and scholars, go a string of Buddhist pongyis or priests, patient and contemplative, looking neither to the right nor left, but stopping in front of each house, the inmates of which, having been warned by the clear, reverberating notes of the half-moon-shaped metal gongs carried by the "kyaung thas" or scholars, are ready with their charitable doles of rice, fish, and vegetables. Then again down that street, wearing huge turbans, go a few fierce-eyed, flat-nosed, dirty, ragged-looking, wiry Kachins, with their shifty and treacherous nature depicted in their every look and action. Arrakanese with their European type of features and hirsute appendages, jolly, mild-faced, converted Karens, stolid, hard-working Maingthas, active Chins, malodorous of "khaung" or rice beer, Hindus and Mussalmen, also swell the motley throng to be met with in this wonderful town of queer tribes and primitive superstitions. In the bazaar, representatives of the above-mentioned races may be seen sitting side by side with the Burman, busily engaged in plying their trade. The panorama now presented before one, of the various bright-coloured dresses of the many different nationalities, is picturesque in the extreme, and the impression thus conveyed to a new-comer is one which will not easily be forgotten.

To one who has any knowledge of the native of India, a marked difference will at once be apparent between him and the Burman. The former, clad invariably in loose, white, flowing robes, turban and hirsute appendages, is easily identified from the latter, who is brightly attired in silks of every shade and pattern, with a face invariably as bare as it was when he first saw the light of day. In character they are quite as strongly contrasted. The Hindu, Mussalman, Corringhee or Madrassie is full of caste prejudice, deceitful, mean, and cringing; the Burman, on the other hand, is more pliable, tractable, honest,

KING THEEBAW AND HIS QUEEN.

From a Photo by Watts & Skeen, Rangoon

and sociable, without caste, more straightforward, frank, and jovial, and showing a deal of independence both in his manner of speech and dealings. His attention whilst wandering about from stall to stall might well be drawn to the bright, amiable, chatty, self-possessed, vivacious manner of their women-folk, whose freedom of action in every respect is unparalleled amongst any other Oriental nation. Their graceful and fascinating ways grow upon us more and more the longer one knows them, and they, like the men, have a great eye to dress and adornment of person, the greater part of their clothing consisting of silks made for the most part in Manchester; he or she is in a very poor way indeed who does not wear some article of silk about the person, or some such ornament as gold bangles, rings, necklaces, and earrings of various designs. They also, however, manufacture by hand-looms or shuttles their own silk, which is really a very strong wearable and good washing material. Many European ladies in Burma wear blouses made from really very pretty patterns and shades of this particularly strong and purely silk material.

The Burmese have well been called the "Irish of the East"; they are full of wit and humour, and are never at a loss for a quick repartee. They are a nation of smokers; their children as soon as they can walk are provided with cheroots quite an inch in thickness, and sometimes quite a foot in length. Often a child at the breast will take his mother's cheroot and take a puff or two. It is amusing to see little boys and girls in the streets puffing away at these torches, handling them with the same grace and ease as is shown by their elders. The men do a good deal of trade in a small huckstering way, in either stalls in the market-place, "ze," or in their own houses; the women, however, do nearly all the real hard work and attend to all the wants of the household, in fact, they do everything except till the ground, and are infinitely superior in every way to their lords. These have, unfortunately, the terrible fault of being inconceivably lazy, apathetic, unambitious, which, coupled with their absolute indifference, conceit, and independence, will eventually, more's the pity, be the means of allowing themselves in the not very distant future to be ousted and superseded in every department of commercial and industrial work by their more thrifty, hard-working, and plodding neighbours, the natives of India and Chinamen. What he will eat and drink to-morrow does not trouble him in the least so long as he has enough for to-day. Such a thing as a starving Burman, however, is unknown, as food may be had from any monastery for the asking, and wages are high; the people are besides noted for their charitable and hospitable qualities. If you enter an out-of-the-way jungle village, where no white man has perhaps ever set foot in before, you are sure to receive a pleasant reception. You may be tired, travel-stained, and disreputable-looking, with regard to dress and general appearance. You may look like a veritable tramp or loafer, in fact, as one often does in out-of-the-way parts of Upper Burma, from deputy commissioners downwards. At any rate, speaking for myself, my appearance, decked out as I have often been in a pair of baggy, dark blue, silk Shan trousers, "baungbees," a banian, a shooting-coat, and an old brown Ellwood's shikar-hat, would certainly lead any one at home, who should see me thus clad for the first time, to suppose that I had either escaped out of a lunatic asylum or was in reality a tramp. It makes no difference to the Burman; he will at once attend to your wants and that of your pony before even troubling you with any inquisitive questions as to who you are, your destination, the object of your journey, etc. Fresh cocoa-nuts, cheroots, the offer of a seat on a strip of brand-new Manchester carpet in the verandah of his house, are at once placed at your disposal. The perfect freedom of the women, as I have already remarked, and the very frank manner in which they reply to your questions and in turn put others to you, is, coupled with their seductive and winning ways, particularly attractive to an Englishman, and very different from what one would be likely to meet with from any other Oriental.

Their food consists chiefly of rice, vegetables, fresh and salt fish; a decoction of pounded fish is also consumed in a state of semi-putrefaction, after it has undergone a process which need not here be gone into, but it is considered amongst them as a *bonne bouche*, and known as "ngàpee," their national dish. His one and only ambition, so far as I have been

BURMESE FESTIVAL. (ONE OF THE PRETTIEST IN BURMA.)

able to gather, is to obtain an appointment in Government service, even though it should only be a minor appointment, such as a clerkship or a court-peon's billet on fifteen to twenty rupees per mensem. To be in possession of a gun and an unlimited supply of ammunition is also one of his dearest hopes, although the taking of life in any form is forbidden in their religion—Buddhism. The recent attack upon the Mandalay fort had no political significance whatever, although nearly all the men concerned, some ten or eleven, were either killed or executed; the conspiracy originally promulgated and led by a fanatical ex-pongyi, or priest, who thought himself bullet-proof, and who was accompanied by a few idiots similarly affected, labouring under the impression that they were going to take the palace and drive the British from Mandalay. Such an action is quite typical of Jack Burman, who is really a very inoffensive fellow, but easily beguiled into believing anything, especially when it emanates from the mouth of one of their priests, who, however, do not now appear to have the same power over the people as when King Theebaw sat on the throne. The faith of the Burman in his charms is beyond all conception. He will wear a piece of silver about the size of a sixpence perforated in two places and secured round his forehead with a piece of string, in the firm belief that by so doing he has made himself invulnerable to bullets or steel. A number of Burmans and Shans have also circular pieces of silver or metal charms inserted beneath the skin of either arm for the same purpose.

I remember very well on one occasion when out on tour through the district of Katha, putting to shame some pongyis or priests before a large gathering of villagers. A priest approached me while I was having breakfast in a "zayat" or rest-house, and said that he had heard that I could shoot, and that he wanted to see whether I could perforate with a shot from my revolver a white handkerchief hung up at thirty paces. Certain charms in his possession, he informed me emphatically, would prevent my being able to do so. This distance being just a few paces too long for straight shooting with any degree of certainty, I stipulated that it might be lessened by ten paces, adding that distance should make no difference to the efficacy of his charms. This the monks, several of them having in the meantime arrived on the scene, agreed to. I took up my stand at the required distance and succeeded, much to their disgust, in sending a hole through the centre of the handkerchief. A dissatisfied murmur from the onlookers, and the speedy disappearance of the priests into their monastery, was the result. The priests afterwards informed me that their charms had been rendered useless by the fact that the fabric was of English manufacture instead of Burmese. Taking their good and bad qualities together we conclude that the Burmese are all round to be preferred to the ordinary native of India.

As a companion in the jungle, whilst camping out under canvas with them after game as I have often done for a couple of months at a time, I have always found them most agreeable, entertaining, and adepts in the art of spinning out many a long yarn, truthful or otherwise, as to how such and such a dacoit "bo," or leader, they knew was sword or bullet-proof, or how such and such an elephant which they had come across in a certain range of hills had to ascend them backwards, owing to its tusks being too long to allow of its walking up them in the usual manner. (This yarn is current in every part of Burma visited by me.—F. T. P.) Hair-breadth escapes from tigers, ghost tales, and gruesome stories of dacoity and murder often form part of these after-dinner yarns, told "far from the madding crowd," in the open, before a roaring camp fire, with only the stars and the moon shining above us. He is a good *shikarie*, an indefatigable walker when he chooses, and an all-round inveterate gambler, and the mains of buffalo and cock-fights and boat-racing in which he revels have none of the brutalities which distinguish these sports in other countries. He is also very often, I am sorry to have to relate, addicted to the vice of smoking and eating opium, a habit which, when once it has obtained a firm hold of its victim, invariably leads him on to mental and physical destruction. Buddhism forbids the use of opium as one of the five deadly sins. There has been a good deal written for and against opium by well-meaning people, who perhaps have not had an opportunity of studying its good or evil effects upon

MANDALAY. THE QUEEN'S KYOUNG.

mankind. "A confirmed smoker may go a day or two without his smoke and only feel incapable of eating or performing his daily work, but within a week or ten days he would probably die from want of it. Yet while his supply is regular he is little affected by the indulgence if not carried to excess, and is to all intents and purposes as well able to go about his daily work as a man who does not use it. Indeed, the opium smoker can bear a much greater amount of fatigue than the man who does not smoke, while, as far as I can judge, the habit does not shorten life, unless, as already stated, the consumer be deprived of his drug." So says one writer who was capable of giving an opinion. It is only when the drug is eaten in excess, not smoked, that its baleful effects are felt. Opium has been the cause of a good deal of trouble and misery to the Burman; he will sell his all to gratify his craving in this respect. On the other hand, he is sober and abstemious in his way of life, drunkenness amongst them being almost unknown, except in a few cases in those towns adjoining the coast where education and European example have led him astray. It has been said, and not without some truth, that to some extent the taste for opium has been cultivated in early youth through its use as an anæsthetic for the painless administration of the tattooing needle. Burmans are invariably tattooed from the waist to the knee with a decoction of sesamum-seed or indigo, in a tracery of figures representing cats, bears, ogres, tigers, monkeys, nats or spirits, and mysterious squares and letters. This painful process is undergone by the "kalatha" or young man at any time between the ages of seven and fifteen. The youth, after recovering from the stupefying effects of the opium and the inflammation which continues for some time after the tattooing process is over, surreptitiously, it is said, resorts to opium in order that he may enjoy all over again the pleasant dreamy recollections experienced from his first dose. This may or may not be the case, of course. Many parents now, I believe, have the needles used upon their children without the assistance of opium.

The Chinese and Shans are also great consumers of the drug, but they have a better physique than the Burman, and neutralize to some extent its evil effects by taking it in moderation, and eating at the same time comparatively good and nutritious food. We will now suppose that the visitor or intending sportsman has had enough of Mandalay, and desires an introduction to the glorious shooting grounds of Upper Burma, where even at the present day the lordly elephant and gaur roam about unmolested, over vast tracts of hill and dale which have as yet, comparatively speaking, been untrodden by either the foot of the globe-trotter, or the relentless searcher of trophies and record heads.

BURMESE BOAT-RACE.

From a Photo by Watts & Skeen, Rangoon.

CHAPTER II

THE SPORTSMAN'S OUTFIT, BATTERY, SERVANTS

THE first matter to be taken in hand by a sportsman after his arrival in Mandalay is to look about him for a good servant, cook, interpreter, and table-servant combined in one, if he wishes to economize. Madrassie servants who have already served in the out-of-the-way hilly stations of Upper Burma, where they have become acclimatized, and who talk English and Burmese fluently, are the most useful men to accompany one on a shooting expedition of this sort, but as a rule these men are great rascals and much too fond of drink. They may also be picked up in Rangoon, and it would perhaps be as well to engage one there if possible, as he would then look after his master's property and wants *en route* to Mandalay. Messrs. A. Scott and Co., Merchants, Bankers, and Agents, Merchant Street, Rangoon, would be able to assist the sportsman in many ways, such as in getting together not only the necessary servants and kit which may be required, but also stores, liquor, ammunition, and, in fact, almost any other thing that may be wanted for making one comfortable during a prolonged stay in the jungle. Should the sportsman have a stock of liquor with him, such as whisky, beer, etc., he should keep these things if possible under lock and key—letter-padlocks are the best—as "Ramsawmy" is particularly addicted to helping himself freely from his master's bottle whenever an occasion offers. Should money be a secondary consideration, I would suggest the sportsman engaging a Burmese "lugale" or table-boy, who will wash clothes, clean boots and guns—the last should always in my opinion, however, be taken in hand by the sportsman himself—and do general all-round work; the labours of the cook would then be considerably lightened. It is always best, in fact, to have at least two servants with one, as should the cook fall ill, as he very often does out in camp, from jungle fever, dysentery, or other causes, the Burman can always be utilized as cook. Burmans do not consider it pilfering helping themselves to tea, sugar, or tobacco, and it is as well not to be too strict in such matters. The "lugale" would also act as a set-off to the native boy, who would then have to be on his p's and q's, as each other's misdeeds and pilferings would then be promptly reported to the master. English-speaking Burmese boys are, however, difficult to obtain, and when they are to be engaged they are not always to be depended upon, as they are so independent and touchy about the least thing. Never strike a Burman servant for a small matter, it is no punishment, as he is inclined to be as hasty as yourself, and would leave you without the slightest warning or hesitation, and sometimes without even claiming the pay that might be due to him. From Rs.25 to Rs.30 per mensem, including food, would be the maximum salary for the best English-speaking cooks or table-servants obtainable in either Rangoon or Mandalay. Burman servants who do not speak English could be engaged for Rs.20 per mensem. The name and address of any servant engaged should invariably be noted in case of desertion, which however rarely happens. The head butler in the dak bungalow or rest-house in Mandalay, should the visitor be staying there, or any other European whom he may know or happen to have letters of introduction to, should be able to put him in the way of at once obtaining without difficulty servants, stores, and liquor, or any other thing that may be required. Stores, liquor, etc. may be purchased in Mandalay at almost the same prices as in Rangoon.

The sportsman's attention should next be directed to his camp equipment, kit, battery, etc. It is better to be comfortably provided with everything if you wish to enjoy sport, but to do so you must live well. Certain articles herein mentioned may be left out by less fastidious sportsmen who do not mind roughing it to a certain extent. But I am at one with the late Mr. Sanderson, who says, in his excellent work, *Thirteen Years amongst the Wild Beasts of India*: "The great principle to be borne in mind in making arrangements for jungle life is, that the sportsman should make himself and followers as comfortable as possible. Any amount of hard work may be done by all during the day if they have dry clothes and a comfortable dinner and bed at the end of it. Roughing it when there is no necessity, and there seldom is nowadays in India or Burma, is a mistake which only the inexperienced fall into. There is rarely any reason why a sportsman should sleep without sheets, drink out of a tin-pot, or dine off a box, though these are merely discomforts. In matters actually affecting the health of a party in jungle localities it is suicidal not to know what are the precautions to be observed or to neglect them." Many people at home seem to be under the impression that Burma is a fever-stricken, unhealthy tract of swampy country, inhabited by an uncivilized people, and that Europeans in stations there are deprived of many comforts and enjoyments of home life, by the want of which existence is rendered unbearable. Let me inform the reader, on the authority of one who has just returned to this country, for the first time after an absence of eleven years, as fit if not fitter than when he left it, that such is far from being the case. Europeans have certainly to take greater care of themselves in many respects, especially with regard to what they eat and drink; more care, I suppose, than has to be exercised at home. Plenty of outdoor exercise and general moderation in everything, especially with regard to whisky, is the key to good health in the East, but I suppose the same maxim is also applicable at home. I attribute all my present health to, in the first place, a good constitution, and next to the greater amount of outdoor exercise I went in for there, and at the same time total abstinence as regards spirits. The two enemies of the European in Burma are the water when drunk unboiled or unfiltered, especially out of standing pools in the jungle, and ordinary malaria or fever, brought on for the most part by one's own carelessness, by either catching a chill, drinking bad water, or sleeping in the open when roughing it out shooting. I have had one or two sharp attacks of jungle fever off and on at different times. These attacks were, I may say, the results of my own indiscretion in sleeping on damp ground whilst in the pursuit of big game. Thanks, however, to a good constitution I pulled through and recovered in four or five days.

The following is a list in detail of articles under different heads requisite for a sporting expedition into Burma :—

Wearing Apparel.

Three shooting-suits made of some strong untearable material such as gabardine, khaki-cord, or shooting-cloth ; the first named may be purchased from Messrs. Burberrys, 30 Haymarket, London. The knicker-bockers should be loose and baggy at the knees.

Three pairs of gaiters to match suit ; these should not be made of leather unless it is very soft like sambur skin, as the noise made against hard leather gaiters by leaves and branches while you are stalking game through bush and undergrowth is very distinct. A light green-coloured shooting-cloth during the rainy season when everything is green, or a dirty brown for the hot weather, should be worn. Personally, I preferred the following kit: an ordinary pair of strong, dark blue cotton Chinese or so-called Shan "baungbees" or bags, pulled up short till the ends are hanging a couple of inches below the knee to prevent tripping when running or jumping obstacles, and hitched up round the waist by a spring or elastic or leather belt. A strong pair of box-cloth or dark-coloured canvas gaiters worn from the knees to the ankles over the boot. This, with a woollen banian, cholera-belt, a strong dark or light green-coloured, untearable shooting-jacket, together with a pair of light strong boots with canvas or leather uppers, and a brown Ellwood's shikar-hat, usually comprised the rest of my shooting attire—the coolest, most convenient, and least cumbrous in every way. These "baungbees" or trousers, which, by the way, may be had in silk as well as cotton, may be purchased from any Chinese, Shan, or native shop, for about Rs.10 or Rs.12. I am not prepared to recommend any new-comer to try this particular article of wearing apparel, first, because it would take him some time to get accustomed to them, and secondly, because the colour comes out and they are expensive.

12 well-shrunk flannel shirts.

12 thin woollen banians.

3 woollen cholera or stomach-belts.

3 dozen strong pairs of soft, thin woollen socks with double-spliced heels and toes.

2 dozen pairs of stout ditto.

6 flannel sleeping suits.

3 dozen handkerchiefs.

1 light ulster and a dressing-gown.

2 pairs of strong braces. These are best got from Thersher and Glenny, who though dear in their prices supply first-rate articles.

2 belts, leather, spring, or elastic.

6 bath towels.

6 small towels.

3 small table-cloths.

6 napkins.

2 pairs bathing-drawers.

6 sheets.

6 common towels for servants' use.

2 or 3 balls of twine.

A canvas housewife, needles, thread, scissors, sponge, soap, nail, tooth, and hair brushes, comb, tooth-paste, and other useful articles you may require.

A light mattress and 2 pillows to fit trestle-cot.

2 pairs of blankets.

1 folding-glass to hang up or stand.

3 pairs of good shooting-boots with light, strong canvas or leather uppers.

1 pair of shooting ammunition boots with short nails on the sole and high uppers for hill work.

3 pairs of tennis shoes with rubber soles for stalking; these should be light and pliable as well as strong and serviceable, as one has very often to walk some distance over very rough stony ground. My plan was always to change into my stalking shoes when my trackers, who are invariably shoeless, had warned me that the quarry was not far off. Very often,

however, one has a false alarm, and the sportsman finds that instead of having to walk only a few hundred yards, he has to cover a mile or two of country before coming up with the animal being tracked up, which may be grazing and walking along steadily ahead of him. This happens over and over again, and the sportsman is compelled by the signs before him, such as warm droppings, mucus from the animal's mouth, freshly-cropped grass, etc., to prepare for a silent stalk on catching sight of the animal, which may now happen at any moment.

1 dozen pairs of cheap canvas hempsoled shoes should also be taken for your servants, gun-bearers, and trackers, who can always be made to take them off when game is near. These may be bought in Rangoon for Rs.2/4 per pair, or about two shillings and eightpence.

2 waterproof capes for your own use, made, if possible, of stout weather-proof gabardine.

6 cheap syces' waterproof capes for your men. These may be purchased in Rangoon or Mandalay for Rs.4 or Rs.5 each.

4 double-texture waterproof sheets, 7 × 7.

6 common, cheap, stout, black cotton umbrellas costing about Rs.2 each. Do not laugh, reader! these are very useful should you be doing any shooting in the rainy seasons. Each man to carry his own waterproof and umbrella. I have always found an umbrella in the jungle very useful indeed, and have often saved my cartridges, guns, breakfast hampers, etc. from many a drenching when a waterproof was utterly useless.

The only portion of his person that a Burman cares about keeping dry is his precious head of hair, of which he is very proud, and the wetting of which disgusts him thoroughly, as it necessitates his uncoiling, re-combing, drying, and oiling it again. Burmans are besides addicted to catching fever or cold by getting the head wet.

2 mosquito-nets, one being made of very fine muslin to prevent the entry of sand-flies.

2 soft-peaked felt caps. These come in very handy during the evenings or early morning, when the hat or helmet may be discarded, or when game is being walked up in cover where the foliage is sufficiently dense overhead to allow of a cap

being worn nearly all day. I have often worn a small cap from sunrise to sunset on cloudy days during the rains; it is not, however, always safe to do so; besides, I was to a certain extent acclimatized. The sportsman should, however, be able to judge for himself whether the sun, although behind the clouds, affects his head or not. It is well known that on a very hot sultry day, when there is not even the faintest breath of air, the sportsman will feel great relief and minimize the danger of catching sun-stroke or heat-apoplexy if he at intervals lifts up his hat above his head 5 or 6 inches so that it may be kept cool. A few plantain or other leaves stuffed into the top of an Ellwood's shikar-hat are also of great assistance towards warding off the sun's rays. These hats should all be ventilated.

2 pairs of riding-breeches made of khaki-cord or any other material suitable for the purpose should also be brought, as the sportsman, to travel comfortably from camp to camp, will require a pony. The latter may be hired, borrowed, or bought almost anywhere in Upper Burma. It would almost be better, however, to purchase a mount in Mandalay, as there might afterwards be some difficulty in procuring an animal, and this would cause a delay. A serviceable Burman pony may be bought in Rangoon or Mandalay for from Rs.150 to Rs.200. Suitable riding-kit and, in fact, any other clothes required for a prolonged stay in Burma may be obtained at short notice in Rangoon, there being several very good tailors there, viz. Messrs. MacFie and Messrs. Harman and Co.

Cooking Utensils, Crockery, etc.

Enamel cooking pots, plates, tumblers, and cutlery of all kinds may be purchased in either Rangoon or Mandalay for a few rupees in any European or native firm. Should money be a secondary consideration, aluminium ware would be more useful, as being not only lighter and less bulky than the iron enamel ware, but because it is easily kept clean. Saucepans and pots should fit one inside the other and should also have detachable handles; a knife with corkscrew and tin-opener combined, together with a spare corkscrew and tin-opener, should also be taken.

6 wood-choppers or Burmese "dahmas"; these are found very useful for breaking up the various animals, cutting down jungle, chopping firewood, and a hundred other purposes.

A pestle-and-mortar for the cook.

A couple of medium-sized iron, copper, or brass cooking pots for servants' and hunters' use.

Carving-knife, fork, and sharpener.

12 ordinary soft metal butchers' or other knives for skinning and cutting up animals shot. Two or three stones for sharpening same.

12 leather chaguls or water-bottles for yourself, trackers, and gun-bearers, and for camp use. I have never seen these in either Rangoon or Mandalay, and doubt very much whether they are to be bought there. Messrs. Creet Bros., Cawnpore, India, supply them, and a letter to them from England with instructions to forward them on to Scott and Co., Rangoon, or any other agent, who should in turn be directed to pay the bill and take delivery pending the arrival of the sportsman, would facilitate matters.

1 sandstone bottle-filter and 2 pocket-filters.

1 zinc pail or bucket.

1 meat saw.

Stores.

Branson's extract of coffee, tea, cocoa, sugar (lump and ordinary), tinned soups, ox tongues, sausages, bacon, Crosse and Blackwell's square tins, yellow; order the very thin ones only. Swiss condensed milk, sweetened or unsweetened, tinned fruits, jam, butter (Esbensen's Danish), ghee or clarified butter for cooking purposes, salt, pepper, mustard (Crosse and Blackwell's, Durham), dried prawns, if you can get them, chutney, pickle, flour, onions, potatoes. "Bovril" or Brand's Essence of Beef should also be taken, as a stand-by in case of illness when living on slops is imperative. Curry powder and paste (Barries' Madras is the best) and the ingredients which go to make it up. The following should also be included for your servants and followers:—chillies, "ngàpee," rice, salt, dried fish, pumpkins, red and white ("buthees and shwépyaungthees"). The rice, "ngàpee," salt fish, and egetables being the staple food of the Burman, the quantity taken out should be sufficient to last throughout the journey.

Matches, toilet-paper, a case of candles containing twenty-five packets, two candlesticks with spare globes; the pattern of the former should, if possible, be in two pieces to allow of its being fixed up on a peg or nail driven into the tent-pole. Oil lamps are a nuisance, as everything in time, one's food included, invariably becomes impregnated with the taste of the oil, kerosene, which does not by any means act as an appetizer. Should lamps however be taken, a couple of Hinks' best hurricane hand-lamps are the least troublesome, most serviceable, and cheapest.

All the above may be purchased either at Mandalay or in any of the cargo or bazaar-boats plying up and down the river, to which reference has already been made. A good supply of pounded saltpetre and alum for the curing of skins and heads of the various animals shot should also be included.

Tents, Camp-tables, Chairs, etc.

Second-hand or even new tents, single and double, may be picked up in Rangoon or Mandalay for Rs.50 or Rs.60. Should the sportsman, however, bring one out with him, I would recommend him getting a light, strong, waterproof V-shaped tent 10 × 8. The best material is green Willesden waterproof canvas. One end of the tent should be closed. The open end should have two flaps fitted with eyelet-holes, so that it can be laced up at night if necessary. The poles, which should, if possible, be of bamboo, should be pointed with rings in them so that they can be tied together when packed. All joints of the poles should be fitted like those of a fishing-rod, metal to metal, otherwise in wet weather, when the wood swells, it is difficult to get them apart. Messrs. Benjamin Edgington, 2 Duke Street, London Bridge, S.E., make these tents. They may also be had at the Military Equipment Stores, 7 Waterloo Place, Pall Mall. A very good pattern of a trestle-cot, an improvement of my colleague, Col. Pollok, may also be obtained at the former place. The double Cabul tents, usually seen in India and Burma, are not to be recommended, as I have always found that they get too heavy when saturated with rain, and were not only easily torn but rotted very soon from damp and mildew. A second and smaller tent should, if possible, be brought, for not only the comfortable housing of your servants in damp weather, but the stowing away of various articles liable to be destroyed by the rain, which often overtakes one without the slightest warning. If there are villages where you can put up, tents are scarcely required, as there are zayats, or a Burman will give up his house for a very slight present.

The success of the whole expedition, in fact, depends on the health and comfort of your servants and hunters. A dozen pockets of various depths and sizes should be sewn on all round inside the walls of the tent, as they are very handy as receptacles for all sorts of things—brushes, comb, sponge, binoculars, novels, razor, strop, note-books, etc. Loops for attaching various articles to the walls and keeping guns in an upright position against the sides of the tent should also be added. Four loops fixed up inside the roof of the tent in such a way as to allow of a mosquito-net being rigged up over the cot are also useful when poles are not used. Four double-texture waterproof sheets 8 × 8 with eyelets; a long arm camp folding-chair with a table fitting in at the back, which may be used not only for writing on but for dining purposes as well. These are the most useful chairs that were ever made, originally invented, I believe, many years ago in Maulmain by an officer in Government service now holding a prominent position in Rangoon. These chairs may be purchased in the workshop of the Rangoon or Maulmain Jails for Rs.12 or Rs.14.

A small folding camp-table and stool would also be useful.

A zinc bath tub or a block-tin metal box shaped like a tub, made by Jones and Co., with a cane wicker framework basket fitted inside, which serves also as a trunk for holding clothes, should also be taken. The removal of the lid and the wicker-basket which fits inside the box, together with all it contains, converts it into an ordinary tub. Should mule transport be used, however, a tub could not be taken. For my own part, I have always found two large-sized strong zinc pails or buckets, one for hot water and the other for cold, quite sufficient for all purposes. A good bath sponge is also a very necessary adjunct.

Six mule trunks, made of strong cane with a waterproof covering of tarred canvas, are also very useful for packing stores, clothes, cartridges, etc., being perfectly watertight. These trunks, which pack on to mules very easily, may be purchased either at the Rangoon or Mandalay Jails for about Rs.16 or Rs.20 each.

A good alarm-clock and pocket-compass; the latter will not be required much, as a Burman hunter never loses his bearing as long as he can see the sun or stars; at any rate, such has been my experience of them.

A dozen empty sacks, which, when stuffed with grass, are used as mattresses for the men to lie upon, are also useful.

Medicines, etc.

The following medicines and other articles will be found invaluable.

Quinine in powder form for your servants, hunters, and followers. Five-grain gelatine-covered quinine capsules (McKessin and Robins) for your own use. A bottle or two of each of the following should also be added—brandy, chlorodyne, raw carbolic acid, for use when diluted with water for washing wounds or sores, antipyrine or phenacatine, Cascara Ṣagrada capsules, citrate of magnesia, a box or two of Cockle's or any other pills you may fancy, blue or otherwise. Castor oil or black draught for your followers. A pot or two of vaseline for blistered feet, a bottle of Rubini's Liquid Camphor, an india-rubber hot-water bag. Do not laugh, reader, at the variety and length of the above list; every article is useful and likely to be required. You may say to yourself: "I have never had a day's illness in my life, what is the use of taking out all this trash?" Allow me to inform you that it is best to be on the safe side, one never can tell what may happen—I speak from experience. Six pints of champagne might also be added to the above list as a powerful stimulant and pick-me-up, should you be unfortunate enough to be laid low with an attack of malarial fever.

Liquor.

Light Pilsener or Lager beer, or any other liquor you may wish to take out with you, such as whisky, brandy, Beaune claret, Vermouth, etc. I would suggest, however, that the less liquor taken the better, as no man can do a real good day's work on foot after big game such as gaur or elephant with a hamper in his immediate rear consisting of a bottle of whisky and half-a-dozen soda. A peg at lunch, and one perhaps during dinner at 8 p.m., is quite enough for any man who wishes to keep himself in condition in a tropical clime like Burma. More men are invalided home from the East from the results of over-feeding and too many whiskies and sodas, hanky pankies, cock-tails, and other mixtures, than from any cther cause. A few bottles of rum, gin, whisky, or brandy should be taken for your hunters, who should have an occasional dram after sunset round the camp fire after a successful day. A Burman "mokso," or hunter, loves his "peg" after a hard day's tracking, but he invariably prefers it neat, without either water or soda.

Saddlery.

A good panel or colonial hunting-saddle with numerous "dees" fixed on all round for saddle-bags should be brought out from home. Saddle-bags should be made to buckle on with straps, and lie flat, attached to the "dees" on either side of the saddle. A thick felt "numdah" or saddle-cloth is also a necessary adjunct, although many people do not use any with a panel-saddle. A strong leather head-stall. Two bridles with chain snaffle; the bit to fasten on to the head-stall at either side of the mouth with two small straps, so that the head-stall may remain on the pony's head after the reins with the bit have been removed.

Two blue spare girths, spare rope, a blanket for pony, curry-comb, brushes, and a grass-cutter's sickle.

A supply of paddy or unhusked rice should be taken out into camp for your pony.

Native blankets for your servants and followers.

Rifles, Cartridges, Camera, and Binoculars.

It will be unnecessary for me to enter into details on this subject, as numerous books on Indian and African sport with excellent advice have been written. A few hints, however, for the benefit of those who have not read the books I refer to may not be amiss. The following is my ideal battery, and for sport in Burma it is in my opinion most suitable.

(1) A double hammerless 8-bore "Paradox," by Messrs. Holland and Holland, burning 8 to 10 drams of powder, top lever action, for use upon big game, such as elephant, rhinoceros, gaur, tsine, or wild cattle.

(2) A double hammerless 12-bore "Paradox," burning 4 drams, for snap-shots and while driving for thin-skinned animals, such as tiger, leopard, bear, sambur, etc.

(3) A double hammerless ·256 Mannlicher for hill shooting and long shots, or double hammerless ·303.

(4) A double hammerless 12-bore shot-gun.

The low trajectory, accuracy, absence of smoke, recoil, and great penetration of the Mannlicher is something marvellous. A small bore like the ·256 or ·303 is all very well when picked shots are obtained in fairly open ground, such as tree or bamboo forest, where the sportsman has been able to approach in an easy, cool, collected manner to within say 15 or 20 yards of an animal. He is then enabled to place his bullet in a fatal spot. The advantage of an immediate retreat behind a tree or bamboo clump in case of failure or a charge is also available. It would be a very different matter, on the other hand, should he, after a hard climb up a steep ridge of say a mile or so through a patch of low dwarf bamboos or "kaing" grass, suddenly find himself face to face with either a solitary bull elephant, gaur, or wild bull. The ·256 or ·303 would be of little use to him in the breathless trembling condition he would then be in. It is in a case of this sort that the heavy rifle, such as an 8-bore "Paradox," acts as a stopper.

One need not necessarily burn straight powder, as the shock received anywhere by an animal of a 4 or 2 ounce ball driven by 10 or 12 drams of powder, would either floor or, at any rate, astonish an animal and induce it to change the direction of its charge, whereas the effects of the small-bore bullet, owing to the minuteness of the wound and the consequent absence of shock, is not felt soon enough to prevent a charge, unless of course, as I have already said, the animal has been struck in a vital spot. An 8 or 4-bore is therefore an indispensable adjunct to the battery of every sportsman who intends shooting big game in Burma on foot, as animals such as gaur, elephants, rhino, and tsine have very often to be followed up into thickets, especially in the case of old solitary bulls, a charge from which, if not met by a good knock-down blow, is very often made good to the detriment and danger of the sportsman. A heavy rifle need not be carried by the sportsman till he is about to use it upon an animal (I think the sportsman should never be without a weapon ready for use—F. T. P.)—one's gun-bearers do all that. And as for kicking, heavy weapons are built in proportion to the charge used, and in the heat of the moment one really never feels that the rifle has gone off at all. I often fired, within the space of five minutes, fifteen or twenty shots from an 8-bore, burning 10 drams of powder, and never felt any recoil. Should the sportsman, however, require anti-recoil pads, indiarubber air-cushions for the butt and cheek are made and fixed permanently on to the rifle by Messrs. J. and W. Tolley, Conduit Street, London, at a small cost. Should the sportsman already have a battery of hammer rifles, he should see that all safety-catches be done away with, as they are a nuisance and quite unnecessary. See that all your rifles for large and dangerous game are double; the danger of a misfire is a fatal objection to single-barrelled weapons. Rifle-cases should be well lined with at least a quarter of an inch of felt, and each case should have a strong waterproof canvas cover to keep the damp out and prevent it from being knocked about.

See that your rifles fit tightly into their cases, as they get shaken about a good deal in transit on the backs of mules or in carts. Spare back and fore-sights for each rifle should also be taken. Slings for rifles are unnecessary, as the belts and (swivels are not necessary, there are loops to any good sling—one goes on to the small grasp end of the stock, and the other over the barrel—but these cannot be used when firing at game, they are only handy to sling a weapon across one's back after the day's shooting is over) swivels not only rattle about and alarm game, but invariably catch on every projection, and are a nuisance to yourself in every way. A Burman does not object to carrying your rifles without a sling, and I have never yet had one of my rifles dropped or damaged through any carelessness on the part of my gun-bearers and hunters. With regard to breech actions, the Westley-Richards breech and top-snap action (said to be the best sporting action in the world) should, if possible, be used. There are several very good makers of rifles and really very little to choose between any of them.[1] It is all a matter of money, and if that is a secondary consideration you can always obtain a good rifle. Each maker has, of course, his own speciality or patent with regard to breech, top-snap action, ejecting and single-trigger mechanism, rifling of barrels, etc. Metford ·461 double rifles by Geo. Gibbs of Bristol are also very highly spoken of by Mr. F. V. Kirby, author of *In Haunts of Wild Game*, who has done great execution with this rifle amongst the pachyderms of Africa, killing elephant and rhinoceros with both the head and body shots. Messrs. Holland and Holland are the well-known makers of Colonel Fossberry's patent, the "Paradox" (this is also made by Westley-Richards); a double hammerless ·303 Lee-Enfield is also a useful weapon for deer, and all thin-skinned animals. For the "Paradox," conical, steel-pointed, hardened lead bullets, conical, steel-core bullets coated with lead, and solid, hardened, conical lead bullets are used.

For the Mannlicher, soft-nosed, nickel-coated, copper-coated, and slit-up bullets are used. The cartridges made abroad for this weapon—in Austria, I believe—are said to be superior to those of English manufacture. The ·303 bullets are similar to

[1] I got my own rifles recently from Messrs. Jas. Dickson and Sons, Prince's Street, Edinburgh, and they turned them out to my entire satisfaction.

those mentioned above for the Mannlicher. Two cartridges may be used for Gibbs ·461 Metford rifles, one taking a charge of 90 grams powder and 570 grams bullet, hollow and copper-sheathed projectiles, and the other 90 grams powder and 360 grams bullet, hollow. All cartridges should be hermetically sealed in tins of twenty-five each to protect them from the climate and damp; they are then always fresh and give better results than if they had been lying in a cartridge magazine exposed to the air day after day. Each tin should state on the outside the gauge of the cartridge, bullet charge, etc. If you have paper-cases (get Eley's brass shells, they are dear, but never or scarcely ever fail) for your double 8 and 12 Paradox's, a cartridge-extractor for each should be taken for use, should a shell expand and remain in the chamber. Smokeless powder in preference to black should not be used for any rifle larger (for all rifles if possible) than a ·450-bore or ·500 at most. Many gun-makers will not recommend the use of nitro powders for even small bores, as the pressure is so great as to allow of an accident happening to the breech at any time. Smokeless powder should never be used out of any rifle not originally built for the purpose, unless the maker has first been consulted as to the feasibility of doing so. All rifles should, if possible, be hammerless. There is no reason why big bores should not be hammerless any more than small bores. Many men are, however, under the impression that big bores should not be hammerless, because the second hammer is apt to go off by the jar or recoil occasioned by firing the right barrel. This is altogether an erroneous idea, and, if such ever happens, it is entirely the fault of the weapon and the firm who made it. (I perfectly agree.) Rifle-sights, both fore and back, should be screwed down to the rib of the rifle, as sights that are let in from the side or front without screws are apt to slip or be jerked out of their places when, with head down, you are engaged in boring your way through jungle in hot haste after a wounded or other animal. Strong waterproof covers for each weapon should also be taken; white enamel night-sights to fold down flush with the rib should be fitted on to your 8 and 12-bore "Paradox," as many opportunities occur of sitting up at night over a "kill" for a tiger or leopard, or in an elevated Burman's paddy "Hté" or hut adjoining the rice-fields for elephants (luminous paint is the best thing to put on to one's fore-sight even if it is only a make-shift, nothing else answers thoroughly; if you can catch a fire-fly it is the best thing for a few hours, but the insect soon dies and then the light goes out). Gaur, tsine, leopard, bear, sambur, etc. may also be shot in the same way over a water-hole or salt-lick, but this sort of sport is to be deprecated except in the case of the three first-named animals. Several bottles of Rangoon oil and a quantity of cotton "waste" or tow, such as is used by engineers in steamers, should also be taken out for gun-cleaning purposes. A good camera and a light pair of Aitchison's best collapsible aluminium binoculars should also form part of the equipment. A light rope-ladder, about 25 feet in length, with iron hooks at one end for hitching on to branches of trees, would be very useful to enable the *shikaries* to get a view of the surrounding country whenever it is desirable. If this is not available, a light bamboo ladder will do, or better still one of the ladders made for use for getting into and off howdahs, procurable in Calcutta and Bombay.

CHAPTER III

MANDALAY TO THE RUBY MINES

Large and small game to be found there—Best time to find it—Burmese hunters, trackers, transport available—Hints on tracking game.

LET us then suppose that all arrangements have been made for a journey up the river, and that the sportsman has together with all his belongings arrived on board the steamer. Two services of paddle-boats leaving Mandalay for Bhamo are available, viz. the mail or express and cargo boats. The former leave Mandalay every Monday and arrive at Bhamo on Thursday. The latter leave Mandalay every Thursday and arrive at Bhamo on the following Tuesday. It is an amusing sight to watch from the river bank, as the cargo boat arrives alongside with its two huge flats or barges on either side, the busy motley crowd, consisting of nearly every nationality, Burmese, Shan, Karen, Chinese, Jew, natives of India, Eurasian, and an occasional European, who are all ready to rush on board the moment she has been made fast, some for the purpose of buying stores for the forthcoming week, and others again as passengers. For fifteen minutes at every halting-place the vendors of the numerous shops or stalls on board do a roaring trade with the villagers. Pins, needles, pick-axes, and spades, rice, fruit, vegetables, fish and stores, tinned or otherwise, silk and cotton goods, lamp oil, and, in fact, everything, from a sack of potatoes to a box of Pears' soap or Beecham's pills, may be obtained on board these steamers. How anxiously the advent of these boats is looked forward to by European officers living in small stations along the river bank and inland who have run out of stores, and who are expecting their weekly supply of aerated waters, liquors, ice, and other luxuries ordered from European, Chinese, or Jewish firms in

THE ANGLE ROCK, UPPER IRRAWADY.

From a Photo by Watts & Skeen, Rangoon.

Rangoon or Mandalay. A loud blast or two from the whistle, a few revolutions of the paddle, and we are in mid-stream. It is wonderful with what dexterity and skill these huge river steamers are manœuvred and made to answer their helm by the skippers in command, most of whom are, by the way, Scotchmen, who have very often, as I have personally witnessed, found themselves in very tight places. The greatest caution is requisite in turning sharp corners, avoiding sand-banks, and the many large unwieldy Burmese "paddy" or rice junks, and huge teak or bamboo rafts which come swinging along with the wind and current regardless of all rules of the road. The steamer after leaving the wharf at 8 a.m. proceeds on its way up-stream, passing numerous islands and sand-banks. The hills which may be seen on approaching Mingûn to the west of the river are the Sagaing hills. A huge pagoda-like-looking building composed of bricks, with the massive Mingûn bell alongside it, a description of which has already been given, may now be seen. On theright bank three miles above Singu, Kyauk-Myaung, in the Shwebo district, is next reached after a run of twenty-four hours, and *en route* are passed several large islands. This village is situated on the sloping banks of the river. Singu is the head-quarters of the northern subdivision of the Mandalay district.

Ten miles further on, on the right bank, we come to Kabwet, the head-quarters of the Burma Coal Mining Co. The coal found here is said to be of good quality. The third defile is here reached, the river contracting considerably for some miles, and the hills, which are covered with luxuriant vegetation, rising up boldly from the banks on either side. Towards evening the village of Thabeitkyin, prettily situated on the rising banks of the river, is reached. This place is the quay or river port for the Ruby Mines district, the head-quarters of which is Mogok, situated some sixty-one miles inland from the river bank at an elevation of about 3000 feet above sea level. A good metal cart road at great yearly expense is maintained between this town and the Irrawady. Five years of my service were spent in this district, and it was here that some four or five months of my short leave were spent, in the pleasurable excitement of big-game shooting. I may also be permitted to say that I was the first European who laid himself out to tap in earnest the big-game tracts of this glorious district. I would therefore ask the would-be sportsman to leave the steamer here and accompany me into the wilds. It was thought at one time that no big-game shooting worth having was to be obtained in Upper Burma, and that to get at what there was necessitated a great expenditure of time, money, and labour. Such is certainly far from being the case, and the men who first circulated this announcement were, I presume, invariably those who had had no practical experience of this particular kind of sport, and who were unacquainted with the language of the people, their customs, and habits, a knowledge of which is an indispensable factor in securing successful sport. Some of the best big-game shooting in the world, with the least possible trouble and expenditure so far as transport, food supplies, comfort, guides, and trackers are concerned, may be had in Upper Burma, if the sportsman will only go about it in the right way. Inland, a few miles from Tagaung, a subdivision of the Ruby Mines district, situated on the left bank of the river a little more than a day's journey by mail steamer from Mandalay, a distance of some seventy-seven miles, and only about forty-five miles above Thabeitkyin, some of the finest big-game shooting in Upper Burma may be had. Some eighteen months of my service were spent in this subdivision, and I was, I may say, the first police-officer—none of my predecessors apparently being sportsmen—to indent on the vast herds of gaur, elephant, wild cattle, and other animals which roamed about the jungle and hills to within, I might almost say, a mile or so of my very doors. I have often on a bright moonlight night, when all was still and silent, save perhaps the occasional splash, splash of a paddy-boat's oars, the faint wailing of a child, or the yelp of a pariah pup from the village, heard, while seated in my verandah in a long arm-chair, and under the soothing influence of a cigar, the dull rumblings and mutterings of elephants as they wandered about only a few hundred yards off, amongst the tall dense "kaing" or elephant grass which skirts the river's banks often for miles along its course. The verandah of my house commanded a lovely view of the river, both up and down-stream for miles, and on a clear night its waters rolled past to within 20 yards of my steps, with a shimmer and a sheen, beautiful, and far surpassing my powers of description. Across the river again, whilst I am leaning on the rail of my verandah in a meditative mood, with my eyes fixed on the low, rugged, dark range of scantily wooded hills which skirt the river within the jurisdiction of the Shwebo district, the sharp distinct bark of the "ghee" or barking deer, and the startled bell of the sambur or rusa deer as he starts away from the near proximity of the dreaded midnight prowler, who spares neither man nor beast, may also be heard floating across the river. The rasping "waugh, waugh" of the prowling leopard as he stalks forth to find his midnight meal is also wafted across through the stillness of the night. All these sounds, reader, Nature's music, are greedily drunk in by all of the same craft as myself. Glorious bags of snipe and shooting of all kinds may also be had at nearly all the stations where the steamer stops *en route*. There are numerous inland lakes, off the river a short distance, caused for the most part by an overflow of the river's banks during the rainy season, or an old diverted course of the river, where geese, duck, and teal abound in amazing numbers; snipe are also very plentiful along the banks and in the surrounding paddy fields. I have often, without exaggeration, seen hundreds of these birds, when out shooting on one of these lakes, and have never come away without having got a mixed bag of at least twenty to thirty brace. One of the lakes or sheets of water I refer to is situated about thirty miles above Tagaung, and within a mile of a village named Kyetta-gaung, which is accessible to steamers, being situated on the left bank of the river. The best time for duck, geese, teal, etc. in Upper Burma is from November to January. The snipe season begins in September and continues till December or January. The following numerous varieties of feathered game abound in nearly every district of both Upper and Lower Burma. Green and imperial pigeons, several varieties of doves, peacocks, and pheasant, jungle fowl, partridges two or three varieties, quail, plover, woodcock, snipe, whistling and cotton teal, godwit, curlew, coolen, sarus, duck, and geese. These last four are more plentiful in Upper Burma than in Lower, and as for waders, storks, and water-fowl, as distinguished from the regular duck and teal tribe, they are numerous but scarcely deserve mention. The best snipe shooting is, however, to be found in Lower Burma.

The following are the mammalia to be found in Upper Burma :—

1. Elephants.

2. One-horned rhinoceros (*Rhinoceros sondaicus*).

3. The Asiatic two-horned rhinoceros (*Rhinoceros sumatrensis*). This animal is the smallest of living rhinos and the most hairy.

4. Gaur, miscalled bison (*Bos gaurus*). Bur. "pyoung."

5. Bur. "tsine," wild cattle, the banting (*Bos sondaicus*).

6. Buffaloes (*Bos bubalus*).

7. Sambur or rusa deer (*Cervus unicolo*).

8. "Thamine," brow-antlered deer (*Cervus eldi*).

9. Hog deer (*Cervus porcinus*). Bur. "dayai" and "dalaél."

10. Rib-faced or barking deer (*Cervulus muntjaa*). Bur. "ghee."

11. Wild pig (*Sus cristatus*). Bur. "wet."

12. Serow, Burmese goat antelope (*Nemorhædus*).

13. Tiger (*Felis tigris*). Bur. "kya."

14. Leopard, panthers (*Felis pardus*). Bur. "kya thit."

15. Bears. Two varieties, *Ursus torquatus* and *Ursus malaymus*, the Malay bear, a smaller species. Bur. "wet wun."

16. Wild dogs (*Cyon rutilans*), Malayan wild dog. Bur. "taw kwe," or "cyon dukhunensis," the Indian wild dog.

There are also numerous species of wild cat and other vermin, such as porcupine, jackals, etc.; the latter are not, however, found in Upper Burma proper. Hares may be shot in some districts of both Lower and Upper Burma; they are not, however, plentiful. The tapir, mouse deer, and I believe the larger species of rhino are to be found in the Tenasserim Provinces, Lower Burma. It will be seen from the above list that game is plentiful, and that magnificent shooting may be had. The best time of the year to get at the big game of Upper Burma is, in my opinion, during the months of April,

May, June, and up to the middle of July, when the rainy season begins in earnest. During March and April most of the dense undergrowth, dry leaves, twigs, branches, etc. have been burnt. Rain begins to fall in most districts of Upper Burma about the middle or end of May, and stalking is not then such hard work. Should the sportsman, however, not be able to stand the heat and rain with its accompanying discomforts, which is really, taking it all round, not so great as in Lower Burma, I would recommend his starting for the jungles about the middle or end of November, when delightfully cool and dry weather may be experienced till the end of January or even February. I have often shot during the rainy season in the Ruby Mines district, and have not been troubled in the least by leeches, mosquitoes, or sand-flies. On the other hand, the shooting, which will in all likelihood have to be done on foot, no elephants being available, will be much harder work then than in the hot and rainy season. During the commencement of the rains the ground would be soft and denuded of all superfluous undergrowth, allowing of easy stalking and tracking, whereas in the former case the hard ground would not only make it up-hill work for your trackers, but stalking would be well-nigh impracticable, owing to the dry leaves, twigs, undergrowth, dense jungle, and "kaing" or high elephant grass, which has sprung up during the rains, and which, to a sportsman unaccustomed to it, would appear to be at times well-nigh impenetrable. The healthiest time of the year to camp out in the jungles I have, from my own experience, always found to be between the first of April and beginning of July. All malaria and fever-giving germs have by that time been destroyed by the fires which occur all over the country. After the first few showers of rain in May the young grass sprouts up rapidly all over those parts where jungle fires have occurred.

It is then, in the early dawn or at sunset, that game may be seen in herds or in twos or threes browsing on the tender shoots. Gaur, wild cattle, rusa deer, brow-antlered deer, etc. will then invariably be found feeding out in these open patches, and they may often easily be picked out a long way off with the assistance of a good pair of binoculars. From about the end of July to September elephants, gaur, wild cattle, sambur, barking deer, pig, etc. may usually (at all hours of the day) be found in shady bamboo forests feeding on the young succulent shoots. All the above animals are then very easily approached, as the ground has by then been thoroughly saturated, and there never is, as a rule, any undergrowth in bamboo forests at any time to impede one's movements and alarm game. An animal often gives indication of its presence in bamboo jungle when it is feeding on the tender shoots, and should you be standing anywhere within 200 or 300 yards of where it is feeding, the snapping off of a shoot is quite audible and distinct from any other noise. The sportsman is then enabled to make for the spot at once as quietly and quickly as he can, after having, of course, first tested the wind to see whether it is in his favour or not, as a gaur, tsine, or elephant will wind a man at a distance of from 300 to 400 yards, and of course make off. The easiest way to test the wind is by lighting a match and then blowing it out; the direction taken by the smoke, however slight a current of air there is, at once indicating whether the wind is in your favour or not.

Hunters, gun-bearers, and trackers are to be found in every district in Upper Burma. The best way for a new-comer to obtain their services is as follows:—

He should first of all write a polite letter to the head of the district, a Civil servant known as a deputy commissioner, and inform him that he wishes to shoot in the said district, and ask whether there is any objection to his doing so, and if he would kindly assist him in obtaining transport, hunters, trackers, etc.

The Deputy Commissioner, or District Magistrate as he is sometimes called, will usually depute one of his subordinates, a Burman "myook" (minor magistrate or "thugyi," head-man of a village), to do the needful. It would perhaps be wise at the same time, if the sportsman wishes to shoot elephants, to ascertain where these animals have been destroying plantain or banana crops, and damaging paddy or rice fields, in which case, a permit to shoot them will also be required from the Deputy Commissioner, as the shooting of elephants has now, as in India, been prohibited. It would perhaps also be as well to inform the sportsman that should he receive permission to shoot one or two elephants, he should not be in too great a hurry to slaughter the first small tusker or female he comes across, as there are plenty of very fine tuskers to be met with in Burma, and if his trackers and hunters are worth their salt he will soon come across one of these monsters.

It must be understood that game, however plentiful, will not be found unless a good deal of trouble, one way or another, is taken by the sportsman. Some men who are not particularly keen go out for a day or two, and because they happen to have bad luck in not coming across anything, they return in disgust to their head-quarters dissatisfied with themselves for having ventured out into the jungle, and vowing vengeance on those who have misled them into believing that there was game. Such is not the case with the true, keen sportsman, however unsuccessful he may be. However plentiful the game, all men have disappointing days. I have often been out in jungle teeming with gaur, elephant, and wild cattle and other game, and on several occasions for two or three days at a time have failed in even catching sight of an animal. But I have always stuck to it in the hopes of eventually coming up with something, be it only a fresh track, and have eventually been rewarded on the third or fourth day by obtaining several shots.

It is, as I have already stated, those men who are not very keen who give it up early, those who cannot do without their "pegs" during the day. These are not the men who will follow a wounded tusker elephant, solitary bull pyoung, or tsine for twenty miles or more, and then come up with it and administer the *coup de grâce.* I have been out with some men who, after marching all day under a hot sun without seeing any signs of game, have turned round in a sudden fit of rage upon their unfortunate *shikaries*, and rated them severely, simply because no game had been seen, as if his men were really to blame for that, and could tell to within a mile or two where animals would be found grazing or lying up for the day. Burmans are very independent, and a sportsman will find that it is always best to keep his temper with them if he wishes to have a successful issue to his expedition. It is a very different thing from India, where, I believe, your *shikarie* marks down game and then comes to you with the information. The Burman hunter, than whom a better never followed a spoor, will often mark down a herd of elephants or bison, or even a solitary bull for you, and tell you that he had seen certain fresh tracks in such and such a place, but as a rule he much prefers you, and expects you, to accompany him when he looks for game, and for my own part I think half the excitement of big-game shooting is that derived from the tracking up and finding of your own animal.

Some of the Burman *shikaries* I have known were marvellous trackers, and one man especially, Moung Hpé, whose name will often be mentioned in connection with the various hunts narrated hereafter, never once made a mistake, or failed to bring me up with an animal whose tracks he had once taken up as being fresh. Tracking was the one thing, besides being a good shot, that he prided himself on doing well, and that with an energy and dogged determination that at times surprised me. I have often come on tracks which, to my unpractised eyes, appeared perfectly fresh. Moung Hpé, when taxed as to its freshness or otherwise, would say, "Well, sir, that animal" —supposing the hour to be 9 a.m.—"passed last night about dark; you will notice how the morning's dew has dulled its freshness, and that a tiny cobweb has been spun across the hollow of the slot or track; we might come up with it if you care to take on the tracks, but it is hardly advisable, as he may have travelled a long way by this, besides we will come across other more recent tracks." Of another track he may say, "That track was made yesterday afternoon; look at the little insect-made earth furrows thrown across it; it is useless taking them on, besides the animal who made them is making for such and such a tract of jungle," mentioning a particular patch of cover or tree forest known to himself a long way off. And of yet another track, some nine hours old, perhaps he might say, if we had had bad luck and there was not much game about, "I think we might take on these tracks, sir; if we keep at it long enough we may come up with the owner before nightfall."

A good "mokso" tracker or hunter, who knows every foot of the country thoroughly, can tell you almost to a certainty, on coming across the trail of a solitary bull or herd of animals in the open, what particular patch of jungle or cover the animals are leading for. Fresh signs, such as the bark scraped off a root by an animal's hoof, exposing the white wood with the juice oozing out before the bruises have turned yellow from exposure to the air, smoking ordure, steaming urine, with the froth and bubbles *en évidence*, freshly-cropped grass, a muddy pool, an animal's resting-place where the ground and grass is still warm, and where the odour of the animals still pervades the surrounding atmosphere,—these and many other tokens are all distinct indications, which are quite intelligible to the experienced sportsman, of the near vicinity of an animal. To become proficient in the art of tracking and stalking an animal is, in my opinion, one of the most difficult of all the arts of woodcraft, and no European sportsman can ever become an adept at it unless he is a close observer of nature, and has spent a good many years of his life in the wilds and jungles, far from social and political strifes, with only his guns, dogs, and hunters as his companions.

Burman hunters and trackers are to be found in nearly every district of Upper Burma where game is at all plentiful. The best method of getting at them is by invoking the aid of a myook or (a myauk, as he is sometimes called by strangers, in Burmese means a monkey) a subordinate magistrate, or a thugyi, the head-man of a village, as previously mentioned in this chapter. Many of the myooks speak English, but through the medium of an interpreter all difficulties would be removed. It is difficult to fix on a rate of pay for your men; they have not as yet, thank heaven, been spoilt by the sporting millionaires of England and our cousins across the water. As a rule, 12 annas per diem and his food, with perhaps an occasional coat or a blanket thrown in, and the right to dispose of the meat of all the animals shot, is sufficient. A present of Rs.5 or Rs.10 should, however, invariably be given on the close of a successful shoot, if the sportsman finds his *shikarie* has been working hard and doing his duty faithfully. Two hunters or trackers, the qualities being usually combined, and one gun-bearer should be engaged. Two out of the three men should have a thorough knowledge of the country you intend shooting over. The interpreter, who should, if possible, be a Burman, as no half-breed is, as a rule, to be depended on, would also accompany the sportsman for several days till he gets into the run of things. It would be to his interest, however, to see that he did not overwork him, for should he fall ill he would have to return, and then the sportsman would be deprived of his valuable services.

A BURMESE MATRON AND HER CHILDREN.

From a Photo by Watts & Skeen, Rangoon.

The native English-speaking boy or cook, of course, can always be fallen back upon, but he would not be able to accompany you when you leave camp to shoot, as he would be too tired to do any cooking on his return. The transport men would also come in handy for carrying anything in the way of eatables. The "boy" should, every second or third day, be dosed with quinine, as on him largely depends the success of the expedition, good food and good cooking being essential to the health of the sportsman.

When I started out from camp at dawn to shoot I was invariably accompanied by three men, viz. my head-tracker, who carried my lightest rifle, a bag of cartridges, and a pair of binoculars, a second hunter who carried my heavy 8-bore, and a third man with eatables, a leather chagul or water-bottle, and any other necessary article. The sportsman should himself travel as lightly as possible, but should *always* have a rifle of some sort in hand when after game.

I remember once travelling listlessly through some very open country sparsely wooded here and there by bamboo clumps, accompanied by my hunters, at about 10 a.m., a blazing sun overhead, with only a light walking-stick in my hand, never for one moment expecting to see any game, when a huge solitary bull gaur got up within fifteen paces from behind a bamboo clump, where he had been having his mid-day siesta, and with a snort dashed down a declivity and disappeared from view behind a piece of rising ground before I had time to even put the rifle, hastily snatched from one of my men, to my shoulder. One is sure to meet with disappointments like this if a rifle of some sort is not carried. Of course there are times when there is no possibility of seeing any game, but it is always best to be on the safe side. An experienced tracker will warn you at once when to be prepared for a shot. Your shooting-boots should then be discarded for a pair of light rubber, tennis, or other shoes, in order to be able to stalk up to the animal noiselessly. The snapping of the smallest twig, the rustling of a few branches, or, in fact, any sound out of the common would startle the quarry at once. Should you be wearing a hard Ellwood's helmet or "shikar" hat, it should be exchanged for a soft fore-and-aft peaked cap at once, as it is then easier to bend about through the shrubs and trees without noise, whereas the sounds made by branches and leaves against a hard hat are audible a long way off.

There are three means of transport available in most districts of Upper Burma, viz. mules, carts, and carriers, or porters as they are called in Africa. Mules are certainly to be preferred when obtainable, as they are very handy, carry three times as much as any single porter, and can cover twice as much ground over hilly country in a shorter space of time. They may be hired at the rate of from Rs.25 to Rs.30 per mensem per mule (about £2), and the services of one muleteer for every three mules is included. The mule men are also very useful in assisting one's servants in pitching camp, erecting tents, getting together firewood, and cutting down jungle. These Maingthas, or Shan Tayouks as they are called, come of a very hard sturdy race, and at first sight with their pig-tails one would take them to be Chinamen. They are, as a matter of fact, of Chinese extraction. Burmans are absolutely useless as muleteers, as they do not understand how to lace up packs on to the Shan or Maingtha pack-saddle, which is really one of the simplest, lightest, least galling, and most serviceable articles of its kind I have ever seen, and in my opinion to be preferred to any Government commissariat or other pack-saddles ever invented. Should the sportsman not be able to hire mules in the district he intends shooting over, and should money be a secondary consideration, I would suggest his getting an agent in Mandalay or Bhamo to purchase mules for him. Good serviceable mules may be bought from sums varying from Rs.80 to Rs.120 each. Carts drawn by bullocks may be hired in any district throughout Burma for sums varying from Rs.1 to Rs.2 per diem; they are, however, a very slow means of locomotion, and the sportsman can only keep the beaten track; all hilly country would be quite inaccessible to them. A good deal of baggage can be conveyed by cart, and when rough cart roads intersect a flat game country, it would perhaps be as well to take them, for part of the journey at any rate. The feasibility of this would of course first be ascertained by the sportsman. I have often used carts myself in the Tagaung subdivision of the Ruby Mines district, but found that I was unable to get as deep into the jungle as I should like to have gone, owing to the absence of cart tracks and to the continual breaking of an axle-tree, an accident which requires a halt of a few hours. No journey by cart could be undertaken into a hilly, rocky country, such as is likely to be met with in parts of the following districts of Upper Burma, where the best big-game shooting is, namely, Chindwin, Katha, Myitkyna, Singu, in Mandalay district, Shwégu in Bhamo district, Momeik and

Tagaung subdivision of the Ruby Mines district. Big and small game abound in all the above districts, and especially in the vast tracts of forest lying around Shwégu in the Mandalay district, up to Thabeitkyin, Chaukhlèbèin, and Shwényaungbin of the Mogok or Ruby Mines district. Coolies or carriers may be engaged at most villages after arranging with the head-man or thugyi of the village. It is always best, however, should the sportsman engage carriers, to apply to the nearest Magistrate, stating exactly what he requires, and he will invariably, if not in a disobliging mood, and there are not too many cases on hand, issue instructions to the thugyis of the villages from which he intends starting for the jungle to supply him with all he requires in the way of transport, etc. It would be as well to state at the same time, prior to his departure, the period for which the coolies were required, as then proper arrangements could be made with regard to the quantity of rice, dried fish, pumpkins, salt, etc. which would have to be taken out for their consumption.

CHAPTER IV

ELEPHANTS

My first tusker—My second, and the peculiar circumstances connected with his death—A good tusker.

ELEPHANTS are perhaps the most docile, timid, intelligent of animals, and yet when thoroughly roused and in full charge with curled-up trunk they present a most furious and fear-inspiring spectacle. There are two distinct varieties of the Asiatic elephant, although of the same species, to be found in Burma. I quite agree with all Colonel Pollok says on the subject with regard to the marked differences between tuskers and "hines," or tuskless elephants. The first are known in Hindustanee as "goondas," the tuskers; the second as "mucknas," or in Burmese "hine." I have no intention of going fully into particulars as to their habits, etc., as Colonel Pollok, whose experience of them is much more varied and greater than mine, has already, in the beginning of this book, dealt with the subject at some considerable length. I should like, however, before relating my experience with them, which covers the death of some twenty-two animals, to give the sportsman some idea as to the method of approaching and shooting them, their haunts, peculiarities, and any other observations which, to one who has never seen an elephant in his wild state, may be of some service. The elephant is, as a rule, very easily stalked, provided one has the wind in his favour. I have often been standing within a yard or two of the hind-quarters of one of these animals waiting patiently for the huge beast to turn round and expose a vital part. Their powers of scent, as is well known, are very keen, and they can easily detect the presence of a human being at a distance of a quarter of a mile. Their senses of sight and hearing, on the other hand, are far from good; I have often approached an elephant, which was directly facing me, while it rested under the shade of a tree during the heat of the day, and have not been observed. He does not seem to be able to comprehend matters till his head is turned a little to one side, when apparently you come into view more easily; he then immediately backs or wheels sharply round as if on a pivot, and makes off. Under these circumstances a male elephant will not charge once in a hundred times.

At other times I have been within 80 to 100 yards of a herd right out in the open, with hardly a tree or a bush between, and have not apparently been detected although stared at suspiciously, and it was not till a slant of my wind had been obtained by an uplifted trunk that the usual dull rumblings of alarm were sounded, preparatory to a sudden and swift departure. There are various sounds uttered by elephants denoting different meanings, which are well known to all who are familiar with the habits of these animals. Colonel Pollok has remarked on them. It is marvellous how after an alarm a herd will collect together and then swiftly and noiselessly take its departure.

An inexperienced sportsman will often be exceedingly surprised on approaching a cover, which he has every reason to believe contained a number of elephants, to find that not only have they all disappeared, but that there are also no sounds to indicate that they are even anywhere in the immediate vicinity, so quietly, quickly, and orderly have the whole herd in single file melted away. I have never had any difficulty in approaching a solitary elephant or even a herd to within a few yards; gaur, tsine, deer, etc. are very much harder to stalk, their sense of hearing, compared with that of the elephant, being more acute. Elephants will often stampede when suddenly alarmed, and the whole herd will rush off pell-mell in the greatest confusion in different directions with a noise so terrific, especially should it be in bamboo cover, from the smashing and falling of the canes, that it somewhat resembles an independent musketry fire.. Should the sportsman be in the line of flight in a stampede of this sort he should always stand firm behind the trunk of some tree or solid clump of bamboos. He will then be in perfect safety, as the terrified animals are intent only on getting away as far and as quickly as possible. A herd alarmed in this manner will often travel ten or fifteen miles without stopping. The only danger to be apprehended is from a female elephant when accompanied by a young one, of whose safety she is very solicitous. An old female, when the herd has been alarmed, invariably takes the lead, and the rear is usually brought up by a huge "muckna" or tusker. The large tuskers more often, however, are the first to get out of danger's way, and are, so far as my now experience goes, never found near a herd, but always on the outskirts, at distances varying from a few hundred yards to a quarter of a mile. A large tusker will often during the night wander away miles from a herd, in order to visit rice fields or a certain favourite banana plantation. These visits are often repeated at intervals, till the animal has either been fired at or in some other manner effectually scared. Elephants in Upper Burma do a great deal of damage annually to the rice crops, and in a single night a herd of twenty animals will utterly demolish a field of rice, in fact they destroy more by trampling on it than they eat.

I remember very well once on a pitch-dark night vainly endeavouring to get a shot at a huge solitary elephant, that night after night visited a certain patch of "paddy" land in the Twingé jurisdiction of the Tagaung subdivision, Ruby Mines district. The Burmans in this locality, being unarmed, had done their utmost to drive away this animal by making huge bonfires along the paths by which he was known to enter the fields, and by throwing lighted brands at him; all to no purpose, however, as with a slight, suppressed scream of rage and feinting charge he used to put them all to flight. He would then stalk calmly in amongst the standing rice and begin uprooting it; the swish, swish of the earth being knocked off the roots of the rice-stalks as he banged them across his fore-legs prior to stuffing them into his capacious mouth was distinctly audible. I succeeded eventually in shooting this animal, which turned out to be a huge "muckna" or "hine." The circumstances connected with his death will be related in another page.

No forest can contain a herd of elephants for more than three or four days, as, destroying more than they eat, they consume all fodder in a very short time. They are therefore continually moving about from one locality to another. The denser and more luxuriant the vegetation the better is the chance of falling in with them. Elephants are found at almost any elevation. I have shot them at a height of quite 3200 feet; they do not as a rule, however, remain at such a high elevation for any length of time. During the end of April, May, and June elephants, gaur, and tsine resort to hilly, open places where there is a breeze, and where they can escape from the tormenting gad and other predatory flies which infest the low-lying country. An elephant's skin, although very thick, is just as sensitive as that of many other animals to the proboscis of the various insects which prey upon mammalia. Solitary elephants are always worth following and shooting, as they are usually large and have the best tusks. Should the tracks of an elephant with a diameter of 18 to 20 inches be found, and it prove to be a tusker, it will invariably be noticed that he has one if not two good tusks. Burman hunters say that they can always tell by examining the toe impressions whether the animal possesses good tusks or not, or whether the right tusk is heavier than the left, simply by the deep and distinct impression or otherwise of the two front toes of the fore-feet in the soil. This depends a good deal upon whether the earth is hard or soft at the time. My hunter has often remarked to me of a track, "Sir, look at the deep toe impressions of this elephant's right fore-foot compared with his left, which is very indistinct; he has only one tusk." Again, of another fresh track, which shows only the huge circle-like impression of the foot without the toe impression, he would say, "We need not take on these tracks, sir, it is only a 'hine,' ah-swè-ma-she-bu," or in other words a tuskless male. I am convinced, from my own experience of tracking up elephants, that large tuskers invariably leave a very distinct and deep impression of the two front toes of the fore-feet in the soil, though a similar impression may sometimes be made, and has, within my own experience, been made, by a huge "muckna" or "hine." I have personally tracked up and shot several large solitary "mucknas," which had done a great deal of damage to crops, and found that in most cases there was always the huge circular imprint with a perceptible impression of the toes, but the latter not so well marked as in the case of a tusker. A solitary bull should always be approached with the greatest caution, as he is generally an old stager, who is on the alert for the slightest sound, and has often been stalked and fired at by Burman hunters. A solitary bull which has often been fired at or disturbed by hunters generally rests during the heat of the day in dense "kaing," tall elephant grass, quite impenetrable to the sportsman, or in some thicket where he is practically unapproachable. Sometimes, however, he is found stretched out at full length on his side on some breezy bamboo-wooded slope sound asleep, snoring away quite unconcernedly.

I remember once very well when out in camp shooting with Captain Clements, then Chief Commissariat officer at Bernardmyo, how the latter suddenly came on a solitary tusker elephant sound asleep and snoring loudly, and it had eventually to be wakened by throwing little pieces of sticks and stones at it, to be laid low again by a well-planted shot from Clements, which took effect in the temple. The circumstances connected with the bagging of this elephant recall to my memory a sad accident, which resulted in the death of a Karen military police naik of the Mogok battalion, who was accidentally shot by me under rather peculiar circumstances during a false alarm in camp one night over a tiger. Mr. C. E. Daniel, D.C., who held the inquest, and Captain Clements, who was on the spot when the accident occurred, can corroborate my story, which to be intelligible must be related in detail.

Clements and I were encamped in the jungle at the foot of the Shwé-ū-taung hills in a small natural clearing some six miles from the village of Chaukmaw, on the banks of the

Kanawzo choung or stream. On the first night of our arrival in camp a tiger suddenly made us aware of his presence by roaring at intervals in a most determined, monotonous, and somewhat mournful manner. We had altogether a following of some twenty-five men, consisting of our servants, syces, "drabies" or muleteers, two Karen military policemen, hunters, and trackers. Early on the morning of the second day, Clements, thinking there might be a kill somewhere in the neighbourhood, went to look for it, without however finding it or seeing any signs of the tiger, and eventually finished up the day by shooting the tusker already mentioned. I had no luck, although I came on a herd of gaur, which winded me and made off.

I remember getting back to camp that night about 7.30 p.m. feeling rather done up, having had some very stiff climbing and a long tramp. Almost immediately after my arrival, as we were about to sit down to dinner, the tiger started roaring again as on the previous night. We had no tent with us on this occasion, as the rainy season had not then set in, but slept side by side on a raised split bamboo framework platform, which our hunters had put up for us. This make-shift was about 8 feet broad by about 7 feet long, and stood in the centre of the clearing at a height of between 2 and 3 feet from the ground. Our mattresses, waterproof sheets, bedding, etc. were laid on this, the space some 18 inches between our respective beds being occupied by our rifles, cartridges, my revolver, and a few odds and ends. I had also rigged up overhead waterproof sheets and blankets to keep off the damp and wind in such a way as to form, as it were, three sides of a mosquito curtain over my own mattress. I had a sheet stretched out overhead, another behind me, and one on my left, the windward side. Clements was sleeping on my right.

Some ten or fifteen villagers from Chaukmaw, I may mention, had, on hearing that an elephant had been killed, turned up in camp early in the evening, so as to assist next day in cutting out the tusks and taking away the meat. The tiger, strange to say, continued his roars or calls till about 10 p.m., at which hour we retired to rest, feeling anything but safe, and that we would much rather have been lying in a canvas camp-cot beneath the shelter of a good tent. I overheard various remarks made by the Burmans as we were turning in, about the "nats" or spirits of the woods being displeased over the death of the elephant, that some one was going to be carried off that night by the tiger, which was an evil spirit or "nat" in disguise. A bird of bad omen amongst the Burmans called the "aungwa," a species of night-hawk, I think, which is never seen during the day, settled on a tree overhead and uttered its disagreeable calls of "aungwa, aungwa." I have seen in the Shan States or Momeik quite a number of villagers turn out and endeavour with shouts, and sticks, and stones to frighten away one of these birds, which had settled in a clump of trees near the village. Both the Burmans and Shans are very superstitious in this respect, and implicitly believe that if one of these birds settles in a house or a tree anywhere near and utters its peculiar cries, some person within that house is sure to die before the year is out. All this seemed to cause a general feeling of uneasiness amongst the more nervous of the villagers and our servants. For my own part, I must say I did not feel by any means comfortable, lying as we were out on an open platform exposed to the attack of an animal which can carry a man in its mouth and make off as quickly and as easily as a cat with her kitten. Our servants, muleteers, hunters, and villagers were lying scattered about on the ground amongst the bushes and under bamboo clumps to the rear on our right. No one was sleeping to our immediate front, that is to say in the direction towards which our feet were pointing. The Karen military policemen and the hunters were sleeping alongside one another under the shade of a huge bamboo clump on the right side of the platform nearest Clements, and only some 10 or 15 yards away. My dog "Jumbo," a thorough-bred pariah, which had been in my possession for some eight years (now, alas, no more, having been lost in the streets of Edinburgh), and who was really the cause of the whole mishap, was tied to the corner post of the platform at my head. The night was a very dark and cloudy one.

At midnight, when the whole camp was hushed in slumber, a fire flickering here and there, Jumbo woke me with a start by biting through the rope which secured him to the post. I remember turning drowsily over from my left side to my right, and saying to Clements, "Confound it, Clements, Jumbo has got loose," after which I dropped off to sleep. At about 2 a.m. I was suddenly wakened by hearing all our camp-followers shouting at the top of their voices, every man, as I afterwards found out, with his head under his blanket. I immediately sat up, and on hearing the words—"Kya, kya, lu-ta-youk-pa-thwa-byi-ah me lé péya!" (A tiger, a tiger, a man is being carried off; oh, my God!), I came to the conclusion that one of our followers was in the act of being carried off, or had already been taken away by the tiger. Thinking that perhaps by firing a few shots I might be able to startle the tiger sufficiently to make him drop the man he was carrying, I whipped out my loaded revolver, as I sat, and with a hurried ejaculation to Clements of, "My God, Clements, somebody is being carried off by a tiger!" I stretched out my arm at full length before me, and, aiming up into the trees, fired two shots in quick succession, sufficiently low to avoid boring a hole through the waterproof sheet some 30 inches or thereabouts above my head, after which I put the weapon down between us and waited events. All shouts had ceased after my two shots, with the exception of a few inquiries as to who had been carried off. While these inquiries were going on the fires all round which had burnt down were blown up and re-kindled to a bright blaze. All this was, of course, the work of a few seconds. Moung Hpé, my favourite head *shikarie*, who was seated round a fire some fifteen or twenty paces off to one side under a bamboo clump, suddenly made my heart throb in a way that I have never experienced since or before, or ever hope to again, by saying, "Thakin, thakin, lu-ta-youk-hman-thwa-byi!" (Sir, sir, a man has been hit!). Clements and I, on hearing this, immediately leapt out from beneath our blankets on to the ground, and there stretched right out at full length on his back close alongside the foot of the bamboo platform, grasping tightly with his right hand his snider rifle, was the poor unfortunate fellow, a Karen corporal

Moung Bya, breathing his last. It was a ghastly sight, and one which will never be effaced from my memory. We were not sure at first where the bullet had taken effect, as there was only a little clotted blood on the head, and at first we were buoyed up with the hope that it might perhaps, after all, only have been a graze. But it was not, as we found, on examining the head carefully under lamp-light, that the bullet had entered the left temple and passed out at the top of the head, the brain protruding. It was a dreary wait till daylight, and I do not remember ever having spent such a miserable night; all sorts of fancies and fears of trouble to come chased one another through my mind in rapid succession. We were unable to come to any satisfactory conclusion as to how the unfortunate Karen had managed to find his way alongside the foot of the platform, and as to whether my first or second bullet had killed him, but we could only presume that on hearing the outcry he had started up from his couch, rifle in hand, and rushed across to protect us from danger at the moment perhaps of my pulling the trigger. The unfortunate man did not utter a sound when shot, the bullet passing through the brain.

There was nothing to indicate on the other hand that I had in any way lost my head; my intention, as already stated in firing the shots, being to startle the tiger, so that it would drop its prey. As it happened in this case, however, it turned out that no one had been carried off and that it was a false alarm, caused by my dog Jumbo, which, after biting through the rope which secured him to the platform at my head, had trotted away towards the cooking-place in search of bones. Our men were sleeping scattered about on the ground amongst the bushes, and Jumbo, whilst sniffing about for bones, had jumped over a prostrate Burman who woke with a start, and on hearing an animal trotting about amongst the bushes and dry leaves close to him, immediately took it for the tiger, and shouted out an alarm at the top of his voice, the whole camp joining in with a vengeance. The alarm was very realistic, and under the circumstances I was perfectly justified in firing as I did, knowing that there was no one sleeping anywhere in front at our feet. The Karen to be hit must, after running some 10 or 15 yards, have stood close up alongside the platform to receive the shot, which had been fired at an angle up into the trees. I could not have fired in my immediate rear as the men were all sleeping about there, besides, I should have had to shoot through a blanket. A shot fired over Clements to my right would also have been dangerous, as a number of villagers, hunters, and the two Karens were sleeping in that direction, and again, a shot on the opposite side on my left would have bored another hole through a waterproof sheet. The perforation of a sheet or blanket would of course have been a very insignificant matter indeed, if I had thought there was the least danger in firing as I did. An inquest was afterwards held by Mr. C. E. Daniel, then Assistant-Commissioner of the Shan States of Momeik, at which it was shown that my actions were under the circumstances perfectly natural.

There are four or five shots by which an elephant may be killed; these are well known, and have already been pointed out in detail in an earlier chapter of this book, by Colonel Pollok. The shoulder-shot by reaching the heart, which lies exactly between and protected by the massive bones of either fore-leg, was a favourite shot of mine. The heart may be reached without touching the shoulder-bones by firing at an angle behind the elephant, or with a raking shot forward into the chest through the small of the ribs. Should the heart be missed by this shot the lungs are penetrated. I have always found that two well-placed bullets from an 8-bore behind the shoulder brought an elephant to a standstill in a few minutes. Most of the elephants bagged by me in Upper Burma were killed by the shoulder shot, although I quite agree with the late Mr. Sanderson, who says that head shots are the poetry, and body shots the prose of elephant shooting. Elephants as a rule are not given to charging unless suddenly confronted by a human being. When wounded, however, and in fairly thick cover they are most dangerous, as without the slightest warning, although seemingly rendered *hors de combat*, they will spin round and charge through undergrowth, and then woe betide the sportsman or follower who, whilst fleeing, should make a false step, trip, and fall, for he would in the space of a few seconds be converted into a mass of unrecognizable pulp. I remember once asking a famous old Burman hunter in Wébaung, Momeik State, Ruby Mines, named Moung Aung Gyi, how he had come by certain weals and scars across his thighs and legs. He said, "Ah, yes, sir, these were connected with circumstances which I bring to memory even now with a shudder; it was a very narrow escape I had from a large solitary tusker elephant, which I, together with two or three other hunters, had succeeded in wounding severely. I was young and active then and a good shot, although only armed with a flint-lock. The elephant, which had a magnificent pair of tusks and was badly wounded, had taken up a position in a fairly open tree forest, with a thick undergrowth of thorny wait-a-bit bush through which, naked as we usually are from the feet to the hips, it was rather painful to travel at any great pace." (I may here mention that Burmans when shooting elephants often use a short, strong, pointed iron spear, about two feet in length, which is inserted into the muzzle of the gun till the end rests on the wad over the powder, the barb only showing over the muzzle. This is a very effective powerful missile when fired as is usually done at a range of from 10 to 12 yards into or behind an elephant's shoulder. The poor beast, although often not touched in a vital spot, is very soon brought to a standstill, as it cannot travel through the forest without suffering great pain owing to the butt of the spear, which, protruding several inches from his body, comes in contact with every branch and bush which the animal brushes against. Many elephants in Burma have been slaughtered in this manner by Burmans; others again, I regret to say, have escaped with these fearful iron shafts buried in their bodies only to die lingering deaths, or should the wound not be very severe, to be a source of danger to other sportsmen and villagers who come across them.)

"As it was getting late, and thinking that the elephant was unable to charge, I made my way up cautiously to within a few feet of him and, aiming for the temple, fired. The shot did not reach the brain, and with a shrill, short, sharp scream, he wheeled round and bore straight down on me like a 'miyeta'—railway train—and as you can imagine, sir, I fled through those thorny bushes as fast as I could go, regardless of the pain I was enduring; but such great difficulty had I in keeping out of reach of the elephant, which was at times only a few feet behind me, that I would most certainly have been caught up and trampled to death ere I had gone very far, if by a good chance I had not stumbled head-first into a dry water-course, some 7 or 8 feet deep, and about the same in breadth, and escaped. I was laid up for days afterwards, owing to my legs becoming inflamed by the very severe tearing and scratching they underwent when running away from this elephant."

It is a well-known fact that elephants cannot take all four feet off the ground together, and that they can only step over a crevasse or gap that comes within the compass of their stride, which is never more than 7 or 8 feet at the outside, so that a man chased by an elephant can clear a fifteen-foot nullah or chasm, land on the other side, and turn round and fire at the animal, unless of course the ground permits of it running down the side of the one bank and up the other. As a rule, however, a narrow nullah, 8 or 10 feet wide and the same in depth, is quite impassable to an elephant. I had a short conversation at Edinburgh the other day with the owner of perhaps the best troupe of performing elephants in the world, and he informed me that he had taught these animals to do almost anything except jump, and although he had tried again and again, he had so far utterly failed in his efforts; whether he has since succeeded I cannot say. These elephants were, by the way, procured from Maulmain, in Burma.

My first elephant, a small tusker, was bagged in the Nampan forest in the Shan States of Momeik, Ruby Mines district, whilst on a two months' shooting expedition. My hunters and I were on the move one morning early through the jungle on the look-out for fresh gaur tracks, when the snapping of a twig in a bush skirting a water-course about 20 yards ahead of us attracted our attention. On hearing the sound I thought we had either got on to a herd of gaur or a solitary bull, and immediately pushed forward as quietly and as quickly as the conditions would permit; but what was my surprise on gaining a piece of rising ground to see, not what I had expected, gaur, but a solitary tusker elephant, standing perfectly still, with its ears cocked forward, and trunk up in a listening attitude. It was quite a rude shock to my nerves, as this was my first elephant, and the distance between us only about twenty paces, with no trees or bamboo clump behind which to retreat, so I felt very much inclined to go back quietly by the way I had come. Not wishing to show any signs of funk in the presence of my hunters, I managed to screw up courage to creep up a little nearer, my heart and pulse all the time going like sledge-hammers. When within about fifteen paces I decided to fire for the point of the shoulder from a little behind, in order to rake the vitals and penetrate the heart. Bang! went the report from the heavy 8-bore, followed by an angry, shrill, half-suppressed scream from the elephant, which, wheeling suddenly round as if on a pivot, came straight for us. I hardly waited to see the result of my shot, and, as you can imagine, did record time over and through the bushes and fallen timber, hampered as I was with the heavy 8-bore, which, however, at the time felt like a feather. I very nearly came to grief all the same, as, while jumping a fallen tree, a hidden stump tripped me up and sent me sprawling frog-fashion, rifle and all, on the other side. Moung Hpé, one of my hunters, was fortunately equal to the occasion, as, running up, he at close quarters effectually stopped the charge, by letting the animal have the contents of both barrels of my double-twelve Lang smooth-bore, burning 4½ drams of powder. My rifle and I were fortunately none the worse for the fall, so hastily jamming in another cartridge I ran round to where the elephant was standing in rather an undecided manner, and at a distance of about twenty-five paces succeeded in getting in a right and left behind the shoulder. This seemed to have the desired effect of disabling him, as after first staggering from side to side in the vain endeavour to ascend a slight incline, he lurched heavily to one side against a bamboo clump and then collapsed stone dead in a kneeling position. My last two shots I afterwards found had, after raking his lungs and

PREPARING TO START.

grazing the heart, lodged in his chest. We extracted the tusks and also took away with us to camp the tail, liver, and heart; the latter is, if my memory does not deceive me, about the size of a Rugby football, or a little smaller perhaps, and is capital eating. The tail stewed or as soup is simply excellent in my opinion. The elephant was afterwards cut up, and the meat divided amongst my camp-followers, who dried it in the sun and over a slow fire, eventually disposing of it, together with the meat of other animals shot by me at the expiration of my shoot, to the neighbouring villagers, thereby netting a round sum of some Rs.300 to Rs.400. I have always made it a point when out shooting to allow as little meat to be wasted as possible. The proceeds of sale of all meat of animals shot was always given to my hunters, who were afterwards all the more keen in furnishing information as to the whereabouts of game.

My second elephant was bagged under rather peculiar circumstances, and for some days after its death disagreeable arguments by outsiders, who had nothing whatever to do with the matter, and who had never before shot an elephant amongst them, but who were keen on having their say, were continually being raised as to who was entitled to the tusks. The reader will, however, judge for himself.

I was out on a ten days' shoot with two officers from a regiment at a neighbouring hill station, Bernardmyo, whom I had invited to shoot with me. I shall call them A and D; the latter was a hardy old veteran of over fifty, who had lived a long time in the East, and was, besides being excellent company, a keen and enthusiastic sportsman. A was a young subaltern who had not, I presume, been long in the East. Both knew how to use the rifle well. After getting out into the jungle under canvas, some ten or fifteen miles away from any village, we managed to work up separately, each with his own gun-bearers and trackers, towards the Shwé-ū-taung range of hills. Our beats were arranged so that we should not interfere with one another's sport. I had not been out half-an-hour before my hunters struck the trail of a herd of gaur; these tracks were, however, according to Moung Hpé, about twelve hours old. Nevertheless, I was determined to stick to them. So we took them on, and worked steadily up a steep ridge. At about mid-day, after being out since day-break, my attention was attracted to a herd of elephants trumpeting in the valley to my left, somewhere in D's neighbourhood; not wishing to relinquish the bison, however, or to interfere with D's sport, we held on. We were then at an elevation of some 2500 feet. Whilst moving along in this manner I heard a faint noise on ahead, and suddenly to my surprise a magnificent tusker elephant stalked majestically into view down the same ridge we were on. It was amusing to see how the animal kept the flies from his body by whisking from side to side a small branch covered with leaves which he had broken from a tree, and which he used as dexterously as a lady does her fan. This elephant was a much larger animal than my first, and his tusks protruded from his mouth quite three feet. The wind was fortunately in our favour, or else the animal would soon have scented us and made off. I waited till he had approached broadside on to within about twenty paces, and fired for the temple shot between the eye and ear. The 8-bore was the only weapon with the exception of the double smooth-bore I had in my possession at that time, a single ·303 and double 12-bore rifle not having been purchased till a year later, and I had unfortunately left the smooth-bore in camp. As I was on lower ground than the elephant when I fired, I immediately retreated out of the way to one side, taking up my stand behind the trunk of a large buttress tree, which had huge parapet-like projections on either side at the base. The smoke after the shot obscured everything for a few seconds, and the next thing I saw was the elephant rolling down the side of the hill exactly to the spot I had just vacated, where it was brought up by a slight depression in the ground. It was a sight never to be forgotten to see that elephant struggling on its back, with all its four legs in the air, vainly trying to recover its equilibrium, having only been temporarily stunned by my shot, which had passed into the right side of the head, missing the brain by a very little.

An elephant invariably recovers from a head shot wound, when the brain is not touched, as there are no large arteries, the severing of which would cause it to die from loss of blood. Sanderson says, "A shot that goes through the skull nto his neck without touching the brain may kill him, but it will take time." While the elephant was in this position I was only about six paces off behind the tree already spoken of, vainly endeavouring to extract the empty cartridge case which had somehow expanded in the chamber, so that I should have two shots instead of one to meet him with should he get up. I did not succeed, however, in getting it out. In the meantime my plucky hunter had been doing his best to hamstring the unfortunate beast with his sharp "dah," or fighting sword; this, however, owing to the frantic endeavours made by the beast to regain his legs, he failed to do, and as I saw that the elephant was about to regain his feet, having got on to his fore-legs, I aimed for the forehead bump shot between and below the eyes, and fired; but whether through nervousness, or excitement, I cannot say, my shot did not reach the brain, nor did it seem to have the slightest effect, as, slowly regaining his hind-legs, he swept majestically down the hill-side without uttering a sound, evidently making a bee line for the herd already referred to in the valley below. I was awfully disgusted with my bad luck, or bad shooting, call it which you will. We took on the tracks immediately, and followed on as quickly as possible; after about half-an-hour's tracking we suddenly heard two shots fired down in the valley somewhere in D's neighbourhood, which showed that he had got on to something. An interval of about half-an-hour then elapsed, when eight or ten shots were fired at intervals. My hunter, then turning round to me in an excited state, said he was convinced that D had come upon my elephant, which might have been partially disabled by my last shot passing through the forehead into the neck or body, and that he was now all unconsciously killing my animal. This was too much for me; it was about mid-day, and the whole jungle had been thoroughly disturbed by our shots, so I thought it useless looking for game, and returned to camp, intending, if D had not already killed the animal I had wounded, to take on the tracks next day. Towards evening D returned to camp triumphantly waving an elephant's tail in his hand, jubilant at having slain his first tusker in Burma. I jokingly said to him, that I hoped he had not shot the elephant I had fired at and floored.

Next day, A, D, and myself visited the spot, accompanied by our trackers. The elephant was lying in a kneeling posture with both tusks driven deep into the ground. It was impossible to tell from an examination of the bullet-holes in the animal's head whether any of the shots had been fired by my 8-bore or by D's 12-bore rifle, or the 10 smooth-bore which he was using, as the skin had contracted and the holes appeared exactly alike. I made my hunters take on yesterday's tracks, and after an absence of about three-quarters of an hour they returned, having taken up the trail right up to the spot where D had first fired at the elephant. Poor D would at first hardly believe me when I told him that the elephant now lying dead before us was in reality the one I had wounded. I knew, however, that my trackers would never have played me false over such a serious matter simply to curry favour, so I suggested cutting out the bullets, which we did; and after a great deal of labour, one of my 8-bore, solid, hardened, spherical bullets was to D's utter astonishment and disgust then brought to light. A, who was rather incredulous, suggested weighing the bullet; D was, however, quite convinced that it was mine, and although it had been very much knocked out of shape, the lead was all there, and it certainly presented the appearance of having at one time been an 8-bore spherical ball.

The rule amongst sportsmen is, that the animal belongs to the one who first draws its blood, so long as he sticks to it and follows it up till he kills it; should he relinquish the chase, however, and give up the animal as lost, then any other sportsman would be entitled to shoot. I then proposed to D, who had naturally by this time become very crestfallen, that we should split the difference by taking a tusk each, although I suppose both tusks rightfully belonged to me. D made no demur, but assented to this proposal. The rightful ownership of these tusks was, as I have already said, afterwards made the subject of many a heated argument, and I was often told I had no right to them. This may or may not be the case as it happened; however, I think I was quite entitled to one tusk, if not both. D's first two shots, I afterwards ascertained from the Burman hunter who was with him at the time (a villager of Chaukmaw, near Sagadaung, Momeik State, Ruby Mines district), had been fired at the head of another elephant altogether, which had gone clean away, practically not having been hit in a vulnerable spot, or even floored. It was while following up the tracks of this elephant, according to the account afterwards given me by D's tracker, that they came upon the one I had wounded standing stock-still under some trees looking quite disabled; it was then an easy matter for D, who mistook it, according to the Burman's story, for the one he had first fired at, and whose tracks he believed he was still following, to pump lead into it, which he did with a vengeance, firing no less than ten shots, the animal being apparently too done up to either charge or put on enough speed to escape. The surrounding country in the neighbourhood was very hilly and rocky, and a wounded elephant would therefore find escape, having a lot of climbing to do, well-nigh impossible. My second shot I afterwards found proved, on examination, to have done all the damage, having entered the body after passing through the neck.

There is no sport which entails a greater amount of endurance and hard walking than elephant hunting, and the sportsman has to be in fairly good condition if he wishes to indulge in this particular branch of big-game shooting with any degree of success. I have repeatedly marched on for miles on the seemingly fresh tracks of a solitary bull elephant, sometimes in despair of ever coming up with the owner, so steadily and over such an immense stretch of country do these animals wander; at other times after walking for many a weary mile I have come on the animal, only to find that he has winded me, and made off. In cases of this sort, should it be after mid-day, it is well-nigh hopeless to take on the tracks of the elephant again that day, as the animal, if it be a large tusker which has often been disturbed in this manner will travel for miles without stopping once.

One day in July, in the rainy season, while cantering along the road between the villages of Chaukmaw and Pinkan, I came across the large tracks of an elephant; having nothing of any importance to do at the time, I dismounted from my pony, hitched it up to a tree, and waited till my transport and servants arrived. The tracks had a circumference when measured of quite 4 feet 8 inches, which would approximately make the elephant's height to be about 9 feet 4 inches. On the arrival of my men and transport I unlimbered my guns from their cases, a double 8-bore rifle by Tolley, burning 10 drams, and a double 12 smooth-bore, burning 4½ drams, and started on the tracks accompanied by two villagers from Chaukmaw, who were not much use as trackers. The tracks which, according to my companions, had passed the road early that morning, about 3 a.m. probably, held steadily on for about three miles, in which distance the animal had not apparently stopped once to feed, except on an occasional bamboo shoot which happened to be growing within reach of its trunk.

An elephant, in fact no wild animal, cares to cross a beaten track or highway during the day; they often do so, but in great trepidation and fear, and the pace is invariably increased. A gaur, tsine, sambur, barking deer, or pig, will either bound across or trot over quickly after a little hesitation; a tiger will walk across, if not disturbed, with a long, quick, stately step. An elephant will shuffle over noiselessly by turning his head slightly to either side as he passes, to see that none of his human foes are in sight. Should any of these animals suddenly cross your newly-made trail in the jungle, they invariably dash off at a great pace; gaur, tsine, and the deer tribe gallop away with a snort, or a bell; the elephant will back suddenly and make off at right angles, bringing his trunk at the same time down to the ground with a rap, emitting often a sharp, clear, metallic sound of alarm. I have watched a whole herd of elephants which had been alarmed and were going at full speed, recoil from human scent in this manner and refuse to cross the trail, as if they had each one received a severe blow on the forehead.

Within three hours of the time of my taking on the tracks we came upon the animal's fresh warm droppings; this raised my hopes of at any rate being able to come up with the

A GOOD TUSKER.

From a Photo by Mr. Hannyngton.

elephant that day. The rain about this time came down in torrents, and in spite of a waterproof cape, so heavy was the downfall that it was with the greatest difficulty that I could keep my cartridges dry. On one or two occasions I almost despaired of ever finding the tracks, as they were often nearly obliterated by the rain. The men with me, however, who were, as I have already said, by no means experienced trackers, stuck to it, stimulated by my promises of plenty of "sūngwé" (reward money), and assisted by my little knowledge of tracking, by making now and again wide casts, always succeeded in striking the trail again. We were at last rewarded by hearing the snapping of a bamboo a few yards ahead. I then tried the wind by striking a match, and blowing it out; the direction taken by the smoke indicated that the wind was fortunately in our favour. Another 30 yards brought me in sight of the tusker, who was standing on the edge of a steep, rocky piece of ground, feeding on some young bamboos. I crept up with the 8-bore to within about twenty-five paces, having just instructed one of the trackers to be in readiness with the 12 smooth-bore should I require it. Fixing on a small bamboo clump in my immediate rear, behind which I could retreat after firing, I walked up to the elephant and fired when about fifteen paces off for the shoulder-shot, after which I immediately retreated under cover of the smoke, which hung in the damp air, to the bamboo clump fixed upon. The elephant on receiving the shot stood perfectly still for a few seconds, and then, with a shrill scream of pain and rage, charged up and passed within six feet of the flimsy bamboo clump behind which I had taken up my position. I had in the meantime succeeded in getting in another cartridge, and as the elephant passed me at a quick shuffle I gave it a right and left immediately behind the shoulder which caused it to stumble slightly. The huge beast on receiving the shots turned round and faced me as if about to charge, but after regarding me for a few seconds in an undecided manner it wheeled round and made off again. My two companions at this critical moment had, on seeing the huge beast loom up alongside the bamboo clump, thought discretion the better part of valour and ascended trees.

The rain all this time had simply been coming down in torrents. After shouting myself hoarse for the two trackers, who looked very sheepish when I began to chaff them for making themselves scarce, we took on the tracks of the elephant, whose route was now plainly indicated, not only by its tracks, but by splashes of blood on the ground and surrounding bushes. We had not gone half-a-mile before I caught sight of the elephant standing in some open "indaing," bastard teak forest, with its trunk up in the air, through which at intervals blood appeared to be issuing; this was a sure indication that he had been shot through the lungs and was practically disabled. On seeing me approach he made feints of charging, but I could see from the bubbles and bloody froth which dropped from his trunk that he was helpless and that the end was near. I then walked up to him accompanied by a Burman with a spare gun, and at the distance of about ten paces administered a *coup de grâce* by planting a bullet in the centre of the bump with my Lang smooth-bore. The elephant on receiving the shot toppled over on one side with a dull thud, falling on its right side, the heavier tusk being the right one. I have noticed that tuskers, when shot through the brain, invariably, when they fall on their sides, collapse on the side which has the heavier tusk. Elephants very often, on the other hand, when killed by body shots, succumb in a natural life-like kneeling posture. His measurements, taken as he lay, were as follows:—

Vertical height at shoulder, 9 feet 4 inches.
Length from tip of trunk to tip of tail, 26 feet.
Right tusk, length 4 feet 9 inches.
Right tusk, weight 38½ lbs.
Left tusk, length 3 feet 9 inches.
Left tusk, weight 28 lbs.

A piece of the right tusk had, at some time of the animal's life when he belonged to a herd, been broken off in an encounter, or perhaps through an accident. The pulp cavity in both tusks had decreased considerably, showing that the elephant was an old one. It will be noticed that the hollow or pulp cavities of large massive tusks are as a rule very small.

CHAPTER V

ELEPHANTS

Shoot my largest tusker—Death of a huge solitary "muckna" or tuskless male—Shoot solitary "muckna," noted for destroying rice crops and plantain plantations—Fire at large tusker in herd of five tuskers; am charged by remaining four; succeed in bagging two—Shoot my last tusker on New Year's Day 1897, after a long chase.

SOME of my readers, I dare say, think that sportsmen are unnecessarily cruel and callous in their methods of killing game, and no doubt wonder how one can find any pleasure and excitement in doing to death such a harmless beast as a gaur, or an animal so intelligent and useful as the elephant. Granted, but we have all still, more or less, implanted in our breasts a taint of the savage instinct of our forefathers to take life, and there is also a natural craving for some form of excitement amongst the majority of people, which has in some way or other to be satisfied, and what better form of excitement or what more manly and healthful sport could one desire, than the tracking up and stalking of these wary denizens of the jungle? We sportsman have, however, whilst standing over an animal newly shot, a momentary feeling of regret or remorse, call it which you will, but this feeling is only momentary and is more than counterbalanced by the satisfaction of having obtained another noble trophy.

The largest tusker elephant which it was ever my good fortune to shoot fell to my 8-bore one lovely evening in November 1895. It was then about the beginning of the cold weather, and the evenings and early mornings were quite chilly.

Whilst travelling through the subdivision in the neighbourhood of Twingé, one of the police posts under my charge, I got word of a huge tusker elephant which had, according to rumour, been fired at and wounded by Burman hunters, who were still tracking up the animal. As these hunters had all previously been warned by me not to disturb or shoot any of the solitary elephants, gaur, or tsine in the neighbourhood, there being numerous herds upon which they could indent, I was naturally not a little annoyed at their behaviour, more especially as I had promised them "sũngwé" (Bur., reward money), and plenty of powder and ball, should they furnish me with information regarding the whereabouts of "solitaires."

Proceeding to the village of Wăpyũdaung, which lay within the sphere of my duties and where the hunters lived, I ascertained that the rumour was true, and that three of them had come on a huge tusker asleep, in some bamboo jungle about six miles from Wăpyũdaung, and that while the animal was lying asleep they had fired simultaneously at his head with their old Tower muskets, and then followed up the beast for three successive days without coming up with it, eventually giving up the chase in disgust, as the animal had not shown any signs of being disabled. Whilst *en route* to Wăpyũdaung I fortunately met these hunters on their way home on the day of their return from the jungle. They gave me full particulars regarding the locality in which they had relinquished the tracks, but absolutely refused to accompany me, on the grounds that they were foot-sore and tired, and that there was not much chance of my coming up with the elephant, the direction of whose tracks plainly indicated that it was making for the Shwé-ũ-taung range of hills. No amount of bribes would induce them to come with me, not even the promise of the value of one tusk, should I bag the animal.

It would have been quite a different matter if I had had my own hunter, Moung Hpé, with me; he, however, lived at Sittone, a village distant from Wăpyũdaung some twenty-five or thirty miles, and could not therefore be sent for to arrive in time to take up the tracks. Eventually, I heard that the thugyi or head-man of the village of Ontabu, situated about nine miles from the village ot Wăpyũdaung and about three miles from the spot where the hunters had given up following the elephant's tracks, had at one time been a *shikarie* and tracker of some note. The Wăpyūdaung hunters had on their way back imparted to the Ontabu thugyi the whereabouts of the elephant's tracks. So, early next day I left for Ontabu with a few coolies, determined to follow up and sleep on the trail of the elephant till I came up with and bagged him. I was all the more determined to do so, after the opposition I had received from the Wăpyūdaung hunters, who were, I have no doubt, somewhat vexed and disappointed at having lost an elephant whose tusks were worth at least Rs.600. As a tracker the old Ontabu thugyi turned out to be all that could be desired. I started out with eight or nine coolies, taking as little kit with me as possible, and armed with my double 8 and 12-bore rifles.

We struck the tracks of the elephant at about 9 a.m., and followed them all day without coming up with the owner. I camped that night in the jungle, sleeping on a waterproof sheet with a few branches rigged up overhead to keep off the dew. At daybreak we were off again, and soon came on fresh signs of the elephant having been in the neighbourhood. Some cultivators, whose clearing we passed, informed us that the animal had, during the preceding night, eaten and trampled down a large quantity of standing paddy or rice. This was good news to us, although rough on the cultivator, and it showed that the elephant was in no way disabled, nor had it apparently any intentions of making for the Shwé-ū-taung range of hills, or leaving the neighbourhood.

Hitherto my tracker was under the impression that the elephant had, as predicted by the Wăpyūdaung hunters, headed for the Shwé-ū-taung hills, but now he informed me that it had altered its line of flight, and from various signs *en route*, we noticed that it had quite settled down again and got over its recent alarm, as it had begun to zigzag from one place to another, and had fed on several bamboo clumps, which had been stripped bare of their leaves. My coolies, boy, and Burman "lugale," or servant-of-all-work, were now instructed to follow my hunter and myself at a respectable distance, while we moved cautiously forward. At the same moment the loud cracking sound of a breaking bamboo was distinctly audible some way ahead. It was amusing at this juncture to see with what longing eyes my servants and coolies looked about them for suitable trees amongst whose branches, should the elephant charge, they would find a safe retreat. I then lit a match, blew it out, and noticing that the current of smoke was in our favour, I moved quickly and noiselessly forward. The elephant had in the meantime moved into a shady patch of tall young bamboos, whose stems were nowhere thicker than a man's wrist, and about 12 or 15 feet high; there was also a number of small saplings, but not one of a sufficient thickness to furnish a retreat in case of a charge. We could now distinctly hear the animal as he stood in the shade lazily flapping his ears.

I have always found it the best policy, when possible, before firing at large game such as elephants, rhino, gaur, or tsine, to fix on a good solid bamboo clump, tree-trunk, or rock, behind which to retreat after firing in case of a charge. It is not always necessary, of course, and there is not always a retreat available, but it should always be taken advantage of when possible, as it is quite unnecessary to risk your life and become foolhardy.

An elephant or gaur, I have always found, when disturbed or wounded will invariably be found standing or resting in cover, head on towards the point by which danger is expected, namely, the trail by which he has just entered. Animals have sufficient instinct to know this, and, as happened in this case, I found the elephant standing facing me. I crept up to within about twenty paces, backed up by my gun-bearer, and then for the first time got a glimpse of ivory that convinced me that for once the Burmans had not exaggerated, and that the animal now standing before me was the possessor of the best pair of tusks it had ever been my good fortune to see, and which now seemed within easy grasp.

The animal's head was unfortunately hidden amongst the bamboo leaves and branches, sufficiently to prevent my obtaining the head-shot; so creeping quietly round, fearful of treading on dry leaves or twigs, I gradually worked round to his flank. The wind must, however, have shifted, as wheeling suddenly round with a low sharp snort of alarm, like the sound emitted from a steam-pipe when suddenly turned on, off he sailed away at a great pace through the slim bamboos, which bent, cracked, and waved about beneath his strides like reeds. I immediately dashed away in his wake, determined to get in a shot somewhere, with the intention eventually, of course, of following him up to the bitter end, even though I should have to sleep on his trail for another week.

After keeping up with the animal in his immediate rear for some 200 yards, and finding that I could not outflank him so as to obtain a raking shoulder-shot, I fired in desperation at the huge target that presented itself, my shot apparently taking effect under the tail. The effect was magical in the extreme, and, contrary to all my expectations and experiences with elephants, the huge beast wheeled round with a shriek and charged straight down upon me at a great pace. I was too breathless and jumpy from the sharp run I had just undergone with the heavy 8-bore, to shoot straight, and having only one chamber loaded I fired wildly, aiming for the bump or forehead shot, jumping to one side immediately after.

The shot could not have hit the elephant, as he did not stop or swerve from his course in the slightest. My friend with the 12-bore was *non est*, poor man; he thought, I have no doubt, that the weight of three-score years and ten warranted his getting out of danger's way. As can be imagined, I did not wait to see any more, but dashed off at a tangent, jamming in two cartridges as I fled, the heavy 8-bore, although weighing quite 18 lbs., feeling as light as a feather. I was, however, in the pink of condition and as hard as nails. The elephant caught a glimpse of me as I dashed to one side, being then not quite ten paces off, and swerving round slightly towards me, stood for a few seconds, after which, wheeling round, he sailed away again in the direction he had first taken when fired at by me.

After collecting my men, who scrambled like so many monkeys down from the various trees outside the patch in which the elephant had taken up his quarters, and instructing them to follow behind slowly, my tracker and a gun-bearer and I took on the tracks, and kept steadily on. It was then about

9.30 a.m., and my guide informed me that he did not think we would come up with the animal that day, as we would not be able to travel very quickly, owing to the many difficulties which would be thrown in our way, such as the tracks becoming mixed up with those of other animals, a herd of which had been seen in the neighbourhood.

Some people may imagine that to track an elephant is a very simple matter, and so it is in wet weather, when the ground is wet and soft and the elephant leaves a deep impression. It is a very different matter, however, in dry weather, on hard stony ground or on hard laterite soil, when the ground is bare and denuded of all vegetation.

I know from experience that it is really much easier often to track up a solitary gaur or tsine under these circumstances than an elephant, whose flat feet leave hardly any impression. The utmost capabilities of my tracker were on this occasion called into play about an hour after we had taken on the tracks; in fact, on one occasion, for half-an-hour I almost despaired of ever finding them again, as they had become so mixed up with those of a herd which had been in the vicinity the day before, so that it was almost impossible to distinguish between them. Some of the best Burman *shikaries* and trackers I have known have been at sea when it came to the tracking up of a solitary bull elephant, but were, on the other hand, in their element when on the trail of a gaur or tsine; the reason for this being that some hunters made a living by mostly following and shooting elephants, whilst those who were afraid to tackle these monsters stuck to the other game. After making a number of wide detours or casts we did, however, eventually strike the trail, and immediately pushed on again.

It was now well on to the evening, and, as tracking was made much easier by the ground being softer and covered with more vegetation, I suggested to my hunters that we should push on as quickly as possible, leaving the coolies and servants to follow. This we did, each of us scanning eagerly the ground, with the determination of not again losing the trail.

After having covered some eighteen miles of country from the time I fired at the elephant, we struck the banks of the

Péthaung stream, which was about 30 yards wide, strewn with huge rocks and boulders and high shelving banks. The elephant's tracks now headed down-stream, and as there did not seem to be much chance of our coming up with him that evening, it being then about 5.30 p.m. and some time past sunset, I called a halt, and sent back the tracker to ascertain how far off our coolies were. About a minute or two after his departure, my gun-bearer and I were startled by hearing a crash in the jungle on the opposite bank some 150 yards down-stream, and at the same time an elephant, with a magnificent pair of tusks, walked down the side of the bank into full view, and came up the middle of the river-bed in our direction, and stood motionless beside a pool, facing us 50 yards off. My gun-bearer and I were fortunately lying down out of sight at the time, resting under an overhanging clump of bamboos by the river-side, and also hidden by a few low stunted bushes which were growing in mid-stream close to us. At this moment the all-unconscious tracker, who was fortunately some way off, began blowing on a hollow bamboo, with the intention of bringing up the coolies. The elephant, fortunately, did not seem to notice the noise, and after standing in mid-stream for about half a minute, lazily flapping his ears, he began to move up-stream slowly towards us. The wind was, fortunately, in our favour, so wriggling into a kneeling posture, I crouched down to receive him with the 8-bore when he came near enough. My gun-bearer in the interval, who was sitting crouched down behind me with my spare rifle, was in a great state of excitement, as he was continually urging me to shoot, saying: "Shoot, sir, shoot; he will wind us and be off!" The elephant in the meantime was walking along steadily and slowly towards us, with the intention of apparently returning along the route by which he had come. I waited till he approached to within about 15 yards, and then taking a steady aim with the 8-bore, fired for the bump or forehead shot. On receiving the bullet he swerved quickly to one side, with a loud, sharp, shrill scream of pain and anger, and made for the opposite bank. Before reaching it, however, he received my left barrel; the ball, a hardened spherical one, entering behind the right shoulder, penetrating the heart, and bringing him to the ground after a preliminary lurch or two, where he lay uttering a low, deep, rumbling sound, resembling distant thunder, while life ebbed away. I rushed up, having in the meantime reloaded, thinking he might get up again, but saw from the way the blood gushed out that the heart had been pierced. He was a magnificent beast, with massive tusks. The space between the tips of his tusks measured, as he lay, 4½ feet across; the following were the other measurements taken after the tusks were extracted :—

Weight of right tusk, 55 lbs.

Weight of left tusk, 45 lbs.

Length of right tusk, 5 feet 5½ inches.

Length of left tusk, 5 feet 1½ inches.

Circumference right tusk, outside gum at thickest portion, 17 inches.

Circumference left tusk, at thickest portion, 16 inches.

Circumference of fore-feet, 5 feet 1½ inches.

For an Asiatic elephant these were a very fair pair of tusks, and much beyond the average size shot by sportsmen, and at the time I was proud to think that I had succeeded in beating the largest pair bagged by Sanderson, the well-known author of *Thirteen Years amongst the Wild Beasts of India*, now, alas, no more. I do not think I exaggerate when I say that elephants with larger and heavier tusks have been shot in Burma than in India. The following are the measurements of a very large pair of tusks, the record for India, I believe, till last year, when the honour fell to Burma :—

	RIGHT TUSK	
	feet	inches
Total length, outer curve	8	0
Greatest circumference	1	4·9
Weight	90 lbs.	

	LEFT TUSK	
	feet	inches
Total length, outer curve	3	3
Greatest circumference	1	8
Weight	49 lbs.	
	Total 139 lbs.	

The above elephant was shot in the Mysore jungles by Sir Victor Brooke and Col. Douglas Hamilton, in 1863, and up till April 1896 the 8-foot tusk was, I presume, the record for the Asiatic elephant. Mr. Clough of the Burma Police, a young sportsman, shot a very fine tusker on April 18, 1896, in the jungles near Chaungwa Kyaikto, subdivision of the Thaton district of Lower Burma. All measurements and weights of the two tusks were published under the signatures of Messrs. R. C. Syms, of the Burma Commission, and H. P. Pedler, District Superintendent of Police, Thaton, in an issue of the *Rangoon Times* in May 1897. These tusks, the following of which are the measurements, are believed to be, for Asiatic elephants, a record pair.

	Right Tusk		Left Tusk	
	feet	inches	feet	inches
Length, outside curve	7	9¾	8	5½
Length, inside curve	6	9½	7	6
Length from centre of base to tip (direct)	5	8½	6	4¾
Greatest girth	1	5	1	4½

Weight, right tusk, 2705 tolas, 69·156.
Weight, left tusk, 2780 tolas, 71·136.
Total weight of pair, 141·12 = 280 lbs.

Another very large pair, weighing over 100 lbs., were found last year in the jungle near Mogok, Ruby Mines district, Upper Burma.

One morning early one of my hunters woke me with the welcome news that the tracks of a huge elephant, which must have passed during the night, had been seen within 100 yards of camp. I was then on two months' privilege leave, and had been out in the jungles for over a month and a half. It was then well on to the middle of the rainy season, and the ground was very sodden, and vegetation and undergrowth dense.

After hurriedly dressing and partaking of some "chota hazri," consisting of tea and toast and a little bacon, I mounted my pony and took up the tracks, hoping that the animal might be in possession of a good pair of tusks. I had low jungle-fever on me at the time, and did not feel equal to a long walk.

A pony, as I have said before, will always be found most useful in camp should you get knocked up, be laid up with fever, or meet with an accident. I invariably rode to the particular tract of country I intended shooting over, which often lay at a distance of from three to four miles from camp, and then dismounted, thus saving me many a long walk. A riding or transport pony can be taken anywhere over the country throughout either Upper or Lower Burma. Game in Burma cannot of course, like that in Africa, be run down on horseback, the country is not sufficiently open to allow of this style of hunting. My hunter used to give me ample warning when to dismount, by saying, "Sir, you had better get down here, we may see game now at any time," or he might wait till we had struck the fresh trail of a solitary gaur, tsine, elephant, or rhino before asking me to dismount. The pony would then be handed over to a Burman, who would walk behind my tracker and me, keeping us in sight, at a respectable distance. Fodder in the shape of bamboo leaves, "kaing" grass, known as "doop" grass, may be found pretty nearly all over Burma from July to February. A sack or two of paddy or unhusked rice, upon which all Burman ponies thrive, should always be taken.

A pony will also be found very useful should the sportsman have covered a long stretch of country, and find that he is unable to return to camp before a late hour. He may then, if he cares to venture, return alone quickly on pony-back.

This is not always safe, and it might be productive of serious consequences should he take the wrong route and get lost in the jungle. A Burman pony will invariably find his way back to camp alone if left to himself. At any rate, I have done it over and over again, and been in and had a comfortable warm tub and dinner hours before the return of my men. A pony, to know the camp, will naturally require to have been fed there for at least two or three successive days, before his instinct can be relied upon. On several occasions, when some six or seven miles from camp, and having no further use for my pony owing to the dense jungle and undergrowth, I have turned the animal loose, after hitching up the stirrups and bridle in such a way as to prevent their becoming detached, and found the animal on my return quite safe in camp. But I am afraid I am digressing.

On arriving at the place where the elephant had passed, I saw that the tracks were enormous, the tape-measure showing a diameter of 21 inches. My trackers were very doubtful as to whether the animal possessed tusks or not, although there were occasionally distinct toe impressions which, from the theory already aired by me in a previous chapter, pointed to the presence of tusks.

The tracks led through some open, undulating, bamboo country for about two miles, and then entered a dense patch of jungle consisting of bamboo, bush undergrowth, and the forest. Here the tracks became mixed up with those of a herd of elephants which the solitaire had apparently joined.

I dismounted, and with my trackers made various detours and reconnaissances, in the hope of being able to see the monster. Various rumblings, squeakings, and an occasional flap, flap of an ear suddenly made us aware that we were in close proximity to the herd, which was apparently resting during the heat of the day. After making several circuits round the patch in which the elephants were, we took up our stand under the shade of some trees distant some 200 yards from the elephants, intending to wait till evening, when the animals would leave the dense cover to feed.

After the lapse of about an hour and a half we were suddenly startled by hearing the elephants apparently charging in a body at a great pace through the dense undergrowth in our direction. The noise was terrific, and sounded as if a tornado had suddenly sprung up to the accompaniment of a sharp musketry fire. My pony, usually a very quiet beast, accustomed to all sorts of noises, and even standing alongside of an elephant, snorted and trembled with alarm. My men, who had been dozing on the ground, leapt to their feet. Screaming jungle fowl, pheasants, barking deer, and chattering monkeys, all thoroughly alarmed, flew or ran past us at a great pace. Moung Hpé, jumping excitedly to his feet, said: "Get ready, sir; the elephants, while wandering about on the outskirts of the cove, have scented us by coming on our trail, and are now coming straight in our direction." Seizing my 8-bore, and handing my 12-bore to Moung Hpé, we took up positions behind the thickest trees we could find; these were not, however, of a sufficient girth to be any protection. My pony was unhitched from the tree to which it had been tethered, bridled, and then made over to one of my followers, who did not by any means feel comfortable at being held responsible for the pony's safety. The elephants, which were now only about 150 yards off, changed their mad rush into another direction, only, on meeting our trail in the new direction also, to recoil and head back again in our direction. The noise of the terrified charging elephants as they came nearer and nearer, crushing and trampling down everything before them, was simply indescribable. Telling my men to stand firm and not to be alarmed, I took up my position alongside my pony, which had by this time got quite accustomed to the noise. Within about two minutes of the time the stampede occurred, the leading elephant, a huge bony-looking female, came bobbing along, followed in single file by a numerous progeny of all sizes and sexes. It was a wonderful and unique sight, and I had the full benefit of it as they filed noiselessly past me, having moved up from my position to within fifteen paces of their line of retreat, there being no undergrowth to impede the view, and as they followed one another in single file there was no danger of any of the animals coming in my direction. What would I not have given for a camera? The various expressions in the eyes and faces of the different animals, indicative of temper, were very noticeable. Some with bland, good-natured, stolid, or stately faces, others with a fierce or mischievous twinkle in their eyes. Nearly every one of them, the small tuskers especially, turned their heads slightly in my direction, a half-left turn of the head as they passed, evidently scenting danger from that quarter. I noticed that after leaving the dense cover and reaching the open the animals seemed to have recovered somewhat from the panic, as they all moved along in a more methodical and mechanical manner one behind the other. Out of the number that passed me, some thirty in all, there was not

ELEPHANTS WASHING.

a single animal with tusks sufficiently large to warrant my shooting.

Almost immediately after witnessing this march-past, another contingent of the herd, consisting of some seven or eight animals, suddenly appeared on my right, bearing straight down at a quick shuffle towards the position occupied by my pony and companions. Thinking that, as often is the case, the rear of the herd would be brought up by a large tusker, and hoping that the animal whose large tracks we had followed that morning, be he tusker or muckna, would now show himself, I ran back and took up my stand beside the pony, as the foremost elephant, a large female with short tushes, arrived within ten paces of us. I had previously warned the Burman who was holding my pony, should the elephants pass close by, to remain perfectly motionless and not to attempt to lead off the pony or drive off the elephants by shooting, the latter proceeding being most dangerous. My warning was, however, entirely disregarded, as the Burman holding my pony bawled out several times, and at one time I really thought the old female would charge home. Fortunately for us, however, she did not, and with the rest, some seven or eight animals in all, she recoiled with lowered head and swerved off to one side. In the meantime, the large elephant we were on the look-out for did not put in an appearance. My men, meanwhile, had become rather annoyed at my not having shot one of the small tuskers of the herd for them.

After waiting patiently for about a quarter of a minute we heard a faint sound in the direction of the dense cover from which the herd had come. Thinking this was probably the monster we were on the look-out for, and which would be sure to follow in the footsteps of the herd, I waited. Presently, at a distance of about 100 yards, I caught sight of a large elephant making off slowly in a direction at right angles to us. I immediately ran forward with the hope of being able to cut him off, and to see whether he was a tusker or muckna. I did not succeed, however, as he winded me, and it was all I could do to run up and, at a distance of some 30 yards, fire a raking shot into the small of his ribs from behind; this quickened his pace considerably. We followed as quickly as possible, being guided by the breaking and cracking of bamboos and branches, never for one moment expecting to see him, at any rate for the next ten or fifteen miles, but what was our surprise to come up with him suddenly standing broadside on, on a rather thickly wooded knoll. I immediately gave him a right and left behind the shoulder, and Moung Hpé, who was armed with my single ·303, also gave him a shot in the same place, but the brute moved off. I was unable to make out at the time whether the elephant possessed tusks or not, as its head was hidden from view behind some foliage. It being by now late in the evening, it was decided, very much against my wish, to relinquish the chase till next day. I was not by any means keen on continuing the pursuit, as I was under the impression that it was a muckna, but as the poor beast had been badly wounded I determined to follow it up, and if possible put it out of its misery.

We took on the tracks again at an early hour next morning. It was a weary trudge, through one bamboo cover into another, till I felt as if bamboo jungle, trees, earth, stones, streams, and elephant tracks had been indelibly photographed on my brain. We kept steadily on the trail for some hours, an occasional drop of blood, the size of a threepenny piece, showing here and there at intervals. After marching from 6 a.m. till 9 a.m., the tracks led us through some rice and maize cultivations, to which the elephant had helped himself liberally. The cultivators, an old Burman and his wife, who appeared rather concerned about the destruction of their crops, informed us that they had heard the animal pass about 2 a.m. that morning. After refreshing ourselves with the milk of some fresh cocoa-nuts, which the owners of the cultivation hospitably offered us, we pushed steadily on, having an occasional difficulty where the tracks passed over dry, hard, stony ground; Moung Hpé was, however, indefatigable, and was never really at a loss. We only halted once for about half-an-hour for something to eat, my own breakfast consisting of cold gaur tongue, chicken, a few biscuits, figs, and prunes, washed down with water from a neighbouring stream.

I made it a rule to eat as little meat as possible when marching during the heat of the day, in fact I had an abhorrence for meat of any kind when the weather was at all warm, and found that a meal of dried fruits, such as figs, dates, prunes, with chocolate and biscuits, was very sustaining and quite as nutritious, and as for liquor, I never touched any whilst out walking. Spirits I never drank at any time.

After having covered some twenty miles of country we almost gave up hopes of ever coming up with the animal again, but eventually, towards the afternoon, we came on fresh indications of the elephants having at last settled down to feed and wander about in an aimless fashion. The jungle was now becoming denser, and Moung Hpé informed me that the animal, whose droppings were now quite warm, was certain to be found in a cover some three or four miles ahead which he knew, and where the animal would most likely be either found asleep or resting.

I may mention that I had on this occasion, besides the ·303 and 8-bore, a double 12-bore rifle, burning a maximum charge of 6 drams of powder and carrying heavy conical steel-pointed bullets.

We now moved forward very cautiously, as we were in cover where there were no large bamboo clumps or trees behind which we could retreat in case of a charge from the elephant, which was sure to be in a very irritated and dangerous state after the wounds which he had received. While moving along in this manner, my 8-bore in hand, loaded with steel-tipped conical bullets, and backed up by Moung Hpé with the Lee-Metford and another Burman with the 12-bore rifle, we suddenly came across the elephant lying down on its side with all four legs stretched out at full length, apparently sound asleep. At first I thought the animal was dead, but being only some twenty paces off, I made out, from a closer examination, the regular up-and-down breathing motions of its body.

With a whisper to the Burman who was carrying my 12-bore rifle (the thugyi of the Tsaizingon village) to stand firm and be ready with the rifle should I require it, I aimed for the region of the heart, and fired, jumping immediately to one side to see the effects of my shot. The result was startling in the extreme, and I was astonished to see with what rapidity the huge animal had regained its legs and was bearing straight down upon us with curled-up trunk and head held high in the air. This was too much for our friend from Tsaizingon, he disappeared. A shot from the Lee-Metford and another from the 8-bore was immediately fired, neither of which seemed to have any effect, as, sweeping past within a few feet of us, the elephant rushed down the steep almost inaccessible banks of a stream strewn with logs, fallen trees, and blocked with dense jungle, ascending the other side, and making off as if untouched. I now saw to my sorrow, for the first time, that the elephant was a tuskless male.

After severely rating the thugyi and informing him that he was not fit to hold an appointment under Government, we followed on, hoping that the animal would not be able to go very far. We had not gone two miles before we came up with it leaning against the trunk of a large teak tree, looking very sick. It was a magnificent beast, standing, as I found from a careful measurement taken on the spot with a metallic tape, 10 feet 4 inches between uprights.

All the differences pointed out by Colonel Pollok, already referred to by me, between "mucknas" and tuskers were now quite apparent. The poor beast, on seeing us approach, turned round and faced us as if to charge, but eventually collapsed slowly on to its knees after a preliminary lurch or two, when it died uttering low rumbling sounds and looking, with its wide-open bright and mischievous eyes, still most life-like. The rain about this time came down in torrents, and as it was now getting late and we had covered some twenty miles of country, too far to be able that night to return to camp, we decided to head for the nearest village, Pauktabin, distant about three miles, from whence I intended sending out villagers next day to bring in the two fore-feet and rudimentary tusks of the muckna, which were in themselves curiosities. About 100 villagers surrounded the dead carcase of the elephant next day like so many vultures, and soon cut up and carried away all the meat, leaving nothing but bones. This elephant I afterwards ascertained was the animal which had been so destructive to the crops of Tsaizingon and other neighbouring villages, so after all I felt that he had not been wantonly slain.

Some three or four days after the death of the elephant, while tracking up a solitary bull tsine or *Bos sondaicus* about two or three miles from camp, I came upon the large tracks of another solitary bull elephant, which my hunters declared from the impressions of its foot to be a certain tusker which they had often come upon but failed to bag. The reader will perhaps think it strange that any one would be able to identify an animal by the impression of its foot. It is nevertheless true, and I have often recognized the tracks of certain large tuskers, muckna, solitary bull gaur, or tsine from peculiarities in the formation of the huge circle-like depression in the first case, and the great breadth and length of the slot in the other. The tracks of female elephants, as indeed in the case of gaur, tsine, are all much smaller and narrower than those of the bulls. Mahouts, whose elephants have strayed, are often able to distinguish from amongst other tracks those of the animal they are looking for, simply because their eyes are accustomed to the peculiarities of the print. Burman hunters from being continually out in the jungle recognize the tracks of all solitary animals, and can very often tell you, if they are themselves acquainted with the locality, in which cover they are most likely to be found lying up during the heat of the day. Solitaires, as a rule, have their own beats, and are always to be found day after day, if not disturbed, within a certain area. I remember once after shooting a solitary bull tsine in the neighbourhood of a patch of cover, situated some four miles from my camp, and for which my hunters and I were heading, as I hoped to get a shot at a huge solitary bull gaur, whose tracks had for several days been seen by bamboo-cutters, finding that the gaur whose fresh trail we had struck had been feeding on the young shoots in some open bamboo forest, and had become alarmed on hearing my shots and galloped off in consequence. I was awfully disappointed at the time, although I succeeded two days afterwards in bagging the animal, when it had got over its alarm and returned to its old haunts. I have noticed that solitaires, when disturbed from a certain cover they have been in the habit of frequenting, invariably return to it again. But let me go back to the elephant whose track we had discovered. My hunters positively asserted, this time from the formation of the footprints, that the owner was really a tusker. We had not been following the trail long, before sounds from a neighbouring bamboo cover informed us that the elephant was close by. After ascertaining in the usual manner whether the wind was in our favour, I moved forward cautiously with the 8-bore, followed by Moung Yauk, another favourite hunter of mine who was armed with my 12-bore. Both weapons were loaded with solid, hardened, conical bullets, driven in the case of the 8-bore by 10 drams of powder, and in that of the 12-bore by 6 drams.

After picking our way carefully through some rather thick undergrowth we came into more open bamboo forest, where, to my utter astonishment, five tusker elephants instead of the one I had expected to see came into view walking along slowly in single file, broadside on, at a distance of about 35 yards, apparently heading for an adjacent cane-brake, where I have no doubt they intended resting during the heat of the day. Picking out the leading elephant, the largest tusker, which, from a side view, appeared to have only one tusk, I fired, aiming for the heart. The elephant on receiving the bullet charged straight ahead, and crashed into dense cover, some 50 yards further on, when all sounds ceased. The other four tuskers, none of which carried large tusks, wheeled round and came bobbing along, in full charge, straight down upon us. It was rather a startling spectacle, and for the moment I felt very much inclined to get out of the way as quickly as possible. Moung Yauk, at this critical juncture, seemed very undecided what to do, and looked as if he would like to clamber up into the branches of the tree behind which we had taken our stand. The tree was not by any means one of massive girth, and could easily have been knocked down by a butt from an elephant's forehead. After warning Moung Yauk to stand firm and be ready with the 12-bore should I require it, I aimed for the forehead of the nearest elephant, which was by this time some fifteen paces off, and fired. The effect was instantaneous ; the elephant on receiving the shot rolled right over and turned a complete somersault, like a rabbit hit in the head, rolling right over on to its back and then on to its side, stone dead, the blood spouting out of a bullet-hole in the centre of the bump or forehead. The other three animals changed the direction of their charge, and swerved slightly to one side, being met by a hurried right and left from Moung Yauk, who nearly burst the drum of my right ear by firing within a few inches of my head, the bullets taking effect amongst the upper branches of a tree some 20 or 30 feet from the ground.

As I was suffering at the time from a rather severe attack of low malarial fever, my temperature being about 103, I did not feel by any means keen on following the animal I had first fired at, as I was sure it would go clean away and cover some fifteen or twenty miles of country before we should see it again, having only received one shot, and that perhaps not in a vital spot. Judge my surprise when, on entering the cane-brake already referred to, and into which the elephant had gone, we heard the well-known flapping sounds of an elephant's leathery ears. The jungle here was very dense, and our position was now extremely ticklish should a charge be made, unless I could stop it with my heavy rifle.

There were only passages here and there, originally made by elephants, through which we could follow in single file. There was no escape right or left, should the animal come down on us; the only means of exit was by running back along these narrow passages, which were often not by any means clear of overhanging creepers, branches, stumps, and very strong hooked cane thorns. There were, besides, no bamboo clumps or trees of sufficient girth and stability behind which to take refuge. The flapping sounds seemed to come from a dense patch of jungle some 25 yards off, but do what we would, not a single portion of the animal was visible, although I reconnoitred his position from every available point. At last in desperation I collected a few stones and threw them one after another into the patch as quickly as possible. The result was electrifying, for with a smothered shriek the elephant charged through the thick cover, which bent, broke, and gave way before the huge beast, straight towards us, and pulled up to within ten paces of where I was standing. I dared not make a hurried movement for fear of bringing the infuriated beast upon me, but slowly raised my rifle to the present, and, taking aim for the right ear-hole, which was, however, partially hidden by foliage, fired. The elephant staggered slightly to one side, and then wheeled round and sailed off again through the dense undergrowth, carrying everything before him. We followed in his wake as quickly as the inequalities of the ground would permit for about a hundred yards, when we suddenly perceived him standing stock-still stern on and in a listening attitude, and only some 10 yards off. To crouch down and make ourselves as small as possible was the work of a moment. We had not been in this position more than a few seconds before the huge beast spun round quickly and charged straight for us. It was a very close thing, as he passed within a foot or two of the spot where I was crouching, in fact one ponderous foot was within touching distance. Moung Yauk had only time to throw himself to the other side of the narrow lane out of sight, ere the elephant passed between us. Fortunately, instead of bringing up and looking for us, he held straight on for about 100 yards, and then came to a halt in some dense cover, where he stood grumbling angrily and banging his trunk violently on the ground, sure signs these of pain and rage. It was now getting late, and as the fever was making me feel very wretched I thought it high time to bring matters to a climax. So telling Moung Yauk to back me up I edged up carefully towards the elephant, in the hopes of being able to get in a head-shot and thus finish the business. It was very hard work, however, and only those who have followed elephants, especially a wounded animal, through thick cover can understand the magnitude and danger of the undertaking. While pushing our way carefully through the undergrowth, and when quite 25 yards from the beast, it suddenly seemed to be aware of our presence, and without the slighest warning charged in our direction at a great pace, the thump of its feet on the ground, strange to say, being very distinct and unlike the comparatively noiseless advance of the elephants which I had previously encountered. As before, we had just time to step out of his way, one on either side. Instead of passing us he stood between us, in an undecided manner, at a distance of about fifteen paces; I immediately covered his left temple, which was exposed, and fired, the bullet taking effect in the brain and bringing him to the ground with a dull thud.

He was a magnificent beast, and measured at the shoulder 10 feet 6 inches. His tusks were not so large as I had expected, the right one weighing 40 lbs., and the left 25 lbs., total 65 lbs. I mounted my pony and returned to camp alone, feeling very ill, leaving my men to bring in the tusks, together with the fore-feet, heart, and liver.

My five transport ponies were sent out to the spot next day early, and returned laden with the tusks and feet and as much of the meat as could be packed on the saddles. The delicacies already mentioned, such as the heart, liver, and elephant's tail, were specially reserved for my own consumption.

I was quite incapacitated from doing any shooting for several days, as apart from the fever I had contracted, my "boy" or cook had been bowled over with jaundice and liver, and I was consequently unable to get any good food, such as soups, broths, egg-flips, custard, puddings, which were necessities in the condition I was then in. For the next ten days, however, I had to manage as best I could under the circumstances, dieting and doctoring myself to the best of my ability. The great secret of good health in the East, and particularly in Burma, is to eat sparingly, and in the case of the hunter over-eating is fatal.

I shot my last tusker on New Year's Day, 1897, in the Ondan valley, at the junction of the Ondan and Nakayin streams, at the base of the Shwé-ū-taung hill, having first picked up his tracks in the jungle between the Mogok, Thabeitkyin road, and Ondan rice-fields, a locality some twenty miles from the spot where I eventually succeeded in getting him.

My hunters on sighting the spoor pronounced it that of a

tusker, and, indeed, it was soon patent to every one, as he had left marks of his tusks in the steep clayey side of a river bank where he had been eating the earth, which, being impregnated with a certain amount of soda or salt, is eagerly partaken of by all ruminating animals. There are a great many of these salt-licks and tepid brackish streams (yénganbauk and myéngan) scattered over both Upper and Lower Burma, and animals such as elephants, rhino, gaur, tsine, buffaloes, and deer frequent them periodically, and often travel great distances to indulge their craving for salt. Burman hunters often sit over these pools or licks and pot the game from trees.

Well, to return to our tusker, I first came on the animal's tracks on Thursday afternoon, December 31, 1896, and took them on for some five or six miles over very hilly country partially covered by open tree and bamboo forest, with occasional patches of old "tounyas" or deserted cultivation, which had grown up into a perfect jungle, and through which at times it was very hard work to make one's way. We did not succeed in coming up with the animal that day, as he winded us and made off while we were 100 yards off, so we returned to camp, fully intending to try for him again next day.

"Chota hazri" at dawn next morning, and then taking a hamper containing breakfast we started on the trail, determined to come up with the animal before dark. The usual slow, steady, wearisome trudge then ensued for several hours, the monotony being occasionally broken when a difficulty occurred in tracking, or when some startled sambur or barking deer roused from his morning slumber fled, uttering a loud bell or bark as the case might be. Occasionally a porcupine or solitary boar would cross our path in front, as if aware that I could not shoot without alarming the nobler quarry whose tusks I was bent on having. Occasionally a question would be put by me to my trackers, such as, "Howki-la, thee-chi-ya-hman-the-la?" (Is that so—are these the correct tracks?) "Gané-chi-ya bè-daw twè-mi is tin-the-la?" (When do you think we shall come upon to-day's tracks?)

After covering some ten or twelve miles of country in this fashion, steadily on over hill and dale, we at last came on signs of the animal having passed early that morning. The difficulties sometimes were great, but I need not go into details, as they have already been enumerated elsewhere, how we worried around and made casts when the animal had stopped for a short time and fed round here and there in circles, crossing and recrossing its tracks, or what trouble we had to pick out his trail from amongst those of other elephants which had recently been in the neighbourhood. Let it suffice to say, that after travelling in this manner from 5 a.m. till about 2 p.m., we eventually heard sounds of breaking bamboos on a neighbouring hill-side some 300 yards off, which plainly indicated that we had at last come up with the animal and that it was feeding.

It is much easier to approach an animal when it is feeding than when it is resting or even on the move, as in the two latter cases it seems to be more on the alert, whereas the noise made by an animal feeding naturally drowns to a certain extent all other sounds in its immediate vicinity, such as the breaking of twigs, the rustling of leaves and branches when the sportsman brushes against them, and so on.

I had only my 12-bore rifle with me on this occasion, my 8-bore rifle and ·303 having been sold, as I was about to proceed to England on long leave.

I soon caught sight of the elephant standing broadside on, feeding away quite unconcernedly on bamboo leaves, oblivious to all danger. He was standing with his back a little above the top of a ridge on the edge of a steep ravine, a most advantageous position for a quiet approach, although I must say I felt an occasional qualm pass through me, as there was not a single substantial tree behind which I could retreat in case of need. I moved forward very cautiously to within about fifteen paces, when a brute of a monkey, the common brown species, jumped from one branch to another on a tree overhead and knocked down a rotten branch, which fell with a loud crash almost on top of the elephant, which, swinging quickly round, faced me. I immediately stopped dead, and, thinking I was discovered, was preparing to raise my rifle slowly to my shoulder, when he turned round and began feeding again, the monkey, which had apparently seen me, keeping up all this time an incessant chatter.

After composing myself, and placing spare cartridges in a handy pocket, I crept a little nearer, and, aiming for the shoulder-shot, fired both barrels in quick succession. The smoke hid everything for a few seconds, then I heard a great crashing and smashing of branches, and saw that the elephant had charged straight down the side of the steep ravine, leaving great ruts behind, where he had slid along on his haunches. To ram in two fresh cartridges, close the breech, and take aim and fire both barrels again at the elephant, as he clambered up the steep bank on the other side of the ravine, was the work of a moment. Both shots took effect between the neck and hind-quarters near the spine, and must have gone well into his vitals. I was now pretty certain of getting him, as I knew that one of the four steel-tipped bullets driven by 6 drams of powder was sure to have penetrated a vital spot, probably his liver or lungs, and would prevent his travelling any distance.

We followed in his wake very cautiously, as the ground was strewn with boulders, fallen logs, and branches; the undergrowth was also fairly thick. There was plenty of blood along the trail, and my clothes from contact with the blood-besprinkled leaves were all stained. The elephant now made us aware of his immediate vicinity by uttering at intervals sounds like distant thunder, and by thrashing the ground with his trunk. This was a sign that he meant mischief, if possible, but it also meant that he was partially disabled.

We were now very deliberate in our movements, as we might come suddenly on the animal in turning a corner, for the elephant was evidently on the look-out for his aggressors.

But luck was in our favour, and after going through some very ticklish jungle we caught sight of the quarry standing in some fairly open bamboo and cane jungle, with his ears cocked well forward listening. We were about 35 yards from him and on higher ground, and as he was standing broadside on, I thought I might as well try to disable him from where I was, as the nature of the ground would have prevented my getting any nearer without being discovered.

So, aiming for the shoulder, I fired. The elephant stood stock-still as if carved out of stone. I fired the second barrel, on which he turned round and made off at a great pace towards the stream (the Ondan or Kin river). We caught him up as he was crossing, pulling one huge leg after the other over the large boulders which lay in his path in mid-stream, the water, some three or four feet deep, seething and boiling all around him.

I did not care much about attempting to ford the stream carrying my heavy rifle, as the water rushed like a mill-stream, but managed eventually to scramble across by jumping from rock to rock. The elephant had now got a start of quite half-a-mile, but we caught it up again. We rushed along rather recklessly at times, I am afraid, being guided not by the foot-prints but by splashes of blood, and risked running into the wounded animal at any moment. As it happened, we did nearly come to grief, as the elephant had, after crossing the stream and holding on for some distance along the bank, turned off and doubled back upon its own tracks for some twenty or thirty paces, and stood amongst the jungle close to the path we were following. Fortunately he betrayed his presence by flapping his ears, and we were warned in time, but only just, for hearing our approach he charged out of cover straight at us. We were about ten or twelve paces off at the time, and it was a very close thing. I had no idea the brute had so much life left in him, for he charged at a terrific pace. I had barely time to jump to one side and take up my stand behind a tree, Moung Yauk doing likewise, when the elephant rushed past us, over-shooting us a few yards from the momentum of his charge, then swinging round with curled-up trunk and a shriek of rage he again made for us. All this was the work of a few seconds, and Moung Yauk being unarmed had made himself scarce. It was only natural; and as I had everything with me, including spare cartridges, I did not mind. The elephant, on reaching the tree behind which I had taken up my stand, began uprooting the small trees and bushes in its vicinity, and hammered the ground at intervals with its trunk, trumpeting shrilly with rage. Stones and clods of earth were kicked in all directions, and my position was far from comfortable, as there was no other place of refuge within a radius of 30 or 40 yards.

A change of position on the part of the elephant exposed the temple, a chance of which I promptly availed myself, the distance between us being only about three yards. The huge beast on receiving the shot collapsed all of a heap, and after a few subdued murmurs lay lifeless. His tusks quite repaid me for all my hard work, the pair weighing 80 lbs.

As it was too late to extract them and cut off the fore-feet that night, we wended our way to camp, thinking little of the tiresome walk we had before us in our pleasure at the satisfactory ending to our day's toil. On my way back I saw several fresh signs of *Rhinoceros sumatrensis;* these animals will be treated of hereafter.

We got back to camp about 7.30 p.m., where I found a comfortable warm tub awaiting me, a pint of beer cooling in a neighbouring stream, and a well-cooked dinner prepared, for my Madrassie cook thoroughly understood the art of catering for a hungry hunter.

CHAPTER VI

INDIAN GAUR (MISCALLED BISON), THE *BOS GAURUS* OF NATURALISTS

BLANDFORD'S description of this magnificent animal, the grandest and largest of all the existing bovines, may not here be amiss :—

"General form massive, body deep, limbs and hoofs small. Ears large. A high ridge along the anterior half of the back, terminating abruptly about half-way between the shoulder and the tail, and caused by the spinous processes of the dorsal vertebræ being long and those of the lumbar vertebræ short, the change in length taking place suddenly. Skull bearing a high ridge convex on the vertex between the horn cores ; in front of this ridge the forehead is deeply concave. Horns, considerably flattened, towards the base curved throughout, the tips turned inwards and slightly backwards. Thirteen pairs of ribs. Tail just reaching the hocks. No distinct dew-lap. Hair short, thin on the back in old bulls.

"*Colour.*—Brown, almost black in old bulls : less dark and sometimes more rufous in females and young males, especially during the cold season, and in those inhabiting drier parts of the country where there is less shade. Lower parts rather paler, hair about axil and groin golden-brown. Legs, from above the knees and hocks to the hoofs, white. Head, from above the eyes to the nape of the neck, ashy grey, becoming in some animals whitey-brown or dirty white. Muzzle, pale coloured. In calves, according to Blythe, there is a dark stripe down the back. Horns, pale-greenish or yellowish, with black tips.

"*Dimensions.*—This appears to be the largest of existing bovines. Large bulls are said to exceed 6 feet in height at the shoulder, but this is rare and exceptional, 5 feet 8 inches to 5 feet 10 inches being the usual height. Cows are much smaller, about 5 feet high. A huge bull measured by Elliot was 6 feet 1½ inches high, 9 feet 6 inches from nose to root of tail, tail 2 feet 10 inches long, girth behind shoulders 8 feet. A cow 4 feet 10 inches high measured 7 feet from nose to rump over curves, and 6 feet 9 inches in girth. A large male skull from the Western Ghats measures 18 inches in basal length and 9·9 inches zygomatic breadth. Average male horns measure 20 to 24 inches round the outside curve. Horns from Travancore have been recorded 39 inches in length and 19 inches in girth at the base; whilst other Travancore horns measure 20·75 in girth, and a pair from the Malay Peninsula 22, though only 32 long.

"Large cow-horns measure 23 and 24 round the outside curve, with a girth of 13·25. The girth of each horn in freshly-killed specimens is about an inch more than in dried skulls.[1]

"*Distribution.*—(With regard to India and Burma) All the great hilly forest tracts of the Indian Peninsula, Assam, and Burma.

"The gaur keeps to forest or high grass generally, but not always near the hill, and is found in herds of from five to six to about twenty or occasionally more. Bulls often wander by themselves, and the finest and oldest bulls are said always to occur solitary; still, very large bulls are found with herds, and young bulls are frequently seen alone, or two or three together. All are shy and avoid cultivated tracts as a rule, though instances occur in wild parts of the country of gaur feeding on growing crops.[2] Their food consists chiefly of grasses; they do not commonly browse, though they occasionally eat the leaves and even the bark of particular trees, and they are fond of the shoots of bamboos. They feed generally in the early morning and evening, and lie down to rest from about 9 a.m. to about

[1] This applies to Indian gaur—the Burmese variety has been described accurately by Col. Pollok.

[2] I have seen whole fields devastated by a herd of gaur in the northern Circars.—F. T P.

ELEPHANTS CROSSING RIVER.

From a Photo by Sir B. Simpson, Bart.

4 p.m. and at night. They drink, as a rule, in the afternoon. These bovines inhabit the hills of the Indian Peninsula to an elevation of 5000 or 6000 feet, or occasionally even higher; but they do not ascend the Himalayas to nearly the same extent. They are admirable climbers, and ascend or descend steep hills with wonderful facility. They are timid animals, but in wild places where they are rarely subject to attack and disturbance they are by no means remarkably wary. Wounded animals occasionally charge, and solitary bulls have been known to attack without provocation; but the tales of the gaur's ferocity recorded by some sportsmen are not confirmed by any of the later writers who have had good opportunities of studying the animals. A bull gaur is one of the noblest animals in the world, a model of strength and symmetry, and his formidable appearance has led to his being unjustly credited with a savage disposition.

"The period of gestation is not known with any certainty. Breeding is said to take place in the cold season. The calves are mostly born (in the peninsula of India) in August or September, a few early in April, May, or June. Gaur suffer from the same diseases as domestic cattle. In India all attempts at domestication of this bovine have been failures. The calves appear always to die in captivity, none, it is said, having been known to attain their third year. But there can be little doubt that the gaur has been tamed and kept tame in some of the hill tracts between Assam and Burma,[1] and quite recently a young male animal, now nearly four years old, has been brought to England from Pahang in the Malay Peninsula, and is still (1891) living in the Zoological Gardens, Regent's Park (London). According to Sanderson three distinct sounds are uttered by this species. The first is a sonorous bellow used as a call, and unlike any of the usual bovine sounds. The second is a low 'moo,' indicative of apprehension or curiosity. The third is the well-known whistling snort of alarm with which the animal dashes off when frightened. I have heard the

[1] This is a mistake. It is the gayal and not the gaur that has been domesticated in the hill tracts between Assam and Burma. Mr. Sanderson was misled by the similarity of name common to both, "mithun," in supposing there were no wild gayal.—F. T. P.

tame animal in Regent's Park utter a prolonged call not very unlike the lowing of *Bos taurus*, but utterly unlike the lowing of *Bos indicus*."

I trust I shall be excused for giving in full Blandford's description of the gaur and its habits, etc. I have done so in order that I may compare my own experiences, acquired through having shot on foot some twenty-five bulls, with the observations published by him.

Having lived and spent most of my short leave in a part of the country (the Ruby Mines district of Upper Burma) where these animals roam about in large herds numbering in some cases as many as thirty animals, I had many opportunities of studying their habits, haunts, and peculiarities.

The gaur is usually known under the misnomer of bison, but is not to be confused with the American, which in point of size and appearance is quite an insignificant animal compared with the Indian gaur; an old bull is, in my opinion, one of the grandest and noblest prizes that can fall to the rifle of any sportsman.

It shall be my endeavour in this chapter to relate, for the benefit of those who intend hunting gaur, detailed accounts of the death of some six or seven of the largest solitary bulls shot by me.[1] I hope on the other hand that I may be excused if, to some of my readers, these narratives should have an appearance of baldness and similarity about them, which is, however, a *sine quâ non* when one is relating true statements of facts taken from diaries written on the spot.

The first gaur I ever saw was one that had been shot by a hunter of mine, Moung Yan Gin, whilst we were tracking up a herd; I remember how annoyed I was with him, and very naturally too. Moung Hpé, my favourite *shikarie*, was also with us at the time. We had struck the fresh tracks of a herd which led up a steep hill some 500 feet above Sagadaung at the foot of one of the outlying spurs of the Shwé-ū-taung range, when somehow or other Moung Yan Gin, who was tracking up a bull on his own account, became

[1] Gaur shooting, principally off elephants, has been described by my colleague, Col. Pollok, who has shot over one hundred in Burma and India.

separated from us. The next intimation I had of his whereabouts was the report of his flint-lock piece, and a shout informing us of the death of a bull. I remember rushing up the steep ridge and feeling anything but charitably inclined towards Moung Yan Gin, whom I now saw standing beside a huge bull which was kicking in its last throes, having been shot neatly through the heart. Moung Yan Gin excused himself for having shot the gaur by saying that he had come on the animal suddenly, which, having seen him, would have given the alarm to the rest of the herd. I accepted his excuse, but told him he was never to shoot any animal again when with me unless by my permission.

Having applied for and been granted a month and fifteen days' privilege leave due to me, and having previously made up my mind to spend it in shooting, I started from the Shan states of Momeik one morning early and plunged into the jungle well equipped with everything. My transport consisted of mules, ponies, and coolies, and I had three hunters, my servants, and a camp-following of some twenty-five men in all, a goodly number to feed.

My camp equipment was as follows:—A double Cabul tent, a Maulmain jail-made camp folding-chair, which is, having a table fitted on at the back, a dining-chair, writing-desk, and easy-chair combined in one. A small iron frame folding spring-mattress camp-cot.

All the above, including wearing apparel, my guns, three cases of stores, a case of ammunition, bedding, cooking utensils, a patent winding fan lamp, a tin of kerosene oil, together with my servants' kit, made up all the baggage, which was carried by four transport mules and ponies. The cost of rice, tobacco, betel, ngàpee, dried fish, chillies, cheroots, cooking oil, etc., for the consumption of my followers, was met by me.

These latter, after a fair division, were divided amongst my men, who carried their loads in wicker baskets called "kyingyas," woven from thin strips of bamboo, which contained, amongst other things, the owner's blanket, strip of carpet or "kawzaw," betel-box, without which he never travels anywhere, a "lue aik" or haversack, a chopper or hatchet, "dahma," and a cutting-up or skinning knife, named a "da myaung," the well-to-do men probably stowing away a spare jacket and a "loongyi" or loin-cloth.

The above is about the sum total of a Burman's kit when travelling or out on *shikar*. The trip from beginning to end, including rations for myself, servants, and camp-followers, together with the hire of two mules, the other two being my own (excluding cost of tinned and other stores), would be as follows: Rations for camp-followers from April 3 to May 15, Rs.100. Hire of two mules at Rs.1 per diem per mule, Rs.86. Total, Rs.180 As many of the licensed gun-holders had had their licences withdrawn, game was plentiful in the neighbourhood. There were numerous signs of *Bos sondaicus*, the banting or tsine, as well as gaur about, but the ground was still rather dry and parched after the recent fires, and tracking was rather hard.

The places most frequented, apparently from recent tracks, appeared to be those parts where large areas of grass had been burnt and the young shoots had sprouted. After the fires, April, May, or June is certainly the best time for big-game shooting in Upper Burma,[1] more especially for gaur and tsine, as, being easily seen a long way off, they can be approached and stalked without difficulty.

After we had been out in camp two days, one of our mule-men, on his return from cutting fodder, informed me in the evening that he had seen fresh tracks of a herd of gaur near a patch of "kaing" or elephant grass, about four miles from camp, which had recently been burnt. Moung Hpé and I immediately pricked up our ears on hearing this piece of information, and as he was acquainted with the locality referred to by the muleteer, we decided to visit the spot next day. Early next morning we were up, and well on our way when day broke. Moung Hpé, who knew the patch well, said that the gaur were sure to be found grazing on the young shoots of "kaing" grass, which ought to be about a foot high. While nearing the patch in question, a piece of ground some 40 yards square, a few loud snorts and stamping of feet were heard some 50 yards off. I immediately rushed up, but arrived at the patch only

[1] Also in Lower.—F. T. P.

to find that the gaur had winded us, and were making off. I just caught a glimpse of one animal as he was charging off, but did not care to fire and needlessly alarm the herd, as I hoped to obtain a shot later on, by taking on the tracks when the animals would probably lie up in some cover during the heat of the day.

After taking on the tracks for about a mile, Moung Hpé informed me that the animals had settled down into a steady walk, and had even begun to crop the grass here and there whilst on the move, which was a sure sign that they had got over their alarm. After keeping steadily on through some open "indaing,"[1] or bastard teak forest, the tracks led into a dense patch of tall elephant grass some ten or twelve feet high, in which, according to Moung Hpé, they would most likely lie up during the heat of the day. This patch of grass, which was about half-a-mile long by about 200 yards broad, would have completely hidden out of sight the tallest elephant. The dry and parched state of everything on the ground rendered our stalking the animals in this cover quite an impossibility. It is on occasions like these that a howdah elephant is useful.

We then arranged to set fire to the grass, and to place myself in a position where I should be able to get a shot when the animals broke from the cover. This was easier said than done, however, as it was almost impossible to tell at which particular spot the herd would break from the grass. The patch appeared to be about a quarter of a mile long by about 150 yards broad, shaped like a parallelogram. We eventually decided that I should station myself at one of the angles of the patch furthest away from the spot where the bison had entered, and that the grass at the end round about the track taken by the gaur should be fired simultaneously in a dozen different places.

I may mention that I had with me on this occasion, besides Moung Hpé, two other men.

The grass was then fired, after I had taken up my stand. About an hour afterwards, I heard the gaur make a tremendous charge, but for the life of me could not tell in which

[1] Often called Eeingeen in Lower Burma.—F. T. P.

direction to expect it from, as the prodigious noise made by the roaring and crackling of the burning grass nearly drowned every other sound. Eventually I succeeded—after running as fast as I could for a distance of about 50 yards through fairly thick tree jungle, which grew right up to the edge of the patch of grass—in getting a snap-shot at a large bull as he burst out of the cover some 25 yards off. He dropped like a stone to the shot, but struggled on to his feet again immediately, only to be laid low by my second barrel, which hit him on the neck, bringing him to the ground with a thud. My first shot had passed through his dorsal ridge close to the spine, giving him the temporary shock which floored him.

Always give any animal which drops like a stone to your first shot a second barrel, as it may have been only stunned temporarily by the brain or spinal cord having been grazed. An animal shot through the heart, or even in the brain, will not fall dead on the spot; they will often stagger away a few yards before dropping. Again, an animal shot through the neck or back, when the spinal cord has been severed, will drop like a stone.

This was my first bison, an animal standing some 17½ hands high, with small horns.

Two days later I came upon the tracks of a couple of solitary or "neenaung" gaur in the bed of the Nampan stream. Whilst we were taking them up, however, and when within about thirty paces or so of the two huge brutes, which were sleeping close to one another, we were suddenly startled by hearing a number of girls laughing and shrieking. Both animals on hearing the unusual noise had jumped to their feet, and dashed away before I could catch even a glimpse of them. This was most annoying, to say the least of it, and I was astonished to think that women should have come so far away from any habitation unattended by any men. Villagers often travel miles into the jungle on expeditions of this sort, some for the purpose of cutting cane, bamboo, or "shaw"—the bark of a tree used for making rope and binding purposes—others for collecting honey, berries, mushrooms, iguanas' eggs, or catching fish, which abound in nearly every stream. The noise seemed to come from the bend of an adjacent stream, so Moung Hpé and I, on curiosity bent, made our way to the spot to see what all the merriment was about. On arriving at the spot and looking down into the river we saw three or four young girls of from seventeen to eighteen years of age, disporting themselves in mid-stream and along the banks *in puris naturalibus,* perfectly unconscious that any one was looking on. Moung Hpé recognized the girls to belong to the village of Sagadaung. We retraced our steps without making our presence known, and returned to camp.

It has been said by a critic in *Land and Water* that Burmese women are very modest in all their actions and *pourparlers* before the opposite sex, and that they never, when bathing in a river, enter the water *in puris naturalibus.* In contradicting this, and without wishing it to be thought for one moment that it detracts in any way from their modesty, I may say that I have over and over again seen girls, both old and young, disporting themselves in the water in the above-mentioned state, not only in outlying jungle streams, but in those which flowed through or close to a village.[1]

Some days later my men, who had gone out to cut out the tusks of an elephant I had bagged, reported on their return that they had seen the tracks of a huge herd of bison on the outskirts of a large tract of cane jungle some three miles off.

After arriving at the spot where the tracks had first been seen, we took them on through some patches of "kaing" and cane jungle. At times the tracks were very scattered, wandering in and out and round in circles, and it was no easy matter often to hit on the right line taken by the animals. After threading our way in this manner through a long stretch of thorny cane and bamboo we eventually came on fresh signs of the herd's immediate vicinity, and were at the same time warned by a low "moo" and the faint snapping of a twig that the gaur were close by. The cane and grass at times were rather dense; fortunately for us, however, elephants had

[1] During thirteen years' residence and extensive travel all over the country, from Mandalay to Mergui, I have seen girls bathing without a stitch of clothing, hundreds of times. It was a common occurrence in my day.—F. T. P.

recently been in the neighbourhood, consequently numerous lanes had been trodden down, affording an easy passage.

Two of my hunters who were with me on this occasion, Moung Hpé and Moung Yan Gin, were both armed with muzzle-loading Tower muskets. Finding that the wind was in our favour, after testing it in the usual way, I took my 8-bore and moved cautiously forward, sending Yan Gin and Moung Hpé round on either side of the herd, so that they might also obtain a shot after I had fired. I had not gone forty yards before I heard a gaur breathing stertorously whilst browsing. A whisk of its tail brought it to my view standing broadside on beside a clump of bamboo, all vital parts, however, being hidden behind the clump. To glide off to one side and take up my position behind another clump, some fifteen paces from the animal, was the work of a second or two. I had not long to wait before the gaur, stepping out, exposed his whole body. I immediately fired, aiming, as he was standing away from me, for a little behind the shoulder. The shot took effect through the heart, as dashing away for about thirty yards she collapsed all of a heap. Moung Hpé succeeded in bagging a huge bull with one shot through the neck, the animal dropping dead in its tracks. Moung Yan Gin wounded another, which, charging in my direction, was bowled over by me with a right and left. The animal shot by me turned out to be a large female, standing about 18½ hands with a fair head. Moung Yan Gin's bull, finished off by me, stood 18½ hands, and measured from tip to tip 11 feet 6 inches. Moung Hpé's animal stood 3 inches higher, but was the same length to half an inch. I am aware that it is not supposed to be the correct thing amongst sportsmen to shoot females unless you are badly off for fresh meat, but I can only plead guilty to my want of discrimination between bulls and cows.

It takes, in my opinion, no little experience to be able to pick out at a glance the bulls from the cows in a herd when you have only got, say, some ten or fifteen seconds to do it in, and where the gloom of the jungle is great. Should you by chance happen to come across the animals in dark tree jungle where the gloom is great, it is well-nigh impossible to discriminate betwixt the two. It is harder still to obtain a clear shot, as not only in the majority of cases has the bullet to penetrate many small intervening twigs, which are apt to turn it from its course, but the gloom is also so great in many parts of the jungle, especially in cloudy weather, there is a want of contrast between the foresight and dark hide of the animal, which adds to the difficulty of planting a bullet in the right spot.

There is a distinct difference, nevertheless, between the male and female gaur, which is, however, only noticeable at close quarters. Colonel Pollok gives this difference. He says that the Burmese cow bison has a longer head, nose more arched, and the points of the horns bend slightly backwards, and are, of course, much smaller; the frontal ridge is also prominent.[1]

Having made up my mind to change my camp from the Nampan Tankta-kugyi forest, and work up the Shwé-ū-taung hill and its outlying spurs for rhinoceros, elephants, wild goats, and the like, I issued orders accordingly, and we were soon *en route*. The climate in the neighbourhood of the Shwé-ū-taung hill would also be more enjoyable and cooler, having an elevation of some 4000 to 5000 feet. The water was not only cooler at that time of the year—May—but was also purer and more wholesome than that found in the low-lying country of the Nampan forest, which was invariably brackish, and nearly always in a tepid state.

After arriving at the village of Pinkan, near Sagadaung, Moung Hpé and I started for the hills, leaving our camp people to follow, having previously arranged with them as to a suitable spot for camping, in a gorge some eight miles from Pinkan. Moung Hpé and I, after wandering about for some time without seeing any tracks, were thinking of returning to camp, when a loud, long, deep, sonorous roar or bellow proceeded from an adjacent ridge. I was quite convinced in my own mind that the noise had been made by elephants. On the sound being repeated, however, Moung Hpé, although himself rather doubtful, informed me that it was the call of a gaur, and that a herd must be in the neighbourhood, as solitary animals seldom, if ever, call or bellow. After pro-

[1] These I have noticed in all I have seen or slain.—F. T. P.

ceeding cautiously in the direction of the sound for a distance of about 300 yards, I caught sight of three gaur, standing stern on, under some trees; others, from the sounds of breaking bamboos and an occasional low deep "moo," were moving about and feeding in the hollow beyond. With a whispered injunction to my men to lie down, I took my 8-bore, stuffing at the same time two spare cartridges in a side pocket, and stealing quickly forward, I took up my stand behind the trunk of a tree distant some forty paces from the animals, till an opportunity of obtaining a clear shoulder-shot presented itself.

After waiting for nearly twenty minutes in this position, one of the animals, which had apparently become suspicious, although the wind was in my favour, turned round broadside on and afforded me the coveted shot, which I immediately availed myself of, planting—as I thought—a bullet behind the shoulder. There was a general stampede and crashing of bamboos, etc., at the sound of the report, and before the smoke cleared, the herd, including the animal fired at, was out of sight in the valley below.

I ran up to the top of the ridge, in the hope of being able to get in a second shot, as the smoke from the charge—10 drams of powder—hung before me in the damp air like a cloud, and prevented my getting in another shot in time.

While looking for the tracks of the wounded animal on the summit of the ridge, Moung Hpé drew my attention to a sight which it has not been the fortune of many sportsmen to behold, viz. two young gaur calves. Both animals, probably a few days old, were lying down on the ground, watching us in the most calm, placid manner with their large liquid eyes, ears twitching backwards and forwards, eyeing us in turn without seeming in the least degree alarmed. No sooner, however, did we approach to within a yard or so of them, than that intuitive dread of man, inborn in all wild animals, showed itself. Both animals staggered to their feet, and swaying from side to side, attempted with staggering and uncertain steps to escape. Being still too young to use their legs with any degree of stability, they were easily captured. On being laid hold of, they bleated piteously for a short while, and then seemed to become quite reconciled to their fate. After a thorough inspection of the ungainly and yet pretty little beasts, which were about the size and appearance of young calves, we released them and left them in peace—to be shot, no doubt, at some future date, when developed into beasthood. Both animals, I noticed, had a faint dark stripe down the back. I have since regretted not having made an effort to try and get them brought in and have them suckled by a cow buffalo, as I believe, looking at it from a pecuniary point of view, that I could have made a good thing out of it by selling the animals to some dealer of wild beasts at home. And yet I am not sorry I released them, as I do not think I could have succeeded in bringing them in alive, as, being not only difficult animals to rear at any time, I should not have had an opportunity of obtaining fresh milk for them for probably two or three days, not to speak of the possibility of being unable to purchase eventually a milch buffalo. Besides, I should not have liked the little beasts to die whilst on my hands. But yet another and more important consideration—I should have lost the remainder of my leave if I had returned with them. Taking all things together the risk was great, and I do not think I should have been compensated for my trouble in the end.

After the usual scene of finding blood on the leaves and ground, we took on the tracks of the wounded gaur. Moung Hpé, after we had been following the trail for about a mile, seemed to think that I had hit the animal rather far back, and that we would in consequence have a long chase before bagging it. The tracks showed that the wounded gaur had separated from the herd and taken a line of its own. This is usually a distinct sign of an animal having been badly wounded. It is on occasions like this that the advantage of a heavy rifle is most apparent.

I have often picked out an animal from a herd of either tsine or gaur and fired at them with a ·303 rifle, and then found on going to the spot, should the animal not have been shot through the heart or head, that I was unable to tell which animal to follow, simply because the minute hole inflicted by the Lee-Metford bullet had not caused a sufficient flow of blood by which the tracks of the wounded animal could be followed. On the other hand the wound made by a 12 or 8-bore rifle bullet invariably leaves a big blood-spoor.

My 8-bore bullet had apparently passed clean through the gaur, as there was blood on either side of the trail. After two miles of steady tracking we came up with the gaur, looking very sick, standing alongside the trunk of a huge teak tree. The distance being about 100 yards, rather a long shot for the 8-bore, I put up the 100 yards sight and, taking a very full sight, fired, aiming for the point of the shoulder. The gaur stood stationary for about five seconds, and then, quivering in every limb, sank slowly to the ground, when he died after a few struggles. The bullet, I afterwards found, had, after piercing the heart, passed through the body and lodged beneath the skin on the other side. It was a fair-sized bull, standing 18 hands 2 inches, with a very good head and horns well ringed or corrugated at the base; the signs, it is said, of an old bull.

My camp-followers left for the spot early next day, and returned late in the evening with the head and meat. The latter was cut up into square junks laid on a framework of split bamboos, shaped like a parallelogram, erected some three feet above the ground, and then gradually smoked and dried over a slow log fire. This fire is sometimes maintained for a whole day before the meat has been thoroughly smoked and dried.

After a sufficient quantity of it has been cured it is put into woven wicker baskets made of thin strips of bamboo, called by the Burmans "kyingyas," and taken away for sale at the end of my shoot to neighbouring villages. It is then sold, my men making as much as 12 annas or even a rupee per viss—a viss is about 2½ lbs.—eventually dividing amongst themselves the proceeds of the sale, amounting to sometimes as much as Rs.300, about £18.

It is by allowing my men to dispose of all the meat of the animals shot by me for their own benefit, and by giving them the use of my transport animals to forward it to neighbouring villages, that I have always been able to obtain their services and get information regarding the whereabouts of game. Kind treatment, and an occasional present of an old coat, blanket, or pair of boots or shoes, a few cigars, a bottle of beer, or a few rupees at odd times will always repay the sportsman.

When out on *shikar* for a lengthy period his hunters must always be treated on an equal and on a friendly footing; receive them into your hut occasionally after a successful day's shooting, give them a peg, and chat and hobnob with them, if you wish to gain their confidence. This can always be done without lowering oneself or losing in any way one's dignity, or permitting of any undue familiarity or liberties. A Burman, should you treat him in the right way, will always be respectful, and knows how to keep his distance perfectly well. On the other hand, should a sportsman show any signs of temper or impatience by striking any of his guides and hunters, they will not only take jolly good care never to accompany him on another expedition, but will also be very chary of accompanying any other European into the jungle after game.

Next day I lost a huge solitary bull gaur through having only my 12 smooth-bore gun in hand. We were walking listlessly along when the bull, which had been sleeping within a yard or two of the track, suddenly jumped up and dashed away without even the customary snort of alarm. I had only time to fire an ineffective shot with the smooth-bore, taking aim for its ribs. A few spots of blood, the size of a threepenny piece, appearing now and again for a distance of over two miles, during which time the gaur had not slackened its pace, convinced me that it was useless following any further.

While tracking up this animal we ran into a nest of hornets, which stung one of my men most unmercifully. These hornets were in size quite an inch long, of a black colour, and as thick as my little finger. I happened to be leading at the time, and hearing the warning "buzz" overhead of a single "boodwho," which was, I have no doubt, on sentry-go over the rest, I dashed forward, leaving at the same time my hat, an Ellwood shikar, behind me. The two men who were walking behind at the time, and who had also stepped on to the nest, dashed off at right angles uttering yells of pain. On looking back, at a distance of some 30 or 40 yards,

I saw that my hat was literally covered with a black, enraged, crawling mass of hornets. We had actually walked over the nest, and I was the only one who had escaped. My two companions fairly writhed and groaned in their agony, so excruciating was the pain. Two or three stings from this particular species of hornet, it is said, is sufficient to kill a man.

I had a few days before this incident received a letter from my friend D——, already referred to in a previous portion of this paper. I may mention that his was a hornets' nest in a tree in the garden of a Buddhist monastery, occupied by several monks, who had asked D—— to destroy the nest by firing a charge of shot into it. D—— had arrived that day from Bernardmyo, with a friend, G——, and they were both putting up in a rest-house adjoining the monastery a few yards off. I shall read an extract from his letter. "That affair with the wasps was awful. I had a very narrow squeak; I just managed to get into a very dark place in the jungle in time, there were hundreds after me; G—— took refuge in a dark room in the 'pongyi khoung'—monastery. They were a small-sized wasp with dark brown bodies and no stripe. They killed both our dogs, two of my transport mules, and G——'s pony. One of the mules had only six stings, and many Burmans in the village had a dozen or more, so that the poison evidently effects animals more than men."

I had an awful business recovering my hat; quite an hour and a half elapsed before I eventually succeeded in dragging it away by tying bamboos together. These hornets seemed to be able to see at a distance of from 15 to 25 yards, as one of my men was stung a second time by one of them, which shot out from amongst the cloud hovering and crawling around the nest, and made straight for him, stinging him on the back as he ran off. I remember, on one occasion, being nearly killed by my pony, which, maddened by the stings received from them, ran away with me through jungle, regardless of curb-chain, fallen trees, stumps, and overhanging branches. I had to dodge them as best I could, thinking all the time that my last hour had come. When a thing like this happens to an elephant, especially should there be a howdah in the question, it becomes a more serious matter, as the huge brute, maddened by the stings, often travels miles over and through the most awful jungle ground before bringing up. My colleague has, I have no doubt, seen and experienced a good may mishaps of this kind.[1]

A few mornings afterwards, when camped out near the village of Chaukmaw with D—— and A——, two officers from Bernardmyo, I came upon the tracks of a solitary bull gaur within half-a-mile of camp.

The ground at this time of the year was dry and hard, and it was consequently rather difficult to walk along noiselessly through the low dwarf-stunted bamboo shrubs, as the ground was covered with dry, feathery bamboo leaves and stems which cracked at every step. If any person, unacquainted with the art of stalking, had been watching Moung Hpé and myself, he would have come to the conclusion we had gone mad, so cautiously and carefully did we pick our way along, as if the treading on a single leaf or twig was a matter of life and death.

Those who have not experienced the pleasure and excitement of stalking a large animal like a gaur in jungle, will never understand the intense excitement and thrill of suppressed expectation which is felt.

It is not the shooting of the animal alone which is the exciting part of it, but the getting within sight and shooting distance of him without being discovered. But let me go back to the gaur we were stalking.

The animal had lain down twice, and the odour of gaur and other signs well known to a hunter with any experience, such as a number of flies hovering over the impression left by the animal's body on the ground, smoking ordure, the froth and bursting bubbles of its urine, pieces of freshly-chewed vegetation, freshly-cropped bamboo twigs or tufts of grass, fresh white juice oozing out of a root bruised by the bison's hoof, showed us that the gaur was in the immediate vicinity. Moung Hpé now warned me to be careful, as there was little or no cover behind which to retreat in case of a

[1] I have been stung and chased by bees and wasps many times, but don't remember coming across hornets.—F. T. P.

charge, and we might now come upon the bison at any moment. I shall never forget the excitement of that moment, and how carefully we crouched down and stalked along at the rate of about two steps to the minute, eagerly scanning with lightning rapidity the surrounding jungle, with every sense on the alert. The low overhanging bamboo shrubs afforded admirable shade from the sun's rays, and as it was then about 9 a.m., Moung Hpé said the animal would be sure to be either asleep or resting, chewing the cud. After gliding along in this noiseless manner, like two human leopards, for a distance of about 100 yards, Moung Hpé, who was a foot or two away on my right but abreast of me, suddenly sank down on one knee and pointed out a dark mass to me which lay motionless under a low, overhanging bamboo clump. At first I could hardly believe it was the gaur, as not only was it quite motionless, but, which is unusual in a solitary bull, its breathing was also inaudible. Our position was a most awkward one, as I was not only unable to make out any vital portion of the gaur's body, which was partially concealed from view by overhanging bamboos, but I had to sink down on to both knees before firing—which I did, aiming for what I took to be the chest and neck, rather a risky shot considering the position I was then in. For a second or two after the shot the smoke hung and obscured everything, during which time I heard a tremendous snort and thumping of feet. On the smoke clearing, I caught sight of the gaur struggling to its feet; a second shot through the shoulder, however, finished its career, as, struggling to its feet with difficulty, it lurched heavily from side to side, and after crashing through several small bamboo clumps, sank slowly to the ground, when it died after a long-drawn bellow and an interval of a tremendous quivering and stiffening of every muscle and limb. This was a very fine old bull, standing at the shoulder 19 hands. The horns were not, however, for the size of the animal, as fine a pair as I expected them to be. I gave the head to my friend D——, who expressed a wish to have them.

Several articles have appeared in the *Field* recently regarding the presence or absence of a dew-lap in the gaur. Col. Pollok, who has been more observant than I have in these matters, has also referred to the subject at some length, so I need not go into details. I have shot altogether about twenty-five of these animals, mostly old and solitary bulls, but have never noticed a distinct dew-lap. That there is a heavy skin appendage where the dew-lap ought to be goes without saying, but it can hardly be given the name of dew-lap, which is a loose fold of skin descending from the neck to within a short distance of the ground. With regard to the dew-lap being loose in the calf, I may say that there was absolutely no appearance of one on the two animals captured by me, referred to in a previous page of this chapter.

One evening, a short time after sunset, I was strolling along a ridge near the top of the Shwé-ū-taung hill with my binoculars, amusing myself by examining the surrounding country, and watching the movements of a herd of sambur which were browsing on a ridge about 300 yards off, when a large black object, which I at once recognized to be a gaur, emerged from a strip of wood and walked up the side of a ridge, grazing on the tender young shoots of grass as it moved along. As it was then late in the evening, and the animal was distant about two and a half miles, Moung Hpé, who was standing beside me, thought it advisable to leave the animal undisturbed till next day, when we would have more time to come up with him, as he was sure to be found in the neighbourhood. We started next morning early, long before the sun rose, after a cup of tea and some biscuits. Moung Hpé and another gun-bearer accompanied me. After a steady tramp of about three hours through fairly open tree and bamboo jungle, we came upon the bull's fresh tracks. The animal had been wandering about here and there, backwards and forwards, grazing on the young shoots of grass, and had apparently taken up his abode in the neighbourhood, as a number of his old tracks and droppings were visible all over the place. The trail now showed us that the gaur was not far off, so we were on the alert. It was not long before the animal was heard labouring along up the hillside straight towards us, evidently on his way back over old ground again, his deep breathing being audible at quite 100 yards off. I had in the meantime taken up my stand behind the trunk of a tree, and loaded up with hardened spherical ball. Moung Hpé stood in readiness beside me with the 12 smooth-bore. The wind, although I had not tested it, must have been in our favour, as the gaur moved steadily on till within about 20 yards of my position, when he stopped, evidently suspicious that all was not right.

I did not care to fire at once, as I wanted to watch his actions and methods of feeding. I noticed particularly that whilst walking slowly along he browsed on the rough leaves of a certain bush called by the Burmans "kyan-sa," or rhinoceros food, the rough tongue of the animal being used to pull the leaves and small twigs into his mouth. At intervals, whilst standing, he would whisk round his tail on to his ribs with a resounding thump, thump, emitting at times the low deep breathing sounds. Old bulls can never graze on very short grass if they are standing on level ground, as their necks are too short to allow of their mouths reaching low enough. In the same way, many a charging gaur could not toss or reach with its horns a man lying perfectly flat on the ground.[1]

After waiting patiently for a few seconds he veered suddenly round, and stood in a listening attitude as if expecting something to approach, and exposed his shoulder. I immediately availed myself of the opportunity and, raising the 8-bore slowly, fired, aiming for a little behind the shoulder low down. Instead of turning off and crashing away down the hillside, or dropping dead, the gaur stood stock-still for about thirty seconds, and then made a sort of half-hearted blundering rush towards the tree behind which I had taken up my stand. A second shot, however, from the 8-bore turned him, and he went staggering away down the steep incline into a nullah, where he fell with a tremendous crash, stone dead. I found, on opening him, that my second bullet had pierced the heart. My first bullet had entered a little too high. The tape showed his height to be 18 hands 3 inches, and 10 feet 3 inches in length; the horns were very massive at the base, with a circumference of 19½ inches, but were short.

One has to be particularly careful when firing at gaur not

[1] Disproved in the case of Captain Syers, who, when lying on his back, was tossed and killed by a gaur: *vide* page 366 of this chapter.

to aim too high, as is often done, owing to the target presented by the huge dorsal ridge. A bullet may be driven clean through the hump or ridge in question without even bringing the animal to the ground.[1] If hit near enough the spine, however, the shock will stun him temporarily, and he will fall to the ground as if dead, but will be up in a second and off again as if untouched. I have, however, referred to this elsewhere.

I remember an instance of this happening to myself on one occasion, and how awfully disgusted I was at losing the animal, which was a very large gaur—the largest, in fact, it has ever been my fortune to see. I lost this animal partly through being too impatient and partly through bad shooting.

Whilst encamped at a place called Mézli Sakan on the Tha-na-da choung, we struck the fresh trail of a large solitary gaur, which, however, winded us and made off. We again took them on, and after crossing some three miles of country the tracks led into some rather thick cover. Leaving my men outside, I entered with the 8-bore and worked my way cautiously into the jungle. I noticed while moving along that there were numerous fresh tracks of elephants about, and was only hoping that I shouldn't come across any of the brutes in the cover I was then in, as I was not very keen on tackling an elephant in such thick cover.

After having crawled along carefully for about 100 yards, I suddenly caught sight in the gloom of what I took to be the huge dark posterior of a young elephant. Thinking I had got into the middle of a herd of these animals, I immediately backed out to where I had left my companions in order to arrange as to the next move. On getting outside the cover, I heard a crash and a tremendous chattering of monkeys near the spot I had just vacated. We returned to the locality and found, much to my disgust, that the supposed elephant was in reality the gaur we had been following up, which had again winded us and made off.

I was awfully annoyed and ashamed of myself. We picked up the tracks again, however, which, after crossing the Tha-na-da choung—stream—near the camp, entered the jungle on

[1] I once shot a gaur through the dorsal ridge, a little in front of the hump, and he was paralyzed.—F. T. P.

the other side. When we reached this spot, Moung Hpé advised me not to follow any further till the gaur, which had now settled down to a walk, had quite recovered from its alarm, and as it was near evening, Moung Hpé rightly argued that after resting in the cover ahead of us the animal would be sure to be found feeding in the neighbourhood later on in the evening. I was too impatient, however, to listen to any advice, as I was under the impression that the gaur had gone on much further. The responsibility of what followed now fell on my own shoulders.

We crossed the stream, which had only a thin current of water flowing along its sandy bed, and entered the jungle on the other side. We had not gone 200 yards before the now thoroughly alarmed gaur, which had been lying down resting, rose up and dashed away with a loud whistling snort of alarm. I had only time to catch a glimpse of him, and fired a snap-shot in the hopes of hitting him somewhere. The animal, I afterwards found, dropped to the shot, and from blood-stains on leaves and bushes some five feet from the ground, my hunter concluded that my bullet had passed through the dorsal ridge. I was too disgusted to continue the chase, as the bison had gone away practically unhurt. It was thus that I lost my chance of bagging the largest gaur I have ever seen. The animal stood, I am certain, quite 21 hands at the shoulder. I took on his tracks again next day and followed them on for several miles, but eventually gave them up and fired at one of a pair of solitary bull tsine, which were feeding along directly in our track, and which I succeeded in bagging. I often came across the tracks of this monster gaur afterwards, but never managed to come up with him.

Two days after this occurrence I again struck the trail of a solitary bull gaur in the neighbourhood of my encampment, "Mézli Sakan" (Bur. "mézli," the name of a tree, "sakan" Bur. for camp). We found the tracks of gaur and took them steadily on all day, covering, I am sure, some fifteen or eighteen miles of country before coming up with him. The sportsman has to be very keen indeed to go in for tracking up an animal to the bitter end, as it is not only very hard work but it tries the patience severely. The trackers, if not experienced and trustworthy men, will often try to discourage and put the sportsman off if they don't know him well, and think there is the least likelihood of having a long tramp after an animal. He should not be deterred by such hints as "Thakin thee kyi-ya ah-haung tin dè gané ma hmee hnine bū" (Sir, these tracks are old, we will not come up with them to-day), or "Mochok la bŷi thakin, pyan thwa gya zo, yakū ma pyan yin sakan gané nya ma yauk hnine bū kyi ya knepan, ma neh pyan kaukhli mè" (It is getting dark, sir, let us return; if we do not return now we will not reach camp to-night; we can return to-morrow and take on the tracks again).

There are very few natives who are keen sportsmen, and they cannot understand our mania for big-game shooting when we only collect the trophies and discard the meat! A Burman hunter, of course, takes to the pastime simply to make a living, and naturally he goes about it in a business-like way, and takes good care to do as little walking as possible. Often, when out shooting during the day on his own account, he will have a long snooze when the sun is at its hottest, and only begins to think of business in the early morning and evening.

Three men accompanied me on this occasion, and it was amusing to listen to their remarks *en route* as to the likelihood of our coming up with the gaur before dark. Moung Hpé, my favourite hunter, was not with me on this occasion, or else there would have been none of this uncertainty. One man would say to his comrade, for my benefit of course, "Gané kyi ya ma ho pu tin dé" (I do not think these are to-day's tracks), or "Ah thit lo lo ahaung lo lo a hman ma pyaw hnine bū nya gyi ta gaung gyaw thwa dè tin dè;" literally: "Sometimes they look like old tracks, sometimes new, I cannot say for certain. I think they went last night after 1 a.m."

The sportsman, should he not have a really good tracker with him, must trust a good deal to common sense and his own experience of tracking, as to whether he should continue taking on the tracks of an animal or not.

In this case, after travelling on the tracks of the gaur from about 9 a.m. till 4 p.m., the hunter who had first said they were fairly fresh began to hint that he thought he had made a mistake, and that they had passed during the night at about 10 p.m., in which case the gaur, should he have been on the move since that hour, would now be a long way off. After a little hesitation I made up my mind to stick to the tracks and follow them up, even though we should have to sleep in the jungle. This can always be done, even though the tracks should be a day or two old, and if the sportsman has good trackers with him, he will ultimately—if he is keen enough—come up with the animal he is following.

The sportsman should always let his hunters and guides see that he is not afraid to camp out in the jungle for a night with them, even though he should have to go without a meal. They are always in mortal dread of taking the sportsman too far away from camp whilst in pursuit of an animal, in case they are sworn at by the "thakin" or sahib, when he finds—especially after an unsuccessful hunt—that he has some sixteen or eighteen miles of country to cover before arriving at camp, and that he will arrive there too late for a comfortable tub and dinner. A sportsman, to be successful when big-game shooting, must occasionally undergo discomforts of this kind, and sleep a night in the jungle when necessary. In fact, if he cannot put up with it now and again when it assures success, he is not worthy of the name of sportsman, far less to follow up so noble a prize as a solitary bull gaur. But let us go back to the animal I was tracking up.

At one spot, whilst nearing a dense patch of "kaing" or tall elephant grass, we came on a burnt black stump of a tree some 5 or 6 feet high, at which the gaur had apparently shied and been thoroughly startled. The deep impressions of its hoofs, which were left on the ground, showed that it had dashed away with long leaps; mistaking, I have no doubt, in the uncertain light of the early morning, the burnt stump for a human being. The tracks then entered the adjacent patch of grass.

I now became convinced from the tracks, and after an examination of the animal's droppings, that he must have passed about 9 a.m. that morning. It was now necessary to be very careful, as it was very ticklish work, and almost an utter impossibility to attempt to stalk the gaur in grass of this description, where the animal would most likely be lying perfectly still and make off on hearing the least noise. I now noticed that the animal had settled down from its recent alarm and that its tracks crossed and re-crossed one another all over the place ; tracking, consequently, became very perplexing work. It showed me, however, that the gaur had stayed in the neighbourhood for some hours, and would probably not be far off. After warning my men to use the utmost caution in moving, as the snapping of the smallest twig or grass stalk would have been fatal, we moved along in single file through the various narrow lanes that intersected one another throughout the patch, I led the way with the 8-bore, both hammers at full cock ready for action.

After travelling in this manner for about 50 yards or so, I found it was hopeless work going any further, as there were not only numerous gaur tracks all over the place, but it was well-nigh impossible to distinguish from amongst these the tracks of the animal we had been following. Numerous lanes intersecting one another had been trodden down in the neighbourhood recently. Whilst debating amongst ourselves as to our next move and the advisability of making for camp, it being then well on in the evening, and returning next day to take on the tracks, I heard a low, deep "mooing" or breathing sound, which seemed to emanate from an adjacent cover. Moung Yauk at once said : "Thakin pyaung shu than ah nee galè bè" (It is the noise of the gaur breathing not far off). After examining both chambers of my 8-bore to see that they were loaded, and ordering my men to sit down on the ground and wait for me, I worked my way out of the grass and moved cautiously in the direction of the sound.

I had not gone 100 yards before the deep breathing sound of an old solitary bull gaur was wafted across to my ears like music from a patch of jungle some 40 yards ahead of me. On getting nearer, I could distinctly hear the animal cropping the grass which was growing inside the wood quite luxuriantly. The thrill of excitement which now passed through me can only be realized by those who have gone through the same experience. I had no time to ascertain by lighting a match whether the wind was in my favour or not—there was fortunately hardly a breath of air stirring—and everything round was as still as the grave, except, perhaps, for the distant bark of a ghee or barking deer, or the crow of a jungle cock as he strutted about with his family in some bamboo jungle close by. Without wasting any more time I stepped cautiously forward in a bent attitude, my sense of sight and hearing stretched to their utmost tension. I had not gone far before, in the gloom of the jungle, I caught sight of the black body of the gaur standing broadside on, motionless, except perhaps when he shook the gadflies from his head or brushed them from his body with his tail or horns, or perhaps an occasional stamp from a neat yet mighty hoof. It was a grand sight, and one perhaps to make a sportsman hesitate before bringing his death-dealing tube to bear; but, alas! I was only human, and the feeling to slay—that feeling of exultation and triumph which predominates in every sportsman on occasions like this, especially after a hard day's walking under a broiling sun—overpowered me.

The gaur was now in full view, and although there was comparatively little cover between us in the way of dense undergrowth, he was quite unconscious of my presence. I did not wait any longer, but fired, aiming for the point of the shoulder, the distance between us being about 30 yards. The gaur, on receiving the shot, dashed straight off; but turned, strange to relate, after going about 30 yards, and bore straight down on me. It had not covered half the distance that separated us, however, before it collapsed with a tremendous crash into a clump of small trees, a little to one side of me in front. I was standing behind a tree ready to receive him, intending to give him a right and a left behind the shoulder should he pass me at the charge. He was a magnificent bull, standing 6 feet 6 inches at the shoulder, measured correctly between uprights. From tip round the curve to the base the horns measured 38 inches, 20 inches in girth at the base, 19 inches tip to tip, 42¼ inches widest outside, and inside width 34 inches. After disembowelling the gaur we returned to camp, using dry splinters of bamboo tied together in bundles to serve as torches to light our way, the night being starless. It was simply marvellous how my followers managed to strike the right line to camp in the dark. *En route* to camp we walked into a herd of tsine, which stampeded, snorting, in all directions. I sent my transport mules for the head next day, and all the meat they could bring in for my men.

They returned late next evening with the information that they had come upon the huge tracks of another solitary bull gaur, within half-a-mile of camp, near an old camping-ground of mine called Thanada, after a stream of the same name. During the night rain fell heavily, obliterating all tracks, so that next day—should we come upon any tracks—we would have no difficulty in ascertaining whether they were new or old ones. After striking the Thanada choung, or stream, and walking along the banks for about a quarter of a mile, we struck the tracks of a solitary gaur which were only a few hours' old. The impression of its hoofs were enormous compared to what I had been accustomed to seeing, and at first I thought the owner must be a veritable monster. Moung Yauk, however, pointed out to me that the imprint of the animal's hoof had only been made larger owing to the mud and clay which adhered to the feet, the surrounding soil from the recent heavy rain being very soft. Tracking under these circumstances being comparatively easy work, I took the lead myself, with the hope of being able to come up with the animal before mid-day.

The feeling of satisfaction which comes over one under circumstances like these, when the sportsman is confident of coming up with an animal soon, can only be understood by those who have experienced it. Here I was on the fresh tracks of a huge solitary bull gaur, no dense impenetrable jungle in the neighbourhood to impede my movements, my footfall rendered absolutely inaudible on the leaves and twigs, owing to the sodden and saturated state of everything after the recent heavy rainfall, no treacherous breeze to warn the animal of our approach, and our camp distant only about a mile. The tracks, after crossing the stream several times, and along the banks of which the animal had been grazing, eventually led into a shady strip of jungle, where there was little or no undergrowth, but yet ample cover from the rays of the sun. I was now on the alert; my eyes flashed here and there ahead of me and to either side, and my ears strained to their utmost to catch the slightest sound. It was magnificent cover for gaur, as there was lots of grass growing in patches throughout the wood which afforded admirable grazing ground, and I was consequently hoping that the animal would remain in the neighbourhood. Moung Yauk and another companion were following in my footsteps at a distance of about twenty-five paces. The tracks now showed us that the gaur was about to rest, as he had wandered about from side to side in a listless fashion, as if on the look-out for a suitable place to lie down. The animal could not be far off, as a very strong odour of bison prevailed about the place, and, sure enough, after rounding a small clump of bamboo I saw the huge dark mass looming up standing broadside on, under the shade of a large clump of bamboos not twenty paces off. The animal appeared quite unconscious of my presence. Without turning my head, I lifted up my hand behind my back as a signal for my men to halt, and quietly raising the 8-bore, fired for the shoulder, a very clear shot being obtainable. The gaur dropped to the shot like a stone, shot through the heart.

It was curious to watch its actions then, as it closed its eyelids and shot its tongue out at times into its nostrils. After an interval of about half a minute every muscle became rigid and the whole body trembled violently, after which it emitted one or two loud bellows, struggling the while, and then died, the eyes staring and wide open.

Sportsmen should be very careful never to approach a gaur after it has been floored should it remain with closed eyelids, as this is a sure sign that the animal is not as yet *in articulo mortis.*[1] Many a Burman hunter has been gored to death through carelessness in approaching an animal supposed to

[1] A better is that a stricken animal commences to kick; then passes water, then wind, then evacuates—then it is a sign that he is dead. *Vide* an old copy of the Dragon of Wantley in Bishop Percy's *Reliques of Ancient English Poetry.*—F. T. P.

be dead. Pieces of sticks and stones should always be thrown at the body for some minutes after it is down. The sportsman can, of course, when armed with a heavy rifle and there is a sufficiently solid shelter behind which to retreat, such as a bamboo clump or tree trunk in the immediate vicinity of the animal, approach to within a yard or two and administer a quietus. As little powder and ball as possible should, however, be wasted, as not only is the surrounding jungle disturbed for miles around, but it is useless expenditure of ammunition. It is simply marvellous what a gaur will take in the way of lead before succumbing, even from a heavy weapon like the 8-bore, and at others how easily it is killed.

It is absolute folly attempting to use small-bore express rifles upon such thick-skinned, muscular, big-boned, and massive beasts as gaur. Many sportsmen have, I have no doubt, been fairly successful with small bores, but one day in thick cover with a charging gaur, bull elephant, or tsine in his immediate front, he will discover his mistake. An article in the *Field* of September 10, 1898, entitled "Jungle Experiences in Pahang," gives a very good instance of how an experienced sportsman, Captain Syers, Commissioner of Police for the Federated Malay States, lost his life through having pinned his faith to a ·577 express double rifle. I shall here quote an extract from the above article for the benefit of those sportsmen who may still be of the same opinion with regard to a ·577 and other small-bores upon huge and dangerous game, who may not have seen the publication I refer to.

"We started down-river, reaching Knala Klan about midnight on the 12th. Next morning (July 12, 1897) we went up the Klan river and landed at Padaung Ali. I landed here at a grass plain on the river bank, and found eleven bison and a calf feeding. I went back to the boats and informed Syers. He was armed with a ·577 express, and on his recommendation I carried a similar weapon, leaving my 10-bore in the boat. We started the bull through grass about five feet high, and we both gave him the contents of both barrels; he made off at a terrific pace into the jungle. The remainder of the herd cantered past slowly, and we managed to put the contents of another two barrels each into a cow as she passed us. She ran into a patch of undergrowth, where Syers finished her. In the meantime my Malay tracker, Awang, came up with my 10-bore, but stupidly only brought two cartridges. We then proceeded to follow the wounded bull. We tracked for three hours, when we unexpectedly heard a bison stamping, knocking off the flies from his legs. We made for the spot from which the noise proceeded, and came across a fresh bull in big jungle. He was about 30 yards from us, and we agreed to fire simultaneously. I gave him both barrels of my 10-bore and Syers both barrels from his ·577.

"The beast bolted; we followed up, and about half-an-hour afterwards heard him moving in the jungle ahead. We made a detour, but the bull had been watching us, and charged Syers, who gave him one barrel, turning him; he again charged, and Syers gave him his left barrel; the bull, on receiving the bullet, reared clear on his hind-legs and dashed past at an angle. He then made for me, and I gave him both barrels from my ·577, having in the meanwhile handed my 10-bore to Awang, as I had no more cartridges for it. All these shots had taken effect, but the bull was not disabled. Syers used a ·577 express throughout. The bull went on for about 300 yards and then waited for us; as we came up to him he again charged at a terrific pace. I heard him coming and stepped aside; Syers waited for him, and fired his first barrel at a distance of 20 yards, and his second at a distance of only two yards. Neither shot turned him, and the bull caught him clean in the back, rearing up into the air with him. Poor Syers, still clutching to his rifle, turned three complete somersaults before his head struck the branch of a tree some 35 feet from the ground. He fell straight down on his back. The bull till now had not touched him with his horns, but waiting for him the moment he touched the ground again, tossed him with his right horn, the horn penetrating below his ribs in the right-hand side. I was close at hand, and fired two simultaneous shots, not even putting the rifle to my shoulder, and was knocked endways.

CROSSING THE DRY BED OF A STREAM, AND TIGHTENING GIRTHS.

All this occurred in a few seconds, and I had been unable to put in a shot sooner. The bull left the spot and lay down in the undergrowth close by, kicking and bellowing where he lay. I went at once to Syers' assistance, and found him terribly injured; the lining of the stomach protruding from the wound in his right side. I at once sent Awang to get assistance, and he returned in an hour and a half's time with some sakies, whom he met coming down-river in their dug-outs. In the meantime, I did all I could to bind and dress Syers' wound. We made a stretcher and carried him to the boat.

"At Syers' urgent request I returned to despatch the bull, leaving him in the care of his old servant, Yacoob. I had some difficulty in finding the spot where the bison was lying, but, on finding him, I stalked close up to him. He tried to rise but was unable to do so. I gave him five shots before he was finished. I counted fifteen bullet wounds, mostly on the shoulders, some of them penetrating clean through the body. Yacoob, in the meanwhile, had sent on news of the accident to Knala Semantan by a fast sampan. I left two men to gather the head, and immediately proceeded down-river with Syers. It was about 11 a.m. when Syers met with his injury, and we commenced our way down-stream about 2 p.m. Before proceeding down-stream I dressed the wound with carbolic bandages, and gave him small doses of brandy-and-water. He complained of great pain in his bladder, and I applied hot fomentations and opium.

"We reached Knala Semantan at 9.30 p.m., where Mr. Townley gave me every available assistance. We moved Syers into a larger boat and gave him some chloroform. We left at 10 p.m. with a crew of twenty Malays rowing hard, in the hope of reaching Pekan, where the nearest medical aid was obtainable. Syers was in good spirits and complained of being sleepy, but at 12.45 a.m., on the 14th, he expired.

"I reached Pekan on the 15th, where poor Syers was examined by Dr. Jesser Coope. On examination it was found that the muscles on the right side of his back were completely torn away from the spine, and Dr. Coope expressed the opinion that this alone would have been sufficient to kill

Syers, apart from his internal injuries, which were extremely serious. In fact, he was surprised that Syers should have lived so long as eleven and a half hours after the accident. For the benefit of other sportsmen I may here state that Syers, who before his accident was a firm believer in the ·577 express for big-game shooting, and with which weapon he had shot no less than thirteen bison and other large game, told me, shortly before he expired, that if he had been armed with an 8-bore the bull, in his last charge, would have been stopped; and earnestly entreated me never to go after bison again with so small a weapon. With this sad experience before me, it is needless to add that in future I will follow out this last advice of the best sportsman who ever breathed."

The above narrative speaks for itself, and is a very sad instance of the folly of using small-bore rifles upon large and dangerous game, especially in thick cover where it is absolutely imperative to prevent an animal from making good its charge. I cannot point out too often the danger of using small-bores.[1] I remember on one occasion, shortly after the purchase of a ·303 Metford rifle, having a very close shave from a huge solitary bull tsine or *Bos sondaicus*. I was walking along the top of a ridge covered with dwarf bamboo bushes, when, at a distance of only about twenty paces, I caught sight of a tsine looking at me through some bamboo shrubs, the chest and face only visible. I immediately fired, aiming for the chest with a Lee-Metford; the tsine, on receiving the shot, dashed straight at me, and I had only time to step on one side; as it was, the bamboo branches dashed aside by the animal in its charge knocked my hat off. I never saw this animal again, nor could I even make out if he had been hit, there being no blood-spoor by which to follow. This would never have happened had I been armed with a double 4 or 8-bore.

Two days after the death of my last gaur I changed my camp, and proceeded some five miles higher up the Thanada stream. Here we struck the tracks of a herd of bison that

[1] Yet Van Hohnel shot elephants at 400 yards and two rhinoceros with one shot out of a Mannlicher!—F. T. P.

had been in the neighbourhood the previous day. We took them on till late in the evening, when Moung Hpé said that we would have to camp a night in the jungle if we wanted to come up with the herd. This I agreed to do. After covering some three or four miles of ground, Moung Hpé warned me, from the signs he had seen *en route*, that the herd were probably lying down resting in a shady patch of cover ahead of us. It now behoved us to be very careful, as everything was very still, and there being little or no breeze, the least noise would have alarmed the whole herd. At about 4.30 p.m., while seated for a minute or two on a fallen tree till Moung Hpé and the other two men with me had had a chew of betel-nut and a puff at their cheroots, the deep stillness of the jungle was suddenly broken by a dull, muffled, prolonged roar or bellow, which appeared to come from the jungle, some hundred yards or so from where we were seated. The bellow or call, which lasted for about seven seconds, had no sooner been emitted, than we heard from all directions the sound of animals walking quickly along over dry undergrowth and leaves in the direction from which the call had come. We had very nearly walked right into the middle of the herd, which had apparently been asleep. It was marvellous with what rapidity the animals had obeyed the call of their leader, an old bull or probably a female. I tried to stalk this animal, whose deep breathing could be heard quite distinctly before the herd came up. I had, in fact, covered half the distance between us, when a young bull suddenly stepped into view within ten paces and stared hard at me. I lay in a crouched position, not daring to move, hoping that he would move on and allow me to get a shot at the leader; but no—after staring hard at me for a few seconds it obtained my wind and dashed off, after sounding the customary snort of alarm. I was very disappointed at not having got a shot at the old bull, and yet I was very pleased to think I had witnessed the manner by which the herd had been collected, and with what alacrity the animals had obeyed their leader's call.

After some very stiff walking we reached camp late that night. I succeeded on the way back in shooting a large rock-snake, or "sabagyi," or python. These snakes are fairly numerous all over the province, and some have been found over 20 feet in length. On another occasion I shot one of these amimals whilst it was in a torpid state through having swallowed a doe, barking deer, or "ghee," an animal standing a good deal higher than a collie dog. The Burmans not only ate up every portion of the snake, but accounted for the deer as well. The venison, of course, was perfectly good, as the animal had only been recently killed.

In a previous chapter of this book I made some mention as to solitary bull bison frequenting the same localities for days together, and that they, like solitary elephants, go over the same ground when coming and going from one cover or grazing-ground to another.

An instance of this occurred, in my experience, in the Nampan forest near Ōkshitkōn. I had heard that the tracks of a solitary bull gaur had been seen on the outskirts of a long strip of dense jungle, situated some three and a half miles from camp. Having first verified this information, I started out before daybreak, accompanied by Moung Yauk and another man acquainted with the locality. We made a wide detour, intending to return towards evening past the cover in question where the tracks had been seen, with the hope of finding the gaur in the neighbourhood.

Whilst moving along through a very likely piece of bamboo jungle we struck the fresh trail of a solitary tsine, and heard it almost at the same time feeding off young bamboo shoots some forty paces off. I immediately stalked it, but hesitated about firing, as I was afraid the old bull gaur we intended looking up in the evening might hear the shot and leave the locality. But as the old saw has it, that "a bird in the hand is worth two in the bush," I made up my mind to chance it, and, aiming for the shoulder, fired a right and left. Both bullets from the 8-bore took effect, and brought the tsine to the ground with a crash, where he lay kicking and bellowing till life ebbed away.

After disembowelling the animal to prevent the meat becoming tainted, we proceeded to the spot where the tracks of the solitary bull gaur had been seen, hoping that the animal had not taken alarm at the report of my shots and made off. We had not gone a mile and a half before we came upon unmistakable signs of the animal's presence. His tracks were, in fact, only an hour or two old, and two places where he had lain down appeared to have been only recently vacated, as the flies were still buzzing around, and there was an unmistakable odour of bison.[1] At numerous other places, old tracks, and the remains of bamboo shoots upon which the bison had been feeding, showed us that the animal had been in the neighbourhood for some days. A few yards further on the track suddenly widened, with great gaps between each footprint, and the slots or divisions of the hoofs now showed very deep and distinctly in the soft earth. I now saw at a glance from the tracks that the gaur had become alarmed at my shots and made off at a great pace. After taking them on for about 300 yards, we noticed that the animal had stopped, turned round, and halted for a short time to listen, after which it had continued its flight with long leaps. It was very aggravating, to say the least of it, and as I knew the animal would travel a long distance before halting, we did not think it worth while following him up any further. After taking on the tracks for about a mile and a half along a low ridge, during which time the bison had not once slackened its pace, we relinquished the tracks and returned to camp.

I made particular note of the fact that there were several old tracks going and coming along the route by the gaur in its flight which were exactly similar in shape and size to that of the animal we were following; I concluded from this that the beast we had just alarmed always used this particular track along the top of the ridge when bound for its favourite cover and feeding-ground. I made up my mind, therefore, to go back to the ridge two or three days later on, with the hope of being able to see his return tracks. Three days later, in spite of protests from my men, who did not believe the gaur would come back to the cover, I left for the ridge, distant from our camp some eight miles.

During the interval of two days I stayed in camp and amused myself by writing up my diary and cleaning my trophies. My men were not, however, idle; I made them go

[1] Very like the smell of a cattle-pen.—F. T. P

round and visit neighbouring bamboo jungles and likely covers for solitary bulls, and promised twenty rupees to the man who first brought me "kubber" of a solitary tusker elephant, ten rupees for information of a solitary gaur, and five rupees for a solitary bull tsine. This should always be done if you have men to spare. Three or four of them should always be sent out in different directions, with the promise of a reward should they come upon tracks, solitary bulls preferred.

On arriving at the ridge I saw at a glance, to my utter astonishment, that the bull I had alarmed with my shot a few days ago had apparently only just passed on his way back to his old feeding-grounds. It was a great piece of luck, and I felt quite proud to think that in spite of my hunters' non-belief regarding the return of the bull, my prediction had, after all, been correct.

While we were examining the tracks a herd of tsine, some thirty in number, thundered past us at a distance of about 30 yards. They had been startled in some unaccountable manner, probably by crossing our tracks somewhere in our rear. I could have shot a magnificent bull which brought up the rear, but refrained from doing so, as I was determined to bag the solitary gaur, these animals being scarcer and by far the nobler quarry of the two. Tsine were very plentiful throughout the Nampan Tankta-kugyi forest, and on some days I have come upon two or three herds, not to mention solitary animals.

We had not taken on the tracks of the gaur a distance of 200 yards before I caught sight of the animal coming up the side of the ridge broadside on, breathing deeply and munching away at a bamboo shoot. He was a magnificent animal, and looked an old bull. Beckoning to my men to remain where they were, I moved forward along the track, cocking both hammers of my 8-bore, which was loaded with ten drams of powder and hardened spherical balls. There was nothing to impede my view; in fact, the jungle in the neighbourhood being composed entirely of bamboo, was open and free from all undergrowth, and there was besides hardly a breath of air stirring. I succeeded in getting to within about thirty paces, and, aiming for the shoulder, fired. The bull on receiving the shot dashed off down the side of the ridge at a great pace, but collapsed stone dead against a bamboo clump with a tremendous crash a hundred yards or so off. It was very gratifying to think that I had succeeded after all in bagging this animal. He was a very fine bull, standing nineteen hands to the shoulder, and had a very good pair of horns. On my return to camp I was obliged to send my boy or cook back for medical treatment for jaundice, liver, and a hundred other ailments, which deprived me of decent food for nearly a month. I was consequently laid low with jungle fever for two or three days, but succeeded in pulling through, and was on my legs again none the worse.

A short time after my recovery, and a few months before I sailed for Europe, I bagged my last and record bison after some very hard work. This animal gave me more walking than ever I have had from any animals, elephants included.

One day in October I was on my way to the Military Police Post, "Chaungyi," which, situated on a stream of the same name, divides on that side Singa from the Ruby Mines district, when a Shan trader met me and said he had seen the large tracks of a bison across the pathway some three miles on. I proceeded to the spot at once, and saw from the tracks that the owner must be a magnificent animal. I also noticed that after taking them on for a couple of hundred yards, several good-sized saplings—the knocking down of which would really have done credit to an elephant—had been butted down by the gaur *en route*. This astonished me very much, as I had never seen an instance before of gaur uprooting trees with their horns. The beast at intervals seemed to be in an infuriated state, as the ground was pawed up and the bark on the trunks of several large trees had been scored and bruised.

The tracks, on a closer examination, did not look as if the animal had passed that day, and I was inclined to think that he had crossed the previous day early in the morning. It was now about 9.30 a.m. I had quite made up my mind to take on the tracks till we came up with the owner, even though we should have to follow him up for two or three days. We tracked the whole of that day till 4 p.m. unsuccessfully, only coming up with his tracks of that morning. We were, therefore, obliged to return to camp again that evening, arriving there at 1.30 a.m. Next morning we started early for the spot where we had relinquished the tracks the evening before, and took them on again. For the second time we failed to come up with the beast before it got dark, and were again obliged to return to camp. Next day before daylight, for the third morning in succession, we took on the trail, determined, if possible, to come up with the owner this time. At about 9 a.m. we found signs that the animal had passed late at night; and at last, at about 11 a.m., we came upon unmistakable evidences of the gaur's near presence. The jungle about here was mostly composed of open bamboo forest, with little undergrowth, and hardly sufficient cover for a large animal to lie up in during the heat of the day. We noticed that a herd had been in the neighbourhood, as there were numerous tracks all over the place. The solitary bull had, as is usually the case, been wandering about on the outskirts of this herd for some days. We were now moving down a gentle incline towards a stream, whose rushing waters could now be heard roaring in the distance. Never dreaming for one moment that we should come upon the gaur in such open bamboo forest devoid of all cover, we were walking along rather carelessly, talking in an undertone to one another, when suddenly we were startled by hearing two or three low, sharp, short "moos," accompanied by a suppressed snort, which we at once knew came from the animal we were following. Fortunately there were several bamboo clumps intervening, which partially hid us from view. My men immediately threw themselves on the ground while I peered anxiously round a clump to catch a sight of the gaur. There he stood; a magnificent specimen, a model of strength! It was a grand sight and one not easily forgotten, as he stood gazing at us with heaving flanks and dilated nostrils, through which at times he snorted defiance, challenging us, as it were, to approach nearer. His whole attitude, although fierce and defiant, bore at the same time a curious mixture of fear, uncertainty, and suspicion.

The sharp, short spurts of air which escaped from his nostrils at intervals when he raised his head from side to side or up and down in his endeavours to make out what we were, warned me that I must fire without an instant's delay.

The distance was quite 70 yards, and the shot, considering the position the animal was then standing in facing me, head and cheek only exposed, was not an easy one. I hesitated for a second or two with the rifle at the present, to consider whether I should not attempt to outflank him and get in a shoulder-shot.

He might, on the other hand, have not seen us, and have only been suspicious; or perhaps obtained a very slight slant of our wind, or heard us talking; in which case, should he catch sight of me crawling along to outflank him, there being little or no cover to screen me, all doubt would then be thrown to the winds, and he would either immediately charge me or dash off, and I should in the latter case have lost the opportunity first offered me of a shot. So quietly making up my mind to fire, I squatted on the ground, and taking a steady aim, fired. On the smoke clearing, I saw the gaur making off at a great pace up a steep incline on the other side of the stream which flowed close by, and over which, a leap of some 13 feet, the gaur had jumped. Several bamboo stumps which intervened did not permit of my getting in a second shot. I noticed, when aiming at the gaur, that two or three bamboo stems were in my line of fire, and one of them I now saw had been neatly perforated in the centre.

I became convinced, on sending a Burman to stand at the spot where the gaur had stood when I fired, comparing the height of the bullet-hole from the ground, that the gaur had been hit.

After partaking of a hurried meal on the banks of the stream we took on the tracks of the gaur, which plainly indicated, after we had gone about 200 or 300 yards, from an occasional splash or two of blood, that the animal was hit and was bleeding freely. The latter is not, as a rule, a good sign; and if hit fatally behind the shoulder, internal bleeding invariably takes place; and I noticed during the next half-a-dozen miles, that there was far too much blood for a wound which in the end would become fatal, and I was beginning to think that it might only be a severe flesh wound, in which case we would have a very long, stern chase, not to speak of the gaur being on the *qui vive* when we came up with him. It was twelve o'clock when I fired the shot, and my hunters had warned me that if I wanted to reach camp before dark we would have to return at once. This wasn't good enough, so I told them I wasn't afraid to sleep out in the jungle, and that I was determined to bag the bull, considering he was such a huge animal, and had already been wounded. I informed them emphatically, therefore, before going any further on the tracks, that they were not to attempt to dissuade me from going on, as I had quite made up my mind to follow up the gaur till I killed it. Tracking was now easy work, as there were numerous traces of blood on the grass, ground, and bushes *en route* for the next nine miles or so; we moved along at the rate of quite three and a half to four miles an hour—as fast, in fact, as we could possibly travel. At times, of course, we were delayed, and had some difficulty in finding the tracks when there did not seem to be the same flow of blood, and the animal travelled over hard and stony ground.

Once or twice it was very trying work, sometimes plumping down into a gorge and wading over a stream, then up a steep, densely-wooded ridge, or anon scrambling down a steep hill-side, thickly strewn with undergrowth and bamboos, the stems of the latter lying about interlaced with one another pell-mell all over the place, impeding our movements at times very considerably. All this, together with the intense itching to the skin set up on one's arms, legs, and face from coming in contact with spear grass and the fine hair of the bamboos, was most uncomfortable in the extreme. And what made life still more unbearable on these occasions was the minute parasites, or ticks, which, when a nest of them had been disturbed by the sportsman whilst moving along, crawl all over his person, and cling to him like leeches, after embedding their forceps into the skin, to remain there until picked out carefully by the hand. Sometimes a nest of hornets or red ants may also be brushed against by the sportsman or some of his followers, and then woe betide them, for they are most unmercifully attacked and stung by these pugnacious and infuriated little insects, causing painful blisters which smash and irritate one all day, to say nothing of the inflammation of minor scratches caused by the rays of the scorching sun, which, staring down upon one all day with an unceasing glare, well-nigh takes all the energy and spirit out of one.

All these, reader, and many other discomforts have to be reckoned with the pleasures of big-game shooting, and it is only he who has a hankering after this form of sport who can face the many discomforts I refer to.

We now came upon the first resting-place of the gaur. He had lain down under the shelter of a low-lying overhanging bamboo bush at the top of a steep ridge, and I could see from the position he had occupied that his head was pointing in the direction by which we should have had to approach. It is always best in the case of a wounded gaur, or tsine, to let them settle down and get over their first alarm. Should they be very badly wounded they will invariably lie down and be too stiff and sore to rise and charge at once on the approach of the sportsman. Care should also be taken not to rush away in hot haste after a newly-wounded gaur or tsine when in thick cover, as, after going a few yards, they have often been known to turn round and stand motionless by the side of the track, ready to charge down upon the first person who should approach without the slightest warning. It now behoved us to be careful, as we might come upon the animal at any moment. I had not the least doubt now that my shot had only glanced off the shoulder, and caused a severe flesh wound. At any rate there was nothing to show from the animal's movements that it had been badly hit. It did not lie down every two or three miles, halt repeatedly, or wander about in a zigzag fashion, as it would have done had it been severely wounded.

The odour of gaur now became very strong, and after going up one or two very steep ridges we suddenly came upon the gaur standing broadside on, under a bamboo clump, whisking its tail from side to side to keep off the flies. The head and shoulders were completely hidden from view behind the clump. I was only distant some twenty paces, but so noiselessly had we approached that we had not been discovered. My men had of course immediately made themselves scarce behind neighbouring bamboo clumps. The wind was also fortunately in our favour. I moved slightly to one side so as to get in a raking shot from behind, which would travel well forward.

The gaur stood like a rock, and I had consequently a magnificent shot. There was a tremendous stampede of feet after I had fired, and I saw the bison, when the smoke cleared, standing like a rock, head down, as if ready to charge the moment he could catch sight of his invisible foes. We were all perfectly motionless, however. I had also, immediately after firing, taken up my stand behind a clump of bamboos. A second shot from the 8-bore fired into the gaur's shoulder now rang out. This was too much for him, as, wheeling round, he dashed off down the steep hillside, but brought up after going some 50 or 60 yards, and alongside the trunk of a huge tree, where he stood motionless, evidently done for. I walked quietly up and fired a right and left behind the shoulder, on receiving which he immediately wheeled round and staggered up the hillside straight at me. I had only time to cram in one cartridge as he blundered along up to the clump behind which I had taken up my stand, when he stood some three paces off snorting and stamping at me, the picture of rage and defiance.

I refrained from firing at his head, as I did not wish to damage the frontal bone or the horns. I now noticed the wound on his cheek; the bullet had entered rather high up to one side and passed out, causing only a severe flesh wound, and without, as I afterwards found, damaging any of the bones. So close was the animal that I could distinctly see the white larvæ left by flies on the surface of the wound.

As the gaur remained stationary without showing any further signs of aggression I fired for the centre of the chest. On the smoke clearing I saw that although still standing he was about to fall. After one or two vain attempts to keep his feet the mighty beast sank slowly to the ground. My men now joined me, and we retired to a respectful distance. In a minute or so the gaur began to quiver all over, and in a short time the death throes set in, when every muscle and sinew became rigid and showed up distinctly. After a few tremendous struggles and a loud long-drawn bellow—its last effort, which resounded over the hills—its limbs became lax and it was dead.

He was a magnificent animal, standing 20 hands at the shoulder, and 12 feet 3 inches in length, including tail measurement. His horns measured as follows:—

Length of right horn along the curve, 34 inches.

Length of left horn along the curve, 33½ inches.

Girth at base of horn, 20½ inches.

Tip to tip, 21 inches.

Greatest width outside, 42½ inches.

Tip to tip along curve and over forehead, 81 inches.

After disembowelling the animal and cutting off the head, which was slung up into the branches of a tree to be sent for next day, we turned our faces homewards.

To reach camp, Chaung-gyi outpost, situated some twenty-five miles off, on a stream of the same name, we were obliged to walk down-stream the whole distance, as not only was it late, but the woods along the river bank were too densely wooded to enable us to make our way through them after dark in a locality which was also not very well known to my men.

It was a weary tramp after what we had already gone through, and what with carrying my heavy 18-lbs. rifle and bag of cartridges, it was no joke. My men were also laden with strips of bison meat and other articles, including my 12-bore rifle.

We reached our destination at 3 a.m. next morning, and I turned in, after a warm tub, to rise about 3 p.m. feeling none the worse. I should have felt very differently, however, had I not bagged the gaur. A successful day invariably drives away aches, pains, and any weariness that may wish to overcome the sportsman.

We passed numerous traces of elephant, gaur, tiger, leopard and bear. All the country in the neighbourhood between Manday and the Ruby Mines is simply teeming with big game of all kinds, especially between Singu and Shwényaungbin.

CHAPTER VII

BOS SONDAICUS: THE BANTING OR BURMESE TSINE; THE TRUE WILD CATTLE

BLANDFORD describes this animal as follows :—"This animal appears to be slighter than the gaur, with the legs longer in proportion and the dorsal ridge less developed. The tail descends below the hocks. The dew-lap is of moderate size. The head is much more elongate, the forehead not concave, the horns smaller, cylindrical in the young, flattened towards the base in adults, and curving outwards and upwards at first, and towards the tips somewhat backwards and inwards."

Colour.—Cows and young bulls have the head, body, and upper portions of the limbs, bright reddish-brown, approaching chestnut; old bulls are black; in both sexes the legs from above the knees and hocks; a large oval area on the buttocks, extending to the base of the tail but not including it, a stripe on the inside of each limb; the tips and the inside of the ears are white; calves have the outside of the limbs chestnut throughout and a dark line down the back.

Dimensions.—According to S. Muller, a full-grown Javan bull measured 5 feet 9½ inches at the shoulder; the length of the head and body was 8 feet 6 inches, and that of the tail 3 feet. The largest Burmese specimen recorded was 16 hands high (5 feet 4 inches). A skull from Java, in the Indian Museum, Calcutta, has horns measuring 30 inches in length by 17 inches in circumference at the base. This is unusually large. A male skull from Borneo, in the British Museum, measures 17·75 inches in basal length by 8·75 in zygomatic breadth. The following are the measurements of three magnificent heads which belong respectively to Mr. H. W.

Tarleton of the Burma Police, Surgeon-Captain Evans, and myself.

The head belonging to the first-named measures: length of outer curve, 33 inches; circumference at base, 15½ inches; tip to tip, 29 inches; greatest width between horns, 37½ inches.

The head of the animal in Surgeon-Captain Evans' possession measures: length, 24½ inches; girth, 14½ inches; tip to tip, 30 inches; widest inside, 35 inches.

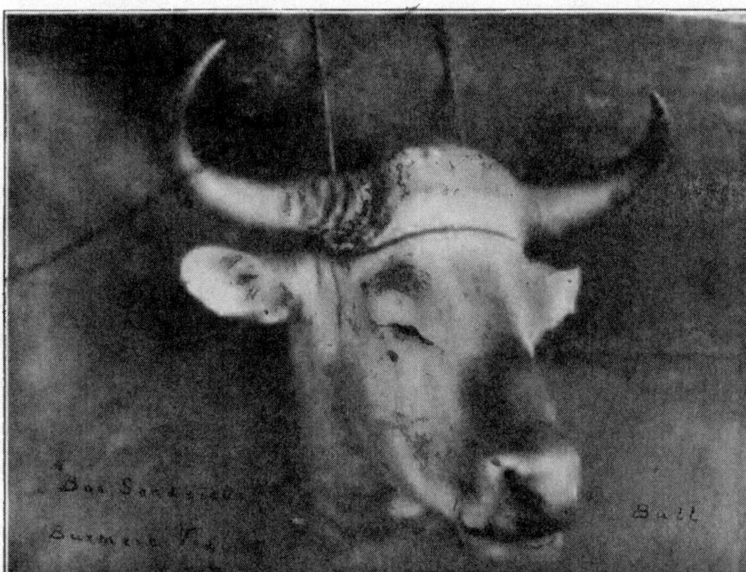

BURMESE BULL (TSINE).

From a Photo by Mr. Hannyngton.

The head of the animal shot by me measures: length, outer curve, 33 inches; circumference at base, 15 inches; tip to tip, 29½ inches; greatest width between horns, 38½ inches.

Distribution.—Throughout Burma and the Malay Peninsula, also in the islands of Borneo, Java, and Bali. This species is probably found also in Sumatra and Siam. It extends north of Northern Pegu and Arrakan, and probably to the hill-ranges of Chittagong.

These animals are also very numerous in all the forests

between Mandalay and the Shweli river, in the Ruby Mines district. I have seen them in the latter district roaming about in herds of thirty and forty.

Habits.—So far as is known, similar to those of *Bos gaurus*, except that *Bos sondaicus*, from the greater proportional length of the legs, is probably less of a climber, and more restricted to the plains of high grass. My own experience of these animals bears out this statement, and I have noticed in the Ruby Mines district that I have never come upon tsine at any elevation beyond 1500 feet.

They are very wary animals, and most sportsmen find them much harder to stalk than gaur, which can often be approached to within a few yards without much difficulty. Their sense of sight, hearing, and smell is very acute, and they can often wind one when quite a couple of hundred yards off. When wounded, and walked up in cover, or driven to bay, they attack and charge home at a tremendous pace, and are considered by Burmans to be as dangerous, if not more so, than gaur. The latter, moreover, are not such fast movers as tsine. I have heard of native hunters being chased round trees by a wounded bull tsine just as a dog would hunt a rat.

They have a very gamey appearance, and it is a very pretty sight to watch a herd of these animals feeding out in the open, or dashing away across an open glade when alarmed. Tsine feed principally upon bamboo shoots, leaves, and grass, and inhabit open tree or bamboo forests, except when disturbed or lying up during the heat of the day, when they penetrate the densest patch of "kaing" grass or undergrowth they can find.

During the hot weather they are invariably found resting in some open shady spot, or on a piece of rising ground, where they can not only benefit by any breeze which may blow, but where the approach of an enemy can also be at once detected. When suspicious of any danger, and no scent of the sportsman has been obtained, a solitary bull will remain perfectly still till the object of its suspicion appears in view, when it makes off, after emitting the customary snort of alarm. As a rule they feed very noiselessly, but when browsing on young bamboos the sounds of the shoots being bitten or broken off are often heard at a considerable distance. When the shoots obtain a height of from 4 to 5 feet, the animal uses his horns to snap off the tops, which are tender till the shoot has attained a height of, say, some 15 or 20 feet.

"Solitary" bulls, singly or in pairs, are often found wandering about the country, and in the month of May, when the animals are nearly driven distracted by the gadflies and mosquitoes, they move along at a good pace, their attention being devoted to shaking off these insects. When surrounded by a cloud of these pests and when not feeding, they are more easily approached.

The early morning, between 5 a.m. and 7.30, or even 8 a.m., and after 5 p.m. till dark, are the best times to find these animals out in the open.

Patches of recently burnt "kaing" grass should always be visited, as after a few showers of rain the young grass springs up and attracts not only tsine, but gaur, barking deer, brow-antlered deer, swamp deer, pig, and sambur. These patches should invariably be visited at a very early hour in the morning or late in the evening, or on some moonlight night. Gaur and tsine, as indeed all the other animals mentioned, except barking deer, are very chary about feeding out in the open, especially should the neighbourhood have recently been disturbed by wandering bamboo-cutters, or shots fired by hunters. Tsine take more killing than gaur, and although they are not such massive beasts, they are more tenacious of life. I have on two or three occasions had very long weary stern chases after tsine, whose fore-legs have been broken by a shot, before coming up with and killing them. If water is scarce and there are one or two pools in the neighbourhood of the sportsman's camp, which from the footprints appear to have been visited nightly by these animals, it is a good plan to sit up close by. In this manner a good head can often be obtained. It is weary work, however, and not in my opinion worth the trouble. More disappointments than successes attend one's efforts in this kind of shooting, and many men consider it unsportsmanlike to indulge in it. Red ants, mosquitoes, sand-flies, and all the other pests of a tropical clime, not to speak of the want of sleep, worry one to such an extent on these occasions, that a sportsman is entirely knocked up for any hard walking he may have to undergo on the following day.

Tsine, especially old solitary bulls, often travel many miles when on the move. I have often been led a long tramp after picking up the tracks of a bull which had apparently only passed an hour or two ago. The trackers must usually follow at a slower pace than that at which the animal is moving. The consequence is, that should the fresh track of an animal be picked up at, say, 7 a.m., it has probably moved into some dense cover by the time the sportsman has come up with it, in which case he will not be able to stalk it successfully. It is always the best plan, in cases of this sort, to leave the animal undisturbed till evening. He will then come out of the cover in which he has been lying up, and begin grazing close by, probably in some open bamboo forest, where he can be easily stalked and shot. It is well-nigh impossible to stalk a tsine when he has taken up a position in cover for a sleep during the heat of the day. The slightest noise will awaken him, and he will be off before you can draw a bead on him. One might just as well try to walk up a sleeping sambur in cover as try to stalk a solitary bull tsine; both are especially wary, the former perhaps a degree more so than the latter. In the cold season, *i.e.* November, December, and January, I have often seen a herd of tsine sunning themselves out in the open till 9 or 10 in the morning. They very rarely lie up in dense cover during these months, unless disturbed or apprehensive of danger, when they seek the thickest cover available. Old bulls which have been shot at or driven out of a herd, invariably lie up in the most inaccessible places they can find. When in cover, they prefer to lie up in kaing grass or thick bamboo jungle where there is some shade, and where they can detect from underneath, without rising, the approach of anything, while remaining unseen themselves. In colour the old bulls have often a dull, dirty-brown appearance, approaching sometimes almost to black. In the distance, some 200 yards off, I once mistook a pair of old bulls for gaur, so dark were they. In the case of some animals in a herd, I have noticed a distinct white ring round the eyes, but in old bulls I do not remember ever having seen this peculiarity.

In the rutting season herd animals seem to be continually on the move. I remember on one occasion following the fresh spoor of a herd, which showed from the tracks, which I was obliged eventually to relinquish, that the animals had been on the trot off and on all day, the result, I have no doubt, of the bull's pertinacity.

Tsine have a very strong and distinctive odour of their own, quite distinct from that of all other animals, and their meat for the same reason is far from palatable. In the case of a female, the odour *à la tsine* is not so pronounced as in a bull. As in the case of a boar, it is necessary to remove the credentials of a bull gaur, in order to make the meat at all palatable.

Burmans as a rule prefer the meat of gaur, or rhinoceros,[1] to that of any other animal except the pig; they do not object to tsine, but their choicest dish, like John Chinaman's, is pork reared in a village.

I have had many opportunities of shooting tsine where they abounded. On many occasions in the course of a day, when out tracking up solitary bulls, I have put up two or three of these animals.

When galloping along on my pony down the bed of the Nampan stream, to see if I could come upon any fresh tracks of solitary gaur, I rode right through a herd of tsine, which were feeding on the long succulent grass which was growing luxuriantly along the bed of the river and its banks. I had no gun with me at the time, so could not shoot. It was very amusing to watch the different movements and attitudes of the animals as, recovering from their alarm, they collected in twos and threes on either bank, and watched my every action, a mixture of curiosity and fear depicted on their faces. It was not till I wheeled round and rode at some of them with an unearthly whoop that the spell was broken, and they dispersed and dashed away with snorts of alarm.

I remember how proud I was when I bagged my first tsine, a veritable solitary bull and a veteran. I had just invested in

[1] I have generally known them to prefer elephant flesh.—F. T. P.

a double 8-bore rifle by Tolly, burning 10 drams, which my hunters always regarded with an admixture of awe and admiration. They expected wonders of me now, as hitherto I had always used a double 12 smooth-bore by Joe Lang, burning a maximum charge of 4½ drams, and had not in consequence always succeeded in bagging everything I had hit.

I had just been granted a month's leave, and had been out in camp for three or four days without having seen anything larger than a barking deer, or a boar, so decided to change my shooting-ground and pitch my tent on the banks of the Nampan stream, where tsine, gaur, and elephants were plentiful. I intended afterwards to visit the Tankta-kugyi stream, another glorious locality for big game, between Tagaung and the river Shwéli.

My camp-followers and servants had been directed to proceed to the site fixed upon, on the bank of the Nampan stream, and make everything snug and comfortable for my return in the evening. Moung Hpé, Moung Kyun Thet, and Moung Yan Gin, three favourite hunters of mine, accompanied me on this occasion.

We left camp at daybreak and struck across country towards a likely part some ten or twelve miles off, known to Kyun Thet, who assured me that we were sure to come across tsine *en route*.

After travelling through open "indaing" forest for some three hours, during which time we had not even come upon fresh tracks, we suddenly caught sight of a solitary bull tsine careering along down the side of a wooded incline in a direction which would bring him near us.

He was moving along at a steady trot, shaking his head and whisking his tail from side to side, evidently maddened by the cloud of gadflies which hovered round and settled on his body. He was so taken up by his endeavours to get rid of his tormentors that he did not notice us. I waited till he came opposite to me, at a distance of some 45 yards, and then gave him the contents of the right barrel, which floored him instantaneously. On rushing up to be ready to fire again, should he get up, I saw that his spine was broken, and that he was completely disabled. Otherwise, however, he was dangerous, as he lunged out with his horns and snorted at us whenever any one approached too near.

A second shot through the neck finished him off; after disembowelling him and breaking him up, we made tracks for camp, which was distant quite eight or ten miles. My men took as much of the meat with them as could be conveniently carried. *En route* we passed numerous varieties of feathered game, such as imperial pigeon, jungle-fowl, pea-fowl, and pheasant.

Not having a shot-gun I did not fire at anything. I make it a point never to take a shot-gun with me when out after big game, as I do not wish to be tempted to fire at birds. No sportsman, in fact, who is out after anything larger than a sambur should ever carry a fowling-piece. Should his larder require replenishing, however, jungle-fowl, pheasant, and even pea-fowl may often be obtained in the immediate neighbourhood of camp. There is always a risk, of course, of disturbing any animal which may be lying up close by.

My new camp had a very pretty site, under a large banian tree, situated on the banks of the Nampan stream.

A pleasure which sportsmen only can experience and enjoy, is to find ready on their return to camp, after a hard day's work, a warm tub, to be followed by a comfortable dinner, washed down with a pint of light ale, and the comforts of a long arm-chair, with the soothing influence of a cigarette or cigar. These make life worth living when one is under canvas.

During the night, should you sit dreamily in your chair or loll in your camp-cot, before dropping off into well-earned sleep, you will hear the hundred and one sounds which emanate from a tropical jungle, sounds which are to the sportsman refreshing and musical in the extreme; the short, sharp, hoarse bark of the "ghee," or barking deer, from a neighbouring hillside, or the bellow of an old bull tsine or gaur comes floating on the night air when all else is still.

Should the remains of any animal which has been shot be anywhere in the vicinity of the camp, the sportsman may perchance have the good luck to hear the roar of a tiger which having scented the meat, intends, uninvited, to make a midnight feast on the remnants. The more common and well-known "waugh, waugh" of a prowling leopard bent on a similar errand may also be often heard in some adjacent thicket. The clear bell of a startled sambur, which has perhaps been feeding close by, resounds through the air as he dashes away, a taint of the occupants of the camp, or perhaps of his more deadly enemy, having been wafted to his nostrils and warned him of his danger. All these sounds send through one a thrill of delightful expectation of good sport to come on the morrow.

At daybreak, should the sportsman be awake, he will hear the familiar sounds which usher in the morn. Jungle-cocks crow, and pea-cocks utter their discordant cries, screaming horn-bills flutter from tree to tree, following one another in single file, a solitary jungle raven croaks overhead, attracted by the hope of picking up something edible, and large flocks of paraqueets and parrots uttering sharp cries pass overhead like fleeting clouds.

"'Chota hazri' ready sir," are always the first words that greet me each morning before I rise, and, after a hurried meal, my hunters and I are soon well on our way towards the ground considered likeliest for our sport.

There were numerous herds of tsine all over the place, but, as I have said before, I preferred looking for solitary bulls, as they not only gave better sport, but carried better heads than those generally found with a herd.

While stalking a particular animal picked out from a herd, the sportsmen is often discovered by one of the smaller fry which alarms and disperses the rest.

I came upon numerous tracks of tsine along the foot of the Thaung-bwet-taung, a range of low-lying hills some ten or fifteen miles inland from the Irrawady, in the Twingè jurisdiction of the Tagaung subdivision, Ruby Mines district.

Game of every description may also be obtained inland either from Tagaung, Twinge, or Thabeitkyin. The steamers which ply on the Irrawady, from Rangoon to Mandalay, and from thence to Bhamo, halt at Tagaung and Thabeitkyin, while a very comfortable "bundobust" or arrangement may be made at either of these places, provided you land there from the steamer supplied with stores, and are equipped in every way, ready for your start inland. Fowls, vegetables, rice, and salt may be purchased at Tagaung or Pôngôn, an adjacent village. Fowls cost from 8 to 10 annas each (about 8*d.*). Other stores, such as tinned milk, biscuits, candles, sauce, flour, lard or ghi, and lamp oil, may be purchased on any of the cargo steamers which ply up and down the river.

Elephants, gaur, tsine, sambur, barking deer, leopards, tigers, and rhinoceros are obtainable inland, within forty miles of the river. To obtain rhinoceros the sportsman should visit Twinge, a village situated on the Irrawady, some thirty miles below Tagaung, and between that place and Thabeitkyin. From Twinge he should proceed to Tsaizin-gôn, and from thence, after getting one or two men acquainted with the locality to accompany him, he should go straight inland towards the hills already mentioned, known as Thaung-bwet-taung (pronounced exactly as it is spelt). The whole range should be thoroughly worked up as far inland as possible. The Tsaizin-gôn thugyi and his son are both sportsmen and fair trackers, and both are thoroughly well acquainted with the Thaung-bwet-taung hills. I have not shot rhinoceros myself there, but have seen their tracks, and know from what I have heard that they are to be found among these hills. Father and son accompanied me on one expedition into the hills ; the former, however, was not very keen on going, as he had his cultivation to attend to, and should his services be required, he will probably say, in order to avoid going, that he knows nothing about the jungles. The sportsman should of course make it worth his while. A present of Rs.25 down, with the promise of another Rs.25 at the end of the shoot, works wonders.

Another locality for rhino is the range of hills known as the Shwé-ū-taung or Kin valley, also in the Ruby Mines district. To reach this part of the country, the sportsman should land at Thabeitkyin, and cart all his kit up the road which leads to Mogok as far as Shwé-nyaungbin, two or three days' journey at the outside from Thabeitkyin, *i.e.* a distance of about thirty-five miles. On entering Shwé-nyaungbin, the sportsman will notice a valley on his left, and a range of hills some 3000 to 4000 feet high beyond it. These hills should be well worked up north, south, east, and west, and the hunter, should he work hard enough, will not fail to come across rhino, gaur, and elephants. The former are not of course plentiful, but this species is never found herded together in large numbers. I have only seen these brutes myself singly and in pairs.

Another good locality for solitary tusker elephants, gaur, and wild goats, is the spurs which run down from the Shwé-ū-taung hill to the village of Yé-nya-u. A good hunter, who is well acquainted with this locality, lives at Yé-nya-u. I have forgotten his name, but if inquiries are made of the thugyi, he will be forthcoming, as there is only one hunter of any note living there.

The following are the names of some of the best hunters and trackers in the Ruby Mines district who have been employed by me:—(1) Moung Yan Gin, Momeik State, Ruby Mines district; (2) Moung Youk, of Pôngôn village, near Tagaung; (3) Moung Hpé, Sittone village, near Sagadaung, Momeik State; (4) Moung Kyun Thet, of Sagadaung; (5) Moung Yan Shin, a retired forester, Tagaung; (6) Moung So, of Wapyu-daung (there are several good hunters who live at the latter place); (7) Moung Pu, of Chaukmaw, near Sagadaung, Momeik State; (8) Moung Hlaing, of Tagaung; (9) Moung Pyu, of Bathin; (10) the head-man of Tsaizin-gôn village.

The best places to pitch camp inland from Tagaung are first, Kyaukôh and then Ôkshitkôn. The first-named village, where there are only one or two huts, is situated some ten or fifteen miles off. Ôkshitkôn is distant from Kyaukôh some six or eight miles. Bullock carts may be driven right out to Ôkshitkôn from Tagaung, and the sportsman can canter along on his pony pretty nearly the whole distance without dismounting. Elephants, gaur, tsine, sambur, barking deer, and pig abound in the jungles round Ôkshitkôn. Thamine (brow-antlered deer), sambur, gyi, and tsine are to be found at Kyaukôh. In fact, magnificent sport may be obtained in the stretches of jungle which extend all round Ôkshitkôn. Excellent shooting may also be had at tsine, gaur, and elephants in the jungles along the banks of the Chaunggyi stream, near Wapyudaung, and between that stream and the village of Chaukhlèbèin. Indeed there are very few localities in the whole district where really good shooting of some kind is not obtainable (see chapter on miscellaneous sport).

I was moving along cautiously through some bamboo jungle one morning early in September, accompanied by two of my hunters, on the look-out for a solitary bull tsine whose tracks we had picked up, when the sound of a bamboo shoot being broken off warned me that some animal was close by. Moung Hpé, who was always near me, now handed me my 8-bore, and after instructing my men to remain where they were, I picked my way along in the direction of the sound. The ground, from recent heavy rain, was quite sodden; I was consequently enabled to pick out the tracks without any difficulty, and move along myself quite noiselessly. Great care had of course to be taken that I did not tread on a rotten bamboo or twig, as the animal, whose sense of hearing is very acute, would have made off at once. I had not gone 150 yards before I heard it feeding on bamboo shoots close by, so near in fact was the animal that its breathing was quite audible. There were numerous bamboo clumps and a lot of undergrowth which impeded my view for some yards, but I succeeded eventually in catching sight of the tsine, a huge bull, standing in an open space, broadside on, some twenty-five paces off. He was slowly munching away at a young bamboo shoot which was dangling from his mouth.

I was just about to fire, when another solitary bull appeared upon the scene, round an adjoining clump, evidently a stranger to the one I had just sighted. On catching sight of the newcomer, the latter turned partially round, lowered his head almost to the ground, stiffened himself all over, and pawed the earth, breathing deeply through his nostrils the while as if challenging the other bull to fight. The other animal acted in a similar manner. I would have given worlds for a camera at that moment, as I could have taken both animals together, and it would have been a unique photograph. Unfortunately, however, I did not possess one, never having gone in for photography. The wind was luckily in my favour or else both animals would long ere this have made off. After regarding each other side-ways for awhile with lowered heads, they made feints of charging at one another, snorting defiance through their nostrils. These warlike proceedings, however, led to nothing; after pawing up the ground and bushes in their immediate neighbourhood, they calmed down and began feeding close to one another.

I raised the 8-bore slowly and fired at the shoulder of the nearer animal. The shot took effect, and the bull collapsed in a dazed manner, and sank to the ground in a sitting posture. He was not dead, however, as a few seconds after falling, and before the death struggle ensued, he uttered a long, loud bellow. The other animal on hearing the report had dashed off a few paces, but on seeing its companion sink to the ground and utter as it were a bellow of defiance, it immediately wheeled round and walked back with lowered head, putting on at the same time a bellicose attitude. It seemed a little puzzled at first and appeared undecided whether to retreat or advance. All this was of course the work of a few seconds. I did not wait a moment longer than was necessary, but fired at the second animal without reloading the right chamber. The shot was quite as effective as the first one, and the bull, after staggering against a neighbouring clump, collapsed, bellowing loudly, and in a few minutes was dead. The animals lay within twenty-five paces of each other. They measured respectively: height, 5 feet 1 inch, and 5 feet 2 inches; length, 10 feet, and 10 feet 3 inches.

As there was a track for carts close by, I was enabled to bring up two, which I had with me on this occasion as transport. The meat of both animals, including the two heads, was placed upon them, and driven away to camp, thus saving my men a good deal of hard work, as otherwise they would have had to carry the meat. My camp was pitched on the Dat Choung at the foot of the Thaung-bwet-taung hills.

Some two or three days later I came upon a couple of solitary bulls or "nyi-naung," as the Burmans call them, while tracking up a solitary bull gaur. We had been following the latter's tracks for some time, through a stretch of rather heavy undergrowth, and had come upon some fresh tracks. Whilst seated on the ground debating amongst ourselves as to whether the new tracks we had struck were those of gaur or tsine, two tsine suddenly appeared on the scene. We remained seated, as it was easier to watch their movements in that position, besides, they were heading apparently straight in our direction. We had not long to wait. Both animals came along at a quick pace, cropping the grass on either side of them as they moved, breathing deeply and sharply the while, as if just recovering from the effects of a long gallop. It was then about 9.30 a.m. and very warm; this may have accounted for their stertorous breathing, as they were not very old bulls. I aimed at the shoulder of the nearest animal and fired; the distance would probably be about 25 yards. Both tsine immediately dashed away. The one I had fired at only travelled a short distance, and then pulled up looking very sick. I was unable to put in a second shot at either beast, so quickly did they disappear through the undergrowth. Moung Hpé now informed me that he could hear the wounded animal close by, stamping its feet to shake off the gadflies. I moved cautiously forward, but had not gone 30 yards before the tsine charged down upon us at a great pace. We stepped to one side, and as he passed us I let him have another shot behind the shoulder, which brought him to a standstill before he had gone 40 yards. He was now limping badly, and as I could see that he would not be able to charge again, I finished him off with another shot. He was a fine bull, standing 5 feet 4 inches at the shoulder, and had a very good head. My men afterwards broke him up, and took away all the meat.

We followed the tracks of the gaur, hoping that he was not in the immediate neighbourhood, but had not gone far before we came upon unmistakable signs of his having been alarmed; the deep indentations of his hoofs and the width between each track showed us plainly that he had heard my shots and made off. I was much disgusted at the time, I remember, because a solitary bull gaur is, in my opinion, a grander prize and more worthy of bagging than a tsine. I used a 12-bore rifle on this occasion, burning 6 drams of powder, and steel-tipped conical bullets, one of which, my first shot, had passed clean through the tsine. I found it to be a most effective weapon upon both tsine and gaur.

On glancing through my diaries, I notice that there are a good many entries such as: "Came upon a herd of tsine to-day, did not fire at them, as I was following up the tracks of a solitary bull;" or "Saw two herds of tsine to-day, but did not shoot, as there were no animals amongst them with heads worth having and I am not in want of fresh meat." Other entries often occurred such as: "Saw two solitary bull tsine to-day, but failed to get a shot at either, as they winded me and made off;" or "Came upon fresh tracks of a solitary bull tsine this afternoon, but failed to come up with the owner before dark." A few entries such as: "Fired at and wounded a solitary bull tsine to-day, and had a long stern chase but did not succeed in bagging him," may also be seen occasionally. It is not necessary to slaughter every animal that one comes across simply for the sake of shooting. I cannot repeat too often that the man who does so is no sportsman, but an itinerant butcher.

I found the ·303 Lee-Metford carbine quite ineffective upon tsine, and when using it I lost a great many more animals than I bagged.

On one occasion I came upon a herd of tsine, numbering, I should think, some twenty-five to thirty animals in all. So tame were they, that they allowed me to come up and fire at them no less than half-a-dozen times within the space of five minutes. My shots, whether aimed too high or too low, did not seem to have the desired effect, and the animals trotted away a short distance and, after each shot, turned round to stare at me, wondering, I have no doubt, what the sharp short reports could mean. But, what was still worse, there were no blood-drops by which I could follow up any wounded animal.

My hands were not perhaps as steady as they might have been, as I had to make several short spurts of 50 and 100 yards on two or three occasions to make up on the animals before firing, a necessity not at all conducive to good shooting.

One animal certainly did fall as if dead; I passed it lying on the ground as I sprinted to try and cut off the rest of the herd, but found, much to my surprise, on my return to look for it, that it was *non inventus*. I concluded therefrom that my bullet had either grazed the spine or glanced off its head, stunning it temporarily. This often happens, and, as I have remarked before, an animal which drops to your shot like a stone invariably gets up again little or none the worse, and makes off. No animal mortally wounded by a body-shot drops thus, and remains perfectly motionless, unless the spine has been penetrated. Sometimes, even in the latter case, animals stagger away before dropping.

Tsine are, as a rule, found near streams whose banks are thickly wooded with bamboo and undergrowth, but they are also sometimes found feeding or lying up a long distance from water. They are particularly fond of sleeping or resting in low bamboo-wooded undulating forest.

The best way to find fresh tracks is to walk along down the bed of some stream, where there is only an occasional pool of water and where tsine are accustomed to drink, and the chances are that before the sportsman has gone very far he will come upon the tracks of both solitary and herd animals crossing and re-crossing the stream. They are often found feeding on the succulent shoots of dōōp grass, which grows along the banks and in the beds of streams.

During the dry weather some of the streams dwindle to a tiny rivulet, an inch or two deep and a few feet broad, meandering along the course, sometimes disappearing altogether to reappear lower down, and forming at times large pools, which are frequently visited by animals during the hottest time of the day.

I remember on one occasion out shooting in the jungles, accompanied by three of my hunters, near the village of "Kyauk oh," which in Burmese signifies "stone pot," coming suddenly upon three bull tsine, or rather, to put the case more honestly, they intruded upon us. Moung Hpé, Moung Youk, and another old friend, whose name I have forgotten, and I had seated ourselves on the ground in a shady spot beside a pool, where we intended having some refreshment.

We had been out all day in the broiling sun since 5 a.m. without getting a shot, and as it was then about mid-day, we called a halt at the pool to cool ourselves and have drink.

The water was not very inviting to look at, being full of green, mossy-looking vegetable matter, decayed leaves and branches; it was nevertheless quite palatable.

A sportsman in Burma must not be too fastidious with regard to the water he drinks. I have often been only too glad to go down on my hands and knees and drink deep draughts of water at the first pool I came to without looking at its colour. Of course, I always make a point of sniffing at it, and if too malodorous or tasty, never drank it. The nose is a very good guide in these matters. I believe the drinking of water does one less harm in India than most people imagine, and I am quite sure that more men in the East suffer from over-doses of whisky than from the evil effects of drinking water.

But to return to our tsine. We had been seated for about half-an-hour, when the noise of animals galloping at a great pace in our direction became apparent. Moung Hpé immediately jumped to his feet, and said, "Thakin, tsine yé thouk-po-la-byi" (Sir, tsine are coming to drink water). On second thoughts, however, he said, "Ma hopu thakin, tsine yé thauk po la-bo-kyan-dè-chunok-do kyi-ya-mya-ah-hnan-ya-thwa-byi yaku pyi nè dè" (No, sir, the tsine were on their way to drink, but they scented our tracks and are now making off).

From the direction in which the galloping sounded, I concluded that the animals were heading in our direction, so, leaving my men at the pool and loading up the 8-bore, I walked out towards the point at which I expected the tsine to put in an appearance. I had not long to wait before some three or four bulls galloped past me at a great pace. A small patch of low kaing grass and some stunted shrubs partially hid them from my view as they charged past my position some 30 yards off, and though an occasional glimpse of them could be obtained, yet it was insufficient to allow of my shooting with any chance of putting a bullet in the right place, or even hitting an animal at all. I noticed besides, after they had passed me, that they were slackening their speed and intending pulling up close by.

I now began to stalk them, and had not gone 150 yards before I caught sight of three of the animals standing on the far side of a small patch of low grass, a space of some 90 yards between us. I was fortunately hidden from their view in a strip of jungle.

All three animals appeared very uneasy, and were walking backwards and forwards in a restless undecided manner when I caught sight of them. I could not see the fourth, but doubtless he was not far off. I noticed that when the tsine were stationary they held their heads high and craned their necks from side to side, looking hard in the direction by which they had come, and from whence they had evidently expected danger. Occasionally they would glance over in the direction of the pool, for which they were presumably bound when they crossed our trail.

I remained motionless for quite five minutes in the hope of seeing them make towards the pool for a drink, but they were apparently suspicious of danger and remained where they were. One animal gave me some splendid opportunities of shooting, but the distance was too great for me to risk it with the 8-bore. With a lighter weapon it would have been a very different matter.

It now struck me that if I did not look sharp my men would be coming to look for me, as they were ignorant of the fact that the beasts were close by. In fact, one of the hunters was already making a clicking noise with his tongue to attract my attention. This noise is peculiar to Burmans. I put up the 100 yards sight and waited. The animal which showed himself before gave me another chance, of which I availed myself. He stood like a rock while I aimed for his shoulder high up. A second animal stepped out from behind some high grass as I was about to pull the trigger, and stood close alongside the animal at which I was aiming. I pulled the trigger; the brutes swerved and dashed off at right angles from each other. The one fired at only went some 30 yards and then pulled up, the other held on with a broken hind leg; my bullet, a conical steel-tipped one, hit it after passing clean through the first animal.

I ran up and despatched the first bull, which was standing quite dazed, the bullet having entered the loins rather far back. My hunters now joined me, and we took on the tracks of the other. There were numerous traces of blood on the ground, and it was not long before I caught sight of the tsine limping painfully along. Telling my men to remain behind, I ran quickly but quietly on, and put in a shot which took effect in the small of the ribs and raked his vitals forward, the bullet making its exit through the right shoulder-blade. The shot brought him to a standstill, but he turned round and faced me with his head down, shaking it at intervals, and stamping the while with his feet. I took good care to have a bamboo clump between us, in case he should make up his mind to charge.

After a little manœuvring I managed to work my way round to his flank, but no sooner did he catch sight of me than he wheeled round again and faced me with lowered head, snorting at intervals. My patience was by this time exhausted, so aiming point-blank for the frontal bone, I fired. The tsine dropped like a stone, and after a few short struggles was *hors de combat.*

After disembowelling him we made tracks for camp. *En route,* while rounding a bend of the Nampan stream, which had at that time very little water in it, we came suddenly upon a pack of wild dogs which had pulled down a sambur. The poor beast was still struggling when we appeared upon the scene. I had no time to change my 8-bore for a smaller weapon before the dogs had disappeared. The sambur had been ham-strung, and its hind-quarters were fearfully lacerated, as also were the neck and throat. The latter was punctured in a dozen places. The deer was a full-grown doe, and on disembowelling her we found she was with young, which would have probably been born in a day or two.

These wild dogs do a great deal of damage to the deer tribe, especially to sambur and barking deer, both of which are run down and winded by these plucky and hardy little poachers. It is not often that one comes across them, as they are very shy.

Richardson of the Police, whilst out on tour in the Ruby Mines district, between the village of Ginnwè and Pinkan, came upon a pack of these animals, which had just pulled down a barking deer or gyi. He dismounted from his pony and fired at them with his revolver in the hope of bagging one. The "gyi," which had not, if I remember rightly, been badly injured, received the bullet instead, and the dogs unfortunately escaped scot free.

Richardson, when telling me about it afterwards, said that the deer's skin had been scored in a dozen different places by the teeth of the dogs, but was otherwise uninjured.

I have gone out, during the hot weather on many occasions, after big game mounted on a pony and accompanied by two of my *shikaries*, who were also mounted. A great deal of ground can be covered in this manner in a short space of time, and it always enabled me to return to my house early enough for a warm tub and dinner. Tagaung, my head-quarters, was a very convenient place for shooting of this kind. It was always a very easy matter for me to ride out in the morning, provided, of course, I had no very important work on hand, bag a solitary tusker elephant or a gaur or two, and ride back to Tagaung in the evening none the worse, in time to change for dinner. Many men overdo the thing on foot, and not only knock themselves up, but lay themselves open to attacks of fever.

The two men, Moung Hlaing and Moung Youk, villagers of Tagaung and Pôngôn, who used to accompany me on these expeditions, could both ride fairly well. Moung Youk carried my 8-bore rifle slung over his shoulders and a bag of cartridges, Moung Hlaing was laden with three Burmese "luèaiks" or satchels, containing our respective breakfasts and luncheons, and their own betel-boxes and other paraphernalia. I carried a single Martini-Metford rifle and a pair of binoculars. We also took two leather water-bottles, or "chaguls," with us. When the ground was soft the three ponies moved along quite noiselessly in single file. I invariably took the lead, and when one of us saw a track which looked fresh, we all dismounted and I took the lead on foot, leaving my men to follow at a respectable distance. Occasionally, I would mount my pony till told we were near the animal, when I would dismount again and begin the stalk.

The pony I rode, a dark bay, would allow me to fire off its back without flinching. The first time, however, that I tried it, I remember the shock of the recoil nearly knocked me out of the saddle.

We had just come on a herd of tsine, which, however, had winded us, and made off. Shortly afterwards, while tracking up a solitary tsine, we came upon another old bull standing stern on between two bamboo clumps, its head and shoulders completely hidden from view and protected by one of them.

All three of us were mounted at the time, but so noiselessly did we approach that we were unheard. I had just time to lean over my saddle, take the 8-bore out of Moung Youk's hands, giving him the Metford, and fire a hurried shot at the animal's flanks. The bullet struck right enough, but the shot entered too far back. The tsine, on receiving the shot, dashed round a clump of bamboos, and disappeared into an adjacent patch of grass before I could get in a second shot. We took on the track and followed in his wake as quickly as possible. After going about 250 yards, we came on him standing in some tall grass. He heard us coming, however, and making his exit on the other side entered another large stretch of tall kaing grass, where we had very hard work to stick to his trail, as there were numerous tracks of tsine which had recently been in the vicinity. It was now necessary to be careful, as, should we come on the wounded animal, it would very likely be at close quarters.

He was still a long way off, however, and it was not till some three hours after that we came upon him lying down under the shade of some bamboos.

The wind being in our favour, I managed, under cover of some shrubs, to work my way up till within 20 yards of him. I was armed with a Lee-Metford, as I wanted to test its efficiency as a sporting weapon. Aiming for the point of its shoulder, I fired, the bullet used being a solid nickel-coated one. The tsine struggled to its feet with difficulty. I had reloaded in the meantime, and aiming again for the head, as it was about to dash off, I pulled the trigger. The bullet made the animal turn a complete somersault and roll over on its side dead. He was a magnificent specimen, standing 16 hands and 3 inches at the shoulder. One horn was a mere stump measuring only a few inches, it having been broken off at the base; the other was 24½ inches.

MISCELLANEOUS SPORT

The following are some of the best shooting districts in Burma :—

1. Ma-u-bin.—Elephant, tiger, leopard, sambur, and hog deer.

2. Tavoy.—Elephant, rhinoceros, gaur, tsine, leopard, tiger, tapir, sambur, etc.

3. Pyuntaza in the Pegu Yoma Hills.—Gaur, rhinoceros, and elephant.

4. Shwegyin and Tongho.—Tiger, gaur, tsine, leopard, buffalo, deer, and elephant.

5. Pegu district, in the jungles near the villages of Panoot and Pagyne.—Elephants, tigers, and thamine, or brow-antlered deer, may be shot.

6. Papun district, Salween.—Elephant, rhinoceros, gaur, tsine, tiger, tapir, and magnificent mahseer fishing.

7. Excellent tiger, rhinoceros, gaur, tsine, and thamine shooting may be had to the east of Tharrawaddy amongst the Pegu Yomahs, and at their base near Tapoon.

8. Mergui, Tenasserim Province.—All large game except elephants.

9. Yai, below Amherst.—Elephant, leopard, tiger, rhinoceros, tapir, gaur.

10. Ruby Mines, Tagaung, Wapyu-daung, Momeik.—Gaur, rhinoceros, tsine, elephant, wild goat, bear, leopard, tiger, sambur, pig.

11. Bassein district, Arrakan Yomahs.—Rhinoceros, gaur, elephant, tsine, tiger, and leopard.

12. Wild buffaloes may be shot between Prome and Arrakan in the Arrakan Yomahs, and near Banlong and Myetquin.

13. Tigers and wild buffaloes are to be obtained in Pyapun.

14. Chindwin district.—Rhinoceros, gaur.

15. Mogaung.—Tiger, gaur, tsine, thamine, and elephant.

16. Elephants in the low flat country of Pegu, viz. Pagaing

and Panoot, leave for Bawni and Zamini in the rains, where they may be shot.

17. Excellent duck, snipe, partridge, deer, bear, and leopard shooting may be had between Wuntho and Tigyaing.

18. Splendid snipe shooting may be had at Dabein and Ledaung-gan between Rangoon and Pegu; the latter is in itself one of the best snipe grounds in Burma.

There is hardly a village in Upper Burma near which game of some kind may not be put up during a drive. Burmans, as a rule, are very good at making a "bundobust" for a drive, and can tell to within a yard or two where an animal will break. Should a sportsman wish to arrange a beat near a village, he should notify the thugyi the night before, and also call up the local *shikaries* and hold a friendly confab with them as to the patches of jungle to be beaten up on the morrow, and the kind of animals that are most likely to turn up in them.

The services of at least twenty or thirty villagers should be requisitioned for driving. It depends very much on the extent of jungle that has to be driven.

I have seen as many as fifty or sixty beaters at work. It is not advisable, however, to have too many men, as they are harder to keep in hand and often go off the line. They should always be cautioned to move along quietly, tapping the trees on either side as they proceed. It is much easier to keep a few beaters in hand than a large number, unless, of course, they are skilled at this sort of work, and each man knows every foot of the ground he is beating, and the point which he has to make for. They often go off the line, and beat up some jungle in an entirely opposite direction to that in which the guns have been placed.

When too much noise is made animals, such as sambur, pig, and barking deer, very often break through the beaters. On the other hand, when the men are moving along quietly, the driven beasts have time to consider from what quarter to expect danger, and after stopping to listen once or twice they invariably move straight ahead towards the guns. The sportsman is posted at some likely spot, a cart-track, for instance, or an open glade; in fact, the most likely spots for

PADDING A DEAD TIGER.

the animals to break out of the cover which is being beaten. These places are well known to the local *shikaries*.

The sportsman should make sure before firing at anything, that he is really about to pull trigger at an animal and not at a human being. Mistakes of this kind have often happened in Burma and elsewhere through the sportsman, whose nerves are, perhaps, through excitement somewhat overstrung, being in too great a hurry to shoot at the first moving object that presents itself; one cannot, therefore, be too careful.

No small-bores, rifled to carry long distances, such as ·303, ·256, and Martini-Henrys, should be used on occasions like this, as one never knows where the bullet travels to. The best weapons to use when driving for any of the following animals, viz. tiger, leopard, bear, sambur, or pig, are a double hammerless 12-bore Paradox by Holland and Holland, or a double ·577 express with solid, soft lead bullets. The Paradox burns a charge of from 3 to 4 drams of powder and carries a conical bullet. A 12-bore shot-gun, burning a maxim charge of 3½ drams powder, and carrying a solid, spherical, hardened bullet or Meade shells for the smaller and less dangerous animals, is also a very serviceable weapon. It cannot be depended upon, however, to carry a ball accurately at any distances beyond 40 or 50 yards.

When the sportsman intends to beat up jungle near villages he should take a shot-gun with him, as jungle-fowl, pheasant, and even pea-fowl and hare often appear, and magnificent shots at the former while on wing may be obtained. I have seen twenty and thirty jungle-fowl fly out of beaten cover overhead in ones and twos at a great pace, and they often rocket and afford excellent sport. Number four or five shot is the size for jungle-fowl and pheasant; for pea-fowl and geese numbers two and three are more suitable. Cartridges loaded with buck-shot to the number of twelve in each should be taken with the sportsman, as barking deer and hog deer often rush past at such a pace that they only afford a glimpse. It is then well-nigh impossible to hit them with a bullet from a rifle unless the sportsman is a second Dr. Carver. The beaters will often try to take their dogs along with them to assist in driving the game. This should not be allowed, as they invariably enter the jungle before the beaters have begun work and start a hunt after some animal on their own account, thereby alarming the whole jungle. When untrained dogs are used, the hunted animals invariably dash away at a tremendous pace in the opposite direction to that in which the sportsman has been posted, and very often the dogs are shot by some one in mistake for a barking deer. Dogs are only useful for bringing big game to bay, to enable the sportsman to walk up and fire at the animal with the best head, for running down a wounded animal, or for locating a tiger, leopard, or bear.

Should the sportsman be the only armed European present at a drive, he should see that he is posted in the best position, which is usually the centre. Two stops, some fifty or a hundred paces off, should also be placed in likely spots on his right and left. These two men should be instructed to turn inwards any animals which may appear in front of them, so as to afford the sportsman a shot.

To avoid any disappointment it is well to see, before a drive is begun, that each beater understands the point for which he has to make.

A wrong line is often taken, and the sportsman is left alone wondering why the noises made by the beaters are growing fainter and fainter, the beaters having moved off in an entirely opposite direction to that in which the sportsman has been posted. The men should also be instructed to stop beating only when they have come within a yard or two of the guns. They have a knack of scattering and stopping to talk to one another, taking it for granted that there are no animals left between them and the sportsman, but I have seen both barking deer and pig break away past the guns when the beaters have been only a few yards distant.

It is simply wonderful what can be turned out of a patch of jungle by beaters. The first animal to put in an appearance, as a rule, is either the sambur or barking deer. Should the former put in an appearance first he will be seen moving along slowly with a wonderfully noiseless tread. He will often appear quite suddenly in front of the sportsman without giving any warning, at other times, when startled suddenly, he will dash out of the cover straight ahead at full speed; occasionally he stops and turns his head to listen, his long bell-shaped ears twitching backwards and forwards restlessly the while, endeavouring to catch the slightest sound. Should the wind enable him to catch the scent of the sportsman, he will immediately dash off at right angles to his former course with long bounds, uttering a sharp bell of alarm. But hark! what is that sharp clattering of hoofs on the hard ground? some animal is pelting along towards the sportsman. Presently with a bound a chestnut-coloured, short-horned animal scurries past like a flash, uttering a sharp bark as he darts off at a tangent on catching sight of his foe. A troop of chattering monkeys next put in an appearance, some running along the ground, others tearing away through the foliage overhead, and all in a great hurry to get out of danger's way. Mothers, clutching their young one with one arm, skip from branch to branch in fear and trepidation. Old scowling males scamper along on all-fours over the ground, stopping occasionally to rise on their hind-legs and look back along their line of flight. In a short time they have all disappeared. A few pheasants now hurry along, uttering the low gurgling cries peculiar to them when disturbed. The beaters soon draw near, and there does not seem to be another living thing in the cover, when suddenly a huge solitary boar charges out at a terrific pace, to be met with a right and left from the sportsman which terminates his career for ever. A more glorious death would have been his if, instead of the deadly tube, the sportsman had met him face to face in the open with the spear. A jungle-cock now comes running along followed by a whole harem of hens, and, passing to the right of the sportsman, they all get up and fly off with startled screams on perceiving him. A few squirrels next scamper through the foliage, and perhaps a porcupine or an iguana scuttles away, the two latter making more noise than a dozen animals of greater worth.

The beaters now come into view with dishevelled heads and garments, their long hair streaming about their necks and shoulders, and perspiring from every pore. Some sit down to extract thorns from the soles of their naked feet and other parts of their persons, which are usually unprotected from the thighs downwards. Others are engaged re-arranging their hair and tying up their "gaung baungs" or turbans, whilst some lie down at full length on the ground to rest themselves. Driving is hard, hot, thirsty work for the men, and the sportsman must take care not to overwork them or lose his patience, or he will find it very hard to obtain their services again. Government officials, as a rule, do not pay villagers for beating jungle, as it is often voluntarily done and payment is not wanted or asked for. The greater portion of the meat of the animals shot is usually made over to them as their portion. Should no game have been bagged, however, and the sportsman had several shots, it is advisable to divide Rs.5 or Rs.10 amongst the beaters according to the number employed. It enables them at any rate to buy cheroots for themselves. The sportsman, should he be driving in a locality where game is plentiful, will sometimes have bear and leopard driven out to him, and on rare occasions a tiger. I remember an instance of one of the latter being driven out by beaters, when only sambur and barking deer were expected. The incident which I am about to relate happened near the village of Sagadaung in the Momeik State, Ruby Mines district. Tom Dobson of the Police, as keen a sportsman and as good a shot as is to be found anywhere in the country, had during a beat wounded a sambur. The animal, which was hard hit, managed to get away into an adjoining cover. The beaters, some twenty men in all, proceeded to beat out this thicket, while Dobson took up a position at the far end.

Dobson, who was only armed with a 12-bore shot-gun, did not of course expect to come upon a tiger so near the village. His right chamber was loaded with 3 drams of powder and a Meade shell, whilst his left contained the same charge of powder but a solid spherical bullet. The beaters had hardly begun when the tiger appeared suddenly on the scene within a few yards of Dobson. I think that at the time the latter was seated on a log smoking a cigarette. At any rate the tiger halted on seeing Dobson, and so composed was the latter, that he cogitated whether it would not be advisable to fire the left barrel first instead of the right one, the solid ball being more effective than the Meade explosive shell.

Having made up his mind on the subject he pulled the left trigger, and the tiger sank to the ground on all-fours with its head resting on its paws, the bullet having pierced its brain.

I remember having a somewhat similar experience with my first bear. I had been beating for sambur in the neighbourhood of Pinlébu Katha district, and had just driven two covers, when a villager turned up and informed me that he had seen a bear enter a patch of jungle some 300 yards off. We proceeded thither without any delay, and after posting two other guns, one on either side of me, some 150 yards apart, the beaters began their work.

My position overlooked the ravine in which the bear was supposed to have taken up his quarters, and I also had a clear view of the ground to the right, left, and front. Before the beaters started work, I had ordered the villagers to tie up three dogs which they had brought with them, as I was afraid the bear would break away in an entirely opposite direction to that by which he was expected to emerge from the cover. The beaters were now making enough noise to awaken the seven sleepers. As the wind was rather high I could not hear anything moving inside the jungle. A barking deer suddenly appeared in view, about 150 yards off, and began to trot along the side of the cover towards me. As I did not wish to alarm the bear I let it go unmolested. A minute or so afterwards I heard two or three sharp hoarse grunts, followed by yells from the beaters, and at the same time saw a number of the latter ascending trees like monkeys. After a few shouts of inquiry, I ascertained that the bear had broken back but had not left the cover. It was now suggested that the three dogs should be brought back and taken into the cover with the beaters, who were to begin the drive over again. The dogs were then let loose, and the beaters recommenced their work with more confidence, perhaps, than on the first occasion. In a few minutes I heard two or three sharp yelps, and knew that the pariahs had given tongue on scenting the bear. It was not long before Bruin appeared lumbering along with a heavy tread. On reaching the open he stopped, and turned round to listen, twisting his snout in every conceivable direction and sniffing the air the while. After satisfying himself that his enemies were in his rear he trotted slowly up the incline towards me.

Fortunately, none of the dogs had followed him, or else he would have travelled much faster, in which case I should not have got such an easy shot. As it was he only moved along at a slow trot. I waited till he had approached to within about 30 yards of me, and as he was moving off broadside on, I fired, aiming a little behind his left shoulder. On feeling the shot he stood upon his hind-legs and, after uttering two or three angry roars, clawed and bit to pieces a small sapling which grew beside him. As he again dropped on all-fours I fired the second barrel, which was too much for him, so he turned tail and re-entered the jungle looking very sick. The beaters and dogs now appeared, and the latter very soon found the bear lying dead on its stomach a few yards inside the cover, with its tongue protruding.

Bears commit great havoc amongst plantain groves, or, in fact, any fruit-bearing trees, Jack fruit especially. They may often be found up trees asleep in wigwams, which they construct themselves of leaves and branches. Burmans and Karens are often severely mauled by them.[1] I know of several instances of villagers having been injured by bears attacking them whilst collecting firewood, fruit, etc. It often happens that a bear is up a tree, like the Thabyè-thee tree, for instance, eating the berries, when some unsuspecting villager appears upon the scene to pick up the fallen fruit or collect dried sticks and branches for firewood. The bear on seeing the person below him generally scrambles down as quickly as possible, usually with the intention of escaping, but should the unfortunate human being be too close to the tree trunk when the bear reaches the ground, he will most assuredly be attacked and badly clawed and bitten, the injuries sustained frequently resulting in death.

I remember the case of a hunter who will carry to the grave with him the marks of a severe mauling from a bear, which had been feasting on Jack fruits in a strip of jungle on the

[1] In Assam more people are mauled and killed by bears than by tigers.—F. T. P.

banks of the river Lemro facing the village of Léhnyindaung, Akyab district. Three hunters, A, B, and C, of whom two were armed with flint-lock guns and one with a dâh only, left the above-named village together to shoot on the opposite bank of the river. While they were seated at the foot of a Jack fruit tree a bear came upon the scene and ascended a tree near at hand. They waited till he had got well into the branches, and then one hunter, A, fired at him. The bear fell to the ground after making one or two vain efforts to maintain its equilibrium, but managed to hobble off into a dense patch of jungle close by. C, who was armed only with a "dâh she," or fighting sword, and B, who had one of the guns, decided to leave the bear alone and persuaded A to do the same, and proposed to return to the village for dogs to hunt up the wounded animal. As they were about to re-cross the river with the intention of going to Léhnyindaung, A changed his mind, and said he was going back to shoot the bear whether his two comrades accompanied him or not. B agreed to wait by the canoe till A and C returned, the latter having finally agreed to go with A. On reaching the cover in which the bear had taken refuge, A crawled into it on his hands and knees, and suddenly came upon the bear face to face. He pulled the trigger but his gun missed fire, and the bear charged, seizing him first by the left arm and then by the right thigh, and began to worry him. A, who was bowled over into a sitting posture with his legs stretched out straight before him, held on to the bear's ears like grim death, shouting all the time for assistance. A was all this time exerting his strength to the utmost to prevent the animal biting him about the loins and stomach, as a nip in those parts might prove fatal. C all this time had apparently lost his head, as he was dancing about, chopping down at the same time the plantain trees in his immediate neighbourhood, and shouting at the top of his voice—" He will be killed ; he will be killed." Fortunately for A, B heard the uproar and cries for assistance, and appeared upon the scene in the nick of time, as poor A was nearly done. The bear's head being held low down between A's thighs, B had to squat on the ground before firing, which he did at a distance of about two paces, aiming at the head. The bullet narrowly missed hitting A on the leg, as after passing through the bear's head it entered the ground alongside A's thigh.

The river Lemro for a distance of quite two miles is thickly wooded on either bank with Jack fruit trees, and bears, sambur, and pigs are often to be found feeding during the early hours of the morning and in the evening; the whole atmosphere is sometimes impregnated with the sickly odour of Jack fruit, and during the night the sounds of the over-ripe fruit falling to the ground may be heard for a considerable distance. Bears are also found in hilly rocky places in deep ravines, and in tree forest where there is a certain amount of undergrowth. The sportsman should always look up those localities where wild mangoes and other fruit trees are plentiful, as bears are particularly partial to fruit. I will now relate the circumstances under which I got another bear in the hills between the village of Chaukmaw and Pinkan, in the Momeik State of the Ruby Mines district.

While riding along the road from Pinkan to Chaukmaw, accompanied by Moung Kyun Thet, one of my hunters, and two of his companions, we came on the tracks of a bear. The animal had apparently been regaling itself during the early hours of the morning on wild mangoes, which were plentifully strewed about on either side of the road. After dismounting and sending my pony on to Chaukmaw we took on the tracks of the bear, which led up a steep ridge. I had with me an 8-bore rifle and 12-bore shot-gun; the latter burned a maximum charge of 4½ drams of powder and carried a spherical ball. The track took us up and down hill over some very rough and steep ground, and, as the sun was extremely warm, walking was, to say the least of it, hard work. The bear having covered a considerable amount of ground, we eventually gave up in disgust, as I saw that if we went much further we should not be able to return to Chaukmaw that night. We accordingly turned our faces homeward and took our way down a very steep rocky incline. Being a fast walker, and having made my gun over to one of my men, I pushed on ahead, intending to take a drink at the stream whose waters could be heard roaring at the bottom of the hill. I told my three followers that I would wait for them there, and requested them to follow slowly and take every care of my guns. I reached the bottom in about half-an-hour without any mishap, and after a good drink of icy water I stretched myself out under the shade of a tree to rest. I determined to lie perdu when my followers put in an appearance, in order to see what they would do. Waiting till they were half-way down the incline, and I could hear their voices distinctly, I hid myself behind a thin fringe of bushes which skirted the stream within a few feet of the water's edge. The men presently appeared picking their way carefully down the rugged incline. One of my followers, I may remark, was armed with a flint-lock gun; as soon as they reached the bottom I could see from the movements of their lips and the expressions on their faces that they were wondering what had become of me, but owing to the noise made by the stream, which flowed close behind me, I could not hear what they were saying although they were only some twenty-five paces distant. All at once I was surprised to see Moung Kyun Thet, the man who was carrying my 8-bore, hand his weapon hastily to one of his companions and receive in exchange the flint-lock gun, which he deliberately pointed in my direction. Thinking he had mistaken me for some animal and was about to fire, I sprang up like a Jack-in-the-box.

Moung Kyun Thet quickly handed back the flint-lock and, seizing the 8-bore, rushed up to me with it, pointing at the same time to the stream behind me, where, to my astonishment, I saw a huge bear enjoying a bath, about 8 or 10 yards from the bushes behind which I had been concealed. I took a steady aim for the shoulder and fired. All this was only the work of a few seconds. A few short, barking roars from the bear were followed by a charge up the bank straight for us. The effort proved abortive, for, on reaching the top, he fell backwards into the water, stone dead. All this while a most ludicrous incident was taking place. One of my followers, the one armed with a flint-lock gun, had accidentally disturbed the nest of a small species of hornet, and the furious little insects had attacked him at all points with such vigour that he was unable to fire at the bear as it charged up the bank.

To see him attempt to bring his gun to his shoulder and immediately lower it again, bobbing and squirming about while endeavouring to crush the insects which were stinging his bare legs and thighs, was, to say the least of it, extremely funny. The bear was an old veteran with hardly a sound tooth in his head, and his skull now adorns my room along with other trophies of the chase.

I will now describe some incidents which occurred in the Akyab district, and request my reader to accompany me at least in the spirit to these well-known and much-appreciated hunting-grounds; if later on he should be tempted to venture there in the body, he need only step on board a B. I. steamer at Rangoon, and in three days he will reach his destination. Steamers for Akyab leave the Boh-ta-taung jetty. In the north-east monsoon, from September till May, on Tuesday mornings. In the south-west monsoon, May till September, on Monday mornings. The language of the Arrakanese differs from that of the Burmese, as much as the English language differs from the Scotch. All words ending in *ya* are pronounced in Burmese as spelt, while in Arrakanese they are transformed into *ra.* There are many other peculiarities connected with the language which need not be detailed. The better class of Arrakanese are more intelligent than the same class amongst the Burmese. Their general appearance seems to indicate that they have a strain of Indian blood in their veins, and unlike Mongolians they often have heavy hirsute appendages.

Some very fine snipe shooting may be had in the neighbourhood of Akyab, and I am told the birds arrive there before appearing in the Rangoon district. It would perhaps be as well to warn the sportsman that the Akyab district is notoriously feverish and unhealthy. Many Europeans who live there seem to suffer greatly from malarial fever even after a stay of only a few days. The best time of the year to visit Arrakan is November, December, and January, the rainy season being generally over in October.

Very good leopard, sambur, and barking deer shooting may be had near Kyauktaw, a village in the Akyab district. I shot my first leopard in the neighbourhood of this village while beating not far from the Kuladan river. Some villagers from the far side of the river had reported that a couple of leopards had recently carried off several goats and pigs, and begged that the animals might be shot. So bold, in fact, had they become that pigs and dogs had been carried off in broad daylight. I determined to rid the neighbourhood of these pests if possible, and as the villagers knew the locality in which the leopards had taken up their quarters, I sent word to say that I would go over the next day if beaters were collected, and that they were to meet me on my arrival at the village. I crossed the river in the early morning and, after a short palaver with the head-man and beaters, we made tracks for the spot where the leopards were supposed to be lying up. We beat several strips of jungle without coming across any signs, and with the exception of barking deer, a pig, and some jungle fowl, nothing was seen. But later on our efforts were rewarded.

The cover to be beaten was a long low-lying ridge with very thin bush extending down either side, scarcely sufficient, one would think, to afford cover for such large animals. There was a small patch of thick cover, however, at the far end of the ridge where the beaters were to begin, and where the leopards proved to have been in hiding. I took up my position on the top, and two men with guns were stationed at the foot of the ridge, one on either side of me about 120 yards away, and these were instructed to turn the leopards in my direction if possible. The beaters now began their work some 400 yards off, moving in a semi-circle so as to prevent the leopards from breaking away on either side. The ground in my immediate front and to my right and left for about 50 or 60 yards was fairly open, so I hoped to obtain an easy shot. The beaters drew nearer, and soon I heard a slow "pitter-patter" on the dry leaves some 20 yards ahead, and a large leopard came into view about ten paces from where I was standing. On perceiving me he stopped and turned partly round as if to pass on my right, showing me his teeth at the same time while he uttered a low guttural snarl. I raised my 12-bore, which was loaded with spherical ball and 3 drams of powder, and sent a ball through his right shoulder.

The animal bounded off as if untouched, uttering as he disappeared a sharp roar. The other leopard, which had apparently been following its mate, broke back and dashed through the beaters with an angry snarl. One man threw his heavy wood-chopper or "dâh ma" at it as it dashed past, but the weapon rebounded off the animal's body with a dull thud without doing any harm. I suppose she was a female, as the one shot by me was a male. A few spots of blood showed that I had not missed, and before we had gone 150 yards the leopard was viewed some 30 yards ahead, lying stretched out on its side with its tongue hanging out and blood oozing from its mouth. My bullet had entered at one side, and after passing through its lungs made its exit on the other.

I remember once on another occasion having a close shave from a leopard which I had wounded. I had just left my tent for a stroll along the bed of the Nampan stream, and was walking some 20 yards ahead of my *shikarie*, who was carrying my 8-bore, when a leopard jumped down the side of the bank and making its way to the water-side began to drink. The 12-bore I was carrying at the time was loaded with 3½ drams of powder and Meade shell. After a little manœuvring I managed to lessen the distance between us to about 35 yards. As I was about to put my gun to my shoulder the leopard looked round and saw me. I fired hurriedly as it turned and bounded off towards the bank, but missed badly with the first barrel; my second shot was more successful, for the brute dropped to the shot and lay motionless. Thinking I had shot it dead I went forward some 25 yards, but was surprised to see the leopard sit up. I now noticed that my shot had taken effect on the jaw, which appeared to be completely shattered, while drops of blood were falling on to the ground, and it seemed quite dazed and helpless. My hunter with the 8-bore now joined me, and at this moment the leopard, which was only some 5 or 6 yards off, regained its legs and charged straight at us. Fortunately, we were watching it at the time and were able to get out of its way; both eyes appeared to have been blinded by the effects of the Meade explosive shell. I succeeded in getting in a right and left as it was clambering up the bank, and one took effect, for it fell backwards amongst some bushes along the river's edge with its back broken. It was now easy to walk up and administer the *coup de grâce*, as it lay snarling and helpless.

Some excellent shooting may be had in the neighbourhood of Maungdaw and along the river Naaf, which is the boundary between the Chittagong and the Akyab districts. Pig, sambur, leopard, and I have no doubt tiger and bear are fairly plentiful, and up in the hills large game, such as gayal, gaur, elephant, and rhinoceros, may also occasionally be met with. This part of the country has not by any means been overrun by sportsmen. Alligator shooting may also be had up the river. The journey to within ten or fifteen miles of Maungdaw, or Teknaaf as it is sometimes called, can be performed in a steam-launch which leaves Akyab at least once a week.

Tigers are not so readily got at in Burma as in India, for howdah elephants are required to beat them out of the cover, and there are not many to be obtained in Burma. It has been said that there are very few tigers in Burma compared with India. I doubt this statement.

Burma is not so thickly settled as India, nor do the people in this country possess so many head of cattle. The consequence is, that tigers in Burma have a large area of unpopulated country to roam about and fewer cattle to prey upon, while the immense jungles, some of which are well-nigh impenetrable, afford magnificent cover where they lie unseen. In India,[1] tigers are often to be found in small patches of jungle, close to villages where there are large herds of cattle, upon which from time to time they levy toll. Goats, buffaloes, and cows are carried off by these depredators in large numbers. Buffaloes, ponies, cows, etc. are without doubt carried off in Burma, but the numbers cannot be compared with those of India. Tigers as a rule only prey upon cattle in those parts where game is not plentiful. The favourite diet of the tiger appears to be the pig or sambur, an immense number of these animals falling victims to the carnivora. Tigers wander about a great deal, and often turn up unexpectedly in the neighbour-

[1] Also in Assam.—F. T. P.

hood of some village, where, for a few days, they commit great havoc, not only on cattle but sometimes upon human beings, and as suddenly disappear again, to be heard of at some other place thirty or forty miles off.

Tigers in Burma are most often shot from a machan over a "kill," or in other words buffalo or cow, which has been killed or dragged away. Occasionally, however, an animal is turned out in a beat near some village.

Colonel Pollok, who has shot a number of these animals, has gone more fully into this subject.

I remember my first experience with a tiger in the days when I was a griffin and had not begun to use a rifle. The incident happened in the Sandoway district. I was out on tour and had just arrived at the village of Sathwa, where the thugyi, who was a half-bred native of India and Burma, begged me to stay for a day and assist him in shooting a tiger, which had been preying upon the cattle of several villages in the neighbourhood, his own included. I was delighted at the prospect of getting a shot at a tiger, so, after collecting some thirty beaters, we sallied forth to beat up all the likely covers where Stripes might be lying. There were three guns in all; a Civil police constable armed with a muzzle-loading Enfield, the thugyi with a breech-loading snider carbine, and myself with a double 12-bore shot-gun, loaded with 3½ drams of powder and 12 buck-shot in each barrel, a very sorry weapon indeed with which to face a tiger. After beating out some eight or ten covers, which occupied the greater part of the day, but without seeing any signs of the animal, we gave it up in disgust and began to retrace our steps homewards. When within 300 to 400 yards of Sathwa, a Burman, who was walking behind me, touched me on the shoulder, and said in an excited manner, "Thakin, thakin, no ma kya" (Sir, sir, there is the tiger). I looked in the direction in which he was pointing, and to my surprise saw Stripes seated watching some cows which were feeding close by, and which were apparently quite unconscious of danger. It was then about 5.30 p.m., and I have no doubt that the tiger intended waiting till it got a little darker before pouncing upon a victim. As the distance between us was only about 60 yards he saw us at once, and, rising to his feet with a toss of his head and a low growl, trotted off into a clump of bushes on a hillock which was quite isolated from any of the surrounding jungle. The thugyi immediately ran round to the other side with the intention of cutting off the animal's retreat, calling me at the same time to accompany him, as the beaters would drive the tiger towards us if he was still in the clump. Unfortunately, there were no large trees up which I could ensconce myself, so I had to remain standing on the ground. The thugyi quickly placed himself on my left, whilst the constable who had accompanied us climbed into the branches of the only available tree some 120 yards to my right. Being the only "Thakin" or European present, I was given the best position in the centre, the one by which the tiger was expected to pass. As the ground in the immediate rear of the constable and the thugyi was open paddy field, the tiger was not expected to pass near them. A short grassy glade some 30 yards broad separated the small clump in which the tiger had taken up his quarters from denser cover beyond, and it was across this strip, in the centre of which I had been posted, that he was expected to break. It was not long before the men began to make themselves heard, and we were soon to know whether the tiger was still in the cover.

The beaters had not travelled 50 yards before I heard a slow heavy tread on the dry leaves and undergrowth. The jungle in my immediate front for some 50 or 60 yards was fairly open and devoid of all thick undergrowth. In the innocence of my unfledged experience, I had imagined that the tiger would come flying past, and that I should then be able to put in a right and left at close quarters, which would be sure to take effect somewhere. Instead of that, however, here he was walking along quite unconcernedly in my direction. On perceiving me he stopped dead for a few seconds, and then, after sniffing audibly, looked first towards the tree which contained the constable, and then in the direction of the thugyi, being all the time apparently perfectly well aware of their presence. My heart all this time was thumping like a sledge-hammer, and I must admit that I should like to have been somewhere else at that moment. The tiger stood long enough to be photographed if I had had a camera. He was not more than thirty paces off, and his tail was twitching all the time with spasmodic jerks. Taking a hurried aim, I banged off both barrels, threw down my gun, and ran like a redshank for the tree up which the policeman was snugly seated. The tiger charged straight ahead with a roar without attempting to come after me, and disappeared in the thick jungle. I then returned to the spot where the animal had been, but except for a few deep scratches on the ground from the tiger's claws and the buckshot, there were no marks to show whether I had missed or not.

I remember on one occasion sitting up over a buffalo that had been killed by a tiger within 150 yards of a small village situated on the banks of the Kin river, some 300 or 400 yards from the village of Sagadaung, Momeik State. I had the buffalo dragged to a suitable spot under a tree convenient for erecting a machan, and staked it down there. The machan was erected some 25 feet from the ground (8 or 10 feet too high). There was no time to alter it, as it was then about 4.30 p.m., and the tiger might turn up at any moment; so, armed with a double smooth-bore loaded with 3 drams of powder and spherical ball, I ascended the tree and sat down on my perch. The erection or platform was very badly constructed, and I had a very uncomfortable seat, being obliged to sit down with my legs stretched out before me. A rail had been constructed in front, on which I rested my gun. My intention was to shoot the tiger if possible through the head, for I did not mean to afterwards follow it up on foot, through heavy cover, if only wounded. The village being close at hand I expected all the different noises emanating from it, women pounding rice, children crying, dogs barking, and cattle lowing, would have tended to keep the tiger away, so I did not anticipate its visit before dark. I had not been seated half-an-hour, however, before the scream of a startled jungle fowl warned me that something was on foot. I was instantly on the *qui vive*, and before long I heard all the "bulbuls" and other small birds chattering and twittering away in the bushes some 20 or 30 yards in my rear. Presently the heavy tread of the tiger was heard, and on looking down I saw Stripes slouch quickly along and pass under my roost to the kill. After walking round the carcase and sniffing at it the tiger lay down beside it, all four legs extended like a dog. I shut my eyes for a few seconds and tried to pull myself together, then, aiming for the animal's head, I fired. The tiger gave a loud "waugh," and was out of sight before I could fire the second barrel. My bullet had missed Stripes and hit the carcase of the buffalo. I was disgusted with my bad shooting, as were the Burmans, for they always expect a European to bag everything at which he fires. I had really no excuse to offer. I would advise a sportsman to always be present when a machan is being erected for him if he wants a comfortable seat, for Burmans are accustomed to squat in any position for hours without discomfort, and consequently put up very rude machans unless properly supervised. There should always be a rest for the feet some 24 inches below the seat, and the sportsman should be enabled to stand up, turn round, and fire in any direction. The machan should be so constructed as not to creak when movement is made inside it. Tigers visit their kill as a rule about sunset, but sometimes, if the latter is too near a village and Stripes is not very hungry, he will not appear till 1 or 2 a.m.

In the jungle, far from any habitation, he will be found feeding on the carcase at all hours of the day, and invariably lies up close to it, especially if there should be water close by. I remember on one occasion, when following up a solitary bull gaur, coming suddenly upon a tiger which was making a meal off a sambur. We were walking in single file, Moung Hpé leading, the tracks winding through a patch of kaing grass, which here and there was rather sparse. We were moving along noiselessly, expecting each minute to sight the gaur, when two or three loud snarling growls were uttered close to us as the tiger bounded away through the grass. We had almost walked on top of Stripes while he was feeding on the remains of a sambur which had apparently been pulled down by him two or three days before. Vultures were perched on the surrounding trees, but not a single bird was on the ground near the kill when we appeared. A tiger has been known to kill a vulture which he caught helping himself to the kill. Solitary wild dogs have been known to follow tigers about, presumably in the hope of obtaining a share of the spoil. I was once sitting over a cow, one of four which had been killed by the same tiger; two carcases had been cut up and removed, and I expected Stripes to visit the one over which I sat sentinel, for the fourth kill was not discovered till the following morning. I waited all night in vain, and at daylight found that the tiger had made a hearty meal of the, till then unsuspected, fourth kill. The tracks of a wild dog were noticed following, and in some instances covering the tiger's pad marks, and I found that the wild dog had accompanied the tiger to within a short distance of the kill, where the dog had apparently laid down, and from this place the dog tracks led straight to the partially consumed carcase, on which the weaker marauder had presumably regaled himself after the departure of the chief actor.

I have heard of a species of grey wolf which is said to exist in Burma. My informant states that he saw them on two occasions in the Shwébo district. On the first occasion there was only one animal, but on the second there were two, and so near was he when he encountered them that they snarled at him before disappearing in the bush. I had never come across any of these animals during my wanderings, in either Upper or Lower Burma, and was unaware till now that they were to be found. I have also learned from another source that a wolf cub[1] was caught in the Zamani forest, Pegu district, and brought down to Rangoon, where it lived for about eight years, only to fall a victim by the hands of an over-zealous Burman constable, who poisoned it in compliance with the municipal rules for destroying dogs.

[1] These were probably wild dogs, and not wolves.—F. T. P.

ASSAM

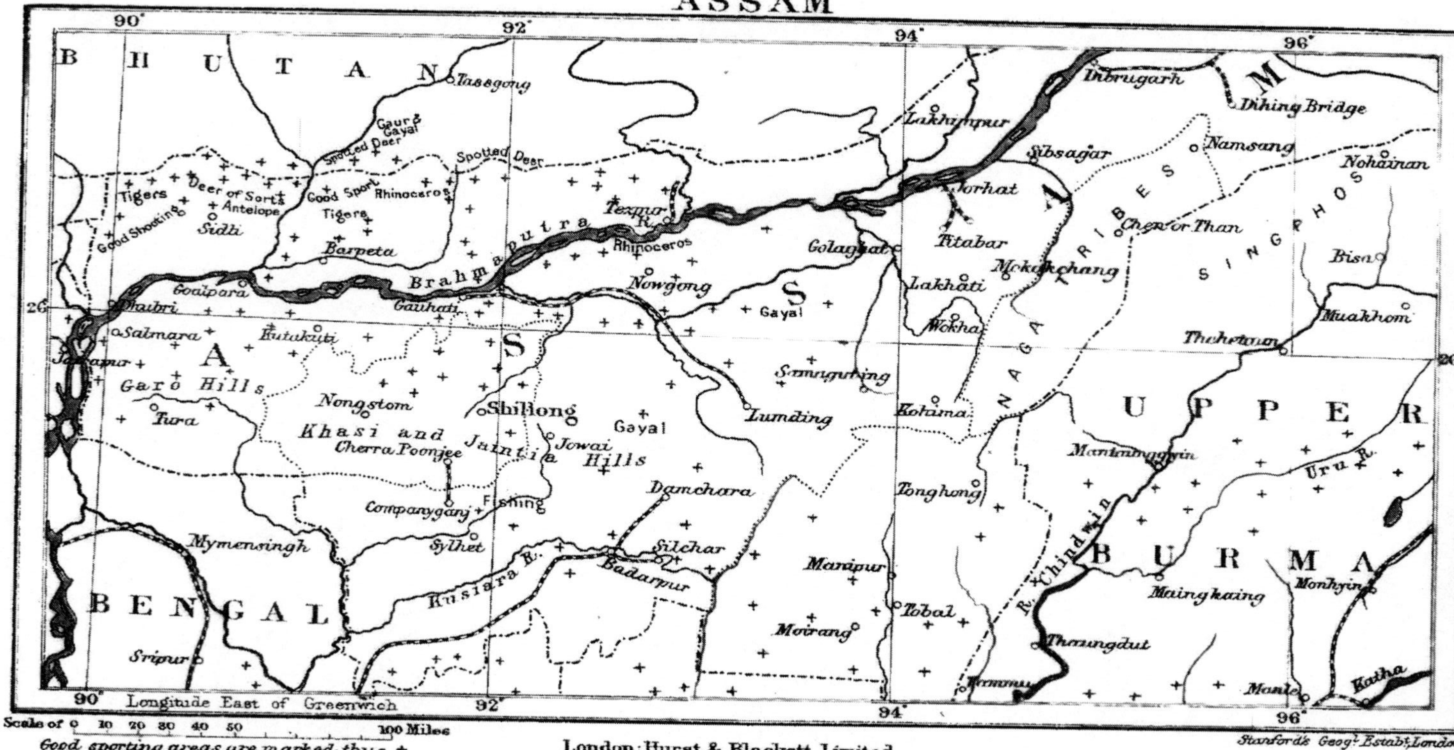

London: Hurst & Blackett, Limited.

ASSAM

[F. T. P.]

Of all our possessions in the East, Assam is probably the richest in natural resources, and up to a very late period, also the most neglected and backward. It came into our possession on the conclusion of the Burmese war of 1824—1826.

During the time the Burmese had possession of it they had devastated it fearfully; they not only wiped out the majority of males, but carried away very many of the younger women.

Although there are evidences that Assam at some remote period has enjoyed a fair share of civilization, good government, and prosperity, there remained to us but ruins of cities, portions of vast embankments and dykes to prove that in a by-gone generation Assam was not the deserted wilderness it was when it became ours. Very soon after we annexed it Mr. Bruce discovered the indigenous tea-plant.

The Province was never popular with the higher officials of India or with Europeans in general. No governor-general interested himself in the Province as Lord Dalhousie did in Burma, or Lord Ellenborough in Scinde. It had no independent Government, but was tacked on to Bengal, already an unwieldy Lieutenant-Governorship; but its patronage was valuable, and any contemplated separation was strenuously opposed. The local authorities and the Board of Revenue were always at loggerheads; the former knew the requirements of the Province—the latter did not, and cared less.

Although Assam has fields of coal, petroleum, slate, and other minerals in abundance, nothing was done to work them, and had it not been for the lucky discovery of the tea-plant

I believe the Province would have been neglected to this day.

But English capital was largely invested in that industry, and the planters gradually but surely forced the Government to introduce a better government.

But the success of a few companies induced others also to embark in tea, and the wildest and, in many cases, the most dishonest speculation took place, and led almost to the ruin of the whole trade.

Assam is a long, narrow valley, bounded on one side by the Bhootan, and on the other by the Cossyah and Garrow hills. It is intersected by the Brahmapootra river, one of the finest in India; as it debouches from the Himalaya it takes a westerly course and finally falls into the Bay of Bengal.

There is scarcely a portion of this valley through which this mighty river has not at some time or other flowed; sometimes approaching the Cossyah range to the south, and at others to the Bhootan hills to the north; it has left deserted channels everywhere, and has at last settled down about the centre of the valley, about half-way between the two ranges which proved insurmountable barriers to its erratic course. Wherever this river has once flowed and receded it has left vast beds, which are now swamps, covered with tangled and high grass, many of which are quite impassable for laden elephants. In these recesses, almost impregnable, vast herds of elephants, rhinoceros and buffaloes live unmolested, save by an occasional European hunter, who, unheedful of the stories told him by the old stay-at-home residents of the deadly malaria prevalent there, has penetrated their wilds.

Assam, like Burma, is subject to a damp heat, totally unlike the hot dry climate of the greater part of India; one suits certain constitutions and the other, others. Men who will thrive in the one won't in the other, and *vice versâ*.

Like in Burma, so in Assam; it does not do for a man to drink freely or to lead a sedentary life. He should wear flannel and be ordinarily careful. I travelled over the whole valley at all seasons, and suffered very little from malarial fever; but there is one thing a man in Assam must avoid, and that is (if he encamps near the foot of a range of high hills)

A SPECIMEN OF JUNGLE.

From a Photo by P. Burges, Esq.

sleeping within the influence of the wind, which nightly rushes down from the elevated plateau to take the place of the exhausted air of the plains, through one of the numerous gorges abutting into the plains, through which almost invariably a river flows.

The great crying evil of Assam was the want of communications; the country is subject to inundation, and to make roads fit for traffic all the year round very heavy embankments are required. Until Captain de Bourbel, Bengal Engineers, became superintending engineer, no regular system of roadmaking worthy of the name had been initiated. When I arrived—not at all willingly, as I did not wish to leave Burma—he asked me to undertake a regular system of surveying various routes and taking levels, so as to have reliable data to go upon.

After considerable obstruction from Bengal I got my own way, and was allowed to purchase four good elephants, towards which I did not hesitate to contribute myself, so as to get really good reliable beasts, not only for burden but also for sport. It was impossible to force one's way on these Goliaths through the vast prairies covered with long grass from 10 feet to 30 feet without disturbing much game, and it was also impossible to decide on the best line for embankments which would also suit hereafter for railroads without thoroughly exploring the country. So for the first two years I lived almost on elephant-back, and had explored the country from the Deopani river down to near Tara in the Garrow hills. I had also to construct a road to Dewangiri in Bhootan, and to lay out and partially construct a cart-road between Gowhatty and Shillong. I had also charge of the Public Works in the Cossyah and Jynteah hills, and also in the Tezpore district; so I had enough of out-door work to look after, which I flatter myself I did thoroughly; but I was also expected to do most elaborate office work, for which I had neither time nor inclination, and in which no doubt I failed, and brought down on me the animosity of the accounts branch in Bengal. The two should be totally separate: no man can excel in both. If useless and minute accounts were required, they should have sent men to compile them—for the most part they are fudged—but red tape must have its way.

The Assamese are difficult to deal with; the people are debased, given to debauchery and opium, and it is impossible to depend on them. Daily payments are very objectionable, as a great deals sticks to the palms of the subordinates. I introduced the contract system, paying for heavy embankments only after measurements; but I ran great risks, as I had to advance often many thousands of rupees to get reliable men to take up the work on my own responsibility and risk, and I got very little thanks for my pains.

The Bengal element prevails in the larger towns, and education does not improve the Bengalie Baboo; they are all adopting Bhramoo Somaj faith, which gives them greater facilities for getting drunk and for aping the vices of the Europeans. The Assamese are most litigious, and will swear to a lie sooner than to the truth.

The Cacharies, who live away far from the larger towns, are a far preferable race—descendants, I fancy, of the Burmese who overran the Province for so many years. When left to themselves they are a hard-drinking, merry race, but they are gradually being Hindoo-ized and degenerating rapidly.

The Bhooteas, who visit Assam during the cold season, are a fine-looking, largely-made race, but abominably filthy in person and habits. They are great beggars, and come with their sheep laden with grain, and with snow-boots, small dogs, ponies, and hybrid gayals for sale.

The Cossyahs are very like the Karens, and wear much the same kind of dress. They are a sturdy, powerful race, carrying immense weights, and being in that respect only inferior to the Hamals of Constantinople and Syria. Like all hill people they are not over cleanly in their persons, but their daughters, when caught young, learn cleanly habits and make capital Ayahs; they are well-made, are well-developed, with shapely busts and small hands and feet.

No Cossyah will go round by a made road if he can go straight up a hillside, even with a very heavy weight. They burn their dead, and erect cairns to their memory. Some of these cromlechs are huge granite slabs ranging as much as

29 feet high; the upright are for the male, the flat for their female relations.

There is a bridge at Nurting made of a single slab of the following dimensions: length 30 feet, width 9 feet, depth 2½ feet. As there is no stone of the description in the neighbourhood, these must have been brought many miles.

The Jynteahs are very similar to the Cossyahs, but perhaps a finer race, but of the same stock. In former days they were possessed of great wealth and power, but successive rebellions and invasions of our territory by them led to their ruin. Our Gurkhas had no difficulty in thrashing them soundly, and they are not likely to repeat their raids in future. Their wealth consists in oranges and betel-nut groves, limestone, coal, slate, and in growing and exporting to Calcutta and Dacca vast quantities of potatoes.

Gowhatty, formerly the capital of the Province, is a very unhealthy place, but since Assam has become a Chief Commissionership, the head-quarters have been fixed at Shillong.

The whole country teems with game, which is never likely to be exterminated, for where it lives the land is useless for other purposes, and its pursuit is too costly to enable the bog-trotters to go in for wholesale destruction, and the chances are, not a few would die of malarial fever. The fishing, too, is unsurpassed in India; the lordly mahseer can be caught in many of the hill streams, and fish up to 80 lbs. have been snared with a rod and line, but the largest *I* ever caught only weighed 44 lbs.

At the foot of the Bhootan range we have elephants, gaur, gayal, buffaloes, rhinoceros, marsh deer, sambur, hog deer, barking deer, spotted deer, tigers, leopards, and bears. In two localities—one to the north, and the other to the south of the Manass in Bagh Dooar—there are a few antelope; the spotted deer are also found at a place called Huttee Muttee Coochgar in the Mungledye subdivision.[1] In the vast plains and in the churs and deserted beds of the Brahmapootra—now quagmires

[1] Also in a valley close to Bagh Dooar there are several herds of the dappled beauties. The *Royal Natural History*, misled by Mr. Blandford, states there are no spotted deer in Assam. Quite an error, as I have seen herds and shot some myself.—F. T. P.

—there are two varieties of the rhinoceros, buffaloes in hundreds, tigers, bears occasionally, marsh and hog deer. The serow is also found in a few of the Cossyah, Jynteah, and Garrow hills. Amongst the Mishmie hills on our north-eastern frontier is found the takin, an ugly-looking brute, somewhat resembling the gnu of Africa. The yak or bûngōorōo is found in Bhootan; hogs are innumerable and of vast dimensions, and afford good pig-sticking in some of the churs below Dobree. The hare is only met with in a few places in Mungledye, but is more plentiful below Dobree. The pigmy hog and the hispid hare are also found in the Dooars at the base of the Bhootan hills. Leopards often take up their residence in cane-brakes in the midst of large towns like Burpettah and Hazoo. The jackal is very common, but the hyæna, as far as I know, is unknown. The tucktoo of Burma is also to be heard in various places, notably Burneyhat, eighteen miles from Gowhatty, and also inland from Goalpara.

The game-birds consist of the Indian variety of pea-fowl, the ordinary jungle-fowl, two varieties of pheasant, the black and the marsh, and three varieties of hill-partridges. There are also quail, and the florikin is very plentiful, but there are no bustard.

GENERAL SPORT

Gowhatty is not a pleasant place to live in, and there was not even a house to be got when I arrived. The Commissioner's clerks occupied the public bungalow, but Mr. Campbell the Assistant-Commissioner, lived in a dilapidated house, and kindly placed half of it at our disposal, and as he was shortly leaving on a tour with the Commissioner, said I should have it to myself ere long. I had a young wife with me, and was rather ashamed of the only accommodation I could offer her, but I got in a lot of workmen and soon converted the tumble-down building into a habitable one.

I had great trouble in getting elephants, the price sanctioned for their purchase being altogether inadequate. The Bhootan war had exhausted the Province of these useful slaves, but after a long fight and much correspondence and telegraphing,

I got a curt reply—"Purchase what you want at the price mentioned" (which was Rs.2000, instead of Rs.1500). I lost no time in procuring the best I could, and where requisite, added out of my own pocket the difference asked. I also bought two for myself. I was offered nearly double what I paid for one, but refused; but she was stolen, her young one left behind, and taken across our frontier, and I never got any redress. I did not know the people, nor the language—Hindoostani was of very little use. My clerks were bad, my subordinates worse—decent workmen would not go to Assam—there had been thirteen Executive Engineers of the Lower Assam division in one year before my transfer. I should have preferred remaining in Burma, but I knew Assam also swarmed with game. Being a willing horse, I had tacked on to me the Nowgong-Darrung, Goalparah, and the Cossyah and Jynteah divisions, in addition to Kamroop. There were military buildings to erect in the stations, surveys and levels to be carried out, and all I had were two assistants. We could never have done the work had I not risked advancing large sums, and getting contractors to undertake the heavy embankments, which eased us a bit, as after marking out the line of roadway or railway curves, we only measured the earthwork every month or so, and then paid for the work done. It was a life of constant activity, and as roads did not exist, to reach the many localities under me I had to go across a country swarming with wild game.

Whilst marking out the road to Nowgong, I used to put up at Chunderpore, Kullung river, a garden belonging to the Bainbridge brothers, both capital sportsmen, as was also their cousin Frank. Between Gowhatty and the Kullung I found that gaur were to be found in some low hills, and hunted them with varied luck, sometimes getting one, at others none. There were also buffaloes about, and in the first six months I shot twenty-two, and then rather tired of the sport.

At Lowqua-ghat I have killed rhinoceros, tigers, buffaloes, and deer. In March 1867 I was shooting there with Sir Charles Reid, of Delhi fame; he shot two with a very small bore rifle, and I lost one on that occasion, but killed many afterwards. I had to go to Burpettah in June 1867, as it was reported that the Government buildings were in danger of being swept away by the river, which was encroaching on its banks. The season was late, as the rivers begin to rise in June, so I sent on elephants ahead, and then dropped down by boat to Tarah-barie-ghat, but no elephants had arrived; but they turned up that afternoon. It was reported that there were many tigers about, and some of them man-eaters; certainly their footmarks were very plentiful.

So on the 11th I started at daybreak, hoping to find one, if not more. The country in the immediate neighbourhood was fairly open, with very short grass and bushes. I saw a broad track, and told my mahout to go along it. It was too dark to see what had caused the trail. When we came to a marshy bit, I found we had been following two rhinoceros. I soon came upon a mound of their droppings; they always deposit their ordure in one spot, until quite a large mound is formed, so I knew the beasts must be pretty close. My elephant began to show signs of funk, but the mahout kept her pretty straight. At last, in front of me, behind a bush, stood a rhinoceros, intently listening to the noise made by the elephant splashing along. Neither the mahout nor elephant saw the game ahead. I tapped the mahout on the head, and he stopped his beast at once. I fired into the mass before me, and as the smoke cleared away, a very large rhinoceros rushed into the open and got another bullet in its shoulder. He pulled up. I dropped the discharged weapon and took up another, and gave him two pills in the chest; he swerved and ran off, squealing awfully. On hearing this noise my steed right-about faced, and raced for her life, and could not be stopped for some time. So I went back to the bheel and took up the trail, and soon came upon the rhinoceros stone dead. Its horn was not long but very massive, weighing 1¾ seers. We got men from the nearest village, who were thankful to get the flesh, cut off the head and took off the shields, and reached Burpettah about twelve, where I put up with Boyd. I examined the river banks, and sent for men to shore up the side nearest the bungalow, and next day went for a few days' trip into the Dooars. I followed a rhinoceros for some way, but it had got into a tangled brake, where it was safe. I then

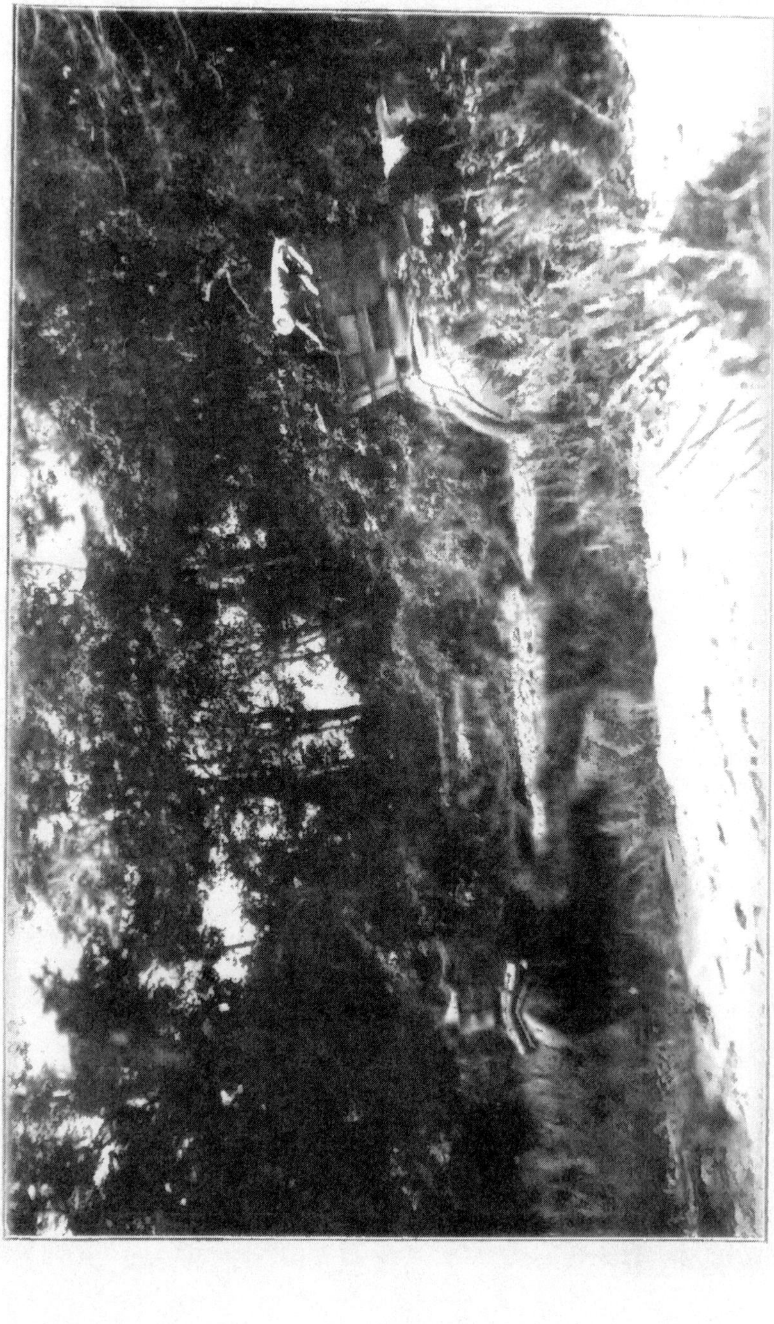

came across some buffaloes, and shot a couple of bulls, one with very curious horns, forming nearly a circle, and all but meeting at the points. I reached Barry's deserted garden about 2 p.m., and put up in his bungalow, and sent for Sookur, his old Cacharie mahout, who was then all but a boy, and engaged him. He was a plucky fellow, and about the best tracker out of India I ever came across.

The next day I sent on my traps to Dowkagong, Barry's second garden. I saw the marks of a lot of game, but all I shot were a couple of buffaloes. At Mina Muttee there is a nice stream of cold water, but no bungalow. Dowkagong is rather out of the way. I sent for the head-man for supplies, but he said they had nothing, and could get nothing without the Mouzadar's orders, so I had him tied up to one of the verandah posts, when everything requisite was forthcoming as if by magic. I paid for everything with my own hands at the prices asked, but the Assamese are an intractable race and will do nothing without being forced by the Mouzadar, who is seldom forthcoming. They don't live in their Mouzahs, but go to some large town, where there are plenty of dancing girls, and they can drink and debauch themselves to their hearts' content.

For the next day I either shot very badly or had the devil's own luck. I came upon rhinoceros after rhinoceros, all at close quarters, but failed to get a single one, though some six or seven were severely wounded. As the rivers were rising I had to hurry back. So on June 16 I went back to Bornuggur. I had heard a good deal of a place called Pākāh, and was told it was not far from Bhowanipore. I was told deer were very plentiful there, and where they are, tigers are sure to be near; but there was no such town or village as Pākāh—it was the name of a district. Whilst in search of it, we had to cross numerous nullahs, all out of depth, so we had to unload the elephants, carry the goods across in boats, swim the steeds, reload on the other side, and so on five or six times a day. Two of my servants had gone off to Burpettah; as I could find no place of that name, viz. Pākāh, I put up in a small village inhabited by nominal Moslems, but they spoke no Hindoostani, and to propitiate the Hindoos who lived round them, they had actually built a namghur and put an idol into it! For the first time I saw nets used for catching game, from deer up to buffaloes; those for the latter were made of jute, the string being as thick as my little finger. I saw these nets at work afterwards, but will describe the process separately. My servants, who had gone on to Burpettah, did not reach my camp till midnight.

On the 18th I was again hunting for Pākāh. I shot some florikan to-day, and also a couple of marsh deer. I saw men going out with nets and agreed to go with them in a few days. I put up in a namghur, but the priests objected, and we very nearly had a row; but before leaving Gowhatty I had ascertained that any traveller of any caste had a right to put up in them. The people were inclined to be bumptious, but seeing my battery arranged in a row, and my two chupprassies ready to back me up, they thought better of it and begged me as a favour not to dine inside, to which I readily agreed, as I always had my table under a tree, only using the namghur for shelter during the heat of the day, or in case it came on to rain. These debased Hindoos will always presume if they think they can do so with impunity. With the greatest difficulty I got back to Gowhatty on June 22, and all the old residents prophesied I'd be dead in ten days, but I did not even get a day's fever.

Round Gowhatty we had many a day's sport, but the wounded game oftener than not got into the low hills densely covered with bamboos, and escaped for the time.

In July 1867 I took my wife and a lady friend of hers up to Shillong, and left them there. There was scarcely the vestige of a road in those days; we had to deposit the money for coolies impressed to carry goods into the Cutcherie, and many of our loads were deposited in the jungles and the coolies fled, we being heavily the losers, but no redress was to be got.

The Lower Assam Company had a bungalow in the station (Gowhatty); there was a good deal of jungle about its vicinity, and twice Fisher, their able manager, had shots at tigers from the back verandah, but failed to bag; and several leopards were caught there in traps.

Near Moirapore, a tea-garden of the Lower Assam Company,

there was very good snipe-shooting, and the officers of the Company shot a good number of tigers there by sitting up over kills. Five miles from Gowhatty on the Beltolah road was the best snipe ground, and we used to get lots of jungle-fowl, pea-fowl, and a few florikan. At Myung wild game abounded; I have shot there at times tigers, rhinoceros, buffaloes, deer, a few hares, lots of florikan, and now and then had capital sport both with the black and kyāh partridges.

In January 1868, as I had to go down to Burpettah, I took with me Bowie of the Police and Barry a tea-planter, and at whose gardens I had put up in 1867. He knew the whole country and could speak the language, which is a bastard sort of Bengali. The Assistant-Commissioner had reported that there were no less than five man-eating tigers preying on the people about Baisah-ghat, so we went there by boat, having sent on our kit and elephants well ahead. At this time of the year the valley of the Brahmapootra is enveloped in a dense fog, which only begins to clear about 9 or 10 a.m. We went all night, but as our boatman was afraid of over-shooting our destination he pulled up about 4 a.m. But of course no objects were visible, and we allowed the boat to drift. When the fog cleared we found we were a long way from Baisah-ghat, so the crew were set to row again. We saw a buffalo on the bank, and he walked into the river and lay down. We ceased rowing and got within some 80 yards without disturbing him; he then stood up and we opened fire. In our first round all the shots missed, but with my left barrel I caught him in the hip and down he went. We jumped ashore and soon killed him, and then found that it was a poor emaciated beast suffering from an old wound, so it was a mercy putting him out of his misery. We did not reach the ghat till 3 p.m. We halted there that day and made inquiries about the tigers, but could hear nothing certain about them, though their pugs were plentiful enough.

We had not enough elephants to carry all our impedimenta, so had to hire coolies, and only those who have been forced to adopt this mode of conveyance can imagine the amount of trouble and bother there is in procuring coolies in Assam. The Mouzadars, themselves Hindoos, will not impress their own religionists, but send miles and miles away and forcibly seize Cacharies and make them do the work which their own villagers ought to do. There is the usual protest by every man that the load set apart for him is too heavy, that he has not had food for twenty-four hours—often but too true in the case of Cacharies. For an hour there is nothing but wrangling and fighting, and it is no use to leave the camp till each coolie

NATIVES OF THE COUNTRY, DOOARS, ASSAM, IN SEARCH OF RUBBER.

From a Photo by P. Burges, Esq.

has started with his load, or the chances are it will be left behind. I would advise no one to go on a shooting trip in Assam who cannot muster enough elephants to be altogether independent of manual labour. It is heart-rending work to have anything to say to the wretched inhabitants. I had enough elephants for my own use, but in all my trips my comrades were dependent on me for everything, carriage included, so shooting in companionship entailed considerable expense, and led to much annoyance. There are no zyats in Assam, so tents had to be carried. There are namghurs, but often they are in the heart of a village, and not pleasant places to put up in; and besides, the Hindoos are not like the Burmese, who welcome visitors, whilst the former would be insolent if they dared.

We found that the villagers, to drive off the tigers, had burnt every scrap of jungle, so all game had gone elsewhere.

We got to Burpettah at 2 p.m. Near a bheel *en route* we shot some duck, teal, and partridges. We halted the next day—I had work to attend to, and everything had to be repacked. In the evening I shot some black partridges; these are generally very good eating, but at times, when they swallow deer droppings, are not fit for table. Jungle fowl in the vicinity of large Hindoo villages, especially if there be a bamboo jungle handy, are very numerous; but avoid them, as they feed on human ordure. Even the cows act as scavengers, and are so pressed for salt that they greedily lick up any urine. The cattle are small, and die in hundreds every year from the rinderpest, from which Assam is never free. It is said that one of the richest Moslems in Calcutta made his fortune by purchasing for a few pice dozens of the skins of the animals that had died of this fell disease. These were imported to other countries and carried the infection with them. These cattle, when they die, are dragged away about 200 yards from the village. If there is a native chumbar he skins them for the pelts; tigers drag away some of their bodies and devour them at their leisure.

After the usual trouble we got off on the 12th, and camped near Sookur's village, re-engaging him and his uncle Seetaram for the trip. I wanted Sookur to take permanent service with me then, but he had just married a young girl who gave him a lot of trouble, and he did not then like to leave her, but he joined me shortly afterwards. In the evening we tried for small game on foot, but did not get much: the florikan were too wild and kept out of shot. All we got were a pea-fowl, three black partridges, and a jungle cock.

The next day we reached Mina Muttee, having shot some small game *en route*. The Deputy Commissioner had ordered huts to be built here; it had not been done, of course; so we pitched our tents and had to do the work ourselves, as we had no tent lascars. We were on the banks of a little rivulet with deliciously cold water, in which we cooled our liquor and also bathed. We made ourselves comfortable before dark, and after a good dinner turned in.

January 14.—Very cold this morning—a fog like a heavy Scotch mist, which wetted us through, and prevented our seeing more than a yard or so ahead. There were numerous marks of rhinoceros about. In about an hour Sookur hit off a fresh trail, and followed it like a bloodhound. These pachyderms feed in circles, and it is tedious following them up. At last we tracked it into grass fully 20 feet high, and we had not gone far when a rhinoceros grunted. My elephant stopped dead, all the others bolted. Sookur hammered mine well over the head and made her enter it with a rush. The pachyderm made tracks, and as it crossed a clearing I got two shots, but it went into heavier grass still. I did not like following it in that, as I could not see it until I came close up to it, and these beasts, when they charge, rip like a boar. I hoped by making sundry noises to induce it to go ahead where the jungle was not quite so heavy, but it would not budge. My elephant, Lutchmie, was in an awful stew, but I told Sookur to force her in, which he did. Barry just then got his elephant up, but Bowie's would not move to the front. As I advanced the rhinoceros retreated; I got shots as it was crossing the dry bed of a nullah; it ran up the opposite bank squealing, and my steed after it. The rhinoceros turned, and was in the act of charging when I gave her—for it turned out to be a cow—two more bullets which turned her, and three more shots laid her low. She was a large cow, with a horn 13 inches long, weighing 1¼ seers. We then breakfasted, and Barry not being well went back to camp, and wounded a leopard *en route*, but lost it.

Bowie and I went on; we soon came upon a fresh trail, and came upon a cow with a half-grown calf. A lucky shot of mine out of a short-barrelled rifle by Lyell of Aberdeen hit her behind the ear, and rolled her over stone dead. Sookur kept calling out "Shănāh, shănāh," and pointed towards some

A MOMENTARY HALT.

From a Photo by P. Burges, Esq.

commotion in the grass ahead, so I fired, and by the worst luck possible brought the animal down, which proved to be the calf! Sookur meant me *not* to fire; I thought it was something unusual and that he wanted me to kill it! These calves are easily caught after the death of the mother, as they won't leave the body, and are worth from £80 to £100 each. Bowie's elephant behaved very badly; she is generally staunch, but her mahout is away, and she was being driven by her grass-cutter, in whom she had no confidence. We got back to the tents soon after twelve, and in the evening shot some florikan.

January 15.—I lent my elephant and Sookur to Bowie, as I did not want to keep all the sport to myself. I visited the Boorie Nuddie and, searching about, soon found a lot of limestone, which was much wanted for conversion into lime for our public works. I saw a lot of marsh or swamp deer to-day, but all does; the bucks were in hiding, having shed their horns, and the new ones not having formed. I followed a rhinoceros, but my steed would not go up to it. Bowie joined me later on; he had wounded and lost a huge bull rhinoceros. We shot some florikan.

The next morning Barry was too ill to go out. So Bowie and I went together, and almost in sight of our tents we came upon a very large rhinoceros in shortish grass. I hit it twice and Bowie once. It ran in circles, and at last stood at bay in the open. My elephant at first refused to go up, but Sookur very forcibly made her do it, and with a few more shots I killed one of the finest rhinoceros I ever got. It had a horn 13 inches long, weighing 2 seers or 4 lbs. I eventually gave it to Colonel Dillon, secretary to Lord Napier when he was Commander-in-Chief of India.

Shortly after finishing off this beast, Sookur took up the tracks of two others; the way he followed them was an art in itself. It was not till fully an hour and a half that we came upon them. Bowie killed the larger with a ball, out of a smooth-bore, behind the ear; the other charged me savagely, but she had no chance; and no sooner was the life out of them than the Assamese swarmed like so many vultures, fighting with each other for the tid-bits. They never leave a scrap on the bones, take the hide and cut it up into long strips and roast them over a charcoal fire, and eat them much as Europeans do the crackling of a pig. Each rhinoceros represents a money value of, I was told, Rs.50. In two days these villagers had five rhinoceros equal to £25 gratis, yet when we wished to move camp, every villager had disappeared, and we could not obtain a single coolie without sending miles away to the Mouzadar. I paid for all our supplies myself daily, to prevent our under-strappers taking "dustoorie" or blackmail. We paid what they asked without haggling, yet I never met with anything but ingratitude from these people. I need give no further details of this trip. We shot enough deer for our wants, and saw hundreds; but they were principally does and a few brockets: the stags, having shed their horns, were in hiding. We also shot a few buffaloes if they got in the way, or were inclined to dispute our right of way, or if we came across one with an exceptionally large pair of horns.

On arrival at Rungiah I found that my overseer Subrooden had just shot on foot a very large tiger. After carefully skinning him we threw out the body, and within less than a quarter of an hour the vultures had picked it clean.

In February 1868 I had to march up to Deopani, some eighty miles beyond Nowgong, to meet the new Superintending Engineer, Sam Davis. I had fair sport, with indifferent luck. At Lowqua-ghat I wounded a lot of rhinoceros, but lost most of them. On the 25th I was in want of venison for camp use, and went to some land higher than the surrounding plain, where marsh deer were abundant. In rounding a patch of unburnt grass, just in front of me, and about 50 yards off, I saw the heads of three tigers, close together, looking in my direction. Neither the mahout nor the elephant had noticed them, so bidding the mahout to stop the elephant and to keep her steady, I took a deliberate shoulder-shot at the nearest; the smoke hung, but a tigress galloped off to my right, and a smaller one bolted much in the same direction; what had become of the third I did not see; but as the tigress went off growling and roaring, I came to the conclusion she was the one I had fired at, and gave her another shot and rolled her

RESULT OF FORTNIGHT'S SPORT (ASSAM).

From a Photo by P. Burges, Esq.

over; but she picked herself up, and with a magnificent bound disappeared into the long grass. There were within 100 yards a lot of villagers returning from fishing, and I had to go towards them and tell them to make themselves scarce, as there was a wounded tiger close by. This delayed me a little, and I then returned and searched about everywhere, but could not find a trace of her. I thought she had sneaked away along the bed of a nullah close by. I was in a rage; it is not often that one comes upon three tigers sitting on their haunches like dogs, and then fail to bag one at such close quarters. I abused the mahout, though when I came to think of it, he was in no way to blame. I told him to go back and look for the trail afresh. He replied, "Sahib, you have killed one—the first you fired at; the second has gone away wounded." I thought he merely said this to flatter me, and I got angrier, if possible.

"If I have killed one," I said, "where is it?"

"I will show the sahib," he replied, and took me back to the spot I had fired from at first, and sure enough, there lay a tiger stone dead. He had fallen without a movement, and what with the smoke and my attention being distracted by the survivors, I had not noticed that he had fallen. In front of the dead tiger lay a fawn, dead, as I supposed, so I told my mahout to get down and secure it, as it would do for the table; but no sooner had the man got almost up to it than the little creature jumped up and ran away, and would have escaped had not I shot it for the pot. My own idea is, that the mother tigress and her eldest hopeful had been giving the youngster a lesson in stalking, and that the hopeful had made a good beginning and had floored its first victim, when I appeared on the scene. I did not search for the mother as I thought she had got away.

February 26.—I hunted for the wounded rhinoceros, saw lots of quite fresh marks, but not a pachyderm. I got into the midst of a large herd of marsh deer, and shot several.

February 27.—I started for Koliabar across country, intending to shoot my way. I made straight for where I had seen the tigers the day before, and after passing it, up flew a lot of vultures. I thought it was the dead rhinoceros at last, but it turned out to be the tigress; she had never moved after the last bound she gave, but must have fallen dead. There was not much of her left, and that very offensive, but I cut off the head and padded it.

I saw lots of buffaloes, but did not fire at them. I reached Koliabar about 2 p.m. and put up with Tye, the tea-planter, a capital sportsman, who had slain numerous tigers and gaur, which were plentiful on his own tea estate. We tried shooting here, but beyond getting a few deer and a couple of buffaloes, did nothing. There were plenty of marks of tigers and rhinoceros about. I bought Tye's two elephants; the larger had a calf which he presented to me; the other elephant was only useful for baggage, as she had been cut by a rhinoceros, and would not go into the same field with one. She was as good as a pointer in that respect.

March 1.—Rode to Deopani, expecting to meet the Superintending Engineer and his brother, who was the Executive Engineer of the Upper Assam Division, but he had not arrived. This was a beastly hole, in dense jungle, so I moved back to a nice open spot on a river five miles distant. There I was kept kicking my heels about for a whole week before the magnate arrived. I saw lots of marks of game, but the jungles had not been burnt.

At last Sam Davis arrived. He was very consequential, and wanted to know why I had not remained at Deopani. I told him I was within call, and that he alone was to blame, as he was a week behind time. I pointed out the unsuitability of Deopani for a camp, and advised him and his brother to accompany me to my huts, where they would have everything they required. This, after grumbling by Sam, they agreed to do, and I went back to have dinner ready for them. We then marched back to Gowhatty, the brother returning to Deebrooghur. Sam was not a bad fellow, but very consequential. He had been very lucky as a speculator, and had shares in the Murree brewery and other companies, and when he died about two years afterwards, he left some £20,000 to a daughter whose existence no one had dreamed of.

Towards the end of April the Superintending Engineer and I were at Goalparah, and Colonel Comber came into camp

TIGER PADDED ON ELEPHANT.

From a Photo by Sir B. Simpson, Bart.

with us. We stopped a day or two at Luckeepore, as guests of the Zemindar there. The Palace is a curiosity shop, which he is very fond of showing to people. He had a large stud of elephants—amongst them a well-known one-tusker *shikarie* elephant, Māinah. His son—quite a young man—was a bit of a poacher, but had been very successful, having killed a lot of elephants, rhinoceros, tigers, and other game. The country is full of game.

On the 29th Comber and I were out after game. My elephant, Lutchmie, began to trumpet in a peculiarly pitiful way, and I called out to my comrade to be on the look-out, as there was evidently a tiger near; we immediately formed line and carefully advanced. The elephants all began to give tongue and did not seem keen to move ahead. The grass had been prematurely burnt, the stalks had only been charred and were still standing, and through them we saw a tigress sneaking away. We both fired and missed; she then ran down the bank of a nullah and up the other side; I fired and hit her through the thigh; she roared and disappeared. We got the elephants close together and steadily progressed. Comber was on Māinah. We had not gone far when the tigress charged, picking out the biggest elephant of course; we reserved our fire until she was within a few paces, then fired and bowled her over. Not an elephant moved. She picked herself up as quick as lightning, retreated a few yards, and then came at us again; this time she picked out Lutchmie, but a right and a left from me and a shot from Comber sent her to the right-about. She ran down the bank of a rivulet, swam through, and as she was ascending the opposite bank I killed her. She was only a small beast, 8 feet long. That was the only luck we had; we shot a deer or two, and saw rhinoceros and buffaloes, but got no shots at them, they were too wild to get near. We got wet through, as a torrent of rain set in, and we were glad to get home and change.

May 1.—Comber and I went on elephants across country to Dhobree, whilst our comrade, who was not a sportsman, went on his pony by a village track. We saw lots of deer, and at Tihri Killah got into rhinoceros ground. Comber killed a cow and called out to me to look out. I saw some beast lumbering through the long grass and fired, and killed a three-parts-grown rhinoceros. We then separated. I came upon a monster; he looked more like an elephant than a rhinoceros, and I hesitated to fire at first; but directly he squealed I put two barrels into him, brought him on his knees, but he jumped up and went off screeching. I chased him some way, but he was going away from camp and it was getting on for evening, so he escaped. We found our camp pitched close to a tank on high ground, quite open all round, very different from other parts of Assam.

May 2.—Comber and I shot our way across country, which, with the exception of a patch of long grass here and there, was open all round and lovely for riding. There were numerous boars, who seemed to care nothing for us. We had no spears and no horses, or we might have had lovely pig-sticking; but I made a note of the locality, and had some fine fun there afterwards with Williamson.

Leaving this oasis, we got into heavy grass, and I shot one of the lesser rhinoceros. Comber wounded one, but lost it. On reaching the river bank, a villager told us a tiger had just killed a cow, and took us to its body, which was scarcely cold; but with the exception of a long narrow tank, the banks of which were fringed with grass about four feet high, the country was quite open, with here and there a baire-tree[1] or a baubul bush. We thought we were sure of this tiger, and that he must be in the grass on the edge of the nullah, so we formed line and beat through it twice without a sign of the tiger, so thinking he had gone to some other chur I shot a small deer, and as we clustered round it Comber's mahout called out, "The tiger!" and there he was sure enough, bounding along in the open, and before we could pick up a gun he had disappeared down the bank, and though we searched for him for two hours, we never saw him again that day, but I shot him near the same spot the next year. He had been lying under a solitary bush in the open, watching a herd of cattle, and had allowed us to pass him within 50 yards without moving, and it was only my shots

[1] The baire-tree bears a fruit something like a crab-apple, not bad eating if thoroughly ripe.—F. T. P.

that disturbed him. The steamer coming in, we sent our steeds back by land and returned in her to our respective head-quarters.

Towards the end of the month I was out on a tour of inspection at Kumblepore, *en route* to Dewangiri. The villagers came to me complaining that a small herd of wild buffaloes had taken possession of a cane-brake lying in the middle of their village, and had gored several people. I was disinclined to go out; I was tired of shooting buffaloes, and I had cut the middle finger of my right hand almost to the bone, firing heavy charges, but the people were so earnest that I got on my elephant and went. I came across one of the buffaloes in the open before reaching the brake; he did not seem to mind me a bit, and allowed me to come within 60 yards, and then walked towards me shaking his head and pawing the ground. I allowed him to come within 40 yards and then floored him with a belted ball in the chest; he fell down, but picked himself up and ran across me. I made a lucky shot, and dropped him dead. I then went in the cane-brake—a terrible place—very boggy, with dense long grass and rattan creepers, through which it is almost impossible for an elephant to go; but by dint of perseverance, and cutting down with my shikar knife the pendulous creepers which these rattans throw out, and which are covered with hooked thorns like fish-hooks, I got sufficiently far in to see two buffaloes. I killed one and severely wounded the other, but it got away and was not likely to return there again.

In January 1869 Barry, Butter, and I were at Kumblepore again. About 4 p.m. on the 18th, just as we were going to bathe, an Assamese came running up saying he had just seen a bear feeding in the open about 300 yards off. We each took a rifle, and my overseer, Sübrooden, accompanied us with one of my guns laden with ball. On reaching the place where the man had seen the bear, we saw its marks, but it had disappeared. There was only one clump of long grass, and we stood round this, with our weapons on the half-cock, wondering where he could have gone to, when there was a movement in the grass. I stepped to the right and full-cocked my rifle. Barry went behind me, Butter to the left, and out walked a large bear within 10 yards of me, looking up at me like an idiot. I fired perhaps a second before Barry, who half-deafened me by firing past my ear, within a yard of it. She rolled over, and another shot from me and two from Subrooden did for her. It turned out to be *Ursus labiatus*, a beast unknown in the Province, where only the *Ursus tibetanus* is generally found. Jerdon, the naturalist, would not credit it until I produced the skin with the head still

PADDING A BEAR.

From a Photo by P. Burges, Esq.

attached to it. How it came there I do not know; I never came across another like it in Assam, though I shot many afterwards.

From the 19th to the 26th we were constantly marching. It is a curious fact that nullahs, or rivulets, which during the night are running streams, are dry during the day. We could scarcely credit it until we ascertained the fact for ourselves. We shot enough black partridges, florikan, and deer to feed the camp, but did not come across anything dangerous.

On the 26th we encamped at Mina Mattee, and sent for Sookur; but he was absent with some elephant-catchers. Without him it was useless looking for big game, but as I had to measure certain cubes of limestone, we took things for a three days' trip and went for the Manass in Bagh Dooar. It is a long march, but the country is very pretty and full of game; we must have seen a thousand marsh deer to-day, but all either does or brockets. We only shot enough to keep the camp supplied with meat. Near where the Manass emerges from the hills the country is beautiful. In the afternoon I tried fishing; I had bought some second-hand tackle from a Deputy Commissioner, but no care had been taken of it, and it was more or less rotten. As there were no boats I went to the extremity of a rock that jutted out into the river, threw out a spoon-bait, and began to drag it towards me; a large fish at once took it, but the line broke in two and away it went with one out of the only two spoons I had with me, and some 30 yards of line. I again baited my line and soon had on another fish, and succeeded in landing it after about twenty minutes' play. It was a fine mahseer, 7 lbs. in weight. As it was getting dark, I would not tempt fortune any more, but went back with my fish to the hut. We had a portion curried and a portion broiled, and found it good both ways.

During the night a wild Muckna elephant visited our females. Fearing he might do some damage—for if these males are baulked in their desires, they think nothing of wrenching off the tail of the coy female—I took a rifle and stood guard within 10 yards of him for three or four hours, not blessing him, as the mosquitoes were very troublesome. I was not sorry when he got our wind and went away across the Manass. Shooting elephants was then forbidden in Assam.

As it was raining in the morning I would not go out shooting, though some Bhooteahs declared they could show me four rhinoceros within a couple of miles. I tried fishing again, landed a beauty of between 8 and 9 lbs., then I hooked another; I played him for some time, but he eventually broke my line and escaped. I tried crystal bait, artificial minnows, and the fly, but had no further luck. Directly I reached camp I ordered out £50 worth of mahseer tackle from one of our leading makers.

We then went to Gohine Goung, then Bornuggur, and on to Burpettah. There I had shots at a tiger, but failed to bag, but shot a few deer and a lot of small game. Barry and I visited from Baromah the Namuttie bheel; the whole place was alive with wild-fowl, but they had been much molested by the police and were as wild as hawks, but we shot a few geese and a lot of duck and teal. I had various sport between March and May, bagging a couple of tigers and three rhinoceros, deer, and buffaloes.

In January 1870, General Blake, Mrs. Blake, Ommaney of the 44th, and Masters of the Police accompanied me as guests to the Manass. The General was a most noted sportsman, but shooting off elephants was to him a novelty. We caught a good many fish, for I had received the tackle I had sent for, killed two rhinoceros, several buffaloes and various deer without any particular incident, and were *en route* back and within sight of Burpettah, when Campbell, the Assistant-Commissioner, joined us. It was getting hot, and no prospect of any sport where we were, so the General and his wife went off, and I proposed we should dismount and try for florikan. The grass was only about three feet high, in which I had frequently shot on foot hog deer and small game. We had scarcely entered this and were about to dismount, when to our amazement we put up a right royal Bengal tiger! Campbell fired and missed; my ball went through the tiger's stomach. Campbell and I being on the fastest elephants, gave chase, but lost sight of our quarry. General Blake, hearing the shots, turned back and joined us; we then formed line, and we beat through the grass without seeing anything; the tiger had allowed us to pass him. We turned back and carefully retraced our footsteps; we saw the tiger with his head down, looking anything but well or lively. Masters and I fired, and one of the shots struck; he ran into the heaviest portion of the cover, growling like the devil. Blake, Ommaney, and I went towards him; the others stood a little way off, one to the right and one to the left. No sooner did we get

CAMP IN THE DOOARS, ASSAM.

From a Photo by Sir B. Simpson, Bart.

within 50 yards of him than he rushed at us, half roaring, half growling, and away went our steeds; he picked out mine and was close to its quarter, when I turned round, and firing down over the back of the howdah, I struck him on the back of the head, and he turned a complete somersault; and there he lay, but kicking up such a row that none of our elephants would go up to him from the front. So I beckoned to Campbell and Masters to take him from the rear, which they did, and rolled him over, dead. In bulk he was the very largest tiger I ever beheld; it took fifteen men to lift him on to a pad. As he lay dead, he was just 10 feet 1 inch in length; after being flayed the skin was 12 feet; after being pegged out, 13 feet 4 inches, and broad in proportion! It was curious afterwards, in comparing notes, to hear the different accounts those present gave; they remembered the 12 feet and 13 feet, but none remembered the 10 feet 1 inch!

On April 15, 1870, Jackson, Adjutant of the 43rd A.L.I., and I started by boat and got to Bassah-ghat by 2 a.m. We found our elephants there and reached Burpettah in time to breakfast with Mr. and Mrs. Campbell. The whole day was devoted to repacking our things. We intended to go in light marching order, as my time was limited. We were hurried throughout our trip, and lost nearly all our wounded game, which was retrieved, if I may say so, by native *shikaries*, who hovered round us, and whilst keeping out of sight got most of the game which had escaped us, sorely wounded.

My comrade had seen a good deal of sport in Central India; he was a capital shot, an ardent sportsman, and right good fellow; but he had never had any experience of shooting off elephants. We generally took a couple of pad elephants with our breakfast and to help to carry game, but the others we sent on by native pathways. Sookur and his uncle Seetaram also accompanied us. We went straight across country to Bāikee; we saw deer and had a few shots, but failed to bag, and we also saw numerous buffaloes that we would not fire at. About half-way I shot a marsh deer and Jackson a hog deer. Our attendant elephants were not with us, so we had to quarter the deer and hang the pieces to the sides and back of our howdahs. My stag had good horns; they were still in velvet, but the horn had formed. We separated, and Jackson shot a sambur, the first I had seen in the plains in Assam, and also a nice young porker for the table. We got to Bāīkee at 11 a.m. We put up in a small shed, taking the precaution before going into it to knock down all the sides. As there was a nice breeze blowing, we were fairly comfortable after we had bathed and put on our pyjama suits. After breakfast we had a snooze, and on waking were told a tiger had just killed a cow within half-a-mile of our abode, but we did not go after it till 5 p.m. We then got all our elephants in a line, close together; Jackson guarded the left flank and I the right. We had not advanced 300 yards when in front of us, nearer Jackson than to me, out sprang a tiger, and ran along through the short grass. The shot was a long and difficult one, but Jackson let fly; the tiger gave a roar and pulled up. I certainly thought he was hit, and called out: "Well done, Jackson, a good shot!" With the exception of the patch of long grass in which the tiger was, the country was open all round. We took up our positions on each side of the bush, and the leading elephants, touching one another, advanced; when within 60 yards the tiger rushed towards them, uttering many a roar and growl, but as not one of them moved, he came down upon me, open-mouthed. I was on the elephant I had bought from Becher the tea-planter; she did not care two pins for a tiger, but the sight of a pony nearly drove her mad with fright! I allowed him to come within 10 yards, when a shell in the chest killed him, and he fell almost at the feet of my steed. I put another ball into the neck to make sure, but there was no need for it, for he was stone dead. On carefully examining him we could find no other recent wound than my two; he had an old scar on his shoulder, the result of a shot from some native. He measured 9 feet 4 inches as he lay dead, and was in height 2 feet 11 inches.

April 18.—We marched straight to Mina Muttee, getting there at eleven. We had great difficulty as usual in getting supplies, not because they were scarce, but because the Mouzadars forbid the villagers to sell except through them. They ought to have known me well by this time, as I had

MR. HANNYNGTON AND TIGER.

From a Photo by Mr. Hannyngton.

been there more than once and had always paid their own prices with my own hand to prevent peculation by our servants. They also knew Seetaram and Sookur well; but the Assamese are only fit to be slaves, and will do nothing unless driven.

April 19.—We started very early for the Manass, for Matagoorie. I rode to-day a very old Muckna elephant belonging to the 43rd A.L.I. He was half blind—I think quite deaf—but very steady; nothing in the world would make him go more than about two to two and a half miles an hour. To be on his back with a wounded beast in front was heart-breaking; but in a scrimmage he was invaluable, for he would not move. We changed our minds, and put off going to Bagh Dooar till the morrow—got nothing but three deer for camp use.

April 20.—This time we started in earnest. We went a long way. I shot a couple of swamp deer, both bucks, but the horn had not formed, so the heads were useless. We then came upon fresh rhinoceros tracks and followed them up. We found one asleep in the bed of a nullah, without even a blade of grass to screen him from the sun; probably it was only a siesta, and that he would have retired to a heavier jungle later on. He looked for all the world like a huge pig. I was the nearest to him, but did not like to fire as there was no vital spot visible. Sookur had the sense to whistle, which awoke the sleeping beauty, and Jackson and I fired at his chest. He was on his legs in a second and came at us open-mouthed, but before he could climb up the bank he fell back dead—our battery was too much for him. We then shot a couple of buffaloes with good heads, which Jackson wanted. We breakfasted, rested half-an-hour, and then resumed our journey. Jackson then shot a stag. We were within sight of Matagoorie, and were going along the left bank of the Manass, when I saw a huge rhinoceros standing under a monarch of the forest. Its head and shoulders were protected by the trunk, but I could see its shoulder, and my first shot with the 2-groove rifle knocked it over. I fired two more shots as it lay struggling on the ground, but it recovered its legs and went off at a slow trot.

I went in chase, loading and firing, but could not gain an inch on my quarry. All the thrashing in the world could not induce the Muckna to go faster than its usual pace. The dense jungle was only a hundred yards ahead, and once in that I should never see the monster again. Just then Jackson on a fast elephant hurried up, ran alongside, and laid the rhinoceros dead. This was one of the largest rhinoceros I ever shot. It length from snout to tip of tail was 13 feet 4 inches; height at shoulder, 6 feet 2 inches; length of horn, 13 inches. I went direct to the huts, but Jackson shot on. He came across another giant and fired seven shots into it, but it got into a tangled brake and there he had to leave it. He arrived at camp at 4 p.m. We then went to the Manass. Jackson caught the first fish, a 6-pounder; I then caught three—19, 8, 25 lbs. each. The mahouts that went to bring in the head of the rhinoceros I had killed came across a tiger eating a deer, but as it was all but dark we put off going after it till the morning. We had pitched our tents too close to the river; the wind came down in a tornado all night, and we had six inches of sand over us in the morning, so moved further away—this night breeze is deadly.

April 21.—This morning, instead of going after the tiger, Jackson persuaded me to search for his rhinoceros. He said his mahout (a Gurkha) knew the place it went into; but these jungles are so alike he could not find it, and we lost some valuable time, so we had to give it up; but seeing fresh tracks we followed them up, and in passing through a narrow belt of long grass Jackson saw a rhinoceros and fired into him. The wounded one spun round and round, uttering the usual grunting squeals, and I should say the noise was echoed by some dozen others. I never heard such a pandemonium in my life, and whilst the pachyderms were making this noise not an elephant would go into the long grass, which was very dense and high. Not wishing to get any of our beasts cut, we waited until all this excitement should be over; we tried to burn the grass, but it was too wet with the night's dew, so we sat down to breakfast under a tree. Before we had half finished, a mahout said: "There is a rhinoceros

SHOT IN MY OLD HUNTING-GROUNDS, DOOARS, ASSAM.

From a Photo by Sir B. Simpson, Bart.

feeding quite near; he looks as big as an elephant." There was a nullah close by, and had we got into it we might have crawled up within a dozen yards, but instead of following this obvious course we got into our howdahs and went towards it. When within about 60 yards the animal looked up, saw us advancing, plunged down the side of the ravine, and was lost to us for ever. We hurried back, finished breakfast, formed line, and went into the long grass—I was still on the Muckna. We told the mahouts to advance almost touching; we had not gone far, when a rhinoceros with a young one charged Jackson; his elephant swerved, but he put a brace of bullets into her; as she crossed me I dropped her dead. Going on, I found myself in the midst of a herd of rhinoceros; they were all round me, kicking up their diabolical row, and threatening to charge from every quarter. Fortunately the old Muckna never moved. I fired four double rifles and a double gun as fast as I could, and it was only with my last shot that I rolled over the most persistent of my foes. There were two dead, two more just crawled away, one of whom lay dead a few yards off, and several more were wounded. My friend had gone a little way off after one he had seen, and was not in time to join in the scrimmage, the like of which I have never seen elsewhere. Sookur, who was on the Muckna, wanted to follow up hot-foot, and I had great difficulty in restraining him till I had loaded my battery. The wounded ones had got into a brake where we could not follow, but we heard that the people who followed us about had found three others dead.

He then went back towards the slain, when a three-parts-grown rhinoceros charged Jackson, whose elephant turned tail and ran for its life with the rhinoceros in full chase. Jackson was so knocked about, it was some time before he could put in a shot; after the brute had actually struck his elephant, but fortunately without cutting it, he killed it. Going homewards, well pleased with the day's bag, we shot a deer and a pig for the camp.

In the evening we went out fishing. Jackson caught two mahseer—20, 12 lbs. each. I also got two—19½, 6 lbs.—so on the whole we did not do so badly to-day.

April 22.—Jackson was ill with dysentery, so we did not start till late. We saw nothing till after crossing the Gatee nullah. We then saw a rhinoceros, but he declined being shot. Shortly afterwards we saw another; as he entered a tope of trees we hurried round, and got there just as he leisurely walked out, and killed him off the reel. Its horn had been injured, the root on the muzzle was full of maggots, the stench dreadful; it would have fallen off in a few days, and in time another would grow up. These horns, naturalists say, are only hairs conglomerated together. We went on to the Pohōomarah river and crossed it. In a tope of trees I had shots at a gaur, but lost it for the time. Jackson shot a hog deer for the pot. In the evening's fishing Jackson caught two, 26, 7 lbs. each, and got upset. I caught also two—17, 9 lbs. each. We each lost some others.

April 23.—We moved camp. We came upon a rhinoceros lying down in a running stream and killed it. I then shot a bear. We then lost three rhinoceros, and came upon a very large wild Muckna elephant. Our servants also saw two rhinoceros, and also, I fancy, the same elephant as we did. Seetaram fired at it, as he declared it followed the females and meant mischief. We halted at Basbarie, where there is a deliciously cold stream.

April 24.—We made rather a mess of to-day's sport. We sent a Gurkha orderly and Seetaram to track up rhinoceros we had wounded, but instead of doing so, they had a hunt on their own account, and disturbed the jungles ahead of us. I rolled over a bear, but lost it. After going a long way Sookur came upon fresh marks of a rhinoceros; the heat was awful, there was not the least shade, or a cloud in the sky. As usual, the rhinoceros had been feeding in circles; my comrade got disgusted at our slow rate of progress and took shelter under the only tree near. I went on, and in half-an-hour, which seemed like several hours, came upon the beast lying down in a patch of heavy grass, and killed it with two shots in the shoulder. We then saw a cow with a young one; we killed the mother and intended to catch the little one, but one of Jackson's conicals glanced off the old one and went into the youngster, so we had to kill it. The udder

CROSSING A RIVER

From a Photo by P. Burges, Esq.

being full of milk our men filled two bottles with it. I just tasted it; it was very weak and very sweet. Going homewards, I saw a rhinoceros in the bed of a nullah on its back, and with its feet in the air. Thinking it was one of our wounded ones that had died, I called out to Jackson. No sooner had I spoken, than up it jumped and came straight at me; for the first time the Muckna swerved a little, and escaped being cut, and the second after the beast was lying dead.

We only shot one more rhinoceros this trip—getting back to Gowhatty on the fifteenth day. We killed a lot more deer than I have enumerated, and also small game; but I have said enough to show what sport is to be had in parts of Assam.

Jackson having still a balance of fifteen days' leave, went to Barry's garden, Kookooriah (which I bought afterwards), and bagged a rhinoceros with a horn 13 inches long, weighing 2½ seers or 5 lbs., besides deer and buffaloes.

I will now describe killing game out of boats during inundations. I had to go down the road to ascertain the highest water-marks, and reached Luckeepore after a very unpleasant trip in July.

The Rajah collected a lot of boats, and as the whole country was under water, he asked me if I would like to see one of their national modes of killing game. The Assamese take only spears and dâhs. I took an old rifle. I did not interfere with the sport as I was only a looker-on. These boats are propelled by a dozen men; they draw very little water. We went along till we reached some small islets covered with long grass. These were in reality only knolls; as we approached one of them our boatmen began to yell, and three marsh deer and two hog deer plunged into the water and commenced to swim for their lives, but were speedily killed one after the other. We went on with various luck until some eight or nine deer had been killed; we then had a chase after three buffaloes; but as we passed the knoll out of which they had started, the old bull, who had remained behind, charged us. We were only in a depth of some two feet of water, which to him was no hindrance. The men tried to pull into deep water, but he was too quick for us, and he all but closed. I fired, and he fell so close to the cockleshell of a boat we were in, that it was nearly swamped by the waves made by his colossal body; but he was by no means dead. One of the boatmen speared him as we passed, but he was up and after us. Before I could load he struck the boat—the men jumped out; he took no notice of us, but butted the bark. The water was up to my waist, but I got a close shot at the beast's chest which proved a sickener, and as he turned I placed the second barrel behind his shoulder. He ran a little way and then fell down, to rise no more. The other boats had chased the cows, but only one was killed, the others getting away. We went on for several miles, looking up all likely spots, getting a hog here and a deer there. One rhinoceros was started, but he got away. About three o'clock there was a cry of "bagh!" and we went full chase after a royal tiger, who was swimming for his life. We were rather behind, but were coming up fast, when a man in the leading boat threw a spear, but missed; another was launched and struck; the tiger roared and turned round to give battle, but he was saluted with such a shower of spears that he right-about-faced; then ranging up alongside, spear after spear was thrust into his beautiful hide, and the water was crimsoned with his blood. Once it closed and caught the gunwale of the dug-out and nearly upset it, but a blow from a dâh laid open the head and it let go of its hold. Still the tiger, though covered with wounds, and dyeing the water with its blood, swam strongly; and what with its roaring, growling, and gurgling when thrust under the water, the yells of its assailants, the scene was an exceedingly savage one. The tiger got to a shoal and charged, seizing the prow of the boat. Fearing injury to some of the inmates, I put the rifle close to its head and blew out its brains. All this time the whole energies of the beast were devoted to the destruction of the boat—it took no notice of the crew. It turned out to be a tigress, 8 feet 3 inches in length. We got home at five with thirteen deer, five pigs, two buffaloes, and one tiger. As the Rajah was going to send his koonkies to catch wild elephants, he asked me if I'd like to see the sport. It is certainly most exciting, and apparently most dangerous, but in reality very few accidents ever occur.

For this sport only the fastest elephants are retained, and regularly trained and fed on grain to give them good wind. Near the root of the tail there is a sore the size of a cheese-plate kept, which is hammered during a run. The elephants are bare-backed, but a stout rope is twined round the body like a girth, then under the neck and tail like a breast-plate and crupper, and all are securely fastened together at the withers, and where the sling is also tied. The mahout who guides the elephant and throws the noose must be a plucky fellow, specially trained to the work, and he must of course also be at home on the beast's bare back. He has a man to assist, who is also trained, and whose business is not only to keep the koonkie going her fastest, but to assist directly the wild one has been lassoed. These two men are quite at their ease, although whilst going at full speed the elephant at times all but topples on her head, and at others almost falls backwards. The ground is covered with matted grass and brambles; its inequalities cannot be seen; there are narrow water-courses to be negotiated (invisible); there are fallen logs of trees, rocks, holes, ant-hills—every device to upset an animal; but whatever the obstacles may be, the elephant's speed must be maintained so as to overtake the quarry before it can obtain its second wind. The mahout as often as not stands up, holding on to a small rope attached to the girth, and it is really marvellous how he sticks on. In my own case I was tossed to and fro, never on the elephant's back for two minutes on end; I held on like grim death. Fortunately I was pretty young, fairly strong, and given to gymnastics; but after the hunt was over my arms felt as if they had been dislocated, and I felt sore all over.

In falling in with a herd, the mahout singles out one, generally a three-parts-grown tusker, a komooriah if possible; but if no good tusker is present, then a good young female is chosen. As soon as the victim has been selected, they endeavour to get as near him as possible, and then lay in as fast as the koonkie can put legs to the ground, and endeavour to separate the quarry from the rest of the herd; then for half-an-hour or more it is a case of the devil take the hindmost. You must go as fast as your steed can amble. The koonkie ranges alongside, the noose is thrown over its head; the wild one, feeling it dangling about its face, curls up its trunk, and in so doing assists in its own capture, for the noose then slips under the neck and is at once drawn tight. The koonkie now plants herself as firmly as possible, leaning her whole weight to the side opposite to the prisoner, with one foot advanced to meet the struggles its opponent is sure to offer, and who, recovering its wind, rushes off with great violence, dragging the koonkie after it; but the noose tightens, and the animal gets half strangled and has again to pull up. A second noose made of stouter rope is then thrown—this has a slip-knot; another koonkie runs up alongside and another noose is thrown, and the beast is safe. The attendants slip off and fasten hobbles round the front and hind legs.

The mahout who first lassoed has now the dangerous task of loosening the slip-knot and of fastening thick ropes round the neck of the victim. So expert are the men, that an accident seldom occurs. Two or three elephants range alongside, get in front, and lavish attentions on the poor half-strangled captive, while the man is attaching a small rope, which he carries for that purpose, to the end of the slip-knot to loosen it, which is often a matter of difficulty, for the sling first cast cuts deep into the flesh, and cannot readily be withdrawn. Directly this is accomplished, the wild elephant is led away between two tame ones, and is tethered at the appointed spot, where water and fodder are plentiful. Sometimes the mahouts, contrary to orders, noose an old elephant, who now and then proves too much for them and has to be cut loose; but generally, as soon as an elephant finds himself in the toils, he abandons hope and resigns himself to his fate.

I have now described most of the wild sports of Assam and where to look for them. I will here briefly note how animals are trapped in nets and speared to death.

On the day appointed I found over a hundred men carrying nets, whilst about fifty more were laden with stronger nets, made of jute of the thickness of my little finger, and who were to follow. These were to form the outer barrier to intercept large animals, such as buffaloes, who would scatter the frailer nets, but could not break through those.

The nets are never made more than 8 feet high; when employed in hunting they are kept upright by bamboos, the lower portion being fastened down with forked bamboo pegs driven into the ground. When a rush takes place, the net falls forward on to the intruder. Men and boys, armed with spears and dâhs, take up their position in rear of these obstructions, hiding behind bushes, long grass or anything, to administer the *coup de grâce* to such animals as are snared. If the first line is broken, the watchers retreat to the second, and if that too be demolished, they take up their final position behind the impregnable nets. It is seldom that any one is ever hurt in these encounters, which look perilous to a degree. The nets enclose a large space, and when every one is in his place the army of beaters commence "tom-toming," cholera-horn blowing, and yelling like demons. As the game advances, the nets in the rear are pushed on, curtailing the circle gradually. In half-an-hour the circle would be considerably diminished, many deer slain, and fallen nets re-adjusted. Some of the deer, scenting the people ahead and the blood of the slain, attempt to break back, but they find their retreat cut off more fully than even the front, so in despair a grand rush is again made, and more animals are killed. On the occasion I particularly allude to, I saw many of these beasts; a tigress at one point, and a three-parts-grown cub at another, were in the meshes. The latter was easily killed by the men opposing it, but the former had only two boys to deal with; they gave her many a stab, but were not strong enough to drive the weapon home. I hurried up, rifle in hand, but the boys said they could manage her; but as I saw she had got her head through the netting, I thought it quite time to blow out her brains. While this was going on at one place several buffaloes had broken down two sets of nets and had carried the third some way with them in their rush. I hurried there and found the natives stabbing the full-grown animals, but noosing the cow-calves. One bull tossed a man, and I had to shoot him. This is about the commonest mode of sport amongst the Assamese. I also shot game in the Durrung and Nowgong districts, but the sport did not materially differ from that already narrated.

PIG-STICKING ON THE CHURS OF ASSAM

Williamson, the Deputy Commissioner of the Garrow hills, and I had been shooting for a few days in the Churs of the Brahmapootra below Dobree, and as pigs were very numerous, my friend proposed that we should have a shy at them. Neither of us were well equipped for the sport; I had got rusty, as, during my thirteen years' residence in Lower Burma, I had been unable to indulge in this the noblest of sports. My spears had got blunted and rusty, and not thinking that I should have a chance of using them in such a jungly country as Assam, I did not carry them about with me; nor had I suitable steeds. I had four good ponies, the best to be got; but none of them were above 13.2—my largest—and the others under. I had put on a certain amount of flesh and was no longer the light-weight I had been in the fifties, therefore these diminutive animals could not carry me as they would have done ten years previously. I had only two ponies out with me; we seldom took any, but moved about and lived almost on elephants. Williamson had a country-bred mare and a couple of short jobbing spears of Bengal; they are barely 6 feet long, heavily weighted at the butt end; those I had been accustomed to were from 7½ to 8 feet long, and were used for thrusting and not jobbing. Williamson had seen a little pig-sticking in Tirhoot. Although neither of us was properly equipped, the temptation to once more follow a grizzly boar was too great to be resisted, especially as they lay out under the very flimsiest of shelter and in splendid riding ground. So we determined to try first the mainland on the left bank, where the pigs were particularly numerous, the country flat, fairly open, the beau ideal for hunting. Fences and ditches there were none, but occasionally a dry watercourse had to be negotiated; but most of these had sloping banks, up and down which it was easy going, so I thought

ALL IN A DAY'S WORK.

From a Photo by P. Burges, Esq.

my two nags, Pekoe and Elgin, would do fairly well, even with a heavyish weight on their backs.

The jemadar of the mahouts was directed where to take the elephants (we had ten with us) at daybreak next morning, and to beat in a certain direction towards us. As I have said, we were hunting under difficulties, for we had no spare spears and were inadequately mounted; but there is a charm in hog-hunting which is impossible to resist, if you have once been entered to it.

Williamson was an out-and-out sportsman, plucky to a degree, a splendid shot, a good rider, and under thirty, while I was over forty. He weighed about ten stone, I twelve or more. His mare was well bred and about 15 hands, and had been ridden to pigs; mine had had no such experience and were a hand and a half lower, so the handicapping was all against me. In a straight run I should be nowhere; but in hog-hunting even the slowest of steeds has a chance, particularly if the boar turn out a jinker.

I was tired of being eternally on the back of an elephant, and welcomed the chance of a gallop, even if I failed to draw first blood. To get to work early, we crossed over from the right to the left bank over-night, sleeping in an unused cattle-shed, so we were ready for the fray at dawn.

The jemadar, on a small elephant, received our orders and went off to execute them, and in about half-an-hour we could see the line of elephants advancing towards us. Williamson was ensconced behind a patch of long grass on the right; I was similarly concealed a little to the left, an interval of about 50 yards between us, having agreed that we were to ride boars only, and to let them pass us and get well ahead before laying in. The space before us, although not quite a plain, was ridable for fully three miles. These boars lead an idle life and have their food at hand, so do not take much exercise and get very fat and disinclined to run, and will as often charge at once as seek safety in flight. So fearless are they that I have in these churs put them out of the same patch of grass as a tiger, the two having been lying within thirty or forty paces of one another. The mahouts were told to advance in line and silently—only to shout when a boar broke. In less than a quarter of an hour there was a hubbub all along the line, the mahouts shouting, prodding their elephants, who were crying aloud and endeavouring to break back and showing all the signs of being in a stew. We at first thought that the commotion had been caused by a tiger, but presently a sounder of fifteen or sixteen pigs appeared. We let them go for a couple of hundred yards, and then W. shouted, "Ride!" I was just about to ram in the spurs, but looking backwards for a moment, I saw a grey old boar trotting along leisurely, champing his tushes and giving glances backwards, as if more than half inclined to charge the leviathans that had disturbed him from his beauty sleep. The sounder that had gone ahead contained two largish boars, but the one now coming up was a veritable Goliath. Williamson had a good start, and in a straight run my nags had not a ghost of a chance with his mare, so I determined to go for the grey boar. I had to restrain my steed, who, generally placid enough, had plenty of pluck in him, and he got excited at hearing W.'s cry and seeing his mare go off full speed, and naturally wished to follow.

By the time the veteran had passed me, my comrade was half-a-mile away; I gave the quarry a hundred yards' grace and then started in pursuit. "Pekoe" was very fresh, and galloped along, pulling double. Hearing a clatter behind him, the boar looked back with his wicked old eyes, hesitated a moment, seemed half inclined to bring our encounter to an issue at once by charging, but the array of elephants was fast approaching; he changed his mind and resumed his flight at an accelerated speed; with his bristles on end he looked nearly as big as "Pekoe," and although not going full speed, for he did not hurry himself, he got over the ground wonderfully. I let my nag go his best; but after going a quarter of a mile I only gained a little, he was still 50 yards ahead. There was a small patch of grass in front into which he bounded, and I too, a second or two after him. Unused to carrying the short spear, which is held with the blade downwards, I was somewhat bothered, but I was fairly ready, though not expecting to come across the enemy for another 200 or 300 yards; but I had not been in the cover above

BEATING ACROSS COUNTRY AFTER TIGER.

a few seconds when a grey mass almost sprang at me, fortunately on the spear side. Mechanically I jobbed and drove in the spurs; the blade missed the vertebræ, but went well into the neck behind the immense head; my speed carried me clear, just escaping a vicious prod. The spear came away, but the gallant quarry—nothing daunted—with a "whoof! whoof!" chased us. I kept ahead, going fast enough to keep out of his way, but no more, until I had lured him well into the open; then, putting on a spurt, wheeled round and went at him again. I fancy some small artery had been severed, for the boar was bleeding "like a pig," as the saying goes, and although he met me in the most plucky manner, there was not the usual vitality, and his charges became weaker and weaker. Ultimately, with a downward job I drove the blade deep into his withers, yet he managed to wriggle round, and with an upward jerk he cut the sole of my boot right through, his enormous head catching us amidship and sending us spinning to the ground, but he was *in articulo mortis.* The pony and I were not much the worse for the spill. Picking up the pieces, admiring the proportions of our late adversary, I withdrew the spear and remounted just in time to see W. coming down towards us at full speed. He had apparently a large, lanky boar before him, who was evidently wounded. I too joined in the chase, but I soon saw our quarry was not of the right gender.

"Why, W.," I sung out, "this is a sow!".

"But look at the tushes," retorted my comrade.

"Yes, I see them; but they are not much to speak of: it is a barren sow."

"It is wounded, so we must slay it, boar or sow," replied W.

Just then she jinked, and my friend's mare, rather hard-mouthed, did not turn as quickly as she ought to have done, so allowed me to cut in. "Pekoe" was quite game, notwithstanding his upset, and took me up nicely, so I gave her a good dig in the ribs, but could not withdraw my blade again, so had to let it go. W. was alongside of me in a moment, but it was no easy matter to get near the brute to administer a *coup de grâce*, for the heavily-leaded shaft remaining upright swayed about woefully, and with these job-spears you have to get to close quarters indeed before you can use one effectively. I was useless, having no weapon, and W. tried to rush in several times, but he got a whack across the shins which made him roar again, and I much doubt whether the victory would have been ours had not the pig rushed through a bush and got rid of the spear sticking upright in her. W. then went up alongside and finished the *mêlée*. Luckily my shaft was not broken, nor even sprung. The male bamboo used for these spears is stouter, shorter, and tougher, with closer joints than those used in the longer weapons. We had our rifles with us, for there was no knowing what animal we might come across.

We then shifted our position, and I mounted my grey, Elgin, who was only 13 hands high, but a very high caste, swift, though headstrong pony. We shifted our ground closer towards the base of the Garrow hills. The ground was not nearly so favourable for pig-sticking there, as there was a quantity of long grass standing. A few pigs broke back through the advancing line of elephants, and then the animals commenced to trumpet and to strike the tips of their trunks on the ground—unmistakable signs to the initiated.

"A tiger!" cried my friend.

We dismounted, seized our rifles, sent the steeds further back, and took up our positions on a couple of ant-hills, not far apart. I saw W. turn round to his left and let fly both barrels. A loud series of roars proclaimed that a royal tiger had been hit.

I ran up just in time to see as wicked a head as it is possible to conceive, not above a yard from my comrade, who was ramming in a couple of cartridges, the man with his extra weapon having vanished. I got a clear shot at the chest; the ball, a solid conical, went right through her from end to end, but she required another shot from me and one from W. before she—for it was a tigress—gave up the ghost.

But some of the men, pointing at right angles towards the river, called out: "Soor! Soor!" So getting astride our steeds, off we galloped, spear in hand. I have before said there was a good deal of unburnt grass about. Elgin, always eager and rather hard of mouth, seeing the mare ahead, took the bit in his mouth and fairly ran away with me. I thought it did not signify, for it looked plain sailing, and there was a good mile or more to the river's bank, so I sat quietly and let the pony have his own way. Passing through a longish bit of grass, Elgin pitched upon his head and turned a complete somersault, and I was sent spinning! and all around there was no end of grunting and squealing. The pony had fallen over a sow in her lair with her progeny and come a cropper, but no harm was done. I was up again and caught my animal before he recovered his legs. Mounting, I went in chase of W., who had no end of start, but just then the sounder took a turn to the right, so by cutting across I made up for lost time.

Wild pigs—sows in particular—form a shelter by biting the grass and piling it up, and then crawl under and form a fair roof overhead. In this the sows litter, and remain during the heat of the day. It was over one of these *caches* that I had come to grief. When I got up to the sounder, Williamson was too close to the only boar to enable me to cut in; his mare was somewhat blown, whilst Elgin, notwithstanding his tumble, was quite fresh. There is no certainty in hog-hunting; boars, when pressed, often "jink," and I hoped this one would do so, and in my favour; so I kept about ten paces to the right, Elgin holding his own in speed. W. got within distance —up went his spear to job, when over the mare rolled. A creeper had caught her across the legs, and the two went a "buster." But there was no time to lose, a sloping bank leading down to a navigable part of the river was close at hand; and however clumsy domestic pigs may be in swimming, wild ones excel in it, and take to water readily. The best place to job a boar is the centre of the withers, but I could not get near enough to deliver that blow. We were descending the shelving and sandy bank; I did the best I could, and dropped my heavily-weighted blade between the hips, which I could just reach. Down went the boar, my pony sprang clear of the prostrate body of the swine, which was rolling down the incline, and I just avoided going a header into the river, which was only some 25 yards across, and on the opposite bank of which basked an enormous crocodile. The boar's back was broken, but he got into the stream. I was off in a moment and grasped a hind leg; Williamson joined me in a second and got hold of the other, and we hauled with all our might; but our feet could not get a firm hold of the ground, the sand kept slipping away from underneath, and not wishing for a bath just then, we let go and ran up the bank, calling for assistance. We heard a snort, and turning round had the pleasure of seeing a knob at the end of a snout project, seize the still struggling but half-drowned boar in his massive jaws and slowly sink into the slimy depths below. We got our rifles and stood there a good half-hour in the hopes of seeing the saurian once more, but never saw him or his prey again. It was now getting hot, and we saw no prospect of any more sport. I went back towards the elephants, but Williamson rode on a little further. There was a cry of "Geddha!" (rhinoceros). I seized the first weapon I could get hold of; it was one of Williamson's double 8-bores. A cow rhinoceros with a three-parts-grown calf rushed past. I saluted her with both barrels; this was too much for Elgin, he broke away from the man who held him and scampered across the plain; the pachyderm, wild with fury, caught sight of him and made for him. They luckily galloped in a circle, so I managed to get in and to kill the rhinoceros. I then had to walk home, for Elgin was not recovered till late that afternoon.

Now took place a most unique occurrence. Williamson on his mare, seeing the juvenile pachyderm fairly out in the open, rode it, spear in hand. His mare at first objected to go near the uncouth beast, especially objecting to its squealing; but W. was a determined rider and forced her alongside, and, holding the spear by the butt, drove it in behind the shoulder with all his might, and was astonished at the ease with which it penetrated. But the youngster, on receiving the wound, made such diabolical noises that the mare reared, and he had to let go of the weapon and become an inactive spectator. The antics of the stricken beast, he declared, were most grotesque; he capered, he shook himself, he sprang from side to side, roaring and squealing the while, the shaft of the spear swaying about like the arm of a windmill; and W. was on the point of riding back for a rifle to give it its quietus, when the rhinoceros tripped up and fell on its side, driving the spear-blade right through him and out of the chest; a few more squeals and gasps, and he lay dead!

When the spear was extracted the shaft was splintered, so our hog-hunting ended. Before the next season came round poor Pekoe had been eaten by a tiger, and I was *en route* to Secunderabad. Nor did W. survive long. He was the most rising man in the Commission, and his death was most painful and inexplicable. Peace to his ashes! for a better fellow never lived.

COSSYAH AND JYNTEAH HILLS

THESE hills may be said to commence about eighteen miles south of Gowhatty, at Burneyhât, and extend in a south-eastern and western direction; they skirt Sylhet and Cachar, and beyond are called the Lushai hills; and both further north and further south they go by various names, but they are all a part of a vast plateau. Towards the east and north they are called the Naga, Mishmee, and other hills, and extend into China and Burma, and there are lofty peaks often covered with snow. Until Upper Burma was annexed, only two or three people (Europeans) had ever crossed from Assam into Burma, but now the provinces are contiguous. The people inhabiting that vast space consist of many tribes, all more or less savages, and give constant trouble—frequently cutting up small detachments, and then fleeing into their mountain fastnesses, where they are pretty safe from attack by regular troops; but the brave Sikhs who have enlisted into our police generally give a good account of them.

Cherra Poonghie, overlooking the Sylhet plains, was occupied by our troops for many years, but Shillong and Jowai and Kohima, as well as Muniyur, are the only places now garrisoned, excepting small detachments at Deebrooghur and other places. These regiments are now Gurkhas, but in my time the 44th was the only real Gurkha regiment.

Colonel Briggs, who had been employed under Major Kennedy in the construction of the hill road towards Nepaul, laid out with his usual skill a road connecting Shillong and Gowhatty, and also Shillong and Jowai. These were far too good for bridle paths, and never completed as a cart road. The distance too was excessive. The consequence was that it was never used; a shorter and a rougher route being preferred by Europeans and natives alike. There is now a capital road from Gowhatty to Shillong; I laid it out and commenced it, but it was finished after my time. By the old route Burney-hât was the first stage, Nongpoh the second; it is 2700 feet high. It is a wild place; there were but a few huts about, and very little cultivation. There was a fair sprinkling of elephants, gaur, sambur, hog deer, barking deer, bears and tigers and panthers about, but the jungle was very heavy—quite impenetrable in places. I shot a few sambur, hog deer, muntjac, two bears, a panther, besides jungle fowl, derrick pheasants and partridges, and saw lots of marks of bigger game; a few gaur have been shot there.

From Nongpoh the hills gradually rise, the jungle is more open, and about half-way to Oomsling it ceases altogether, being succeeded by open undulating hills covered with grass about four feet high, with sholas or belts of trees in the ravines along the water-courses. Many of the hills present a very park-like appearance, and capital stalking can be had; sambur and bears and panthers are always plentiful, and now and then elephants and gaur and tigers are to be found. From Oomsling the old path wound about amongst the hills, which are nearly bare with the exception of a few stunted pine-trees scattered about. There is the usual game to be found there, but it is not plentiful. The Oomean is a pretty mountain stream over which I threw a substantial bridge; it joins the Burneyhât stream, and the two fall into the Kullung near Kookooriah. There are mahseer in it; I caught a few, and knew others caught too, but none above 6 lbs., and those principally with the fly. After crossing this river the ascent of the true Cossyah hills commences, and Shillong, 5000 feet high, is reached.

There was another road *viâ* Ranee to Mooflong and thence to Cherra. The hills commence a few miles beyond Moirapore; near there we shot and trapped in nets some serow, a most unusual place to find them in, as the elevation was only 1700 feet. The first stage was Jyrung, where a tiger killed a valuable pony of mine in the verandah. I had sent it on ahead, and my people, thinking there was no danger, picketed it in the verandah, and placed the pads of the elephants round it; the elephants were close by—the people were all sleeping quite close. A tiger sprang over the pads and the railing against which they rested and fastened on the pony's neck. It was driven off immediately, but his jugular had been severed, and he was dead in a few minutes. The tiger remained close by all night and only retired at daylight. I arrived shortly after and found my pony—for whom I had paid Rs.400—dead. As a window of the bungalow commanded the body, and the night was as bright as day, I watched there all night, but the feline did not put in an appearance. So I lost my steed and obtained no compensation, though I was there on duty. This was the second pony I had had killed by tigers—the other was in Burma.

There is fair shooting along this road. The next stage is Oomloor; *en route*, by starting very early, a good many derrick pheasants and an occasional barking deer may be seen, and if you leave this road at Oomloor and go by Colonel Briggs' road to Palliar, in May and June, gaur are very plentiful there. In three days' shooting there I got four gaur, three sambur stags, two barking deer, and I saw at least thirty more gaur and a dozen tusker elephants, but these were not allowed to be shot then. From Palliar I followed Colonel Briggs' road; it passes over a plateau very like Ootacamund, and 6000 feet high. I had to encamp near a heavy cutting, and strolled off the next day in search of game. I met some Cossyahs, and they said they would show me game if I'd put up in their village, a little off the unfinished cart road; so I sent back a man to bring on my traps and went with them. They took me through beautiful park-like scenery, and I soon saw and shot a noble stag with very fine horns: in a straight line 34 inches, round the curve 38. I saw several does and the pugs of gaur and elephants. In the village they had the head and horns of a very fine gaur, and two or three of serow. My things came up rather late. I tried fishing in a neighbouring stream, and caught but three mahseers, the largest only 2 lbs.

In the night a tiger killed a cow, and going to inspect it, with a view of sitting up over it at night, walking carelessly along with the express in hand, up the tiger got, and on the impulse of the moment I took a snap-shot, and was lucky enough to break its back—another shot behind the ear killed it; it measured 9 feet 1 inch. I then, later on, got a bear, and moved on to opposite Mooflong. At Nungklow there are a good many pheasants and a few barking deer. There is also a cinchona plantation, but the trees were not thriving. The next stage, Myrung, has two deodars, but they are very stunted —quite unlike their kind in the Himalaya. There are also two bushes of tea, originally planted by General Vetch; they were then trees 20 feet high. Mooflong is 6000 feet high. There is any quantity of slate on these hills, and also coal of the best quality and limestone, but the principal industry is potato growing.

From Mooflong the road descends by zigzags to the Kala Panee, which we bridged like the Oomean. We collected disused telegraph wires, twisted them into a cable of five strands, stretched two across the river, and on them built up the bridge. The former bridges were only cane ones, and had to be renewed every year. Cherra Poonghie has the greatest rainfall in the world, the average being 50 FEET per annum. The hills rise abruptly out of the plains and attract the rainfall as the monsoons approach. The plateau is cut up into crevasses or cañons, many of them with sides like those of a wall 2000 feet deep. Notwithstanding this deluge, the place was very healthy, and all English flowers throve exceedingly. Then the earth used to be washed away every monsoon, but it was easily renewed from that of the valleys, and labour was very cheap there; the people would take down their loads of potatoes and bring back goods from Terreah Ghat for two or three annas. Coal cost under a rupee a ton—lime was plentiful, so were rubble stones; the people were capital masons and carpenters, and erected very good bungalows very moderately. Living was cheap, and Cherra throve for many years; but Rowlatt the Deputy Commissioner, a very able man, in his wanderings discovered Shillong, where the rainfall was not above 72 inches, so he persuaded the Government to desert Cherra and to form a station near Shillong, not Shillong itself, which had a bad name even amongst the Cossyahs, who only used it as a burial-place. His idea was for forming the station round where he built himself a little bungalow. But the Government with its usual blundering must needs send up a committee of old Indian officers who had lived in the plains all their lives, and had commanded Oude men to report on the eligibility of the proposed site. They were of course frozen to death, and reported on it unfavourably, as unfit for native troops, forgetting that it was not proposed to locate Bengal Sepoys there, but Gurkhas, whose homes were in Nepal at an elevation of 10,000 feet above sea-level. So as a medium, Shillong, which lies in a hollow, was fixed upon. It is also subject to certain diseases, and even to cholera, but is, of course, an improvement on Gowhatty, and since the province was made into a Chief Commissionership the cantonment and Civil lines have been greatly extended, and now reach to Captain Rowlatt's original site. The cart road, laid out and commenced by myself, has been finished, and now light covered-in carriages ply between it and Gowhatty, and a person can reach it within twelve hours after landing.

Going from Shillong to Jowai, the first stage is Nurting, where there is a Welsh Mission. In my day, the dâk bungalow there was always occupied by the Welsh parson, who seemed to have nothing to do but breed children. I never saw his wife, but she must have been a most prolific woman, for there were some dozen or more children of all sizes, with intervals of barely nine months between them. The school-house was neglected, the pigs had the run of it; it was in a swamp surrounded with human and pigs' ordure—a more filthy and disgusting place I never saw.

There is fair shooting and hunting; there are barking deer, pheasants, snipe, duck, and woodcock. Some of the largest cromlechs on these hills are there; the ducks rest on certain tanks, but if disturbed soon fly far, far away. The only place where I have seen coveys of partridges in the East was on Briggs' road within four or five miles of Jowai. They are peculiar to the hills, and at times are very plentiful. The Cossyahs kill them by throwing loaded sticks at them, and I have been offered as many as a dozen as the result of one man's *shikar* in a day. The birds are, I believe, the ruddy-necked partridge; blacks are also very common; they are of course a francolin. In former days, to judge by the following extract from the Lives of the Lindsays, the Rajahs of the Jynteah hills must have been possessed of large means and had considerable forces at their command; they frequently invaded our territory and made themselves otherwise very objectionable, but they were so thrashed by our plucky Gurkhas that they are not likely to prove troublesome again. All their greatness has departed.

"The Jynteah Rajah of the Cossyahs was my nearest frontier neighbour; he was by far the most powerful and the most civilized of the whole, holding large possessions both on the mountains and on the plains about fifty miles distant. When a younger man he had been misled by a false idea of his own powers, and he had in consequence been the aggressor by entering British territory in a hostile manner. A regiment of Sepoys easily drove him back and convinced him of his insignificance, and he was now endeavouring to show me his perfect attachment to our Government. The Rajah proposed my paying him a visit in his own country, and to partake of a *chasse* he had prepared for me; and after arranging the preliminaries the day was fixed. By mutual agreement we were to be accompanied by a few attendants only. It was during the season of the rains, the whole country being completely under water, looking like an extensive lake. I embarked in a beautiful yacht of my own building, well manned, and armed with eighteen swivel-guns, and arrived at the place of rendezvous at the appointed hour, when to my surprise I found advancing towards me a fleet of boats not less than fifty in number, with streamers flying and fantastically dressed. As this was contrary to our agreement I was not well pleased at the display, but betrayed no kind of alarm. The Rajah proved to be a handsome young man with a good address. He requested me to accompany him to his barge to partake of the *shikar* already prepared for our amusement. We rowed some miles towards a rising ground, on which we landed, and were then carried on men's shoulders to a temporary stage erected for the occasion. On surveying the arena round us I found that the enclosure was not less than 30 acres, surrounded by a stockade, and lined on the outside by the vassals of the Rajah. They had previously driven in the wild beasts of the country to this place, being the highest ground on the plain, and surrounded them. The sight was whimsically wild and magnificent, the concourse of people immense, the whole population of the hills and plains having turned out for the occasion.

"The place into which we were introduced was a species of open balcony; on either side of my chair were placed those of the Rajah, his prime minister, commander-in-chief, and officers of state.

"We each prepared our arms for the magnificent *chasse* now about to begin. Upon looking round me with attention, I saw there were now no fewer than two hundred of the largest wild buffaloes inclosed, several hundreds of sambur, great variety of the smaller description of deer, and wild-hog innumerable. These animals were now galloping round us in quick succession, when the Rajah, turning politely towards me, asked me to begin the sport by taking the first shot. I was no marksman, and afraid to betray my want of skill in so public a manner. First I declined the honour, but the Rajah insisted; I therefore raised my rifle to my shoulder, and taking a good aim, to my own astonishment dropped a bull buffalo dead on the spot. There was a shout of general admiration. I, on my part, put my pipe into my mouth, throwing out volumes of smoke to show my indifference, as if the event were a matter of course. But no power could persuade the Rajah to exhibit, from the apprehension of not being equally successful before his own people. On my left hand sat his luscar, or prime minister; his quiver, I observed, contained but two arrows. 'How comes it, my friend,' said I, 'you come into the field with so few arrows in your quiver?' With a sarcastic smile he replied: 'If a man cannot do his business with two arrows he is unfit for his trade.' At that moment he let fly a shaft, and a deer dropped dead. He immediately had recourse to his pipe and smoked profusely. The loud and hollow sound of the nagara or war-drum, and the discordant tones of the conch shells announced a new arrival. The folding doors of the arena were thrown open, and ten male elephants with their riders were marshalled before us. If it is expected that I am to describe the gorgeous trappings and costly harness of these animals, or the sumptuous dress of the attendants, disappointment must follow. My savage friends were little accustomed to stage effects or luxuries of any kind. The noble animal had not even a pad on his back—a rope round his body was his only harness. The rider was dressed nearly in the garb of nature, and the hook with which he drives or guides his animal was his only weapon. A motion from the Rajah's hand was the signal to advance. The buffaloes at this unexpected attack naturally turned their heads towards the elephants, and appeared as if drawn up in order of battle. The scene now became interesting in the extreme. The elephants continued to advance with a slow majestic step, also in line, when in an instant the leader of the bovines rushed forward with singular rapidity and charged the elephants in the centre. Their line was instantly broken, they turned and fled in all directions, many of them throwing their riders, and breaking down the stockage—one solitary elephant excepted. This magnificent beast had been trained for the Rajah's own use, and accustomed to the sport; the buffalo, returning from his pursuit, attentively surveyed him as he stood at a distance alone in the arena. He seemed for a few seconds uncertain whether to attack him or rejoin the herd. None who do not possess the talents of a Zoffany can describe the conflict which now took place; the elephant, the most unwieldy of the two, stood on the defensive, and his position was remarkable. In order to protect his proboscis he threw it over his head,[1] his foreleg advanced ready for a start, his tail in horizontal line with his back; his eager eyes steadily fixed upon his antagonist. The buffalo, who had hitherto been tearing up the ground with his feet, now rushed forward with velocity. The tusker advancing at the same time with rapid strides, received the bovine on his tusks and threw him into the air with the same facility as an English bulldog would toss a cat, then drove his tusks through

[1] This is a mistake. To protect their trunks elephants curl it up, and do not throw it over their heads.—F. T. P.

the body of the buffalo, and in that position carried him as easily as a baby, and laid him at the feet of the Rajah!"

This story must be accepted *cum grano salis*, as no elephant could possibly lift up and carry a wild bull buffalo as here described; but the account, apart from self-evident exaggeration, is interesting, as showing the power and state of the Jynteah Rajahs of those days. When I knew them twenty years ago they were as poor as church mice, and I do not think there was an elephant in the possession of one of them. Those they had were requisitioned for the Bhootan war, and died of hard work and insufficient food and worse treatment. Their wealth, as I have before said, consists in orange and betel-nut groves and limestone. Many years ago, a well-known merchant entered into a highly advantageous contract as far as he himself was concerned, and rented for a nominal sum immense tracks of orange and betel-nut trees from a Cossyah-Jynteah Rajah, the terms of his lease being written in their language "for as long as he remained above ground," meaning thereby for as long as he lived; but by the time he died these plantations were yielding over £5000 net profit per annum. So his knowing wife had a glass coffin made, in which, up to the time I left that part of the world, his remains lay exposed to view in one of the rooms of his bungalow. The Rajah appealed, hoping the Judge would take a sensible view of the lease, but he gave it in favour of the widow!

When the plains are inundated the deer find their way up the hills, and tigers and panthers follow them. I have seen the fresh pugs of a tiger in the verandah of the dâk bungalow at Cherra Poonghie. Tigers used to find their way up to Shillong, too, and we killed several there on foot, and the Gurkhas accounted for others. Panthers, or rather leopards, were very plentiful; we shot a good many, more were caught in traps; but it was almost impossible to keep a dog for them, for they preyed on them.

I made several trips into these hills, sometimes alone, and at others in company; we generally got bears and sambur. Once I took my family down to Oomseing and beat the neighbouring hills. The grass had not been burnt, so I got together a few Cossyahs and told them to set the hills on fire, but to give us ample time to take up our positions. The grass was very heavy, and we had to force our way through it, so our progress was very slow. Before we got much more than half-way, we found a line of fire, half-a-mile in breadth, bearing down upon us at a terrific pace; *sauve qui peut* was the order of the day. We knew these hills were full of hamadryads, and other venomous snakes, bears and tigers, but there was no time for picking one's way. We tore frantically over the top of the plateau, down a steep declivity, and sought shelter in the bed of a rivulet over which creepers and other plants met. We were only just in time, the flames were upon us and passed overhead, setting on fire the drier of the creepers overhead. It did not last above five minutes, but those minutes were to us like half-an-hour, as we were in a veritable oven, and half-roasted and suffocated before we could emerge. We took up fresh positions, and at a given signal this time the firing recommenced. I shot a fine stag with my ·577 Express, and then finding a cleared spot on a conical hill, I took up my position there, and the grass was set on fire at the bottom all round. The volumes of smoke were dense; fortunately I had undergone smoking out many a time in the fires in Prome and in the jungles in Burma, where three times I was all but burnt to death, so I could stand it; but my two gun-bearers could not, and I told them to lie down, as heated air always ascends. I saw two bears on the move for fully half-an-hour before they came my way; they tried to escape by various routes known to themselves, but were met everywhere by a fiery furnace, so they had to make for the only space free from fire, and that was where I was stationed. I rolled the largest, the leader, over, and was going to fire at the other with the left barrel when the first one picked himself up, so I put the remaining shell behind the shoulder and he dropped dead. Before I could seize my second gun, the smaller ran back towards the circuit of fire. I knew there was no escape that way, so leisurely reloaded and waited for him to return; but I never saw him again, nor did any of the beaters who were behind the fire. What became of him I can't think. I beat these hills for two days with but indifferent luck: one gun was not sufficient; there was no lack of game, but it generally broke away far from where I was stationed. Gaur and sambur and bears were the principal beasts to be found.

In October 1869, General Blake, Ommaney of the 44th, and I went for an excursion over the hills, and Trevor, the Superintendent Engineer, accompanied us as far as Jowai. Skinner, of the Police, also came a part of the way. We started after breakfast, going by the Cossyah paths in preference to the cart-track laid out by Major Briggs. By the route we followed, Pombara was only twelve or thirteen miles, by the latter, twenty-two; but the grass had not been burnt, and the Cossyah paths obliterated, so we had to walk the greater part of the way, and it took us three and a half hours to get to our destination. Pombara is a pretty place. It is colder than Shillong. There is a very deep and widish ravine to the right, with high peaks beyond. The bungalow is very fair. We took our guns and strolled out in the evening; we only saw a few black partridges and quail, but the General went on, whilst we returned home and shot a young barking deer, which turned out when roasted whole uncommonly good to eat.

The road from Pombara towards Jowai is very pretty, with groves of oak and rhododendrons and masses of the common pine. It is pretty level for about five miles, then there is an abrupt ascent of 1500 feet. There was no road then, so we had to climb up the steep hillside, which was no joke; but the view from the top was lovely. We breakfasted there and then went off a couple of miles further, then turned off to Nurting. The road had either lapsed into jungle or had been washed away; we went by Cossyah paths, and worse ones I never wish to see. One nullah we came to had precipitous banks, and the means of crossing was a fallen tree. This was very well for bare-footed Cossyahs, but useless to us with ponies. Ommaney wanted to ride his old screw over the frail bridge, where there was no foothold for a horse; but we persuaded him to dismount at all events. On he went, leading his Bucephalus; but the latter had not got halfway when he toppled over, one hind-leg caught in a fork of the tree, and the horse was suspended head-foremost over the bed of the nullah, which was a mass of huge boulders. The branch gave, and down the horse went, but as his value was but nominal he was not seriously hurt! We sent our beasts by a roundabout way and walked over this temporary bridge, and after a while came to what had in former days been a very good road. It had been bridged, but it had not been attended to for years, and they were impassable and in the last stage of decay.

When we got within sight of the village, I took a short cut and got there before the others. I found, as before stated, a Welsh missionary with a cartload of children in the dâk bungalow, so we had to put up in the school-room, which, from its appearance, could not have been used for months and months, and was a mass of filth. We got it cleaned out, but the odours were abominable, and surrounding the bungalow we were in, were vile marshes; pigs roamed about in dozens and were evidently in the habit of occupying what ought to have been the place of instruction for the village community. We could not stand the stenches and filth, and left the next afternoon for Jowai, having shot some duck, teal, snipe, and a solitary snipe in the adjacent bheels. We had a delicious bathe in the Moūton river, which was a clear, cold stream. The road to Jowai is exceedingly pretty, passing through undulating country, for all the world like the Brighton downs. We had to cross several lovely streams and flooded woods, where in the season woodcock abound. We got to the dâk bungalow at 3 p.m., and our traps arrived shortly afterwards. Mr. Shadwell, the Assistant-Commissioner, soon sent us a quantity of vegetables and also other necessaries of life. There is a detachment of the 44th here, and I was building a stockade for them. Just below the hill on which the bungalow stands there is a deep valley, with a river passing through its centre, and on a former visit I had noticed that it swarmed with fish; so this time I had plenty of tackle with me, and also an india-rubber boat. The Gurkhas used to catch a good many of the fish, but the Cossyahs did not like their doing so, as they said the river was sacred. So Blake, Ommaney, and I went down, thinking to fill our creels; but not only did we not catch a single fish, but did not see one! When I went there a year afterwards without tackle the pools were full of them. The Cossyahs said their gods had sent the fish away to prevent our catching them.

To console ourselves we shot a lot of snipe. The road to Cachar and Nowgong was visible a long way winding over the hills; and on it, a year or two afterwards, I killed the only two gayal I ever bagged, though I had seen numbers dead of the rinderpest. Our elevation was 4300 feet. We got coolies together to start for the river Durrung next morning.

October 30.—Our route to-day lay over the most beautiful scenery possible, high table-land, well wooded and with three fair-sized rivers running through it. One of these rivers, the largest, was spanned by a wooden trestle bridge, the others by huge stone slabs supported by upright slabs. The sholas or ravines reminded me very much of the Neilgherry Hills; one plateau was particularly lovely, very nearly flat, with an elevation of 5700 feet, with a river to the south and one to the north; and looking down we could see hundreds of fish which we took to be mahseer, but some were spotted like trout. The marshy woods had woodcock in them and we disturbed several, but got no shot. I think this place would have made a better military and civil station than Shillong, as water-carriage is nearer. We halted at Jarain, where there is a very good bungalow. On a clear day Cherra is visible, but we did not see it, as it was very misty.

October 31.—The Durrung is still a good eighteen or twenty miles off. We started at daybreak, but found the road so bad that we had to dismount and walk, and to send our ponies back with orders to go on to Jynteeapore and wait there for our arrival. We could not find a drop of water anywhere, and had a weary trudge of it till 3 p.m., when we reached the village of Sankar. Here we rested awhile, and had a good drink of water; but our destination, though not far off, was not at all easy to get to. We had to go down a nearly perpendicular bank, by means of steps cut out, or by springing from rock to rock. We reached the Cossyah village at last, but found the hut built for us in the heart of the village; there was no privacy, and the odours were not pleasant, so we went beyond until we came to a level spot some 15 feet square on the banks of the river, which was as clear as crystal. We all set to work and collected branches of trees and various posts to rig up an awning overhead, as the dews are very heavy at night. Close by, but a little lower, we found another level spot, just large enough for a small camp-table and our chairs. We had brought our tackle with us, and as soon as we could get boats we went out. We could see thousands of fish, from a few inches to three feet long. Ommaney had been here before—the General and I were new to it. We caught nothing, but the Pipon brought in three—7 lbs., 4 lbs., and 1 lb. respectively. By dark most of our traps had arrived, but only two servants, the rest had got drunk at Sankar and did not turn up till late next day. Whilst the servants prepared our dinner, we arranged our beds, rigged up the mosquito curtains, and put several bottles of ale and wine into the river to cool; whilst, after our work was over, we also took headers into the icy cold stream, swam about as hard as we could and then jumped out, and a good rub down made new men of us all. At eight o'clock dinner was ready; but my servant John had excelled himself—we had soup, fish, roasted wild duck, snipe on toast, bread-and-cheese, and washed them down in libations of icy cold Bass' pale ale. We retired to bed soon, and were glad of our quilts, and slept like tops till daylight. The General and I were in the water before the Pipon would wake up, which he did at last, and had tea ready by the time we had finished our ablutions. The place was perfect for bathing; you could take headers off perpendicular rocks into 20 feet of the clearest water conceivable. We each selected a boat; I took the one nearest me, and I found I had perhaps the best man as boatman in that part of the country. He had been out often with Mr. Hind, our padre, and with others. I christened him "wind-up," as that was the only English he knew, and which he repeated whenever we came to a shallow or I struck a fish. This river is divided into rapids, with deep pools intervening. One portion, which we called the gorge, was not less than 60 feet deep, with perpendicular banks of from 200 to 300 feet high, and hills on either side all densely covered with forest jungle. The General made some very pretty sketches of this and other parts of the river.

The Cossyah boats are very light, broad in the beam, have a very small false keel, are safe and easily propelled. I went up stream as far as I could, without getting a run; I was trolling with a spoon-bait, but coming back at a rapid I struck a fish; we were carried down at such a rate the boat could not be stopped till we got into smooth water again, by which time my fish was dead. It was spotted something like a trout, and 2 lbs. in weight. I then passed the village and our camp and four rapids, and to the extremity of the gorge, where there was a weir, without a run; but on my way back I caught two, 3½ and 1½ lbs each. In the gorge itself I heavily weighted the line and trolled very deep; I was using a spoon of the size of a large gravy spoon, treble gut, spinning tackle, and one of Farlow's best mahseer rods; at last I felt a tug and a half, and more than 70 yards of line out of 120 was carried out. I got the boat to a sand-bank, and landed to play it; it fought me for half-an-hour without allowing me a glimpse of it. The morning sun was full on my face, and the perspiration running down all but blinded me. I gradually drew the fish into shallow water, and could note its every movement. It did all it could by lying down on its side and rubbing its mouth into the sand to get rid of the hooks, but I did not give it much liberty and it did not succeed in its efforts. At one time, a fish almost the image of it approached, and my monster went at him open-mouthed. General Blake came up and looked on at the struggle, and after three-quarters of an hour's hard fight I landed about the handsomest fish I ever caught. It weighed between 28 and 30 lbs. My weighing machine was only graduated to 20 lbs., so we had to cut the fish in two to weigh it. The two, after loss of blood, entrails, etc., weighed over 28 lbs. For the next trip I got a proper fish scale showing up to 60 lbs. Always weigh a fish as soon after it is caught as possible—it loses weight as it dries up. We then had a bathe and went back to breakfast. In the afternoon in the rapids I caught two, 4½ lbs. each, and one ½ lb. I then went through the gorge, and close to the weir I caught a monster of 40 lbs., but it did not give half the play of the one caught in the morning. Ommaney had bad luck, losing several fish; he secured only one with a spoon, 2½ lbs.; and with the fly thirteen small fish, weighing altogether 9 lbs. General Blake got two, 4 and 4½ lbs. each, but his sport was spoiled by gar-fish; they take a spoon and offer no resistance, so the fisherman goes on unconscious of what is at the end of his line. No other fish will take the gar-fish as a bait; so unless a line is frequently examined, much time is uselessly expended.

November 2.—To-day I again had all the luck and caught the following—4, 1½, 35, 5½, 3½ lbs. The large fish I caught below the weir, very near where I killed the 40-pounder. I also lost a fish about 8 lbs. I had exhaused it, and hauled it up close to the boat, and told the steersman to spear it; but he made a bad shot, struck the hooks out of the fish's mouth, and in rebounding one went into his thigh, and I had to cut it out. Wilson of the Artillery, an old school-fellow of mine, and Lightfoot of the 44th, joined us to-day. The former caught a mahseer, 9½ lbs., with the spoon, and several small ones with the fly. Lightfoot using a fly only caught about fifty small fish. General Blake with the spoon caught one 18 lbs., and a lot with the fly. Ommaney had very bad luck and got only a few small fish.

November 3.—We went out early, and fished with indifferent luck. I hooked a lot of fish, but they all got off, the hooks either breaking or straightening. I was on to a very large fish for over an hour, but at the last moment the hooks gave, and he got off. I only landed one 6½ lbs—Wilson one 2 lbs. Neither the General nor Ommaney got anything. In the afternoon we moved camp to Joplong *en route* to Jynteeapore; we walked the distance—about four miles. There was only a small stream, in which, in bathing, we came across the gna-booden, a little fish that blows itself into a balloon if taken from the water—a little wretch that takes nips out of one. We had known them in Burma and now made their acquaintance again in Assam. We slept under some fine trees, where there is a weekly hât or bazaar held.

November 4.—We had to walk about two miles to get to the river leading to Jynteeapore; the boats were frail dug-outs without any covering, and I don't think I ever felt the sun more in my life; there was not a breath of wind and our progress was very slow, as we had to pole against the stream the whole day.

By dusk we were still three miles from our destination, and the branch of the river going past Jynteeapore had dried up. We put up in a namghur on the banks of the stream and sent into the town for coolies; the river where we halted was muddy and sluggish.

November 5.—The coolies, for a wonder, turned up at 8 a.m., and we reached Jynteeapore about ten. This place many years before had given us a good deal of trouble to reduce and subjugate; even then there were many dismantled cannons lying about, and the ramparts were in a fair state of preservation.

The people are a ruffianly lot—Sylhetian Moslems—who are not kept in the order they ought to be; these people were too grand to carry loads, so we had to send for Cossyahs, and it was pretty late before we got a sufficient number to carry all our traps. Our ponies were here all right; as neither Wilson nor Lightfoot had any steeds, Ommaney and Wilson took it turn about to ride, and I walked, giving Lightfoot mine. We had only ascended about half-way up the ghat when darkness set in and the coolies refused to go on, as they said there were many man-eating tigers about. So on reaching a fairly open spot, we halted; the coolies lit huge fires and sat up all night, but we turned in. In the middle of the night there was a cry of a tiger; Lightfoot fired his rifle off in the air and there was a general commotion, but it was a false alarm.

November 6.—I saw a peacock-pheasant to-day, but could not get a shot at it. We got off early, passed Jarain, and put up in some huts which had been built for the survey. There was a cold drizzling rain all day, and we were glad to get under shelter and to light fires. We reached Jowai the next day, and Shillong the day after.

I visited these fishing-grounds and also the Lahat river several times afterwards, and always had good sport, which I need not detail here. At Terreah-ghat there used to be good fishing, but the boatmen who ply from Sylhet took to poisoning the river and have ruined it for sport. It is full too of limestone caves, into which a fish dives; and you can't get it out again, for the line gets frayed. The largest fish I ever caught was 44 lbs., but they have been captured up to 60 lbs. In one trip Colonel Hicks, Ommaney, Bourne, and I got in five days 736 lbs. of fish—of which I got 276 lbs., Ommaney 258½ lbs., Colonel Hicks 105½ lbs., and Bourne 96 lbs. At another time in two days I caught 272 lbs. weight of fish.

I may here, I think, conclude wild sport in Assam and the adjacent hills. I had on one occasion good pig-sticking with Williamson of the Garrow hills, below Doobree, and I wonder that the Tent Clubs of Bengal do not pay those localities a visit now and then, for the boars are of the largest and most savage. I have put them up within a few yards of a tiger!

The best lure for a mahseer is a large spoon-bait, about the size of a gravy spoon, silver on one side and gilt on the other; it should spin freely and easily, and the treble hooks should be extra strong and keen of point, for the fish have leathery lips, not easy of penetration; treble gut of the best and fully 6 feet in length; the line should be fully 120 to 180 yards in length. Fishing in deep water, lead heavily, as the big fish remain close to the bottom; strike moderately hard and give plenty of line. Don't be in too great a hurry to land your fish. The scales on the fish are very large and almost as tough as tin, and I found a gaff of no great use—a three-prong spear is better, if thrust into the back of the head with force it will penetrate, and your fish will be secured. Salmon flies are good for moderate-sized fish in torrents, but not of much account in smooth water. Salmon rods for trolling.

THE END